HOSPITALS UNDER FIRE

Strategies for Survival

Everett A. Johnson, PhD
Director, Institute of Health
Administration
Georgia State University
Atlanta, Georgia

Richard L. Johnson
President
TriBrook Group, Inc.
Oakbrook, Illinois

AN ASPEN PUBLICATION®
Aspen Publishers, Inc.
1986
Rockville, Maryland
Royal Tunbridge Wells

Library of Congress Cataloging in Publication Data

Johnson, Everett A.
Hospitals under fire.

"An Aspen publication."
Includes bibliographies and index.
1. Hospitals—United States—Administration. 2. Hospital care—United States—
Marketing. 3. Hospital care—United States—Cost effectiveness. 4. Competition—United
States. 5. Hospitals—Administration. 6. Hospital care—Marketing. 7. Hospital care—
Cost effectiveness. 8. Competition. I. Johnson, Richard L. II. Title. [DNLM:
1. Economics, Hospital. 2. Hospital Administration. WX 150 J66ha]
RA981.A2J57   1986   362.1'1'0968   86-8084
ISBN: 0-87189-364-9

Editorial Services: Jane Coyle

Library of Congress Catalog Card Number: 86-8084
ISBN: 0-87189-364-9

Printed in the United States of America

1 2 3 4 5

Table of Contents

Preface .... **xiii**

PART I—ECONOMIC COMPETITION—THE NEW ENVIRONMENT **1**

Chapter 1—The Driver's Seat in Health Care **3**
The Golden Era 3
The Swing to Competition 4
Moving to Capitation 5
Oligopsony 6
Sharing Ownership 8

Chapter 2—Shifting Roles in a Competitive Environment **11**
Elements of Change 11
Growing Need for Political Skills 12
Evaluating Management 12
Asking the Right Question 13
Changing Relationships 14
Cooperation 15
Risky Risk Taking 15
Medical Staff Attitudes 16
Restructuring Hospital Corporations 17
Leading the Organization 18
Teaching Hospitals 19
The Future 20

Chapter 3—The Quiet Revolution **21**
Looking Back 21
Growing Unrest 22

The Options 23
A Free Marketplace 25
The HMO 27
The Race to Control 30

**Chapter 4—The Unknowns of a Competitive Health
Care System** **33**
The Unknowns 34
Two-Tier Care 35

Chapter 5—Planning and Marketing in a Competitive Climate ... **37**
A New Era 37
Replacing Myths with Realism 39
Selecting Clinical Services 40
Developing the Organizational Structure 42

**Chapter 6—Economic Competition Impacts Hospital
Construction** **45**
Two Schools of Thought 45
Developing Assumptions 46
First Phase 47
Second Phase 47
Third Phase 48

PART II—GOVERNANCE OF HOSPITALS **53**

Chapter 7—Shoring Up the Wobbly Three-Legged Stool **55**
Historical Roots Are Eroding 55
A Risky Environment 56
Tension Will Increase 57
A Bit of History 58
A New Role for the Board 59
Physician Board Members 61
The Solution 62

**Chapter 8—The Changing Role of Chief Executive Officers
and Trustees** **65**
Holding on to Yesterday 65
Selecting Trustees 66
Composition of a Board 67
Expanding the Role of the CEO 68

Chapter 9—Managing the Unmanageable **71**

Chapter 10—A New Look for Nonprofit Hospitals **81**
Debt versus Equity 81
Creating New Entities 82
Capital Costs 83
The Transition 87
Corporate and Management Structures 88

Chapter 11—Management Contracts for Hospitals **91**
Why Contracts? 91
Elements of a Sound Contract 92
Conclusion 96

PART III—RESTRAINTS AND REGULATION **97**

Chapter 12—Should Hospital Planning Continue To Be
Regulated? **99**
Asking Questions 100
Alternative Models 102
An Interim Phase 105

Chapter 13—Cost Control Strategies for Hospitals **109**
Two Forces Shape the Future 109
Differing Viewpoints 109
Developing Strategies 112
Economics Are Key 114

Chapter 14—The Resurgence of a Two-Tier Health
Care System **119**
Entitling the Elderly 119
Controlling Costs 120
Alternative Strategies 122
Two-Tier Health Care 124

Chapter 15—The Basis of a Medicare Crisis **127**
Root Cause 127
Nine Beliefs 128

Chapter 16—A Second Opinion: The Prospects of Medicare's Hospital Insurance Trust Fund **135**
    Report to Congress 135
    Utilization Rates Are Key 137
    An Alternate Scenario 140
    New Programs Needed 142
    Evaluating Options 145
    Additional Modalities of Care 150
    Utilization Pressures 151

Chapter 17—Shooting Oneself in the Foot **153**
    An Aging Population 153
    Medicare Payments to Hospitals 155
    Changing Utilization 159
    Case Studies 161
    Additional Facility Need 163
    Payments to Physicians 164
    Outcomes 166

Chapter 18—Hospital CEOs and Economic Competition **177**
    Speeding Up Decision Making 177
    Regulation May Be Favored 178
    CEOs in Nonprofit Hospitals 179
    New Rules for Economic Competition 180
    Developing the Entrepreneur 181
    Impact on Teaching Hospitals 182
    Changing Board Functions 183

PART IV—EXECUTIVE ROLES IN HOSPITALS **185**

Chapter 19—Retaining Executive Talent in Nonprofit Hospitals ... **187**
    New Ways of Thinking 187
    Measures of Performance 188
    Alternative Career Routes 190
    An Expanded CEO Role 190

Chapter 20—The Changing of the Guard **193**

Chapter 21—The Day After **197**
    To the Reader 206

Chapter 22—The Compleat Executive **207**
    Character, Personality, and Style 207
    Executive Class 208
    The Executive as Generalist 210
    The Dream and the Reality 210

Chapter 23—The Hidden Side of Hospital Productivity **213**
    Fraying of the Social Ethic 213
    A Multifaceted Concept 214
    Lessons about Hospital Productivity 215
    Improved Productivity Won't Offset Shortfalls 219
    Implications 221

Chapter 24—Thinking Conceptually about Hospital Efficiency **223**
    Measures of Efficiency 224
    Comparing Hospital Efficiencies 225
    Limitations of the Concept 226
    Hospital Outputs Are not Additive 227
    Professional Judgment Enters the Equation 229
    Finding a Common Unit of Measurement 229

Chapter 25—The Hospital CEO in Transition **235**
    Increasing Stress 236
    Running out of Time 237
    Organizational Ambiguity 240
    Sizing up the Situation 241

PART V—MANAGING PHYSICIANS **245**

Chapter 26—Changing Characteristics of a Medical Practice **247**
    Environmental Changes 247
    Economic Factors at Work 248
    Physician-Hospital Tensions 250
    Differing Perspectives 252
    Medical Practice Characteristics 253

Chapter 27—Self-Governance of a Medical Staff **257**
    Patient Safety Is Primary 257
    Differing Viewpoints on Self-Governance 258
    Who Represents the Trustees? 260
    The Role of the CEO 262

Fears of Physicians 263
Characteristics of a Medical Staff 265
Self-Governance Has Failed 266

Chapter 28—Perceptions of a Medical Staff Organization **269**
Learning Clinical Skills 269
Entering Private Practice 270
Joint Ventures 272

Chapter 29—Contracts for Hospital-Based Specialists **275**
Private Practice of Medicine 275
Characteristics of Hospital-Based Medicine 276
Medical Malpractice Issues 277
Statements of Medical Specialty Societies 278
Implications 279
Conclusion 280

**PART VI—DEALING WITH HOSPITAL-BASED
    PHYSICIANS** **283**

**Chapter 30—The Supply and Income of Hospital-Based
    Physicians** **285**
Future Trends 285

Chapter 31—The Role of the Hospital-Based Physician **289**
The Dual Position of Hospital-Based Physicians 289
Management Concerns 292

Chapter 32—Structuring the Contract Negotiation Process **293**

Chapter 33—Elements of Incumbent Physician Contracts **299**

Chapter 34—Negotiating the Contract **305**

**Chapter 35—Medicare Regulations for Hospital-Based
    Physicians** **311**

PART VII—THE CHAINING OF HOSPITALS 315

Chapter 36—Old Memories and New Dreams 317
    Forces at Work 317
    Sorting out of Values 320
    Similarities 320
    Differences between For-Profits and Nonprofits 322
    Nonprofit Characteristics 323
    Capitation Offers an Opportunity 324
    Retaining Top Management Talent 326
    Looking to the Future 326

Chapter 37—Going It Alone May Mean Going Broke 331
    Reasons for Growth of Systems 331
    Going It Alone 332
    Hurdles to Going It Alone 333
    Developing Responsive Boards 333

Chapter 38—The Hospital in Chains 337
    Forms of Integration 337
    Internal Strain 337
    External Stress 338
    Organizational Flexibility 340
    Growth of Chains 340
    Developing a New Philosophy 343
    Differences in Chains 345

Chapter 39—The Theory of Multihospital Systems 349
    Purpose of Structure 349
    Corporate Divisions or Holding Company 350
    Focus of a Multihospital System 351
    Components of a Matrix Structure 353
    Grouping Second-Level Functions 355
    Elements of an Effective Organization 357
    Selecting the Right Structure 361

**Chapter 40—Alternative Delivery Systems to Diversify
          Hospital Revenues** 365
    Regulation Efforts 365
    Serious Questions 366
    Founders 368

Front-Runners   369
Prognosis   374

PART VIII—LOOKING AROUND THE HOSPITAL FIELD   377

Chapter 41—Educating Health Care Executives   379
Role of the Faculty   379
Placement Patterns   380
Background   381
Academic Program   382
Relating to the MBA Curriculum   383

Chapter 42—The Rules of the New Game   385
Outrunning the Past   385
Trustees Face a New Reality   386
Major Forces Now Operating   387
Executive Talent   389
Economic Pressures on Physicians   390
Emerging Systems of Hospitals   392

Chapter 43—Looking around the Corner of 2000 A.D.   395
Major Trends   395
The Developing Spectrum   396
Improving Quality of Care   399
Overseas Operations   400
New Training Concepts   401
Lobbying Activities   401
The Middle of the Spectrum   402
Inner-City Hospitals   404
The Widening Gap   405

Chapter 44—Ten Years Hence   407
Societal Forces at Work   407
Demand-Side Economics   408
Governmental Activities   409
The Next Decade   410

Chapter 45—Imperatives in Health Administration Education   413
Administrative Behavior   413
Administrative Judgment   415
Selecting a Decision Path   416

Administrative Knowledge 418
Women in Graduate Health Programs 418
Developing New Knowledge 419

Chapter 46—The Future of Health Field Consulting **421**
Past Growth 421
Future Direction 422
Fields of Competence 422
Competitive Forces 425
Consulting as a Profession 426

**Chapter 47—Reflections on Ray E. Brown: Model Hospital
Executive** **427**

EPILOGUE **435**

Chapter 48—Doing Good—At What Price? **437**

Index **445**

Preface

Until the last few years, hospitals were accepted as an essential part of the social fabric of a community. They provided services focused on the acute medical care needs of the community and gave little thought to economic underpinnings so long as gross revenues covered operating costs.

The hospital industry prospered because the population was expanding and desired the latest in medical diagnosis and treatment, there were ample resources, and there was sufficient discretionary income.

Competition existed between hospitals, but it centered on being the first institution in the area to obtain newly developed medical technology. The emphasis was on maintaining high-quality medical care for all patients, regardless of their ability to pay for their services.

The prevailing belief was social, and hospitals organized to make a business profit were scorned. The philosophy of the times was ''The best possible care at the lowest possible cost'' and was a guiding principle for trustee and management decisions. A corollary belief was that nonprofit hospitals were the best in the land and no investor-owned hospital would ever match the quality of care and scope of service provided by the voluntary institutions.

Internally, the physicians of the medical staff both expected and demanded that hospitals serve their diagnostic and treatment orders, no matter what the financial consequences. Economic concerns of the institution were handled by the hospital administration. In an era of wide support of commercial health insurance and a cost-based Medicare program for the elderly, the physicians' demands were not unreasonable.

Hospitals, as social institutions, were controlled by governing boards whose members perceived themselves as stewards of the public interest and the demands of physicians as the voice of the public. This meant that when there were competing demands for hospital dollars, all issues were resolved by determining the public interest. Internal conflict was overcome by spending hospital resources rather than using cost-benefit analysis and making a cost-effective decision.

Trustees saw themselves as serving the public interest. This was reinforced by the accolades they received as public servants for their unpaid service and the significant time they invested in board and committee activities. Publically, their efforts were perceived as virtuous, reflecting credit on all who were seated at the table of governance. Like the knights of King Arthur's Round Table, trustees believed it was a community honor to serve and they were respected for doing so.

In 1982, with the enactment of the Tax Equity and Fiscal Responsibility Act and in 1983 the Prospective Payment System of Medicare, this world fell apart. Hospital admissions declined, average lengths of stay decreased, new medical equipment carried million-dollar price tags, and business and industry took a hard line on premium increases for their employees' health insurance. At the same time, new outpatient services expanded and alternative ways of delivering medical care arose. It was the new world of marketplace competition.

The social ethic, which had driven hospitals for 50 years, began to unravel. Truisms that had been believed for decades were no longer true.

What had happened was the outcome of the mid '60s enactment of Medicare and Medicaid by the federal government with its cost-based system of reimbursement and expanded entitlements. This fabric, based on social ethics, gradually frayed and finally unraveled. Piece by piece, the hospital financial environment became more expensive and more restrictive.

The crisis of the early '80s moved the social ethic of hospitals to a secondary position as economic interests and a business philosophy became dominant. How far the new ethic will reach, and how much of a social ethic will remain as part of the hospital fabric, has yet to be determined. Clearly, a predominant social posture will not again occur. Whether it will totally disappear is yet an unknown. A by-product of this shift in priorities is the demise of the "old boy" clubiness of hospital administration. No longer do administrative staffs compare salary scales, room rates, and service charges. Internal decisions have become proprietary in the environment of marketplace competition. A hospital's errors in market judgment are now exploited by competitors for improved market share.

The rush is on to expand as rapidly as possible through acquisition, merger, or consolidation. The goal is to have a wide range of health care services at multiple locations, to raise net surpluses as high as possible, and to offer a broad range of services. Unspoken, but of real concern to the growth-oriented hospital, is a fear of being taken over by an aggressive competitor.

In this highly charged, economically competitive environment, a successful hospital, or health care corporation, can no longer rely on a traditional type of governing board leadership. The day of the part-time, unpaid community leader serving as chairman of the board is past because it is inadequate to capitalize on opportunities in a market-driven industry. Nor is a large board of 15 or more trustees capable of coping with the new economic competition.

Hospitals that continue to foster a traditional form of governance will find an increasingly difficult time in responding to the new marketplace. The decisions at the board level will be too late and too conservative. To explain what forces are operating on and in hospitals and why they will prevail is the purpose of this book.

Everett A. Johnson
Richard L. Johnson

Part I

Economic Competition— The New Environment

Chapter 1

The Driver's Seat in Health Care

THE GOLDEN ERA

For the past 50 years it really did not matter who was in the driver's seat in health care. The public wanted more and better health care as well as a payment system that cushioned the costs involved. There were ample dollars, enough to fund all of the activities that were commenced and to support the improving technology. No one group was needed to steer the system and keep it headed in the right direction since there was general agreement about what needed to be accomplished.

The golden era had its beginnings in the early 1930s; hospitals entered a new age when the first Blue Cross plan was formed in the late '20s in Dallas, Texas. Because the country was in the midst of the Great Depression, hospitals were having serious financial difficulties. Many of their patients were indigent and dependent on welfare. When these people became sick and required hospitalization, the county or city government accepted financial responsibility. Because there were insufficient funds in the governmental coffers, local governments typically paid hospital bills well below the costs incurred. Hospitals accepted these monies because the alternative was empty beds with no patients and, therefore, no revenues. When the teachers in the Dallas school system expressed an interest in developing a prepayment plan, the hospitals were quick to respond. From their viewpoint, they could see two advantages. With a plan in operation they would have paying patients and at the same time, by sponsoring the plan, they could insist on being paid their operating costs and avoid providing nonreimbursed services. Thus, cost reimbursement was born. The idea of paying hospitals their costs of operation grew right along with the rapid enrollment in Blue Cross plans.

When Selective Service began in 1940 and civilians were drafted into the United States Armed Forces, a need developed to pay for hospital care for the dependents of servicemen. The result was the Emergency Maternal and Infant Care (EMIC) Program. Hospitals successfully argued the case for payment on the same basis as

3

that received from the nonprofit Blue Cross plans, cost reimbursement. Again, this turned out to be a success.

In 1964 and 1965, when Congress was considering Medicare and Medicaid legislation, hospitals once again successfully argued for being paid on a cost-reimbursement basis. When the legislation passed in 1965, a key element was the provision that hospitals would be paid on the basis of reasonable operating costs. This continued until October 1, 1983, when the federal government adopted the concept of diagnostic related groups (DRGs) and moved to paying hospitals on a price-per-case basis.

THE SWING TO COMPETITION

Until the move to DRGs occurred, hospitals were in a protected position. If their costs increased, for whatever reason, their income rose by the same amounts. In addition, their primary service areas were protected by the Certificate of Need process, which prevented the expansion of the number of beds beyond a predetermined formula that was known to all concerned parties. The pendulum swing then reversed and hospitals found themselves in a climate dominated by economic considerations. The protections afforded by health systems agencies over the marketplace, and payment for all of their costs of operation through cost reimbursement, were swept aside. The riskless environment became risky. The social agency ethic was replaced with the business ethic. Today, in recognition of this shift, traditional relationships need to be reexamined and, if necessary, modified to meet the requirements for institutional survival in the future.

One of the most important areas is the financing of the operating costs of health care. Until recently, hospitals concentrated on capital financing. From the 1940s to the late 1950s, buildings and equipment were purchased by using a combination of funds from philanthropy, government grants through the Hill-Burton program, and endowments. As the speed of medical technology increased and capital needs outstripped these sources of funding, hospitals turned to the debt market for its capital. Since hospitals had protected marketplaces and interest expense was a recognized element in cost reimbursement, hospitals were considered an excellent investment and correspondingly carried good ratings from Standard & Poor's and Moody's.

In the early 1980s, the bond market became aware that hospitals were a mature industry and that an excess bed capacity existed throughout the country. With the advent of the DRG program, it became widely recognized that hospitals were now in an economically competititve marketplace and the protections previously accorded bond holders no longer existed. The result was a drop in bond ratings.

As competition stiffened, hospitals increasingly looked with concern at their marketplaces. Having excess capacity and faced with decreasing occupancy levels in the years ahead, they sought ways to reverse this trend. This led many institutions to consider signing contracts with health maintenance organizations, preferred provider organizations, and independent practice associations at discounted rates. Such a practice is now being followed in the belief that beds that have patients in them, even at revenues that are less than full operating costs, are better than empty beds.

This new attitude is a return to the days of the 1930s. However, conditions have changed and cost reimbursement is unlikely to reappear as a method of paying hospitals. Instead, the movement away from cost reimbursement will continue and all payers will probably adopt a pricing mechanism that will be similar to the DRG approach by Medicare. The price-per-admission system will likely vary from carrier to carrier depending on the volume of patients under contract and how important it is to the hospital to have additional patients.

Even though nearly all hospitals have excess capacity, physicians have less and less influence on where patients are hospitalized. This is a consequence of the growth in various forms of capitation. Capitation prevents physicians from selecting a hospital of choice since that decision has been made prior to the time the patient sees the physician. That determination was made at the time an insurance carrier contracted with both the physician and the hospital. The major difference between now and earlier days, when Blue Cross and Blue Shield plans were formed, is that the "Blues" contracted with all hospitals and all physicians in the area, irrespective of whether they were high-cost or low-cost. Now, even traditional carriers are moving in the direction of making selective decisions in favor of those who offer the lowest prices through competitive bidding. Many Blue Cross plans have now formed separate, subsidiary corporations in order to offer capitation coverage through a health maintenance organization (HMO).

In an organizational context, the "Blues" are striving to maintain the same kind of relationship that previously prevailed with hospitals, an arm's length one that links two parties through a contract to pay for services provided to patients covered by the Blue Cross plan. However, capitation is a different concept from traditional prepayment and therefore a different relationship is required.

MOVING TO CAPITATION

In a capitation system, the plan seeks competitive bids from hospitals with the intent of selecting the lowest-cost bidder for a given period of time. Once a hospital has been selected, the plan's marketing program will use the reputation of a selected hospital in its promotional activities. The reputation of a hospital in the marketplace has considerable value in a promotional program since a major concern of potential subscribers is the hospital or hospitals they will be admitted to in the event of a serious illness. If the contracted hospitals are the premier institutions in the market area, the capitation plan has a decided advantage.

Capitation differs from the generally understood concept of a buyer and seller relationship. As a buyer of services, the plan selects a seller or contract hospital based on price quotations from all potential hospitals in the market area. Subscribers choose which plan to join, but have no involvement in a selection of hospital providers. The decision to enroll in one plan as opposed to others offered in the marketplace is based on

1. Monthly premium charged
2. Scope of services covered by the contract
3. Hospitals used by the plan

From the perspective of a hospital, the present-day economic climate is so changed that a reexamination of relationships that have traditionally existed with the various carriers is in order. When there were no financial risks involved and payments were assured, rewards were in the safety of the arrangement itself. Under capitation, this relationship no longer exists. The plans seek bids from hospitals for services to their subscribers and limit hospital selection to low bidders in the market area.

OLIGOPSONY

When there are only two, or perhaps three, capitation plans seeking to contract with any one hospital, the institution is in a difficult position. It is a classic case of oligopsony, where the marketplace has only a few buyers who control demand from a larger number of sellers. For example, assume that there are two capitation plans in a hospital's primary service area and they account for 40 percent of the hospital's patient days, each having 20 percent. In the same market area are six hospitals, all of which are requested to bid for the inpatient admissions from one of the plans. Also assume that the hospital is a voluntary nonprofit corporation that has minimal reserves and no endowment income, with an average occupancy rate of 70 percent. When the chief executive receives the request for a proposal (RFP), he is faced with a difficult situation. In order to secure the contract he knows he has to be the low bidder. His competition has the following characteristics:

Hospital A—A university hospital with the highest cost per patient per day in the state.

Hospital B—A small community hospital on the periphery of the service area that provides limited services.

Hospital C—A district hospital of about the same size that annually receives tax support equal to 7 percent of its annual budget.

Hospital D—A voluntary nonprofit hospital located one block away offering the same range of services and operating at 80 percent of capacity.

Hospital E—An investor-owned hospital owned by a chain operator operating at 65 percent occupancy and located one and one-half miles away.

Hospital F—A specialty hospital for women and children that is affiliated with the local medical school.

Clearly, the concerns of the chief executive will focus on hospitals C, D, and E. Questions that must be addressed are:

1. If a marginal cost concept in pricing the bid is used, how much of a discount can be offered?
2. Will Hospital D, one block away, be willing to do the same thing and, in addition, use some of its endowment income to offer an even more favorable discount?
3. To what extent will the investor-owned hospital use corporate resources to outbid the competition?
4. Will the district hospital use some of its tax support to offer a better discount?
5. If the bid is reduced to the lowest point possible, what will happen the following year when the contract is again up for bid?

As this situation is reviewed, will the question of clinical excellence of the medical staff and the quality of nursing service provided be considered? Upon reflection, a likely conclusion is that these aspects will not be of importance in securing a contract because of the previous efforts of both physicians and nurses over the last three decades to strengthen their education and training programs. As a result of these efforts, there is a remarkably uniform set of professionals that all practice well within acceptable norms and standards. The only remaining consideration then is the utilization rate, which is determined by a hospital's rate structure. Therefore, the original conclusion is reinforced, a decision to contract will be based on the lowest price.

As the various options are explored and discarded, a realization arises that economic competition is a risky business. To lose the bid carries severe economic penalties. To lose both existing contracts would be financial disaster. But to win a contract, at a price that is well below the lowest possible cost that can be attained, commensurate with patient safety, is also an unacceptable situation. These risks can be easily visualized, but there are no rewards. A balance between risk and reward is missing. The hospital is in a "no-win" position. To survive, a hospital has to find an option where, when risks are taken, there are opportunities for rewards as well. This can only be achieved through an ownership position in a capitation plan.

SHARING OWNERSHIP

Shared ownership is difficult to achieve when capitation plans are already in place, since they are unlikely to be willing to share ownership. From the hospital standpoint, it is imperative that an ownership position be achieved in an oligopsony marketplace. Bargaining for a share of ownership in existing capitation plans is difficult because the executives of capitation plans will usually conclude that hospitals are not a credible threat, even when hospitals take the position that they will form their own capitation plan if not accorded a share in ownership, and thereby be in direct competition with their organization.

When hospitals are unsuccessful in securing a shared ownership, they need to move rapidly to form their own capitation plan. Ideally, a for-profit capitation plan should be owned

- One-third by hospitals
- One-third by physicians
- One-third by the plan

Any plan that offers this type of ownership arrangement would have a decided advantage in a local market over an outside organization, even though an outside organization may have been operating for several years. While it is always desirable to be first into a marketplace, the value of having hospitals and physicians in ownership positions will offset the disadvantage of not being first.

The importance of ownership in capitation plans is imperative. The health field will be criticized by the general public for a number of years ahead even though serious efforts have reduced, or slowed, the overall costs of operation. Ownership of financing mechanisms that pay for health care offer the best opportunities for future financial stability. An example of the benefits of ownership of a capitation plan demonstrates this point. Assume a plan has 50,000 subscribers.

Average monthly premium per subscriber	$ 150
Average cost per month to the plan per subscriber	125
Net result, per subscriber, per month	$ 25
50,000 × $150 × 12 months = gross revenues	$90,000,000
50,000 × $125 × 12 months = cost to plan	75,000,000
Net result	$15,000,000

After appropriate allocations to reserves, operating expenses, etc., the net result is a substantial amount, approaching $5 million for each of the three major partnership groups. No combination of shared service programs approaches the potential for rewards as does ownership of a capitation plan. The alternative is to contract with a capitation plan and let a single insurance entity receive the total financial benefit generated by the serious efforts of physicians and hospitals.

Perhaps the single greatest advantage to owning a capitation plan is that it places the physician and the hospital on the same side of the economic table and creates meaningful shared economic interest. This is not the case when a third-party payer wholly owns the capitation plan because the physicians are pitted against hospitals and vice versa, each blaming the other party when financial difficulties are encountered in contracts with the plan.

When a hospital, or hospitals, join together with selected physicians to establish a capitation plan, the new partners can readily become a formidable competitor for any existing plan already in operation. If they carefully develop their marketing strategy and fully appreciate the price sensitivity of the public, they can, in a short period of time, capture a significant market share. If, at the same time that a sales effort begins, hospitals and physicians advertise the reputation of the hospitals and the high caliber of the physicians associated with the new plan, the public can be expected to shift to that plan. As this occurs, there is little that a capitation plan that failed to share ownership can use to compete. If hospitals and physicians terminate their contractual agreements with an existing plan, the only recourse open to a nonmedical capitation plan is to contract with less well-known physicians and less respected hospitals. As long as both an existing plan and a new plan are economically competitive in the marketplace, the medically sponsored plan will soon dominate the market.

There is only one way an existing capitation plan that does not share ownership can win in the marketplace. That is to keep the hospitals and physicians from forming a separate plan. When hospitals and physicians listen to representatives of an existing plan, they will hear a long litany of reasons as to why they should not proceed. Unspoken in the discussions that take place will be a very real fear in the minds of the existing plan executives that the new group will proceed. By blocking a medically sponsored plan, the old one protects itself in the marketplace. Plan executives are acutely aware that if the leading hospitals and physicians terminate their present relationships, their ability to hold on to the market share already in hand is likely to be severely damaged.

Hospitals and physicians need to recognize that leverage in the capitation market rests solely with them—if they choose to exercise it. Existing capitation plans that don't share ownership, and have no intention of doing so at any time in the future, are living on borrowed time. Once hospitals and physicians start their own capitation plan, existing ones can't turn around and offer ownership to bring them back into the fold since they are already committed as a direct competitor.

Capitation plans that succeed and grow in the years ahead will be a composite of ownership relationships between physicians, hospitals, and plans. Patterns may vary, but the crux of a successful equation will be that all three elements are economically linked together through ownership. Shared ownership provides strength and viability by replacing adversarial relationships with a mutually reinforcing economic interest. The opportunity to have physicians and hospitals mutually supportive of each other's roles will forge a whole new set of relationships between them that will lead to a stabilization of the financing of the health field in the years ahead.

Chapter 2

Shifting Roles in a Competitive Environment[*]

ELEMENTS OF CHANGE

As interest in economic competition has grown, hospital executives have accepted the notion that their role will finally be more fully appreciated by both governing boards and medical staffs. They recognize that institutional risks will be economic in nature and therefore be the responsibility of management. Thus far, little thought has been given to how this shift will impact their roles and bring about changes in administrative behavior. Clearly, their traditional characteristics, traits, and attitudes will undergo a shift.

Hospitals have engaged in competition with one another for a long time, but until recently competition has been noneconomic in nature. Traditionally, hospitals have vied for patients by improving their quality of care and broadening the range of services to attract physicians. Competent and capable physicians understood the quid pro quo was to admit their patients to the hospital as long as it had the most up-to-date technology, adequate nursing staff, and a supportive environment that catered to the needs of patient and physician. In a multihospital community, institutions that did so led the field. Because hospitals received adequate payment for patient services from insurance carriers and other third-party payers, neither patients nor attending physicians concerned themselves with cost.

Economic competition between providers of care creates significant change. The role of a third-party payer will no longer be a passive one of paying all bills of subscribers when they are hospitalized. Rather, third-party payers will negotiate with both physicians and hospitals for their services, proposing a larger volume of work with guaranteed payment for a predetermined discount price. They will no

---

*Adapted by permission from *Hospitals*, Vol. 57, No. 12, June 16, 1983. Copyright 1983, American Hospital Publishing, Inc.

longer pay hospitals the costs of providing the services rendered, but only the agreed-upon price. Hospitals will bid for these contracts. When an institution is inefficient and high-cost, its bids will reflect these facts in the proposals made to carriers. When efficient and low-cost, hospitals will bid lower and win contracts. In turn, patients with health insurance will be restricted to receiving care from physicians and hospitals with whom the carrier has contracts. Free choice of physician and hospital by patients will be limited to providers of care with whom the carrier has contracts. Economic competition will have arrived.

GROWING NEED FOR POLITICAL SKILLS

In the present-day hospital, a successful CEO needs a well-developed set of political skills. An ability to negotiate and compromise between differing viewpoints, while at the same time keeping the hospital moving ahead, is a prized commodity in a CEO. Finding the greatest amount of common ground between differing proponents requires patience and often a protracted period of time in order to reach consensus. This set of skills is based on knowing who to involve, when to involve them, and how much to expect of each party. Years of experience in this arena are essential.

In the new era, events will be moving at a faster pace and decisions will not wait upon complex, time-consuming organizational mechanisms. Of necessity, executives will be forced by circumstances beyond the control of an institution to make decisions. A greater degree of managerial authority will be required if the present pace of changing events is maintained. Securing agreement by governance and the medical staff before proceeding on a course of action involving all of the appropriate committees will no longer be workable.

To cope with changed conditions, administrative staffs will expand, with an emphasis placed on planning and analytical skills. Managerial reports to CEOs will need to be in greater depth and more comprehensive than reports now received and considered to be adequate by today's standards. There will be a premium on seasoned and mature CEO judgments based on solid experience. The administrative office will no longer be a training ground for new course graduates. The traditional career path involving a few years experience at the assistant or associate level, under a capable CEO, and then moving on to another hospital at a higher administrative level will soon be replaced. An administrative team composed of seasoned executives accustomed to working under pressure and being held accountable for their results will be the new model.

EVALUATING MANAGEMENT

The criteria used to evaluate a management team will undergo change. Dollars of revenue and costs of operation will become more important as price increases are publically resisted. A CEO will look for associates who carefully monitor operational statistics and take appropriate corrective action on their own initiative to keep costs in line without reducing the quality of services provided. Members of an administrative staff will develop an appreciation that their CEO views being tough-minded as a necessary ingredient to successful performance. They will also learn that being tough-minded must be coupled with real leadership skills to maintain acceptable standards of departmental performance. This combination of skills cannot be learned in a short period of time, but is the result of many years of experience gained in a well-rounded career of increasingly difficult assignments. Junior members of an administrative team will recognize that any one of the senior members could probably step into the position of CEO and be effective. They will not see the CEO as being head and shoulders above immediate subordinates, but rather the senior member of a team of competent executives.

During the early years of economic competition, managers are apt to experience difficulties because of a lack of familiarity with the new conditions they face. The result may be an overemphasis on the price/cost equation. Managers may lose sight of a need to maintain a balance between economics, quality of care, and comprehensiveness of service. There may be a tendency to overly scrutinize all programs that do not break even and then look to eliminating them, even though a program may be a needed community service. The justification for this decision will be made on financial grounds. This reaction to cost considerations will gradually be self-correcting as executives learn to balance economics, quality, and comprehensiveness without placing an institution in financial jeopardy.

ASKING THE RIGHT QUESTION

The problem of an overly developed cost consciousness will gradually moderate because physicians will continue to be attracted to membership on medical staffs that focus on quality and comprehensiveness of services. This will force hospitals to deal with all three of these factors in making their decisions. The result is a more complex equation. Instead of ''Does the proposed activity enhance patient care?'' the question to be answered will be ''Does the proposed activity enhance patient care at a cost that enables the hospital to remain competitive in the marketplace?''

The CEO who is afraid of an economically competitive marketplace will make decisions by answering a different question, ''How can hospital costs be cut to the bone?'' Answering this question is relatively simple, but it is not consonant with physician concerns about patient safety that are part of the traditions of the medical profession.

Economic competition is a new phenomenon for the hospital field. It differs markedly from the previous competition between hospitals. Under cost reimbursement there was no need to have a primary interest in operating efficiently, since any costs that were incurred could be directly passed through to third-party payers. This is not to say that CEOs were unconcerned about operating costs, but given a choice between holding the line or adding to quality or comprehensiveness, the inevitable decision was to make programmatic improvements in order to maintain physician support for an institution. Patient care decisions almost always outweighed cost considerations.

This type of decision making has long been recognized by management consultants. As advisers to hospitals they have seen a need to emphasize productivity to the same extent it is prevalent in the business field. However, the demand for such studies in the past was minimal. Under economic competition, support for this type of project is likely to grow rapidly as costs become a major priority in the minds of executives.

CHANGING RELATIONSHIPS

Economic competition will bring about changes in the relationships between CEO, governing board, and medical staff. Modifications will not be accepted readily by either trustees or physicians. Trustees who are in business will be supportive of the concerns of the administrative staff for increased productivity because they have the same kinds of interest in their own businesses. In nonprofit hospitals, a productivity drive may well pose a dilemma. Because trustees receive no compensation for their governing board services and have a strong sense of participation in a community/social agency activity, economic competition is at variance with their philosophical roots. Even though trustees recognize a hospital as a social enterprise with deepening economic overtones, they tend to consider their responsibilities as being conservators of community assets. They do not see themselves as entrepreneurs when serving as hospital trustees.

This concept of trusteeship is a deeply ingrained attitude. It has served the public well and has produced a hospital system unparalleled in the world. The very success that has been enjoyed will act as a deterrent to changing the formula.

Many trustees view a CEO of a hospital as being similar to a public official appointed to his position by an elected body, much in the same way that a professional city manager is seen by members of a city council. They are in favor of cooperation among hospitals and health agencies and tend to think that competition leads to higher costs because of unnecessary duplication of services. A lack of cooperation is apparent when viewed from the perspective of the community. On the other hand, competition may be a reality for survival when seen through the eyes of an individual institution. City council members often have the same kinds of feelings when they learn that the Streets Department has an active dislike of the Water and Sewer Department, which rips up roads to replace broken water mains.

COOPERATION

Given trustees' desire to have hospitals cooperate rather than compete, CEOs who aggressively seek to increase market share are likely to find less than enthusiastic support from governing boards. This reaction is particularly acute when service volumes increase as a result of reducing the market share of nearby hospitals or attracting patients away from practices of physicians on the medical staff. Some doctors believe the hospital should be prevented from competing with them for patients and services that can be performed in their own offices.

With public support for trustees that favor cooperation rather than an unregulated competitive environment, there is bound to be considerable support at the grass roots for continuing to regulate the hospital industry. A highly structured environment sits more easily on the conscience of trustees because it is less risky, since marketplaces tend to be protected as though hospitals had franchises. As trustees of community resources, they are uncomfortable in risking a substantial percentage of resources in programs and projects that have a degree of uncertainty. From their own business experiences, trustees are aware that a competitive environment often involves taking steps that they would prefer not to take. However, they understand that for an enterprise to remain competitive additional resources must be pumped into it. Trustees know that the specter of failure is always the companion of success.

RISKY RISK TAKING

CEOs need to have a high regard for the reluctance of trustees to support aggressive marketing programs and expenditures aimed solely at remaining competitive. Since governing boards have a preference for regulation, cooperation between institutions, and an orderly environment, a CEO of a nonprofit hospital is apt to be in a lonely position when it comes to risk taking. To their dismay, CEOs in the nonprofit sector will learn that the rewards for successful risk taking will be different from those of their colleagues in the for-profit sector. The not-for-profits will take risks to protect or strengthen market share or assure fiscal viability, but not to put as many revenue dollars as possible on the bottom line. Stated another way, nonprofit hospitals will take risks to avoid failure, while for-profit hospitals will take risks to achieve greater financial success. The difference may be subtle, but will profoundly affect the way a CEO is regarded by a governing body.

In the case of the CEO of a nonprofit hospital, should the risk taking be a failure, board members will put some distance between themselves and the CEO. On the other hand, if the venture is successful, the CEO will be regarded as simply doing a job for which he is employed. Those who philosophically see themselves as conservators of community funds are likely to look for a scapegoat if a risk turns out badly. Successes may be buried, since the rewards of risk taking will become part of the stream of revenues required to keep the hospital up-to-date in new technology or to offset bad debts and charity allowances.

Under economic competition CEOs of nonprofit hospitals will find their judgments on the line. No longer will they be able to hide behind decisions of governing boards. The fact that a governing board has approved a risk-taking activity will not let a CEO off the hook; accountability for performance and good judgment will receive greater attention in the coming era.

MEDICAL STAFF ATTITUDES

Relationships between members of a medical staff and their CEO will also undergo change. Difficulties will be encountered by the CEO from the medical staff when a need arises to move away from the status quo. The compelling reasons will be economic, but physicians will be hard put to think of it in terms of having equal priority with patient care and comprehensiveness of services. Physicians have been accustomed to their role as the initiator of important hospital changes: deciding on new procedures, or new clinical equipment, or new programs. From this viewpoint the role of a CEO is to provide the support systems needed to respond to diagnostic and therapeutic orders of attending physicians. The hospital is seen as a patient care institution, where all other concerns are secondary in importance.

In a period of ample resources, when noneconomic competition prevailed and health care saw a rapid expansion of clinical technology, this viewpoint was to be expected. Physicians were not only gatekeepers to the hospital but had an advantage over the hospital because economics was not a major concern. There was no abridgement of a physician's decision to admit patients to the hospital; the institution was a bystander, as were third-party carriers to the decision. Payment for hospital services was given and would automatically occur after the care was rendered.

Under economic competition the terms of reference are likely to be drastically altered, which in turn substantially affects the hospital CEO relationship with the medical staff. In the future, when economic competition is in full force, a hospital can look forward to receiving a request for a proposal (RFP) from a third-party carrier wanting a quotation on providing services for x numbers of days of inpatient care. If the hospital is entrepreneurially oriented, the quotation that is prepared will be the result of a collaborative effort with the medical staff. The response will likely include a combination of hospital services and the professional component, where both parties discount their usual prices, hoping that by doing so the result will be the low bid received by the third-party carrier. When this approach is first proposed, physicians may react negatively, since they believe that hospitals should have no concern in setting their professional fees. However, when physicians participate in a proposal and the result is successful in winning the business that has been put out to bid, other hospitals and medical staffs can be expected to follow suit.

Should medical staffs cling to their traditional attitudes, they can look forward to a continued loss of business. Third-party payers are concerned with the total cost of each case, not with component parts, and they can be expected to award contracts on this basis. A few rounds in this arena will lead medical staffs to conclude that the hospital has an important role in securing contracts for both hospital and professional services. No longer will physicians attempt to keep the hospital an economic neutral to protect their incomes. They will realize that hospital executives are an important ally in winning contracts.

During the early stage of economic competition, CEOs are not likely to use this approach on the medical staff. The first skirmish inside the hospital is more apt to be with the hospital-based specialists who will be asked, as part of the hospital bid, to accept 75 to 80 percent of their ''usual, reasonable, and customary'' fees. Their reaction to this proposal is predictable. When asked, hospital-based specialists can be expected to marshal support among private practitioners on the medical staff to prevent an intrusion into their professional prerogatives. Recognizing that if the CEO is successful, the next step may also include them, private practitioners may rally to the support of the hospital-based specialists. Some CEOs will not survive this internal battle. Others will recognize a danger to their positions and will not pursue this approach. Only those who are risk takers will proceed.

RESTRUCTURING HOSPITAL CORPORATIONS

In hospitals that have undergone corporate restructuring and created a parent/ subsidiary model (i.e., where the hospital is a subsidiary of a health care corporation that operates several subsidiary corporations), the perils of dealing with a medical staff will be lessened for the CEO of the parent organization. Removed from daily operations of the hospital, he is not easily accessible to members of the medical staff. Since the CEO's interests, of necessity, involve other subsidiaries of the health care corporation, as well as that of the hospital, the CEO will have a more detached and objective perspective that is required for successful bidding. Given the importance of a contract to the total corporation, the CEO can push harder against medical staff attitudes without fear of retaliation, knowing the governing board of the parent organization will probably share this viewpoint.

The taking of risk by a parent corporation in a health care corporation will be a well-traveled route by the time economic competition arrives in full flower. As the number of subsidiaries increase, and as more and more health-related activities are spread to multiple sites, the CEO will think and behave as an entrepreneur. The challenge to develop new programs and services in a risk-filled environment will be appealing and satisfying. Previously, the main challenges encountered included testing of the CEO's administrative ability to reconcile differences between key figures of the medical staff and the governing board, and the result was progress on programs, if any, at an inch-by-inch pace.

LEADING THE ORGANIZATION

As entrepreneurial instincts develop, a CEO will slide into the role of leader of the total organization, rather than remain a servant of the governing board. As a CEO gains confidence as an entrepreneur, concerns that were previously felt in tackling board or medical staff problems will be minimized. Gradually, a CEO will come to appreciate a risk-taking environment as generating more real satisfaction than any experienced as a hospital administrator. In turn, there will be less and less reverting to consensus finding and more and more reliance on hard data and objective thinking. In the event a CEO leaves a health care corporation, it is predictable that he may remain in the community where roots have been established and establish some kind of enterprise where the skills that have been honed in the previous position can be utilized. Within the field of hospital administration, there will be more movement of CEOs out of the profession to develop businesses of their own.

There will also be an attitude change among CEOs of nonprofit hospitals toward the investor-owned chains. Under economic competition they will increasingly come to understand that for-profit hospitals make substantial net profits by carefully segmenting the marketplace and then filling in the gaps by providing service and quality care at an economically attractive price. When they see colleagues in for-profit hospital organizations receive substantial bonuses and equity positions for outstanding managerial performance, those who are talented will leave the nonprofit sector for greater rewards. As capable executives they will seek tangible recognition of their abilities.

From a management standpoint, economic competition will force nonprofit hospitals to adopt management information and reporting systems that are carbon copies of those in use by for-profit hospitals. Interpretations of reports received and actions that follow will parallel those that occur in investor-owned hospitals. Instead of casually reviewing ratios (such as employees per occupied beds on a monthly basis), under the new game plan, CEOs are apt to call for this report on a daily or weekly basis and follow up adverse reports with corrective action on the same day.

The budgeting process can be expected to be tightened. Instead of establishing new vacancies at the beginning of the fiscal year and letting department directors fill them at their leisure, a two-step procedure will be adopted. The slotting of new positions, or the filling of vacancies at budget time, will depend on the demonstration of increased workloads. When it is time to fill a position, a review of workloads to date will be made to assure that what was expected has in fact occurred. Only then will a position be filled.

TEACHING HOSPITALS

Teaching hospitals, under economic competition, will be particularly hard hit. CEOs will face the severest problems of CEOs in all hospitals. Their dilemma will be to successfully compete on an economic basis for patient care contracts and at the same time continue to provide residency and postgraduate education for a large house staff. If they continue to lump together patient care and education, they will be able to attract only those types of patients for which they offer a unique service unavailable elsewhere in the community. Since this is too limited a volume to keep overall hospital occupancies at acceptable levels, other steps will be necessary.

When economic competition ripens, teaching institutions will probably have to separate out patient care costs from educational ones and reflect these differences in their accounting system. This may turn out to be a difficult task, but one that must be accomplished. Once achieved, it still leaves unsolved the problem of paying for educational programs. Teaching hospital executives will be hard pressed if they accept no financial responsibility for educational programs; they will be confronted by a hostile teaching faculty. If, on the other hand, they acquiesce to supporting the educational commitments of the institution, they will run the risk of pricing patient care services above the going rates of the marketplace—with dire financial consequences. Leaning too far in either direction or hanging on to the status quo may both lead to unfavorable results.

Given existing constraints, the first responses of teaching hospitals under economic competition are predictable. Third-party carriers will be asked to accept university hospital bids that are higher than those of community hospitals because of the unique nature of their services. This same argument has been effectively used since the early days of third-party coverage.

In university hospitals the CEO will have an especially difficult situation. Where the hospital is part of the university, and the CEO reports to an academic dean or vice-president, educators dominate the decision-making apparatus, so that the necessity for competing on a price basis in the marketplace may not be squarely faced until the medical center is confronted with the very real prospect of bankruptcy. Should this crisis occur, the result will be an organizational wrenching in which administratively oriented executives are replaced with educational administrators. When the results of this choice become clear, it will be observable that the problem was not management but the pricing of services at a noncompetitive level. When that point is driven home to faculties, the next step will be to seek funding for education from alternative sources. Since tax monies are the most likely support, they will be sought at all levels of government. Where positive results ensue, there is likely to be a quid pro quo involved; the university medical center will get tax dollars in return for patient care to welfare and indigent patients. The wear and tear on university hospital CEOs in making this kind of transition will be the most difficult burden experienced by anyone in the field of hospital administration.

THE FUTURE

The events just outlined will markedly affect CEOs but will also bring about structural changes in the organization of the hospital. Hospitals will grow in size and complexity, with many of them turning into health care corporations operating multiple kinds of health services at several locations. The hospital/health care corporation will have annual revenues many times larger than at present.

As the pace of activities increases, a CEO will have to be granted wider latitude in decision making, by the transfer of authority from the governing board to the chief executive. Making hard decisions that balance quality of care, comprehensiveness, and price will become administrative responsibilities because of the complexity of issues. This delegation of authority will lead to a reduction in the number of governing board committees and ultimately the size of a board. Because of the necessity for rapid decisions most matters will move directly to the governing board for action instead of first going the committee route. Board decisions will be based on recommendations of the CEO rather than of a committee. As this procedure becomes standard operating practice in a hospital, governing boards will seek to put into place improved and expanded evaluation techniques to avoid becoming the captive of the CEO, hearing and acting only on matters brought to them through that channel. Feedback mechanisms will increase in sophistication and will lead to improved and strenghtened accountability on the part of the CEO to the governing board.

Economic competition will separate the brave from the timid in hospital management. Those who survive will be seasoned, tough-minded hospital executives who thoroughly enjoy taking risks in an environment where winners and losers can easily be identified. It will be a high-stakes game where balanced judgment, experience, ability, and courage will be needed in large measure. Those CEOs who seek such a challenge will find economic competition to be the most satisfying period of their professional careers.

Chapter 3

The Quiet Revolution[*]

Over the next decade the health delivery system will undergo radical change; change that is not now being given substantial consideration by either physicians or hospital executives. It will occur quietly without fanfare, but when viewed from ten years hence it will be identifiable as a revolution, much to the surprise of many who lived through the turbulent years of the '70s when hospitals and government were locked in a seemingly never-ending struggle. There will, of course, be problems, but they will not be ones that now dominate the daily diet of hospital administrative life. Long gone will be bruising battles with health system agencies (HSAs) and state rate review commissions. Concerns about bureaucratic meddling and tinkering with the system will be replaced with thoughts about improving productivity, the application of pricing services based on marginal cost concepts, and the realities of living in a free marketplace.

LOOKING BACK

To understand the future course of events a look at the past is needed, as well as a perspective as to what is going on at the present time. Looking back over the past century, Odin Anderson identified the major thrusts of the hospital field.[1] He characterized the period from 1870 to 1930 as one in which all of the developed nations were concerned with growth and expansion of hospitals. In the United States the number of hospitals grew from 450 to over 5,000. From 1930 to 1965, all hospitals had a common problem, the putting in place of financing mechanisms for purchasing hospital care, and from 1965 on, a mutual interest in controlling

---

*Adapted from *Hospital Progress* (now *Health Progress*) with permission of The Catholic Health Association of the United States, © November 1977.

costs. This last phase was fueled by a rapid expansion of residency training, which took place immediately following the end of World War II.

The growth in specialists and subspecialists led to a metamorphosis in hospitals. Whereas in the past they were patient-care institutions offering limited diagnostic and therapeutic services, they now have become large, technologically oriented enterprises that cost ever-increasing sums of money to operate. As a result, the public has come to believe that hospitals are out of control. This is where we are today. It is clearly evident that the point has been passed where doing a better public relations job of explaining costs will be all that is needed to soothe the tempers of a disbelieving public. The answers of the past are no longer acceptable.

The evidence for needed change, any kind of change, is piling up. There is a growing recognition that cost containment may be required to stem the continued rise in hospital costs; that both labor and management are now serious about restraining additional dollars for higher and higher premiums for health coverage; that cost reimbursement is not a satisfactory method for reimbursing hospitals; that inefficiency is not penalized nor efficiency rewarded under present financing mechanisms; that competition is noneconomic between hospitals; and that the present system is disjointed and uncoordinated. There is also a growing recognition that life styles need to be altered if better health for all is to become possible. As the list lengthens those calling for change grow in numbers.

GROWING UNREST

Significantly, government has now been joined by labor and management in desiring a change in the health field. This has been brought about as an outcome of collective bargaining. Over the years negotiations between the two on health care benefits centered on the items to be included, without any real knowledge of the amount of dollars that were involved. After the fact, it was discovered that the costs were often much higher than had been anticipated, but the door was closed to reopening the matter at the next round of negotiations because it had been agreed to as a fringe benefit in a health package without dollars being attached. Because the benefits are often comprehensive the only practical solution is for corporations to maintain their commitment to the established range of services and absorb an annual hike in premium rate. The increased cost then becomes a bargaining point for the corporation, which correctly points out that it has added dollars to the fringe-benefit package and wants it recognized by union representatives. From the other side of the table unions may be unwilling because to do so represents a benefit already in the fringe-benefit package and their membership will not acknowledge it as a new or additional benefit. The point has now been reached where both groups are looking for ways around this troublesome issue and recognize a mutual interest to be served if they can contain hospital costs.

As the number of premium dollars has escalated in corporate budgets, there has been a growing interest in using these dollars to secure bids to provide health care on a competitive basis to benefit large block purchasers of health care. For better or worse, the mutual interests of management and labor are now joined with those of government to bring about a major change in the way they plan to do business with the health industry.

THE OPTIONS

Assuming that change will occur because of a deep interest in controlling health care costs, the question to be addressed is what avenue is most likely to be followed. Five options can be identifiable:

1. Continue the status quo
2. Continue to increase regulation
3. Introduce meaningful economic competition
4. Alter physician behavior
5. Alter consumer behavior

The first two options hold little promise for the future, as past events clearly indicate. The status quo route of minding the store, of doing things in the way they have been done in the past, will only see a continuation of past trends in costs and public attitudes. The same outcome holds true for the second alternative, of continuing to increase government regulation.

Behind the governmental posture on controlling costs lies a belief that hospitals are inefficient and mismanaged. Unfortunately, it is difficult to refute this opinion so long as cost reimbursement dominates the payment mechanism. To pay a hospital an additional dollar of revenue for each additional dollar of expense seems to the public mind a way to encourage inefficiency. Hospital people deny this generalization and legitimately claim that the Economic Stabilization Program of the early 1970s far more seriously penalized efficient institutions than it did inefficient ones. They correctly point out that the fat became leaner and the lean nearly starved to death. Notwithstanding this experience, the public disbelieves, and will continue to do so, until cost reimbursement is totally abandoned.

Public dissatisfaction is heightened when confronted with the costs of an emergency room visit, the problem of securing regular medical attention when moving from one community to another, the lack of sufficient numbers of primary care physicians, the array of medical bills to be paid for a major illness; all of these elements are laying a groundwork for change.

The last three alternatives provide hope for the future and are linked together. Moving away from payments that are cost reimbursed is not easy to accomplish, yet it is essential to establishing meaningful competition. The barriers are substantial. The present contracts between hospitals and Blue Cross will need to be modified. In most of these contracts, there is a provision that the carrier is entitled to pay the hospital "costs or charges, whichever is lower." This effectively precludes differential pricing and results in requiring a hospital to offer its lowest contract price to other carriers. The hospital is forced to apply an average cost or average price to all of its services, preventing the use of a marginal cost concept. Under this type of a Blue Cross contract, a hospital is effectively deterred from seeking to competitively bid for small service volumes because, if it were successful, the same rates available would have to be made available to Blue Cross.

In states with rate review commissions, a similar problem is found. For instance, in Connecticut, the commission insists that all carriers be charged an identical amount for each unit of service, irrespective of the numbers of units of service provided. State rate review agencies, under this policy, are a barrier to competition.

Internally, hospitals reflect entrenched viewpoints that represent barriers to change. Medical staffs of community hospitals can be characterized as having attitudes overwhelmingly in favor of fee-for-service and free choice of physician. The establishment of a free marketplace runs counter to these attitudes since it necessitates patients selecting both physicians and hospitals from approved lists where contractual relationships have been developed and defines a range of service to be provided and the rates to be paid. If, as a part of bringing about economic competition, hospitals find they must negotiate for physician services and fees, medical staffs are apt to resist.

Whenever possible, physicians usually attempt to keep the hospital as an economic neutral with regard to their services. Anesthesiologists prefer separate billing, as do many radiologists and pathologists. Other specialists, such as cardiologists, emergency room physicians, neontologists, and physiatrists, usually feel the same way. Given a choice, physicians prefer that a hospital have no role in determining charges for their professional services.

To shift from these concepts is to move away from the status quo. When hospitals attempt to do so they can anticipate that physicians will consider their actions as a violation of the concept of the corporate practice of medicine. State statutes limit the practice of medicine to natural persons. Overlooked, by this line of reasoning, is the number of physicians now employed by hospital corporations in university medical centers, state mental institutions, community hospitals, emergency rooms, industrial medicine, chronic care institutions, and in the rapidly developing health maintenance organizations. To avoid confrontation on this issue it is desirable to repeal these laws.

Even a section of the planning act, PL 93-641, has built-in barriers to effective competition. Three of the ten guidelines used to evaluate a hospital's application for a Certificate of Need relate to cooperative planning. Under these guidelines, a hospital is expected to develop a plan, share information with other institutions in the same service area, and secure agreement from them. This same kind of cooperation is being forced by various state rate review commissions that examine hospital budgets to ensure that rate structures are similar for the same kinds of services. Not only is there no penalty for exchanging price and cost information between institutions, the activity is considered desirable. When such a practice occurs in other industries it is seen as illegal since it is a collusion or restraint of trade. The Department of Justice views hospitals as it does other forms of enterprise. It sees its responsibility as one of encouraging competition, not of encouraging cooperation and sharing arrangements.

If economic competition is to become the road to follow, then the hospital field needs to work with Congress to remove barriers that are now in place under PL 93-641. Price fixing and cooperation are as undesirable among hospitals as they are in American industry. To force either, or both, of these end results on hospitals is not in the public interest. Thus far, hospital executives have been unwilling to take public stands against these guidelines, though privately they admit that they are a farce because they do not square with the real world and the competitiveness that exists. A poll would probably show that, given a choice between the position of the Department of Health and Human Services (HHS) or the Department of Justice, hospital executives favor the stand of the Justice Department since it would allow them to use their managerial talents to the maximum, rather than having to use manipulative skills as they now must do.

One of the most difficult barriers to overcome will be moving hospital governing boards away from the status quo. Trustees listen thoughtfully to medical staffs and if they sense that physicians associated with a hospital do not want to make any changes, they are likely to take the same position. They see physicians as surrogate customers and are not apt to take a position that alienates the prevailing viewpoints of the medical staff. This bias suggests that the hospital, particularly a community, nonprofit institution, will react to changes in the marketplace, but will not attempt to reshape the marketplace to protect the hospital.

A FREE MARKETPLACE

Before addressing ways in which the health delivery system can be restructured to bring about changes in physician and consumer behavior through economic competition, a look at the advantages of a free marketplace is useful. Price competition does not occur when a cost-reimbursement system pays for hospital care. The patient neither knows, nor is concerned, about the size of the hospital bill, and in many cases, is not even concerned about the monthly premium paid by an employer. A large percentage of patients using hospitals are shielded from both cost and price impacts. Under economic marketplace conditions, both the hospital and the physician are placed at risk since the purchaser is contracting for large blocks of service on behalf of individuals, with the best price available likely to be the determining factor. This is quite different from the past when dollars were not even considered. When a hospital found itself losing market share, its response was likely to be to increase its operating costs and charges for its services because the hospital developed new diagnostic or treatment services, or renovated plant and equipment, all for the purpose of attracting new physicians to the medical staff. In some situations it included a physician recruiting program that guaranteed incomes and underwrote the costs of office space.

The lack of economic competition is evident when hospitals are compared by size ranges. The smallest hospitals nearly always have the lowest costs and the largest hospitals the highest because large hospitals have the most comprehensive range of services to make them more desirable to physicians. Thus, higher cost became associated with better quality of care and low cost with an inferior level.

When competition enters the picture, cost becomes a primary factor and typically leads to improved efficiency. Those hospitals that remain inefficient discover that they are pricing their services too high to be competitive. Bidding makes hospitals sharpen their pencils and resort to the application of marginal costing in determining their bids.

In a free marketplace, hospitals become reluctant to cooperate with other hospitals or to exchange pertinent financial information. As in other forms of enterprise, they come to appreciate that the pricing of hospital services is proprietary information.

Gaining acceptance of the idea of a free marketplace for hospital and physician services is difficult, not only because it is a shift from the status quo, but because it also moves the risk taking from the third-party carrier to the hospital and the physician. Cost reimbursement to hospitals, and reasonable and customary fees to physicians, embodies no financial risks to either of them. By introducing competitive factors the leverage shifts and both hospitals and physicians find that managerial acumen is a valuable asset.

The shifting of risk, which now rests with third-party carriers, can be accomplished through the adoption of a capitation method to pay for health care services. By putting out bids and having them accepted, paying for hospital and physician services largely becomes a fixed cost to the prepayment agency and a variable cost to the providers, depending on the number of units of service used during the contract period.

In the past, entering into a competitively bid contract made little sense to either physicians or hospitals since both were paid for each unit of service furnished to a patient. There was no need for a provider to bid for patients; the marketplace required only that a third party be billed for services rendered.

THE HMO

A new phenomenon is developing that will bring about significant changes in the next decade. The early steps in the formation of health maintenance organizations (HMOs) climaxed with the passage of a federal act in 1973. Even though such organizations had been in existence since before World War II, their influence was primarily restricted to the West Coast with the Kaiser-Permanente Plan, to New York City with the Health Insurance Plan (HIP) and to Washington, D.C., with the Group Health Association (GHA). In some circles, the HMO Act was viewed as a way of triggering widespread development of capitation payment systems. For unknown reasons, the expected surge in HMOs did not occur until 1977 when enrollments moved sharply upward.

Though an individual can never bring about the kinds of results that big block purchasers of health care can achieve, the result is the same when one enrolls in a capitation plan. The elements of such a plan call for the formation of a corporation that will enroll subscribers, either individually or through groups, and in turn contract with hospitals and physicians for large volumes of service at a fixed cost to the corporation. Both free choice of physician and hospital are restricted to the parties of the contract, except for highly specialized services.

With government, labor, and management now all in the same camp with respect to containing hospital costs by fostering growth in capitation plans, the stage is now set for rapid development. An annual growth in membership of 20 percent per year will result in 1988 in 41,300,000 persons being covered, or 17 percent of a population of 242,000,000. It seems likely that this projected result will take place.

As HMO plans grow in numbers and increase in size, they will loom larger and larger in importance. In sections of the country where their growth is the most rapid, it will become evident that managerial abilities of the hospital administrative staff are a crucial factor for the viability of an institution trying to survive in a highly competitive economic situation. Efficiency and control of costs will be of much greater significance than is now the case. Three trends will then be recognized:

1. As enrollments in capitation plans grow in communities, there will be a proportionate growth of interest among hospitals to achieve increased efficiency.
2. As capitation plans grow, the reasonable and customary fees concept to pay physicians will proportionately decline in importance as a method of paying for their services.

3. In communities where the majority of physician and hospital care is delivered through capitation plans, the role of the Health Systems Agency (HSA) will be markedly different from its present one.

Instead of attempting to put roadblocks in front of hospitals wishing to make capital expenditures, HSAs will, of necessity, move from this negative stance to a more positive one where the HSA will become an agent to encourage competition. In communities where hospitals are deeply involved in competition, HSAs will have no meaningful role in monitoring capital expenditures, since marketplace forces will automatically come into play. Once several capitation plans exist in the same service area the need for an HSA disappears.

When a hospital wishes to expand, renovate, remodel, or reequip, the final decisions will be based on the effect on future bids to a capitation plan. If a hospital decides that a proposed capital improvement program will put it at a competitive disadvantage, it will forego the proposed program.

The HSA's future role will be to advocate adherence to established standards of performance and quality in the construction of facilities. In many ways HSAs will probably evolve a role similar to that performed by the Federal Aviation Administration, which establishes and monitors standards of aircraft performance. Under economic competition it will not be necessary for an HSA to concern itself with the number of beds per 1,000 population, average occupancy rates, numbers of computed axial tomography (CAT) scanners in a service area, or other ratios or numbers.

If hospitals elect to join with labor and management in bringing about meaningful economic competition, they need to take a hard look at the role of government in the development of HMOs. The 1973 HMO Act had a number of provisions that proved to be detrimental to rapid expansion. The scope of services turned out to be so comprehensive that the monthly premium charged proved to be too costly to be salable in an open market. Groups considering the formation of health maintenance organizations would be wise to avoid seeking federal grants or certification. Nor can a new HMO plan afford to attract low socioeconomic groups since this might deter middle-income families who will view it as a program for the poor.

To be salable, a capitation plan must provide a range of services dictated by a monthly premium level that is competitive against all other offerings and appealing to middle-income families. This approach is similar to the pattern followed by Blue Cross in the early 1930s when it was established for the teachers in Dallas, Texas. Wide social acceptability of a program by the public is as necessary now to the marketing of capitation plans as it was to Blue Cross 50 years ago.

If economic competition becomes a moving force in the health field, a number of advantages will result. Its greatest strength is that it will be responsive to conditions that exist in any given community.

Since less than 7 percent of the population of this country is now enrolled in a capitation plan there are going to be many more such plans formed in the next few years. Those that can be expected to develop a capitation system include Blue Cross, commercial insurance companies, groups of physicians, investor-owned hospital corporations, community hospitals, and industrial corporations. Examples of each are already on the scene. Blue Cross is involved and commercial carriers are experimenting in selected areas along with some of the investor-owned groups; physicians are forming independent practitioner associations (IPAs) in California, Colorado, and Massachusetts; large nonprofit hospitals in metropolitan centers like Chicago are gaining experience; and industry is carefully observing the HMO of the R.J. Reynolds Tobacco Company in Winston-Salem, North Carolina. The results to date are mixed, but interesting, as enrollments commence climbing at a rapid rate.

With all of this increasing interest, hospitals are going to have to move decisively or they will abdicate their pivotal role in the health delivery system to those that do. As capitation plans grow and multiply, hospitals will come to appreciate that they have both much to protect and much to offer to the changing health scene. Over the past 50 years hospitals have become a technologically oriented industry that is both labor and capital intensive. These high-cost, specialized institutions need to be used as productively as possible and must remain alert to changes in their community and market share. They will face competition from other groups that will also be as interested in forming capitation plans. A variety of arguments will be used to keep hospitals from taking any initiative. The most difficult argument to cope with for a hospital will be from the medical staff. It can be anticipated that its members will favor the formation of an IPA to sponsor a capitation plan and that they will be opposed to the hospital moving into this position and will bring pressure to bear on governing boards to prevent it.

With a growing concern in industry for capitation systems, industry can be expected to use its leverage to ensure maximum results. Once industry supports capitation, physicians will quickly appreciate that the size of their practices may be reduced as plan enrollment increases in a local community. Once this is a general awareness among physicians, the attitudes of physicians will shift. Hospitals can proceed to take leadership in forming capitation plans, and they may eventually have the support of their medical staff. When physicians feel threatened, they view the hospital as offering the best alternative among available options, even though under other circumstances, it would have been undesirable. The least undesirable then becomes acceptable.

Hospitals that fail to take the leadership in the capitation movement will, in time, find themselves competing for a smaller and smaller share of a market. There will be exceptions to this trend, but in general it will hold. Only those hospitals in communities where capitation plans are not available will escape, along with highly specialized services in medical centers where the service is one of a kind.

THE RACE TO CONTROL

The race to control capitation plans has just commenced in earnest and their importance to the health delivery system has just begun to be recognized. These plans bring a new set of problems with them that are different from those now faced by hospitals. But they also provide an avenue for reconciling public attitudes and hospital viewpoints through a previously untried approach, a free marketplace where economic competition becomes the determinant of who survives and who does not. The thoughtful application of economics to the hospital scene will not only strengthen the ability of this industry to respond to the public but can be woven together with ways for altering physician and consumer behavior through economic incentives or disincentives.

The events of the coming decade lead to a conclusion that a positive program is essential. Plans must be developed and can be built around the following conclusions:

1. Hospitals now engage in noneconomic competition but need to operate in a free marketplace.
2. Cost reimbursement as a method of paying hospitals is being replaced with a pricing system.
3. Hospitals need to operate in an environment that rewards institutions with managerial expertise. Conversely, hospitals that operate inefficiently have to be automatically penalized by economic forces at work in the marketplace.
4. Management and labor are now serious about a need to develop appropriate alternate health delivery systems.
5. Hospitals should take the leadership in bringing about a rapid expansion of capitation plans as the best method to encourage economic competition.
6. Even though physicians will want to keep hospitals economically neutral with regard to their economic interests, these attitudes must be handled in a tactful manner.
7. The need for health systems agencies will decline at an inverse rate to the growth of subscribers in capitation plans.

Within the broad dimensions of the quiet revolution in the next decade several practices may be helpful in speeding up the coming changes:

1. Hospitals should be encouraged to take the lead in the formation of capitation plans by mandating preferential treatment by HSAs.
2. State laws on the corporate practice of medicine should be eliminated.

3. Requirements in third-party reimbursement and state rate review commissions that prevent the application of marginal cost pricing of hospital services should be removed.
4. Hospitals should develop working coalitions with local industry groups to foster the rapid expansion of capitation plans as the best method to encourage economic competition.

These steps are not a panacea to solve the problems of the future for the hospital field as it redefines its relationship with the public. They represent only a beginning effort to find a new pathway that will establish hospitals in the forefront of the quiet revolution that is now just evolving.

There are departures from the traditions that built the health care system of this country, but in a broader sense the road just outlined will lead hospitals into the mainstream of American life with an ability to successfully compete in a free marketplace. It is worth the effort.

NOTE

1. Odin Anderson, personal communication with author.

Chapter 4

The Unknowns of a Competitive Health Care System

AN AMERICAN CONCEPT

Discussions about developing a competitive health care system have progressed from the question of what is it, to how can it be accomplished, to studying a variety of proposals. The time is now at hand to begin an effort to understand what is afoot and whether it is good or bad.

Essentially, the title of a ''competitive health care system'' is a shorthand way of identifying proposed control of rates and payments to physicians, hospitals, and nursing homes by making the public price sensitive to medical care services. For the past 50 years, the health field has been busily creating mechanisms that insulated the patient's bank account from the costs of care. The popular motto of the past decade has been equal access and equal care for one and all.

Now that we are spending 10 percent of our gross national product for health care services and all of the planning laws, Professional Review Organizations (PROs), voluntary effort, utilization reviews, and rate reviews establishing commissions have not turned the tide, the issue of the effectiveness of existing reimbursement practices and governmental regulation is under siege. The only way out of the present dilemma is to discard the existing system and replace it with the tried and true American notion of competition in the marketplace.

The argument for a competitive system hinges on an opinion that further efforts at regulation are only band-aids.

How do we go about setting up a competitive system? Whether or not the health care system is amenable to the forces of price competition is still unknown. The logical step would be to buy a country, say, about the size of Ecuador, and give the concept a test run. This, of course, is foolishness, and we might very well adopt the rules of economic competition, untested, and have a great national experiment.

One should be clear about the use of the word competition. There is competition now in hospital care, but not in the rate structures. Hospitals compete for physician support, for philanthropy, and for favorable regulatory treatment. The more hospitals in the same market area, the more the competition.

This means that one-hospital towns have no competitors and both physicians and patients will continue to use the local institution as they have in the past. In two-hospital towns, institutional competition does occur; particularly, if one hospital is investor-owned and the other is either a community nonprofit or hospital authority facility.

In metropolitan areas, there is a substantial level of competition, not directly for patients, but through the attraction of physicians by providing a broad range of comprehensive services and state-of-the-art technology.

THE UNKNOWNS

The largest unknown in a competitive system is based on the reality that a patient, in order to purchase hospital services, must also buy a physician's services, and the effect of hospital competition can be attenuated by the decisions and behavior of the physician. Physicians tend to center their hospital practices primarily in one institution, because of personal convenience, familiarity with operating procedures, and friendship with medical staff colleagues.

The unknown is, to what extent will patients change from one physician to another because of higher-cost hospital services?

Another unknown is the difficulty patients encounter in obtaining relevant information through comparative pricing of hospital services. The multitude of separate hospital rates for specific services makes the task of comparing prices complex. Moreover, a patient cannot determine what services will be required prior to admission and, therefore, is unable to ask for the appropriate rates. The total number of rates used in a hospital are probably between 2,000 and 3,000.

A third major unknown is the degree to which inefficient, or noncompetitive hospitals will be allowed to fail or to go into bankruptcy. Community pride in a hospital often keeps uneconomical institutions afloat. When a financial crunch occurs, a path to survival is usually found one way or another. To what extent this will continue to occur in a competitive system is a guess.

There are many other imponderables—how insurance companies will deal with their set of problems, whether or not a Medicare and Medicaid voucher system will work, how politically feasible is capping the deductibility of health care insurance premiums for tax purposes.

It is realistic to believe that if in fact real price competition can be brought to bear on hospitals, the economic decisions they make will be altered and greater cost containment will be achieved. The question is really how to ensure the creation of marketplace economic competition.

TWO-TIER CARE

If competition can be accomplished, there is one essential fact that should not be ignored—an economically competitive health care system will assuredly drive the system backwards again to a two-tier health care system. There will be one system for middle- and upper-income families and a second system for poor families. The latter will be characterized by inadequate quality and insufficient amenities.

In addition, the hidden subsidization of medical education and research in the operating costs of medical center hospitals will be forced out into the open and a realistic, workable financing solution will evolve, or medical education and university hospitals will significantly deteriorate.

The American frustration with the high cost of medical care is not uniquely one nation's, but is experienced worldwide in the developed countries. No matter what the mechanisms are for a health care system, they are all high-cost, impervious to cost pressures, and still moving to higher cost levels.

The reality of the situation is that no political system, particularly in a democratic society, is willing to freeze the development of a new medical technology or access to medical care. If it is thought desirable, for one or another part of the system, some abstract rule is put in place, such as only x number of CT scanners in a service area, and the next one is not authorized because the ceiling has been reached. This is a modest example compared to a wholesale freezing of technology or services. The bad guy is not visible to the consumer.

The basic fact is that medical knowledge and technology are bumping against new high-cost technology, with only modest effects on mortality and morbidity. Eradication of the causes of disease are not being found as rapidly as better methods of diagnosis and treatment are being developed, which results in a low cost-benefit payoff. For example, why are renal dialysis treatments provided for people who are seriously limited in their life styles and have no hope for recovery? The fact is that we think of ourselves as a humane society and let the physician or hospital staffer tell the patient there is no more room at the inn. Unfortunately for the economics of health care, both the physician and hospital personnel scramble to find a way to accommodate the patient and service is provided.

As citizens in a free country, we want quality medical and hospital care available when needed. At the very least we want an opportunity to find the service and pay for it. More desirably we prefer to be insured. No one wants a system that prevents access at any price. This is one of the reasons employers and unions both seek health insurance coverage and do not want to monitor or control its usage. That nasty job is jaw-boned on to physicians and hospitals, and when they act with the same rationality of the company president and the union business agent, they are criticized.

Economic competition for health care reflects a recognition of this reality and implies that dollars will be used as the rationing device to lower demand by the public or that medical care providers will limit their scope and quality of services. In both cases, there is no individual who must stand up and be counted in any specific instance; the mask of anonymity protects the decision makers against the frustration of the individual patient. What the patient will face is "Too bad, Charlie, but that's the way it is—wish I could be of help, but things are beyond my control."

The way things are now going in health care costs, they are beyond control by our existing system. A competitive system is not an ideal solution for achieving the humanitarian goals of medical care, but it recasts the perspectives into new, and as yet unthought of, ways to approach providing greater flexibility, more opportunities for creative thinking, and increased incentives to do so. Only time will tell if competition is a better or poorer way to deliver medical care. It should be tried because the existing situation is critically sterile and bankrupt of new ideas.

Chapter 5

Planning and Marketing in a Competitive Climate

A NEW ERA

From the late-1930s until the late-'70s a hospital could borrow as much money as investment bankers would approve and use it for any acute health care program that physicians or trustees had in mind. Even when projected utilization and expenses were badly misjudged, unmanageable financial problems rarely occurred.

Medical care and its cost have now entered an era of saturation: from too many beds, hospitals, physicians, malpractice claims, government, and dollars. The reaction is an expected one: a wringing out of the medical care system. Certificate of Need, pricing systems for care, institutional closings, freestanding primary care centers, closing of medical staffs, independent practice associations, and a dozen more concepts have been developed to limit further expansion. The countermove by health care organizations has been to begin to use business and marketing plans to identify and implement specialized approaches to the delivery of health care services.

The result of these actions and reactions is to make it abundantly clear that past successes are no longer an assurance that traditional planning practices will have even limited success. Hospitals and physicians with foresight to set in place strategic plans and marketing strategies are providing themselves with a way of monitoring their performance over time. By frequently reexamining their market position in light of changing conditions, there is a greater probability of future success than if they continue to use traditional planning and operational practices.

In the last ten years all forms of businesses have experienced rapid shifts in market demands, radical pricing changes, and new competitors that have jeopardized their future stability and growth. The hospital field, however, has been perceived as different. In fact, hospitals have been different: they were isolated from economic impacts, controlled by a strong, conservative sense of trusteeship, and influenced by an elite group of medical professionals who legally and organizationally managed the access of patients.

Perpetual isolation for hospitals from community forces is not going to happen. In the past isolation may have been easy because money was available. A new world is coming into focus. Underlying this new viewpoint is the reality that the only way to abate large annual increments in health care expenditures is to bring about the common use of pricing mechanisms for medical services based on economic competition. An awareness of the gradual application of market prices, as the preferred payment mechanism for purchasing hospital services, is the force causing many institutions to scrap traditional planning techniques and to adapt strategic marketing concepts.

A second major force, which is only beginning to be recognized, is the growing availability of specialized physicians and the substantial increase in the total number of physicians. In a few areas of the country this has already occurred, while in most regions this development is still under way. Some far-sighted physicians have already anticipated its future impact on the economics of their practices and are initiating new ways to deliver medical care.

Both major forces have impacted some hospitals and are awakening many others to a future substantially different from what they had previously expected would be the case. The interaction of these two forces in large general hospitals is particularly acute. For the last 40 years hospitals have gradually and steadily experienced a shift in the composition of their medical staffs from a preponderance of family practitioners to specialty staffs.

With few opportunities remaining for additional specialist appointments to medical staffs in large hospitals, residents completing their advanced training are obtaining medical staff appointments in small city and rural hospitals that previously referred patients to metropolitan area hospitals. The result is a slow, persistent decline in the volume of referrals to large hospitals. At the same time, freestanding medical services providing prompt and easy access are evolving in metropolitan areas. These include emergi-centers, ambulatory surgery, renal dialysis, primary care centers, abortion clinics, home health services, and gerontology centers.

When these inroads into traditional hospital services occur at the same time prices are fixed for specific packages of hospital services, a need is created for hospitals to seek out additional sources of revenue. It is similar to a television repair service losing its retail market for new televisions and radios and having its repair prices fixed as an average so that customers will be charged only for the most serious problem on their TV sets, no matter how many other parts need repairing, with the bill audited to assure compliance. The owner of a television repair service in this situation would analyze his local market to figure out what else he might repair or sell. In other words, the owner would develop a strategic marketing plan that would utilize the existing skills and resources of his present business and apply them to unregulated and new business opportunities in the local market.

REPLACING MYTHS WITH REALISM

A good strategic plan is one that replaces myths and traditional practices with realism and acceptance of reasonable market risks. The skills and techniques used by business are the same ones needed by hospitals. However, the basis of health care delivery judgments is different because of the need to blend medical and business decisions in a hospital situation. Hospitals also are characterized by their atypical organizational structure involving a medical staff and the unusual complexities of licensure, regulation, and reimbursement.

The quality of a strategic master plan, therefore, depends on the quality of the minds involved in its preparation. Typically, two perspectives are needed to adequately develop a plan. One perspective is a detailed knowledge of the local health care market and the other a broad knowledge of national trends and regional responses to changing market conditions. The various factors in society that cause change to take place in the hospital field prevail in various parts of the country at different times and in a variety of ways. A wide knowledge of these affairs, and experience with their effects, are needed to add judgment and balance to an individual hospital strategic marketing plan by identifying which regional forces will eventually occur in a local market.

An example of the need for both perspectives is often encountered when a hospital develops an expansion and remodeling program based on a careful and detailed assessment of services and facilities needed to provide the local community and physicians with up-to-date medical facilities. Once the elements of a program have been defined, financial advice and architectural assistance are sought.

The financial adviser reviews the operating and financial history of the hospital to determine the likely investment ratings of Standard and Poor and Moody's, an interest rate, and the amount of money that can be borrowed so that the issue is a reasonable risk. When the financing system for hospital care is being radically rearranged, as is currently taking place, there is a significant possibility that a financial adviser will underestimate the risk. Whatever the findings of a financial adviser, hospital boards of trustees are likely to accept them without question because of the greater expertise of an underwriter and authorize a construction program that exceeds the hospital's ability to repay. The fact of the matter is that no one knows, with assurance, the effects of the present-day reimbursement changes and what will determine which hospitals in the future will survive, except for those hospitals that already have substantial revenues from non-acute medical services.

At the same time that financial advice is sought, architects are usually working to redesign the facility. Their efforts focus on providing a high degree of functional usefulness and adequate space within the limits of the estimated available funds. In this process enthusiasm and expectations of trustees, physicians, and executives rise as they examine possible alternatives. Rather than considering how small a project is needed for adequate operations, they often expand the project to the maximum.

Because the last 40 years have represented an economic environment for hospitals that was more generous than expected, nearly all excess expansion projects succeeded. For the next few years, until the realities of a reordered financing system for hospital care, with more restrictive reimbursement, are experienced, it is likely that hospital projects that had previously been successful will be likely candidates for failure. To avoid future failures, the perspective of a strategic market plan is needed that includes a view of wider issues and an objective perspective in order to assess current plans against future market realities.

SELECTING CLINICAL SERVICES

Historically, it was believed that hospitals should be full-service institutions capable of providing all types of medical care. This concept is rooted in the days when the majority of physicians were general practitioners and admitted the bulk of medical, surgical, obstetrical, and pediatric patients. The changes of the last several decades in medical knowledge, technology, and specialty certification for physicians have outdated this idea. Yet, today, the most common argument used by physicians and trustees to rationalize a new program or service is the need to be a full-service hospital. The economic realities of the current hospital field are that a hospital can no longer afford to offer all sophisticated medical services to the public, particularly in a metropolitan area with many acute care institutions. The fundamental challenge today is to concentrate on clinical services that are mutually supportive and have a high cost-benefit ratio.

To determine what is an appropriate mixture of services a hospital needs to fully assess its local market area. It must find answers to a series of questions about the present state of local health services and what is most likely to happen in the next five to ten years. The facts needed are much more than the population and demographic data that have been the basis of traditional institutional and health systems agency planning.

There is a need to find answers to marketing questions. Why do patients choose one hospital rather than another? Is it related to physician selection, public image of the hospital, distance, price, range of service, promptness of service, or nonavailability elsewhere? The answers to these questions are different for each specific hospital service. For example, responses for an Emergency Department are different than for a cardiac rehabilitation program, as well as for medical versus obstetrical patients.

Utilization patterns and the size of a market area are different for each individual service and program of a hospital. To determine the primary market area for each service requires either an ongoing information system that records all in- and outpatients by service and zip code or a special study for each hospital service when routine data collection is not practiced. With this data available it is frequently possible to determine why a pattern exists, and if it is not obvious, provide simple questionnaires for patients and physicians to find the reason. What cannot be determined, at times, is the reason a service is not used if it is the customer's decision rather than the physician's. At times telephone market surveys can be used to identify reasons for a lack of market penetration.

Analysis of health care markets should be an ongoing activity of a hospital. Without routine organized data, speculation and rationalization about utilization levels for a hospital service occur. With an ongoing flow of information new market approaches can be designed and their effects measured.

A major segment of a strategic marketing plan involves a close look at the characteristics of the medical staff. A hospital needs to know, in great detail, about its physicians, beyond the typical data of age, specialization, office and residence location, patient days, admissions, deliveries, and surgical procedures. There is a need to know physicians' opinions about the quality and performance of individual hospital departments and services, what is attractive and unattractive about hospital operations, why physicians also admit patients to other hospitals, what trends are occurring in their office practices, and if they plan to recruit additional partners and establish other offices.

Because physicians are sensitive to the possibility that a hospital may use this kind of information to a physician's detriment it may be difficult to obtain responses. However, organizational outsiders can often obtain these responses if physicians feel confident that disclosure to the hospital will not occur on a physician-by-physician basis. In local markets where health maintenance organizations are making inroads into fee-for-service medicine, a composite marketing study is of value to both the physician community and the hospital.

When in-depth studies of physician practices and an analysis of other activities of health care institutions in a local market are completed, potential new marketing opportunities can be identified. Once the opportunities have been explored, organizational schemes can be developed for joint ventures between a hospital and appropriate members of its medical staff. By and large, these kinds of arrangements have not been undertaken by hospitals. However, when joint ventures with members of the medical staff can be organized, a hospital can create physician support rather than opposition and further enhance the value of staff membership and gain support for new hospital enterprises.

DEVELOPING THE ORGANIZATIONAL STRUCTURE

A hospital must also have an appropriate corporate structure to move ahead in developing joint ventures. In the past decade most large, and many small, hospitals have created multicorporate structures. Their stated purpose has been to maximize reimbursement and minimize the restrictions of Certificate of Need regulation, but the motivating force is to have in place a corporate structure that allows greater flexibility in developing additional sources of revenue through health-related businesses.

Existing governance structures of hospitals and the traditional philosophy of trustees have stifled aggressive marketing activities of many hospitals. The decision-making process of a governing board is frequently a time-consuming exercise involving the use of multiple committees. This stretches out to an unreasonable extent the length of time required to obtain necessary approvals before implementation. The trustee awareness of a stewardship responsibility creates a conservative attitude that is often expressed as a reluctance to consider investing hospital funds in a non-hospital business. To cope with an inappropriate decision-making process and trustee hesitancy to invest in nontraditional businesses, hospital executives have encouraged the development of multicorporate structures.

In many instances the business potentials of the multicorporate structure have not developed. The major reasons appear to be insufficient depth and quality in market assessment studies and a failure to project the future financial needs of the hospital. This state of affairs is not a reflection on the concept of multicorporate structures. Rather it represents a lack of commitment by trustees and a lack of experience on the part of the administrative staff in developing new sources of revenue outside of traditional hospital operations.

Multicorporate structures are being created by many hospitals without a clear idea of how many additional dollars will be needed to offset future decreases in reimbursement. Aim is taken in a general direction without identifying specific targets and the resources needed to hit them. This approach is in stark contrast to the marketing and business efforts of the companies now expanding in specialty health care markets.

These for-profit companies are using strategic marketing plans that have five basic elements. They are:

1. A determination of the size, scope, and characteristics of a health service market in a local or regional area.
2. A determination of the availability and absence of institutional and noninstitutional clinical and business capabilities currently existing or likely to develop in a market area.
3. An identification and analysis of existing and potential opportunities and threats for future health care services.

4. Selection of the appropriate health care programs, services, and business opportunities that fit the available resources and skills.
5. Establishment of a system for measuring progress in implementation and monitoring the ongoing state of affairs of the marketplace.

To successfully compete in a rapidly changing health care marketplace, all hospitals will need to use the same approach. In many metropolitan areas, hospitals are just beginning to move into health-related businesses to compete against experienced aggressive entrepreneurs who are already present. This competition does not mean these new markets are lost to hospitals, but that getting into the market will be more expensive and slower in developing.

Community hospitals and physicians in a joint venture have several advantages over outside corporations in a local market: intimate knowledge of the market, existing relationships with patients and local government, and an established presence. They also have disadvantages: a conservative philosophy about taking business risks, sensitivity to local criticism, and existing jealousies. In essence, hospitals have marketing advantages and organizational disadvantages.

The basic rationale for developing a strategic marketing and planning program is twofold; one is to prevent inroads into existing hospital services by competitors in a market area that redirects patients requiring uncomplicated diagnostic and treatment procedures to lower-cost services and thereby increasing hospital costs and the other is to establish additional revenue sources to offset shortfalls in future reimbursement payments for inpatient services.

Conceptually, both of these events are easy to understand. However, both are difficult to grasp in month-by-month reviews of financial statements of a hospital. Monthly differences are small in revenue and expense statements and long-term effects on balance sheets are ignored because of different time perspectives. Until both types of financial reports are projected for several years in the future, and take into account decreasing volumes of service and increasing reimbursement reductions, the need for a more aggressive market posture will not be clearly seen.

Once a board of trustees and administrative staff of a hospital can visualize the net effect of changes in the marketplace and reimbursement, a greater sense of urgency will take over as they realize that tighter and tighter cost controls cannot maintain a satisfactory level of patient services. When that point is reached, the traditional view will begin to be questioned. This creates an opportunity to rethink what is needed to maintain patient service levels.

A strategic plan does not ensure the future of a hospital. It provides an organized way of looking at long-term market trends and their effect on future hospital operations and it identifies market gaps. The quality of the strategic plan is determined by the accuracy of estimating demand, the resources needed to enter a market, and the payoffs to be earned.

Failures to make accurate estimates are usually related to inadequate market and financial data, insufficient administrative time to develop a plan and execute its implementation, and an unwillingness to commit sufficient funds to properly provide for its development. The basis of these inadequacies is a lack of commitment to risk taking in both the short and long term. A good example of inadequate risk taking can be found in the history of health maintenance organizations. A sizable number of HMOs have either failed or been only marginally successful because of inadequate capitalization. The ones that have succeeded have been willing to support high levels of marketing activities and to accept prolonged periods of losses during their development.

The number of subsidiary corporations initiated by hospitals in the past several years is unknown, as is the proportion of these corporations that are profitable. However, there is a general impression that the majority of them are either producing losses or are still paper corporations. The ones that have succeeded are in hospitals that have made a serious commitment of resources and had a well-developed strategic plan.

Until hospitals develop high-quality strategic planning and marketing programs, and commit sufficient resources, they will not have a reasonable chance of success. They will not succeed in developing health-care-related businesses that can protect existing markets and provide sufficient additional revenues to offset shortfalls in patient revenues. The longer the delay in getting to the business of developing strategic planning the less likely a hospital is to remain a medical care institution of high quality.

Chapter 6

Economic Competition Impacts Hospital Construction

TWO SCHOOLS OF THOUGHT

As a result of external regulating forces acting on hospital construction, there is a pent-up demand for construction, remodeling, and renovation of hospital facilities. The shift from inpatient bed care to increased usage of diagnostic procedures, particularly in the Clinical Laboratory and Diagnostic X-ray Departments, has led to an imbalance in many physical plants. This has been fueled by rapid technological changes that require hospitals to continually expend greater and greater amounts of money to keep on the cutting edge of the state-of-the art.

There are two schools of thought as to what is likely to take place. One group tends to think that the present high rates of interest, reflecting a shortage of loan funds, will deter hospitals from successfully entering the bond market unless they are able to secure an A or higher rating on prospective bonds. Since the financial situation for hospitals has deteriorated over the last few years because of restricted revenues, it is believed that they will not be able to meet the rating agencies' requirements and therefore will not be able to market their bonds.

A related scenario is one where the federal act expires, but the legislation at the state level that controls hospital capital outlays remains in place. Instead of hospitals seeking approval from federally created local health systems agencies, applications would be processed at the state level in accordance with state law. This would lead to a larger number of approvals but would still inhibit construction.

The other school of thought believes the reverse. Following the expiration of the existing law there will be a rapid expansion in construction in order to relieve the pent-up demand, with many hospitals borrowing up to their debt ceilings. Should this take place, there might be a public reaction pushing Congress to opt for a strong cost-control program rather than for a competitive stance. Assuming that this does not take place and competition does become a reality, what does this hold for the hospital field?

DEVELOPING ASSUMPTIONS

In order to think seriously about hospital construction in an era of competition, a number of assumptions need to be made. Since it is unlikely that what occurs in the early years will be identical with later years, it is appropriate to divide this period into three phases and to list the major characteristics that will affect hospitals.

In developing these comparisons, emphasis is on the national trend, with recognition that there may be regional variations. For example, the Sun Belt will experience in-migration and have a shortage of beds, while the foundry states will have out-migration and a growing excess of beds. On balance, however, the nation will have excess capacity.

Twelve assumptions have been made about factors that will affect hospital decisions related to undertaking capital construction projects. They are shown in Table 6–1. Each of these factors will influence individual hospitals in varying degrees, depending on the region of the country where the institution is located,

---

Table 6–1 Assumptions about Characteristics Affecting Hospitals

	Early	Middle	Late
1.	High inflation	Moderate inflation	Moderate inflation
2.	Regulation	Beginning competition	Growing competition
3.	High interest rates	Medium interest rates	Medium interest rates
4.	High technology growth	High technology growth	High technology growth
5.	Minimum MD surplus	Moderate MD surplus	High MD surplus
6.	Population over 65[1]— 11.2%	Population over 65— 11.7%	Population over 65— 12.2%
7.	Excess bed capacity	Excess bed capacity	Fewer excess beds
8.	Primary revenue—cost reimbursement	Primary revenue—mixture	Primary revenue—pricing
9.	Imbalanced physical plant	Moderate imbalance in physical plant	Balanced physical plant
10.	Average cost pricing of services	Mixture of average cost and marginal pricing	Marginal pricing of services
11.	Single hospital corporation	Multiple corporations	Integrated health delivery systems
12.	Single site	Multiple hospital site	Multiple sites—multiple activities

[1]Population Estimates and Projections Series P25, No. 704, July 1977, "Projections of the Population of the United States—1977 to 2050, Bureau of the Census, p. 10, United States Government Printing Office, Washington, D.C., p. 10, Series II.

whether it is in the inner city or not, whether the state has a prospective rate program in place, and the extent to which the governing board is forward looking and recognizes that the future will be very different from the past. The answers for all hospitals will not be identical, even though the external factors impacting each hospital are pushing all of them in the same direction.

FIRST PHASE

During the early phase the overriding reaction to the elimination of controls will likely be to play "catch up" without giving consideration to what might follow. A flurry of construction projects will occur as governing boards are pressured by medical staffs to get back in step with state-of-the-art developments. The prevailing attitude in each hospital is apt to be to rush into doing those things that are of a pressing nature to take advantage of the opportunity that has been created. A few voices may be heard expressing caution about cost implications for the future, but they will be ignored, on the basis that legislation will not have been enacted and the fact that no one can really predict what is going to take place anyway. Much of the construction that will result will be of a remodeling and renovation nature because of the imbalances in physical space brought about by the shift to ambulatory services.

Since the sources of hospital revenues will remain largely unchanged in this first phase, with cost reimbursement dominating the financial picture, the costs of carrying the debts incurred will be passed along to third-party payers as an operating expense of the hospital. Because the health field will still be doing business as usual, there will be little fear of economic competition from other hospitals since all will still be adhering to average cost pricing for hospital services, as required by the cost reimbursers and state prospective rate commissions. In short, when a hospital examines all of the factors and determines where the balance is, it will tip heavily in favor of proceeding with as much capital construction as possible, limited only by its ability to secure outside financing. The result will be an increase in construction in the early years.

SECOND PHASE

When the middle period is entered, it will occur abruptly on the date that a pro-competition bill becomes law. Attitudes will dramatically shift overnight. Hospital governing boards and chief executives will quickly recognize that the days of cooperation with neighboring hospitals are over and that cost reimbursement and average cost prices are all but gone. The impact of competition will not be felt, but rather hospitals and third-party carriers will be in a gearing up phase. During these years there will be uncertainty as to how severe the competition will be from other hospitals and physician groups. Not being able to gauge this problem, governing boards can be expected to become conservative with respect to approving capital projects, particularly knowing that all restraints on construction have been eliminated. Because of a growing concern about the marketplace and competition, many hospitals will continue to take steps to attract physicians to use their facilities. A great deal of attention will be paid to new technology and strenuous efforts will be made to purchase new equipment in order to be able to provide a service not available from the competition and therefore unique in the marketplace.

During this phase, hospital trustees and executives will do a great deal of talking about competition, but probably not much hard-headed planning, except to tighten up on operations in nonpatient departments. The new financing vehicles will not be in place to any great extent so that hospitals can take advantage of learning curve problems without disastrous results. Deep concerns will arise about how to protect the marketplace and there will be a surge of projects at off-site locations, which will lead to some tensions with medical staffs. With the growing surplus of practicing physicians, governing boards will probably proceed with plans that physicians may initially think are detrimental to their own interests.

The off-site activities will focus around a generalized concept of health care from wellness to real estate management of professional buildings. At the same time, trustees and executives will become more acutely aware that they need to be more responsive and creative in their relationships with physicians on the medical staff. Out of this sensitivity, hospitals will seek to find ways to facilitate referral patterns among staff members, to encourage a stronger tie between the hospital and its medical staff, and to develop methods of economically linking the interests of physicians with that of the hospital. By the end of this phase many of the freestanding general hospitals will have either restructured themselves into health care corporations, using the parent-subsidiary model, or will have joined chain operations.

THIRD PHASE

By the time the third phase is entered, the directions for the future will be clearly established. Hopefully, the general economy will have stabilized and hospital governing boards will be able to plan with confidence. The parameters of inflation, moderating interest rates, and a growing optimism about the future of health care will generate enthusiasm for the challenges that will need to be met during the years ahead. The concept of a health care corporation operating multiple activities on multiple sites and of applying marginal prices to services offered will be well accepted. Building projects will continue to respond to new technologies as they appear and once again inpatient beds and facilities will be added in response to a growing population that will be in excess of 250,000,000 people, 29,824,000 of whom will be 65 years of age by 1990.

Hospital construction can be expected to experience only moderate growth by concentrating on adding beds cautiously, remodeling older sections of buildings, and responding to technological change. The shifting of as many services as possible to ambulatory approaches will have been accomplished and general hospital physical plants will be in balance. Total replacements of hospital plants will no longer dominate the construction scene. Most change that takes place will be under the aegis of the large national chains. The day of the freestanding hospital replacing itself will have passed.

Within each hospital the trend to increase the average gross square feet per bed will continue in spite of the introduction of competition. This growth will be due to the continuing introduction of new technology in the ancillary departments, as it has in the past. Table 6–2 reflects the growth over the last several years and includes projections to 1990.

Because a hospital cannot afford to lag behind in the state-of-the-art, this growth per bed will not be deterred by competition, but in all probability the reverse will be true. New and updated services will be standard practice for attracting physicians to use the hospital. The more severe the competitive forces the faster will be

Table 6–2 Summary of Historic and Projected Trends in Building Gross Square Feet (BGSF) per Bed for Hospitals 400 Beds and Over

Period Ending[1]	Number of Reporting Hospitals	Median BGSF per Bed
12/72	208	796.17
12/73	183	830.36
12/74	182	845.92
12/75	186	870.79
12/76	207	891.40
12/77	187	908.56
12/78	211	938.72
12/79	217	966.90
12/80	Estimated	987.11
Projected[2]		
12/85[3]	Estimated	1,106.22
12/90[3]	Estimated	1,225.33

[1]Hospital administrative services reporting hospitals, 400 beds and over for period shown, American Hospital Association, Chicago, Ill.
[2]TriBrook Group, Inc., confidential report Oak Brook, Ill.
[3]Least square linear regression-coefficient of correlation r = 0.099.

the rate of introducing new technology and updating facilities in order to retain physician loyalties.

Because of the rate of technology change and the adverse conditions in the external environment for the hospital, the size of individual projects may not be as large as they were during the decade of the '70s. While individually smaller in dollar amount, they will be more frequent and more hospitals will be involved in capital programs so that aggregate expenditures will continue to be significant.

Space per bed can be expected to continue to advance in the diagnostic and treatment service areas and will be the major factor in the upward increase. These areas are also the most costly to construct or renovate. The effect of this can be seen in Table 6–3.

Within a competitive environment, to what extent are these events likely to take place? Hospitals that are presently efficient, or become so within the next few years, can be expected to remain responsive to the needs of the marketplace, as seen from the physician's viewpoint, and will do all they can to acquire new technology as rapidly as feasible, as long as their operating costs remain competitive with other hospitals in the area. Hospitals that are inefficient will tighten up their performance standards and having done so will then play "catch up" on the technology front. Both efficient and inefficient hospitals will be as afraid of losing market share in their service areas because of economic competition. By the '90s there will probably be fewer hospitals in operation. Some will have closed because they recognized too late that their managerial skills were not sophisticated enough for the dynamics of the new era; others, because they failed to keep abreast of technological change and thereby lost members of the medical staff to other

---

Table 6–3 Projected Costs for Hospital Construction 1977–1990

Year	Median BGSF* per Bed[1]	Median Project Cost per GSF**	Median Cost per Bed
1977	908.56	$ 91.32[3]	$ 82,969 [3]
1981	999.02	120.00	119,882
1985	1,106.22[2]	157.68	174,429
1990	1,225.33[2]	219.57	269,045
Increase for 1977–90	316.7	128.25	$186.076
Percent Change	34.87%	140.4%	224.3%

[1]See Table 6–1.
[2]Confidential Report of TriBrook Group, Inc., and McGuire & Shook Corporation, November 14, 1981.
[3]Construction cost only, not including financing and other costs.
*Building gross square feet (BGSF)
**Gross square feet (GSF)

more progressive institutions; and still others because they happened to be located in areas where they already had an adverse financial mix of patients and could not withstand the costs of the transition phase.

If competition becomes mandated, the last decade of the 20th century will require coping with a two-tier hospital system, one for those who are employed, the other for those who fall through the cracks of our society. The latter situation will lead to a resurgence of the public hospital, funded from tax revenues, serving those who don't neatly fit into the model now being developed. Once again, a new set of challenges to the health field will have emerged. Inner-city hospitals and teaching institutions will bear the brunt of the fight for survival. Their future will then have to be considered and appropriate solutions developed out of the experiences of this decade.

Part II

Governance of Hospitals

Chapter 7

Shoring Up the Wobbly Three-Legged Stool[*]

HISTORICAL ROOTS ARE ERODING

As an organizational entity the hospital is rapidly moving away from its historical roots as a charitable, nonprofit institution. The vocabulary now in vogue reflects the shifts that are underway. Every day one hears less and less about dedication, serving the public, charity, philanthrophy, humanitarism, and tender loving care. Instead, the words most often heard are market share, profitability, productivity, strategic planning, clinical excellence, bond ratings, debt-to-equity ratios, fair employment practices, new technology, diagnosis related groups, and efficiency. The philosophical underpinnings of health care are being swiftly eroded.

A look at titles within the hospital shows the same shift: The administrator has become the president. A director of marketing has been added, as has a director of planning. Vice-presidents and assistant vice-presidents are scattered across the organization chart. In the financial area, a reimbursement specialist is often found, along with industrial engineers and an internal auditor. Fund accounting has been replaced by a consolidated balance sheet, which often carries a line item for long-term debt that approaches 50 percent of equity. The revenue and expense statement shows a substantial adjustment in contractual allowances, and the sources of income are divided into categories that indicate downward trends from fixed-price payers. Looking at the total situation, a clear impression emerges that the healing mission has been replaced with the business ethic.

When the organizational structure is examined for similar signs of change, they are absent. Organizational structures have not been modified to reflect the shifts in

---

*Adapted from *Hospital Progress* (now *Health Progress*), Vol. 65, pp. 49–53, with permission of The Catholic Health Association of the United States, © October 1983.

authority and responsibility that new fiscal pressures increasingly require. Even in those hospitals that have undergone restructuring into a corporate parent-subsidiary model, hospitals maintain two of the three traditional major components: the governing board and the medical staff. When the relationships between administration, governance, and medical staff are scrutinized, one can see that they have survived intact. Why has this happened and what are the implications for the future? What modifications may be necessary to cope with the changing world outside the hospital? Why is the organizational structure likely to undergo severe stress in the next few years?

In the expansionist period of hospitals from 1910 to the late 1970s, the organizational structure was not tested; the available resources were continually expanding, and there was a cost-reimbursement method of payment for most categories of patients. The mood was one of growth. It prevailed for so long that medical staffs came to believe that when any new technology that could enhance patient care became available, it was up to the hospital to provide it at the earliest possible time. Furthermore, since physicians believed that self-governance of the medical staff meant they would have little, if any, interference from management or the governing board, there was minimal stress on the organizational structure. The governing board had no serious difficulties in coping with the finances of the institution, and the medical staff was content to know that every effort was being made to keep up-to-date. The need for institutional leadership was not a significant matter, and the chief executive was seen by both groups as a facilitator whose responsibility was limited to that role. As long as he concerned himself solely with the physical plant and the hospital personnel, the wobbly three-legged stool was stable.

A RISKY ENVIRONMENT

Then the health field began to change rapidly as the decade of the '80s began. The once-riskless environment suddenly became full of risks. The federal government, faced with mounting deficits, took a long, hard look at Medicare and decided that it could no longer continue to pay hospitals for whatever costs were incurred, but would instead pay a predetermined amount of money for each case based on the principal diagnosis. Physicians began to worry about a doctor surplus and how it might affect the number of patients they treated. Many became fearful of the future and grew concerned that hospitals would move into programs that had been performed by fee-for-service physicians. Hospitals, seeing their revenues constrained and worrying about a growing number of empty beds, began seeking avenues for alternative sources of income. The stage was set for organizational stress of a magnitude that had never been previously experienced.

TENSION WILL INCREASE

The first major test of organizational stability is now approaching; a confrontation is about to take place between management and the medical staff over the issue of financial viability of the hospital. As the fiscal noose is tightened in the Medicare program, there will be direct repercussions in every hospital. Under Medicare regulations, the rate for each of the 467 categories of diagnosis related groups sets a price for each inpatient admission. The rate for 1983-84 was 120 percent of the median cost to the Medicare program; for 1984-85 it was 110 percent; and for 1985-86 and beyond it will be the mean cost. The belief expressed by government officials is that the establishment of this method of payment will force hospitals to become more efficient. To some extent this has happened. When the mean is reached, one-half of all cases in hospitals in the United States will be above the reimbursement level set by the government. This will drive management and medical staffs into two opposing camps.

Management staffs are going to be closely watching expenses and will be making reductions wherever possible in order to increase productivity and keep hospital costs below the target level for each case. Nonessential positions will be eliminated, overtime will be curtailed, and many steps will be taken to make hospitals as efficient as possible.

While this is going on, medical staffs at the urging of the utilization review committee, will be scrutinizing their use of diagnostic and treatment procedures. Physicians who are high users will have corrective action suggested by their colleagues in order to trim back to target levels.

These activities will occur concurrently, but independently. Each group will make some progress, but the actions taken will not be strong enough to stabilize costs to the level of the mean called for in the regulations. This will create internal stress since both groups are apt to take the same position: that each has gone as far as possible without jeopardizing patient care and it is up to the other to do a better job in finding ways to reach the level called for by the government.

When this point is reached, both sides will take positions that protect their own interests—and both will be defending legitimate positions. The medical staff will indicate that careless ordering of procedures has been eliminated and to go any further would be asking physicians known to practice sound clinical medicine to prescribe differently. Utilization review committees will be unwilling to take such a position. They will stand on the ground that patient safety is their primary concern, not the financial viability of the hospital, and that this is a matter that rests with the management and the governing authority, not with physicians. Such a position should be anticipated because the adoption of a mean for payment is inevitably going to cut too deeply and will affect physicians who are careful and conscientious about their orders in behalf of patients. In order to divert the focus of the argument away from themselves, they are likely to suggest that since they have done all that they can reasonably be expected to do, it is up to management to make up deficits with funds from nonpatient activities.

In turn, hospital executives will also attempt to divert the focus of the argument away from themselves by pointing out that they do not control the clinical decisions of physicians and it is a medical staff's responsibility to meet the established targets since management has done all it can to increase productivity. Given these statements, the members of the utilization review committee can be expected to threaten to resign from this committee. All parties will be overlooking the fact that the difficulty was created by the government's selection of the mean as the payment target, and they will fail to realize that they are searching in the wrong directions for solutions.

Matters will worsen when the government shifts away from regional norms and moves to a national norm. This approach will ignore existing regional differences in the practice of medicine. In 1982,[1] the national average length of stay in community hospitals in the United States was 7.2 days. Hospitals in the New England region had an average stay of 8.06 days, while those in the Pacific area had an average stay of 6.18 days, a difference of 1.88 days per hospital stay. When the national norm is applied, New England hospitals average 11 percent over the mean and Pacific hospitals average 15 percent below it. Since physicians in New England are not influenced by the way medicine is practiced on the West Coast, it can be predicted that the organizational pressures on the hospital structures of East Coast hospitals will be enormous.

A BIT OF HISTORY

There is likely to be a great deal of confusion about the reasons why a stalemate between medical staffs and hospital management is developing. In order to understand the feelings that will arise when this occurs, it is helpful to put the situation in historical perspective.

For the past half century, hospitals have been paid for their services on a cost-reimbursement basis; if the cost was incurred, the third-party payer reimbursed the hospital for it. If the units of service declined and the indirect costs rose, the amount of the payments increased. When new services or programs were begun, additional costs were included for payment; it really didn't matter whether the program paid its own way since reimbursement was guaranteed. If the service was needed, it was started. The volume required to make it break even was not seriously considered. In an economic sense, the hospital operated in a riskless environment. This has continued for so long a time that hospital executives came to expect the hospital to be paid for whatever it did, because the institution was operating in the public's interest. Since the bulk of hospitals were organized as nonprofit corporations or were under the auspices of a public body and no person received dividends, this form of organization reinforced the concept that whatever was done was done solely for the public. The value of having a superior management team, as opposed to a mediocre one, was not important given the prevailing methods for paying hospitals and the corporate form under which hospitals were organized.

Physicians recognized these driving forces and were not shy about pushing the hospital to keep up-to-date in facilities and equipment. Clinical justifications were made on the basis of the ability to improve patient care and did not take into account the economics involved. In time, physicians came to believe that improving patient care was the sole criterion, which led to the expectation that the hospital should always be responsive to their requests as new technology became available. In the physician's mind the criterion for measuring administrative performance was determined by how quickly the management could respond to the need for new equipment and remodeled space for clinical programs.

Because management staffs have traditionally been viewed as facilitators for the medical staff, and to a lesser degree by governing authorities, the collision course brought about by the government will have traumatic consequences. Physicians are going to be surprised when they are faced by a management that is no longer in a facilitator role, but that has situational authority because of the growing importance of finance.

This change in role occurred because the chief executive's ability to function as a facilitator has been greatly hampered by a greatly restricted economic climate. He finds himself increasingly in situations where his alternatives are either restricted or presently nonexistent. Whatever problem he faces he must meet squarely and exercise his best judgment. In a hospital today, it is now necessary to have a leader in the organization if it is to survive. It is no longer a question of whether it is desirable, or whether the medical staff likes the idea or not; the economics of the external environment require that there be a clear-cut identifiable leader. Moving from a need for strong leadership to actually establishing the authority for it will be difficult, but the process will be aided by the stalemate between management and medical staff.

A NEW ROLE FOR THE BOARD

Since the governing board is the highest level in the hospital organization, it will have to accept responsibility for adjudicating problems between the medical staff and management. The board will be very uncomfortable in this position because members will find themselves trying to make a determination without having adequate experience or background in such matters. This will be quickly recognized by board members, who can be expected to search for a mechanism to enable them to avoid being put in this position.

Typically, board members would prefer to deal with only one recommendation, not two, when they are diametrically opposed. As they search for a way to resolve these differences they will eventually reach the conclusion in most hospitals that the chief executive is the appropriate person to become the leader of the hospital and coordinator of all its aspects: governance, management, and medical staff.

In order to assure themselves that all parts of the organization recognize and acknowledge the importance of this role, they will follow one of two courses. The chief executive will be named either chairman of the board and chief executive officer or president and chief executive. If the latter course is followed it can be anticipated that, over time, the chief executive will be named chairman. As such, the chairman will be expected, because of his in-depth knowledge of hospital operations, to be able to reconcile conflicting recommendations that otherwise might be brought to the board for resolution.

Taking the step of naming a chief executive as chairman of the board will be difficult for many governing boards because of the long tradition of having unpaid, service-minded community leaders in this role. It will occur only when trustees appreciate that the formal leader of the organization has to, in fact, be where the buck stops, and when it is recognized throughout the organization that there are no avenues around the chief executive. As long as there is a belief in any part of the organization that the authoritative person at the top of the structure can be circumvented, the coordination of major activities will be delayed or interfered with to the detriment of attaining organizational objectives.

The wobbly three-legged stool is going to wobble even more in the next few years because of a lack of understanding of what is now occurring and a desire to cling to traditions of the past. An argument will be put forth that since past successes were attained under the existing organizational form it should not be altered. Overlooked in this approach is the fact that the general economy has moved from ample resources to scarce resources and economic competition is now dominant. To survive, the health mission must adopt the modus operandi of the business world.

This transition will be more difficult for hospitals sponsored by religious institutions than for other nonprofit institutions. Their desire to serve the needy and the poor will remain, but will be increasingly difficult to fulfill because of mounting fiscal pressures. It will provide little solace for the religious to know that it is precisely because hospitals are important to society that it is necessary for them to compete and to survive financially. Religious hospitals that survive will ultimately recognize that operating more like a business and less like a social agency is the price that must be paid for survival. As it becomes increasingly evident that the business ethic has become primary, a number of religious will seriously question whether or not they should remain in the hospital business. Whatever course is decided upon, the survivors will alter their philosophies and corporate structures, accepting conditions as they are, not as they would prefer them to be.

When these changes take place it will not be because hospital trustees care less today, or that the chief executives of hospitals are seeking an expanded role out of personal preference, or that physicians are only concerned with protecting their economic turf; it will be because the economic climate has changed along with technology and these changes are the impelling forces at work. New pathways will be accepted only reluctantly, but those who attempt to maintain the status quo in terms of philosophy and organizational structure in the face of what is happening will only be ignoring reality.

When economic imperatives facing hospitals crash head on with the economic imperatives of physicians, there will be little, if any, room for conciliation and accommodation. Not only will hospital managements and governing boards have to deal with the medical staff from within the organizational structure, but they will also be directly competing with physicians for revenues derived from programs external to the hospital, such as primary care centers and urgent care programs. Even though hospitals may offer to enter into joint activities with selected physicians, physicians will be somewhat less than enthusiastic about doing so because they believe these activities to be solely in their domain and that hospitals are infringing on that domain by attempting to share in them. Trying to change their minds and gain support before moving ahead is not likely to produce the desired results because the economics are unchanged. The governing board then has to face up to the question of whether to proceed or not, given the opposition from physicians.

PHYSICIAN BOARD MEMBERS

Boards with physician members are apt to be divided on issues that pit the economic interests of the hospital against those of physicians. The trustee-physicians are in a particularly difficult position. They may appreciate the reasons why the hospital needs to proceed, but as physicians they also understand the position of the medical staff. This poses a dilemma: Are they trustees first and physicians second, or vice versa? As discussion takes place around the board table, physician members will be thinking about economic reprisals from other physicians that might affect their own practices. If they conclude that to vote for such an activity will not result in economic reprisals, many physician-trustees will vote on the merits of the issue as trustees. If, however, they conclude that physicians will be upset, they may vote, not as trustees, but as representatives of the interests of the medical staff. This thought process usually goes unnoticed by the other trustees.

With increasing frequency these types of issues are going to arise at the board table. In the future, trustee-physicians are going to be uncomfortable in their roles as board members as they have to repeatedly deal with problems that force them to choose between the hospital's interests and those of their colleagues. At some point in time they will come to recognize that the influence they had in shaping board decisions has lost out to the economic needs of the institution, which are at variance with the interests of physicians.

As hospitals and other health-related organizations enter into a marketplace that is increasingly competitive, they will come to appreciate that the timing and implementation of strategies have great importance. They will learn that the first organization to enter a particular segment of the marketplace has a decided advantage over organizations that follow. Once a hospital experiences a lost opportunity because of slowness in the decision-making process at the governance level, the pressure will be on not to repeat the same mistake again.

Ways to speed up the process will be tried in an effort to compete with the decision-making process of competitors in the marketplace. In all likelihood, these efforts will fail because the voluntary hospital will still be attempting to make its decisions by a collective decision-making process, while the decisions of its competitors will be made by executives with authority to proceed. Stated in other terms, the authority of chief executives of voluntary hospitals will be much more limited than that of competitors, and they will be unable to proceed with plans to commit resources as rapidly as the others vying to enter the marketplace. This loss in timing will be a serious disadvantage to the hospital chief executive forced to operate in a traditional manner in an environment that requires speedy decisions. It will be a classic case of too little authority leading to decisions that are too late.

THE SOLUTION

The only workable solution is to grant the chief executive much broader limits of authority so that he can compete successfully. This requires that the chief executive be granted by the governing board the authority to:

1. Resolve all internal differences, including those with the medical staff
2. Commit institutional resources at his discretion, reporting to the governing board on an after-the-fact basis. Clearly, in a risk-filled environment the risks are greater, both to the governing board and to the chief executive.

In a highly competitive marketplace the abilities of the chief executive and the senior management of the hospital are going to determine the success or failure of an institution. The emphasis will be on solid planning and flawless execution, based less on knowledge of patient care and more on financial expertise. Governing boards will recognize that a top-flight executive is a prized asset and will seek ways to prevent their executives from being attracted to other hospitals or health care corporations. Since competition for executive services may come from either a nonprofit or a for-profit organization, a governing board interested in holding its chief executive must assume that any compensation package offered would include not only salary and the traditional fringe benefits, but also a contract and a way for the executive to obtain equity. If competent management is to be retained in the voluntary hospital system, these same kinds of benefits and protections will have to be provided.

In addition, chief executives are going to need much more authority so they can make decisions and implement them at a speed that is in keeping with the rapidly changing external environment. From time to time, executives may have to exercise their authority even though it may run counter to the desires and thoughts of the medical staff or hospital personnel. To wait until all parts of the hospital organization are in agreement may mean missing opportunities in the marketplace.

A number of issues may arise in the future that require strong and centralized management. These may include:

1. Renegotiating all the hospital-based physicians' contracts as a result of changes in federal regulations
2. Deciding to develop a series of primary care centers in response to competition from other hospitals
3. Developing an on-site professional building
4. Establishing a capitation plan in order to protect an existing market share in the primary service area
5. Creating alternative sources of revenue to offset losses from the operation of the hospital

All of these events have the potential of placing increasing stress on the organizational structure to a degree that has never been experienced in the past. Governing boards that wait until they are in the midst of one of these problems will have a doubly difficult time since they will not only need to deal with the issue at hand, but at the same time, have to face the need for reallocating authority and changing the organizational structure.

The wobbly three-legged stool is not an appropriate structure for coping with the serious competitive issues of our times because they are going to create much internal stress. The three legs must be unified. Unification is necessary even though it will probably meet with internal resistance, much of it coming from the medical staff. Deciding to create a strong central authority figure in the hospital is a matter solely for discussion in the board room. The survival of an institution is a board responsibility that cannot be shared with others. Trustees represent ownership, and ownership carries with it the obligation to decide how best to survive. Making the decision to shore up the present organizational structure by centralizing the authority largely in the hands of a single individual is not in keeping with the tradition of nonprofit hospitals, but it is the only way for the intrinsic values of the hospital field to be retained in an increasingly hostile world of economic competition.

NOTE

1. American Hospital Association, *Hospital Statistics, 1982 Edition: Data From the American Hospital Association 1981 Annual Survey,* (Chicago, 1982), 15.

Chapter 8

The Changing Role of Chief Executive Officers and Trustees

HOLDING ON TO YESTERDAY

Now that hospitals are into multicorporate structures, chaining of operations, off-site businesses, and discounting rates to a variety of third parties, past organizational accountabilities and authorities are no longer appropriate.

Since governance and chief executives are on the cutting edge of this adjustment, they will be the first element in a hospital organization to need to work out new ways of carrying out their responsibilities. Should they fail to adjust, the organization will not adjust to these new circumstances.

Up to this time there have been no published studies that report in detail total number of hospitals in the country reordering the functions of governance and the chief executive officer. However, through daily interactions with a wide variety of hospitals, the impression has arisen that the majority of institutions are doggedly holding on to yesterday and making piecemeal adjustments only during a crisis.

The proof of this impression will be in the current number of hospitals in poor financial condition that eventually will sell out to a multihospital system, enter into a management contract, or merge with another institution. These decisions fundamentally reflect inabilities of governance to come to grips with the new realities in health care.

In many situations, the CEO has been aware of the likely future outcomes and either lacked the courage to force change or was stymied by a board of trustees that was unwilling to face community and medical staff pressures. Only a relatively small number of hospitals have been able to successfully cope with the risks that are a part of the process of change. Indeed, it doesn't seem likely that the percentage of risk-taking organizations will increase. The future institutional survivors will be those organizations that readapt their top organizational structure through a systematic and thoughtful process.

How will responsibilities shift? Whether or not a hospital chooses a multicorporate structure or elects to remain as a single corporate entity, the role and nature of the functions of governance and the chief executive officer must be different from those traditionally practiced if they are to survive.

The composition of a governing board must be altered. How these adjustments will be made is less important than the end result of a reordering of the functions of a board of directors. By nature, voluntary nonprofit hospital trustees are conservative and reluctant to give a higher priority to business rather than social policy. Yet the imperatives of current change require a shifting of priorities. Of course, the unique characteristics and values of quality medical care must be recognized no matter which orientation is primary.

The traditional hospital board of directors is a mixture of experience, perspective, and skills. Too frequently their policy decisions are delayed, or permanently deferred, because a significant number of directors, generally with diverse motives, cannot reach a unified position. When this situation arises no board action is often the result.

SELECTING TRUSTEES

The essence of a useful policy body for a hospital is a board of directors composed of persons capable of coping with complex issues, who think objectively and have an understanding of the milieu of medical care. In a board room the primary criterion for deciding a policy matter should be the good of the hospital, not how it affects an individual director or his friends. Too often, quality patient care and sound financial decisions lose out to parochial interests. A "play-it-safe" approach to policy making is usually the end result of a traditional stewardship philosophy, which permeates the orientation of typical hospital directors.

In a period of rapid change in organizational functions and rising competition, a stand-pat perspective frequently has greater long-run risks than a willingness to be venturesome. A successful risk taker is one who more accurately assesses the probabilities of success and failure than a competitor. Sensible risk taking is hard work. Recognizing the controlling issues, evaluating their impact, and developing workable strategies and tactics is not easy.

The usual historical criteria for selecting a hospital director have been based on what community group a person represented, what specialized experience a person possessed, such as lawyers, bankers, or business leaders, or the fact that the person was a woman or of a particular religious persuasion, or was believed to be influential in the medical field. None of these criteria hinges on a quality of mind that has been deepened and broadened by experience.

There has also been a naive expectation that the diverse community interests of directors will become of secondary importance when hospital affairs are considered. The reality of a board room is that specific areas of interest are of greater importance to directors than the well-being of a hospital. As the intensity of competition continues to increase, a hospital will need to become more selective in assessing the personal abilities and skills of its trustees.

COMPOSITION OF A BOARD

The composition of a successful hospital board of trustees in the future will be significantly different from that of present-day boards. These boards will have some of the following characteristics:

- A membership of 10 to 15 directors
- Inclusion of the top management: Chief Executive Officer, Chief Financial Officer, Chief Nurse, Chief Operating Officer, and the Director of Marketing
- Permanent medical staff chiefs: Chief of Surgery, Chief of Medicine, Chief of Ambulatory Care, and Chief of Staff
- Rotating medical staff leadership: President and President-Elect of the Medical Staff
- Chairman of the Board and three to five business executives

The trend will be to consolidate the internal leadership of the hospital in the board of directors, with selection as a trustee based on one's position in the hospital organization structure. This change will require that the major clinic chiefs in the medical staff be appointed by the board of trustees for relatively long tenure periods rather than elected annually by the clinical departments of the medical staff. The position of Chairman of the Board will continue to be held by an influential member of the local community and not be an internal position.

To accommodate the need for additional input, the committee structure of the board of trustees will include members who may not be trustees. The chairmanship of each committee of the board will be appointed from the membership of the board of trustees.

The committees of the board will be limited in number to the following standing committees:

- Executive Committee
- Finance Committee
- Nominating Committee
- Marketing and Planning Committee
- Professional Relations Committee

These committees will function within broad areas of delegated authority so that the board of directors can primarily operate in coordinating and evaluating hospital functions. This will require substantial changes in the board's typical agenda. More emphasis will be placed on informational items, new technology market opportunities, capital acquisition, quality control, and the competition. There will be an increase in reports summarizing and evaluating operations. Procedural items will be consolidated to save time.

Committee reports will not be debated in detail, as is customary in traditional trustee meetings, but quickly evaluated for their fit into the overall strategy of the hospital with adjustments made when necessary.

The number of meetings for both the board and its committees will be more limited than has been customary in the past. With broader administrative authority, the need for frequent meetings will decrease.

In multicorporate hospitals, the subsidiary boards of directors will be composed primarily of members of the administrative staff. They will function as divisional operations of the parent corporation with coordination and control centered in the office of the chief executive officer. In essence, the governance structure of successful hospitals in the future will closely resemble a typical corporate board of directors of today's successful business firms.

EXPANDING THE ROLE OF THE CEO

As the role and nature of governance changes so will the characteristics, functions, and skills of future hospital chief executive officers. Probably the greatest change that will occur in this position will be a granting of authority to direct and control the administration of the medical staff. The growth of preferred provider organizations (PPOs) and independent practice association (IPA) type health maintenance organizations (HMOs), plus the widespread adoption of diagnosis related group (DRG) reimbursement and a variety of hospital/physician joint ventures, will create a need to centralize authority. Physicians will maintain clinical freedoms in the practice of medicine, but economic imperatives for discounts, utilization controls, and integrated health care businesses will drive the administrative aspects of medical practice into a direct administrative relationship with the chief executive officer.

Because of a need to formulate rapid responses to market opportunities a board of trustees will be required to delegate larger amounts of authority to the chief executive officer, to avoid time delays caused by routing the decision-making process through a standing committee, an executive committee, and finally a board of trustees.

Another reason for broadening the area of administrative decision making will be the increasing number of operating factors that must be considered because of increasing complexity in an environment that is unpredictable. The title of president will not be viewed by trustees as an ego builder for the chief executive officer, but a reflection of this new reality.

The position of vice-president will likewise expand, and for the same reasons. A president will not have the depth of knowledge required to direct the internal functions of the major divisions of the hospital and its related businesses. This change will require a greater delegation of authority from the president's position to the vice-presidential position. Good judgment will become the hallmark of excellence.

As in other types of businesses, the background of the new chief executive officer will become less predictable. Graduates of master's programs in health administration will not be the only candidates for the role of president. In the future, a president will require two types of knowledge and skills, one provided by an MBA curriculum and the other from the industry-specific knowledge acquired in the MHA curriculum.

In addition, graduates will require a greater strength in a major functional area, such as marketing, finance, or economics. There will be a decreased emphasis on the technical knowledge possessed by a physician. Under this new model a president will need to understand the traditional value system in health care and appreciate how the qualities of good medical care are evaluated, but the expectation that this knowledge can be acquired only through medical education and experience will gradually diminish at the governance level.

Market strategies and negotiating skill will be recognized as a key attribute of a president. The role of the administrative staff will be seen as providing the expertise needed to frame the parameters of the possible within the limits of what is negotiable and financially feasible—these will be presidential judgments.

As more and more hospitals become $50-100 million dollar a year enterprises, boards of trustees will increasingly center their replacement executive searches on members of the existing administrative staff because the price of a poor selection will be increasingly apparent and the abilities of the staff will be known. Conversely, when an incumbent president has failed to adequately plan for his succession, there will be a greater use of executive search firms to find an adequate replacement.

All in all, the days ahead will be much different from the past and depend on the degree of change accomplished in the organizational structure.

Chapter 9

Managing the Unmanageable

With the advent of planning agencies in this country, the process of managing hospital development and construction often becomes unmanageable. The past is not instructive for the future, but it is useful for understanding how great the change has been.

A quarter of a century ago, hospital planning was simple. One looked at the waiting list for admissions and decided how many beds were needed to catch up with the demand, called in an architect, and asked him to develop the needed facilities. With Hill-Burton funds providing substantial support and a public fund-raising drive for the rest, the typical hospital stance was to secure interim financing from a consortium of local banks and then proceed with confidence into the project. If it turned out that the construction resulted in more beds and facilities than were needed at the point of completion, the decision would be made to leave a floor or two empty until demand caught up and then open the vacant space as required.

In many instances, governing boards believed the role of administration and consultants was to define needs and they would find the financing. This was easily manageable. Then the noose began to tighten: construction costs started upward, the amount of square footage per bed needed to support the nursing unit activities began escalating, federal funding slipped progressively downward, and the public attitude became increasingly skeptical with respect to health care institutions. The knot tightened in 1966 when Medicare commenced and the federal government began paying directly for hospital care. As this share increased to 40 percent of a hospital's revenue, the government's voice has become louder and louder. It has ceased being the silent partner in the Partnership for Health. As spokesman for the public, it has increasingly demanded heightened accountability.

The voluntary, free-enterprise hospital system no longer exists. It was legislated out of existence and replaced with a series of controls that have led to a highly regulated industry. This has resulted in the creation of a series of high hurdles that must be jumped if a hospital is to undertake any sizable construction program. To trip on any one of them will, at a minimum, be costly and may even be financially disastrous. In order to set the stage for understanding the process that has evolved when a major construction program is contemplated typical earlier experiences can be reviewed by a hypothetical example.

Sometime in the recent past, the chief executive of Central City Hospital became uneasy about the future of the institution. Having been there for 23 years, he knew every nook and cranny of the hospital as it grew from 120 beds to 540 beds over the years. He had just returned from a visit with a former assistant of his who was now head of a brand new hospital of 315 beds in an adjacent state and he was disturbed when he mentally compared the physical plants of the two institutions. It had left him with a deep feeling of the inadequacies of his own physical plant. He realized that the day of the four- and five-bed patient rooms had passed, that central air conditioning throughout the facility was a must, and that the last report of the fire marshall was indeed reasonable. He recalled how, when he received the fire inspection report, he had been visably upset because it would require $12.5 million dollars to correct all the deficiencies and still he would have an obsolete, poorly functioning building. He now appreciated the urgency of undertaking an extensive remodeling, renovating, and expansion program.

Looking out of the window of his office and watching the rays cast lengthening shadows across the lawn of the hospital, he made up his mind that the time had come. Instinctively, he realized this was probably the last pleasant day of work he would enjoy for several years. Yet he personally wondered whether or not this was a wise course of action to pursue. Within the past three years, he had seen four of his classmates terminated by their governing boards as they neared completion of major projects. He knew them to be professionally competent, he respected what they had accomplished, and he remembered their answers to him when he had asked each of them what had happened. To a man, they had made similar comments, something to the effect that any chief executive who took on such a task today was not likely to be around for the ribbon-cutting ceremony. Too many delays, too many unanticipated problems, too many uncontrollable events were inevitable, resulting in a gradually hardening board attitude towards the chief executive that just could not be avoided. How to cope with this set of mind troubled him as he left the window and sat down behind his desk.

As he turned to thinking about what would be involved, he was jolted by the thought that the hospital did not have a strategic plan. Looking up at his desk calendar, he quickly flipped through its pages noting the number of meetings he participated in each day. Knowing his board as he did, he was certain they could expect him to develop such a plan internally if he broached the subject with them. Just looking at the calendar, he sensed this would be a burden he could not shoulder, nor did any of his assistants have the available time for pulling together such a study. As he thought further about it, he knew he did not have the expertise for such a study even if he could find the time. Twenty years earlier, it would have been a snap, but having reviewed several long-range strategic planning documents he had seen as a member of the project review committee of the local health planning agency, he had come to appreciate that statistical approaches were now an integral part of these studies. He smiled to himself as he thought that there probably was no one on the board, including himself, who could apply a multiple regression technique, standard deviation, or queuing theory to a hospital problem. Well, he would worry about how to accomplish this study after he figured out all of the steps involved in moving from planning to design to construction to operation.

Pausing to say good-bye to his secretary who was leaving for the day, he began to consider the problem of selecting an architectural firm. Over the years, he had visited far too many hospitals where it was obvious the architect had been selected because he lived in the community even though he had never designed a hospital. From conversations with administrator friends at conventions, he was aware that the AIA had worked out a method to get around this kind of problem, but he was not sure how a hospital brought it about in the local situation. Thinking about the AIA made him wish that his own professional organization had worked as well on his behalf as did that organization for the welfare of architects. He admired the way the AIA had developed and urged the use of a standard contract for architectural services. Thanks to a chance conversation with another administrator, he had only recently learned that the "percentage of the project cost" charged by architects was in reality a negotiable item, and that it could be substantially reduced if properly approached. He had also learned that the formidable language in the standard AIA contract was rather one-sided and did not include any requirements on architectural performance within mutually agreed upon timeframes. With that idea in mind, he pulled a pad of paper out of a drawer and began to make notes to himself. The first item he wrote down was "Discuss strategic plan with the Board Chairman." Next, he wrote, "Consider strategic planning committee for the hospital—discuss with key administrative staff and develop names of trustees and physicians who should be appointed." The third item was "Ask hospital attorney to think about a contract for engaging an architectural firm."

He stopped writing, looked up at the ceiling, and wondered what the cost of the project he was now turning over in his head would be to the hospital. He knew that early in the game he was going to have to get a handle on how much debt the hospital could carry and the impact it would have on the rate structure of the hospital. He had heard that both Medicare and Blue Cross had become highly upset about hospitals passing through large depreciation and interest expense items and were considering placing strict limits on what they would consider as allowable levels. Their concerns he considered reasonable as he recalled the recent fiasco of the pediatric hospital in town. When planning that hospital, the department directors and physicians on the medical staff had spent months developing their needs and working closely with the architects. When the total costs of construction were submitted to the board after a year of effort, the trustees had been stunned. The estimated costs for the project were 150 percent higher than they had in mind and would have resulted in an increase in the average cost per patient day of 30 percent. When they had looked into the reasons for this occurring, they discovered, too late, that everybody had submitted a "want" list to the architect who had dutifully translated it into space requirements. A trustee of that hospital had remarked to the administrator of Central City Hospital, "Children's Hospital has a million dollars worth of architectural plans sitting on its shelf that has a market value of zero, since it will never be built. It is a mistake that could only be greater if it were actually built." The chief executive wrote down on his pad of paper "Be sure to do a revenue and expense forecast early in the project." On the next line he wrote "Control the project from start to finish or what I start may be my finish."

Glancing up, he waved at his associate who was leaving for the day as he began to wonder about the advisability of a public fund-raising drive for the project. Thinking back 20 years, when he had been at Central City Hospital only a short time, he knew he would have put this up at the top of the list of things to do for a building project. Yet, here he was two decades later questioning the advisability of including such an activity. Hospital projects had become so costly that this source of funds was being less and less used by hospitals. He had heard many a chief executive say they went to Wall Street rather than to Main Street for their capital funds. Having lived in this community for a long time, he was aware of a number of wealthy persons who felt kindly toward the hospital and who, if asked, would make generous contributions. In addition, he believed there were many others who did not have that kind of family money but who would like to make a donation to the hospital. From previous long-term loans to Central City, he had concluded that fund raising should not be overlooked since all the monies received could be applied directly to the cost of the project and therefore serve to avoid interest expense. On the sixth line of his paper he wrote "Find out who are good fund raisers for hospitals."

Looking across his office, his attention focused on a framed aerial photograph of the hospital and its site. Moving from behind his desk, he strode across the room and peered intently at it. As he studied the photo, he began to have some real concerns about the wisdom of some of the past decisions the hospital had reached on prior building programs. He noted that the next construction program would encounter serious site difficulties because the present hospital buildings were all located on one side of the site with the existing boiler plant blocking any expansion in the one logical direction for future construction. He realized other major problems would be encountered. It was obvious to him that the utility services would have to be carefully studied as well and that the existing traffic patterns on and off the site would not be satisfactory. He had received an increasing number of complaints in the last two years from patients, outpatients, physicians, and delivery companies about the traffic patterns and unloading spaces at the front door, the delivery entrance, and the emergency entrance. He had done nothing about them because there was nothing to be done, as he had learned from the study the hospital had commissioned 18 months ago. The problem had remained and become even worse since that study.

Part of this difficulty, he knew, was due to both the lack of parking on site and the poor location of the parking lots. The city council was understanding of the hospital's problem, but was putting pressure on the hospital to provide additional facilities. Reluctantly, he came to the conclusion that a building program would have to include a multiple-ramp garage since it was no longer possible to park all of the cars on flat land. He remembered the furor among the employees when the parking lots were reassigned a year ago and the employees' lot was shifted to the farthest one away. The evening and night shift personnel had been outspoken about the dangers of walking from that lot to the hospital after dark, even though the security force walked women employees back and forth if they requested such protection. Returning to his desk, he wrote the seventh line, "Develop a site master plan with emphasis on parking patterns."

Once again, his thoughts shifted back to the costs of the project. He had heard several horror stories at the last state hospital association convention about architects' inability to correctly estimate project costs. One friend of his had related his own experience that was hard to believe. The architect had known the hospital had planned to spend approximately $10 million, but when all of the costs of the project had been added up, the result was not the anticipated $10 million but $16 million. When his friend delved into the matter, it had turned out the architect had assumed the $10 million was for direct construction costs and had not allowed for such items as interim financing costs, architects' fees, consulting fees, attorneys' fees, contingencies, permanent financing expenses, and start-up costs. On the other hand, the chief executive and the governing board had made the assumption that the architect knew enough about hospitals to take all costs associated with the project into consideration. The result of this misunderstanding had led to the termination of the architect's services and to a project that could not be financed. Reflecting on his friend's problem, the chief executive once again picked up his pencil and wrote on the eighth line "Develop a capital budget that inclues *all* costs of the project."

Looking at the clock, he remembered he had to be home by 6:30 p.m. since he and his wife were playing bridge with another couple in the local tournament that was a weekly affair during the winter months. Straightening up his desk, he turned out the lights in the office and started walking towards his car, still deep in thought about the project. If they were able to get through the eight points he had written down, the next step would be to think about various financing alternatives. He quickly recognized that this was an area in which he had only the sketchiest knowledge. He was aware there were multiple methods available: straight mortgages, revenue bonds, private placement, public sale, level debt, balloon notes, 20- 30- or 40-year maturities, a state-sponsored program, interest subsidy, the federal housing authority, and the Farm Bureau—and he was sure there were a number of others he was not even aware of for consideration. As he thought about the complexities of financing, he made a mental note to himself not to put off this important consideration until the latter stages of the project. He recalled the old methods of handling this aspect were no longer applicable. Again, thinking about his early days in the field, he remembered that architects had usually completed 70–80 percent of their working drawings before a hospital would look around for permanent financing. A classmate of his had recently made this mistake and discovered too late the project could not be funded. He, too, had a set of unusable drawings on a shelf in the administrative office. As he reached his car, he pulled out his note pad and wrote on the ninth line "Examine financing alternatives early in the project."

As he pulled out of the parking lot and onto the boulevard, he began to reminisce about his experiences with the local health planning agency. What went on within that agency was something with which he had an intimate knowledge and it concerned him as he thought about Central City Hospital having to submit an application to receive a Certificate of Need from them. He knew from experience that decisions to approve or disapprove were often based on political considerations that had little to do with the submission of factual information and data that demonstrated the needs satisfactorily. Not only was the agency board too large—it had 41 members—but the majority of the members had no knowledge or prior contact with the health care delivery system except as a patient. In addition, he was aware of the lack of capabilities of the staff. They had been recruited two years before and had indicated their first priority would be to undertake a patient origin study. The board of the agency had agreed, but two years later this study still had not been commenced.

As he turned off the boulevard onto a side street, his attention abruptly shifted as he swerved to avoid a youngster on a bicycle who shot out of a driveway without looking either to the left or right. Regaining his composure and control of the car, he began to add up the amount of time it might take to secure approval through the planning process. Though the federal law that established these agencies was specific on the periods of time permitted for each step, he knew these regulations were not usually followed. He concluded that if Central City Hospital's application got through in six months from the date submitted, he would consider the hospital to be lucky.

As a member of the project review committee, he had watched the agony of a nearby hospital that had been trying to secure approval of an expansion project for nine months, and had, as yet, neither an approval nor a denial of its application. When the application had first been submitted, the project review committee decided not to act on it until the committee had disposed of a pending application from another hospital that wished to build a satellite institution in the same service area. Because the review committee did not want to make a decision, it had instructed the representatives of the existing hospital and those from the one wanting to build in the area to get together and see if they could agree on building only one hospital in the area. This had been somewhat perplexing to the board of the hospital already in operation, but it had proceeded to hold seven meetings with the other hospital over a period of three months, until such time as it became obvious to the staff of the planning agency that neither party would budge from its initial position. By then, the hospital wanting to build the satellite had received approval of its application, but could not secure a zoning variation from the county commissioners for the height of its proposed building.

When the original hospital came back before the project review committee, three trustees, two administrative persons, the hospital consultant, the hospital architect, and two physicians from the medical staff came to the meeting prepared to discuss the expansion plans. As requested, they arrived at the hearing at 5:30 p.m. only to find that seven applications were going to be considered. Because the staff of the agency considered their application to be a particularly difficult problem, they shifted it on the agenda to last. When the group from the hospital was finally ushered into the hearing room, it was 11:30 p.m. Two questions were asked by agency board members, both of which clearly indicated they had not even looked over the application. The applicants had been excused at 11:45 p.m. so the board could deliberate on their request. The next day, the hospital chief executive was informed by a staff member that the application had been deferred for one month since a newly arrived staff member had just been assigned to this application. He would be contacting the hospital within a few days with a list of further information he considered necessary to complete the application to his satisfaction. This was a bombshell to the hospital board since it had paid out over $75,000 in the previous three months to the consultant and architect to ensure complete documentation of its plans for expansion and had been complimented at the project review hearing by the chairman, who had indicated their application was the most thorough one he had ever seen in his four years on the agency board.

A week later, the consultant and the chief executive had met with the new staff member and reviewed his request for additional information. It turned out that 95 percent of it was contained in the original submission and that he had not carefully read the material submitted by the hospital. The missing documentation dealt with developing a table showing the educational levels in the community, the major industries in town, and sources for securing additional nursing personnel for the expansion.

At the next hearing of the project review committee, a staff recommendation was made to approve the project. This time the hearing lasted 20 minutes and three questions were asked of the hospital. One that had stumped the administrator was

"If this hospital expansion is approved and financed by long-term debt, how are the poor people going to pay for hospital care?"

Thinking the agency staff recommendation would be approved, the hospital had been surprised to learn the following day that their application was once again deferred and that they were requested to meet again with representatives of the other hospital. When it was pointed out to the agency staff that such a meeting was no longer a meeting between equals since the other hospital now had an approved Certificate and they did not, the agency staff agreed but said the meeting had to be held or it would jeopardize their pending application. Once again, the consultant, architect, and chief executive met with representatives of the other hospital. At that meeting, the chief executive of the other hospital proposed that he would support the pending application before the project review committee and in return wanted support before the county commissioners on his appeal for a zoning variation. He had been surprised to learn that no such deal would be made.

Thinking over the costs and the time involved in securing comprehensive health planning approval, the chief executive of the Central City Hospital realized it might well cost the hospital over $250,000 to prepare a carefully documented application, still with no assurance it would be approved. Should the application be delayed, he knew inflation would push up the cost. Making some quick mental calculations, he concluded that a $10 million project would increase the cost about $66,000 for each month it was delayed.

Making a mental note to himself, he knew he had to carefully develop a strategy for securing approval. Braking to a stop at an intersection a mile from home, he pulled out his note pad while waiting for the light to change and wrote "Be sure to carefully document the application for Certificate of Need—develop a strategy for securing approval without undue delay."

As he shifted his sports car from first to second gear, he reviewed the elements of the project. Had he forgotten any part of it? Pulling into his driveway, he thought of one other aspect: organizing the project. Realizing that he would be responsible for running the hospital through the planning, design, and construction stages, he knew from experience that two facets needed attention. A carefully developed and monitored project schedule and a shifting of some of his direct responsibilities to others on the administrative staff were both essential if he was to have enough time available to deal with the consultants, fund raisers, architects, and financial advisers who would be beating a daily path to his office. Since they often made conflicting demands on the chief executive, he appreciated the necessity for having enough time to sort out their needs and keep the project on track. As he pulled into the garage and shut off the engine, he entered his last note on his memo pad, "Organize the project by developing and monitoring a project schedule." (His 11 notes are listed in Exhibit 9–1.)

Exhibit 9–1 Central City Hospital Proposed Renovation, Remodeling, and Expansion Project

1. Discuss strategic plan with board chairman.
2. Consider strategic planning committee for the hospital.
3. Ask hospital attorney to think about a contract for engaging an architectural firm.
4. Be sure to do a revenue and expense forecast early in the project.
5. Control the project from start to finish or what I start may be my finish.
6. Find out who are good fund raisers for hospitals.
7. Develop a site master plan with emphasis on parking patterns.
8. Develop a capital budget that includes *all* costs of the project.
9. Examine financing alternatives early in the project.
10. Be sure to carefully document the application for Certificate of Need—develop a strategy for securing approval without undue delay.
11. Organize the project by developing and monitoring a project schedule.

As he walked towards the house mulling over his thoughts of the late afternoon, he realized the complexity of an expansion program in today's world. Summarizing to himself, he concluded that if you plan the project as carefully as possible, it just might be possible to manage the unmanageable.

Chapter 10

A New Look for Nonprofit Hospitals

DEBT VERSUS EQUITY

One of the major disadvantages of a nonprofit hospital vis-à-vis a for-profit hospital is that the source of capital funds for new technology, expansion or replacement, or renovation and modernization is a combination of retained surpluses and long-term debt. By contrast, a for-profit hospital can use these same two avenues, but also has access to the equity market as well. This is a considerable advantage in a mature industry where occupancies have declined and are expected to decline even further in the next few years.

Should a hospital experience a declining occupancy with a high level of indebtedness it may encounter serious difficulty in meeting its annual interest and principal payments. When there is substantial equity, greater organizational flexibility is maintained for easier adjustment to changes in external conditions. Less debt means lower interest expense, an advantage in any community with rapidly developing capitation plans where hospitals must be the low bidder to be awarded a contract. Having low carrying costs on debt enables a hospital to underbid other hospitals with higher debt structures. Nonprofit hospitals need to move in this direction if they are to maintain competitiveness in the marketplace.

Traditionally, the community hospital has been an integrated whole for both the organization and physical plant. It has had two basic activities, inpatient nursing units and ancillary services. In some communities a medical office building was on hospital property and all of the operations were on one site and in one corporate structure. Until recently there was no reason to separate any functions.

As revenues have become more restricted and capital costs have risen dramatically, dependence on long-term debt as the major source of capital financing is no longer adequate. Other avenues of funding, including equity funds, are needed. By dividing a nonprofit hospital corporation into four business entities and linking them together in a parent organization this goal can be accomplished. The four entities involved are:

1. A nonprofit hospital corporation
2. A series of for-profit operating companies
3. A for-profit real estate partnership for diagnostic and treatment services
4. A for-profit real estate partnership for a medical office building

These are depicted in Figure 10–1.

CREATING NEW ENTITIES

Each of the four business entities has a different purpose. The nonprofit hospital corporation entity operates inpatient nursing units, administrative and fiscal services, plant maintenance, dietary and housekeeping services, materials management, and other types of activities, exclusive of the ancillary medical services.

A series of corporate entities are created to serve as operating companies, one for each clinical service or other kind of activity housed in the diagnostic and therapeutic services building. The investors in these companies should be limited to those physicians who customarily utilize the specific services and the manager of each operating company.

Figure 10–1 Parent Corporation: Not for Profit

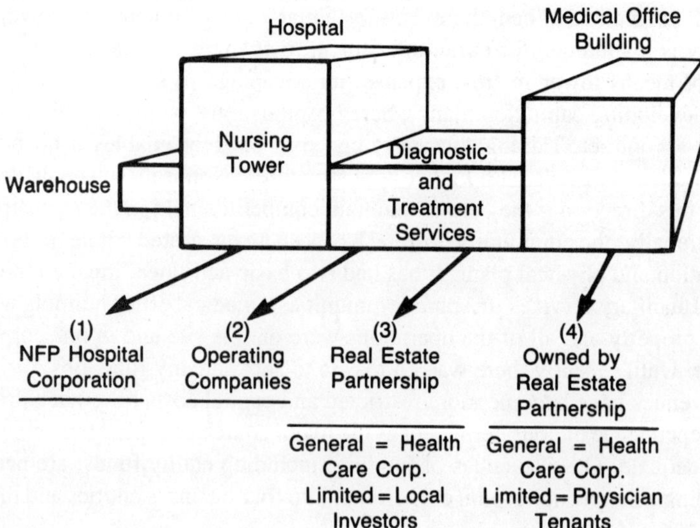

A real estate general/limited partnership entity should own the building and fixed equipment in the diagnostic and therapeutic services entity. The general partner is the parent corporation or a subsidiary corporation and the limited partners are investors, which may include any physicians who wish to invest. The diagnostic and therapeutic building houses all of the ancillary departments and provides services to both outpatients and inpatients.

The medical office building entity is where a number of private practitioners maintain their offices. It is also organized as a general/limited real estate partnership. Selected physicians who can be expected to utilize the diagnostic and therapeutic services should be invited to become limited partners, as well as tenants in the building. Some physicians may desire to be tenants but are not interested in becoming limited partners because they intend to retire in a few years and do not want to make an investment. Others may have just entered private practice and are not willing to go any further into debt at the time of the offering, but as their practices grow they may wish to do so at a later date. In addition, the hospital may want to house a few nonclinical departments in the structure. In this building the parent corporation may desire the right of first refusal on any limited partner wanting to sell. As the manager of the building it may also want to control the tenant mix in the building to ensure the utilization of the diagnostic and therapeutic services.

The parent corporation coordinates all of the business entities just described, as well as engages in other activities. The hospital coordinates all of the departments traditionally associated with its activities, including those housed in the diagnostic and treatment building. Hospital control over the operating companies is assured through a series of lease and lease-back arrangements. The hospital leases the building and equipment from the real estate venture and then subleases to each operating company.

CAPITAL COSTS

The rationale for creating multiple corporations can be demonstrated by examining the sources of capital funds for a 200-bed hospital building project with an attached 40-suite medical office building. Exclusive of the land acquisition and financing costs but based on actual costs at mid-1984, the total project is estimated to be $40,368,000, as shown in Table 10–1. By dividing the total project into three buildings that are linked physically together but separated corporately, a debt-to-equity ratio of approximately 50/50 can be utilized. At this level of debt to equity a nonprofit health care corporation can be financially competitive with a for-profit organization. This is shown in Figure 10–2.

The nursing tower and warehouse building, costing $15.4 million, can be financed in the traditional manner using hospital sources, retained surplus from

Table 10–1 Prototype Project Cost for 200-Bed Hospital (Excluding Financing and Land Acquisition Costs)

Corporation/Building	Building Gross Square Feet (BGSF)[1]	Times: Assumed Construction Cost per BGSF	Equals: Total Construction Cost	Plus: Movable Equipment[2]	Plus: Professionals Fees, Expenses and Contingencies[3]	Equals: Total Project Cost (Excluding Financing)
A. Hospital Corporation						
Bed Tower (570 BGSF/Bed)	114,000	$100.00	$11,400,000	$1,140,000	$2,280,000	$14,820,000
Warehouse (40 BGSF/Bed)	8,000	60.00	480,000	48,000	96,000	624,000
Administrative Space in MOB						
(60 BGSF/Bed)	12,000	80.00	960,000	96,000	192,000	1,248,000
	134,000		$12,840,000	$1,284,000	$2,568,000	$16,692,000
B. Diagnostic and Treatment Building						
D & T Building (330 BGSF/Bed)	66,000	130.00	8,580,000	8,580,000	1,716,000	18,876,000
C. Total Hospital Facilities						
(1,000 BGSF/Bed)	200,000		$21,420,000	$9,864,000	$4,284,000	$35,568,000
D. Medical Office Building						
Physician Offices (40 at 1,250 GSF)	50,000	80.00	4,000,000	0	800,000	4,800,000
E. Total Project	250,000		$25,420,000	$9,864,000	$5,084,000	$40,368,000

[1]Building gross square feet by building and average construction cost per BGSF is based on TriBrook's experience.

[2]Movable equipment is estimated at 10 percent of construction costs for the bed tower, warehouse and administrative areas in the MOB; and 100 percent of the construction cost for the diagnostic and treatment building.

[3]Professional fees, expenses and contingencies are estimated at 20 percent of the construction cost for the diagnostic and treatment building.

Source: TriBrook Group, Inc.

Figure 10–2 200-Bed Conceptual Hospital

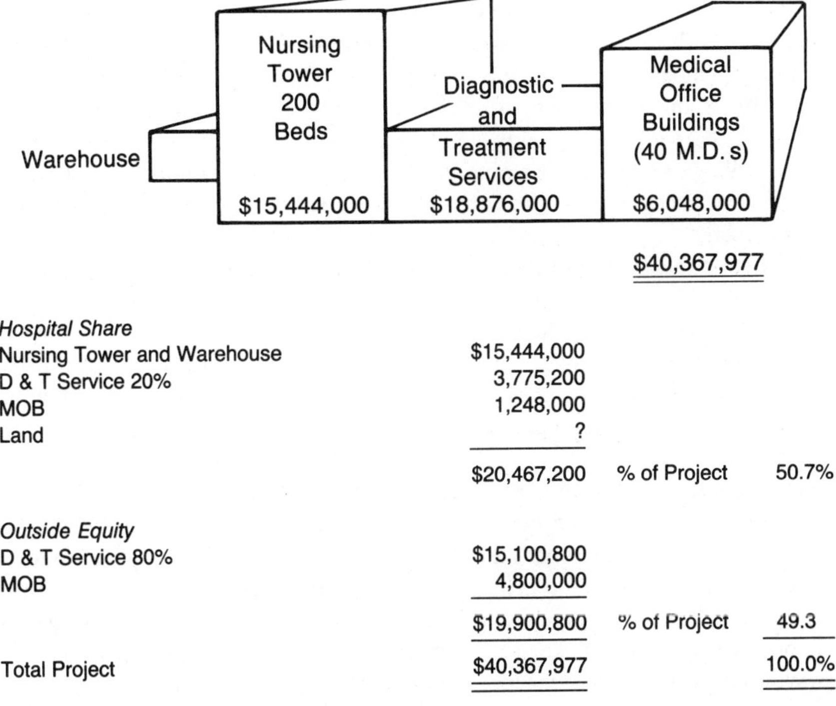

Hospital Share			
Nursing Tower and Warehouse	$15,444,000		
D & T Service 20%	3,775,200		
MOB	1,248,000		
Land	?		
	$20,467,200	% of Project	50.7%
Outside Equity			
D & T Service 80%	$15,100,800		
MOB	4,800,000		
	$19,900,800	% of Project	49.3
Total Project	$40,367,977		100.0%

operations, and long-term debt. The capital for the diagnostic and treatment services building is acquired through the creation of a real estate general/limited partnership with the parent health care corporation (or a subsidiary) acting as the general partner and holding as low as 2 percent of the ownership, which still meets the requirements of a general partner of the investment. Assuming the parent corporation elects to hold 20 percent, then 80 percent is available to the limited partners. In many situations this 80 percent can be financed up to 80 percent of the limited partners' investments so that the initial investment becomes only a minor part of the project cost of the diagnostic and therapeutic services building. If more than 35 limited partners subscribe (and in some cases up to 60), registration with the Securities Exchange Commission may be required. Assuming only 35 limited partners, the individual investment is $431,450 plus financing charges. Although this is too large an amount for most physicians, an offer for their participation should be made. The majority of limited partners are most likely to come from other investors.

The 40-suite medical office building should be a separate real estate partnership from the diagnostic and therapeutic building. If sold in units of 1,250 usable square feet per office, the cost is $120,000 per unit, plus financing costs and profit. First priority for investing should be given to those physicians who invest in the operating companies in the diagnostic and treatment services building. By locating their offices in the medical office building and investing in the appropriate operating company, a stabilizing effect on the hospital's marketplace is obtained. When selling limited partnerships in the medical office building, the general partner (the parent health care corporation) should reserve the right to approve future tenants.

The real estate partnership vehicle has two advantages:

1. Accelerated depreciation can be used to the tax advantage of the partners.
2. After the original investment has been recouped by the partners, the property can be deeded over to the nonprofit health care corporation. A writeoff of the net value of the asset can be taken as a charitable contribution.

The operating companies are created in order to provide opportunities for appropriate physicians and managers of each company to participate in the net profits of each one. The profit motive is an inducement for the physicians to refer patients from their office practices to the appropriate diagnostic and treatment service when needed. By including the manager in the ownership all of the owners are on the same side of the economic equation. In other words, all are concerned with turning a profit. Since the major construction costs are taken care of in the real estate partnership, the purchase of stock in the operating companies can be kept to a modest amount and therefore attractive to physicians and managers alike. Undoubtedly, all operating companies will not return the same earnings per share of stock. The results obtained will depend on the volumes generated in each activity, the relationship of operating expenses to income, and the prices charged. Each company will have to be competitive in the local marketplace.

The medical office building is a real estate partnership and operates in much the same way as a landlord owning an apartment building with leases for each unit. In the event a tenant requires more space, the lease can be changed. In effect, the arrangement separates the investment from the operational use, even though the investors are also the tenants. The lease period should be limited (e.g., for three years), so that the general partner can review the extent to which the tenant has made use of the diagnostic and treatment services. This can be used as the basis of determining whether or not to enter into a new lease with the existing tenant.

As depicted in the conceptual model (Figure 10–1), this is an ideal situation when a hospital is being developed from the ground up. In most hospitals this kind of opportunity will not be available. Existing structures will already be in place and have many years of useful life remaining. However, by having this model in mind an analysis can be made of the steps that can be taken to move as far as possible towards it, given the existing constraints. As future building programs are undertaken they can be developed in keeping with this model.

In the event a totally new hospital can be constructed, there is an opportunity to create a building configuration that embodies the organizational concepts, taking into account the shift from an inpatient facility to one that integrates physicians' offices, inpatients, and a combination of in- and outpatients using diagnostic and treatment services.

THE TRANSITION

Since the end of World War II the emphasis in design has been to develop an efficiently operating structure that would provide flexibility for disproportionate growth rates in the ancillary services. A typical structure is shown in Figure 10–3.

The elevators, as vertical integrators of the system, provided the basic rationale for a structure that was focused on the concept of the horizontal inpatient occupying a bed in one of the rooms of the nursing tower.

Two trends have converged that now make this design obsolete. Hospitals are no longer just for inpatients. They are increasingly providing services for ambulatory patients. These outpatients make an office visit to their physician, follow up with a diagnostic procedure ordered by their physician, and then depart. Convenience in this situation has a high priority and needs to be recognized in the design of the site and its buildings.

The other major factor now is capital costs. Buildings must be designed in such a way that they respond to the organizational and financial imperatives of the

---

Figure 10–3 Typical Hospital Design Scheme

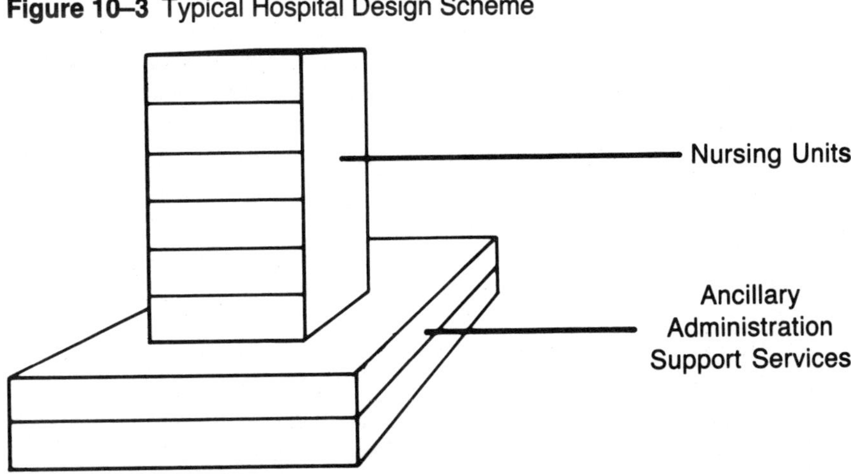

project. In the rapidly changing economic climate of the health field, investing in hospitals is no longer as highly regarded as it once was, so that new ways have to be developed that provide safeguards to the investor. A higher ratio of equity to debt is one of the best methods of meeting this concern.

From a design standpoint three considerations are paramount:

1. A medical office building that clearly identifies itself as a separate unit so that patients view the physicians in it as separate from the hospital organization but at the same time related to it
2. A nursing tower that is publicly regarded as "the hospital," where patients are hospitalized and that continues to be viewed as the modern-day version of the community, not-for-profit hospital
3. An easily identifiable structure where diagnostic and treatment services are provided to a large and growing number of outpatients. This building should be located immediately adjacent to physician offices but positioned for easy access by inpatients.

Buildings that respond to the patients' needs for convenience in both ambulatory as well as inpatient care is now the desired arrangement. In addition, the design must enhance the organizational and financial flexibility that is required.

CORPORATE AND MANAGEMENT STRUCTURES

The corporate structure can be depicted as shown in Figure 10–4. Even though the corporate structure is complex, the management structure can be simple, as shown in Figure 10–5.

The health care corporation (or a subsidiary) also serves as the general partner for the diagnostic and treatment building and as the general partner for the medical office building. In this capacity the control of all of the activities of the hospital is integrated, including ancillary departments. As an alternative, the president of the health care corporation can exercise control since the chief executive of the hospital is a subordinate. Even though numerous corporate structures are created, the management of the total system is straightforward and clearly defined, maintaining administrative authority lines as they were before the restructuring occurred.

In reviewing the overall plan the advantages are:

1. Physicians and hospitals are economically aligned.
2. Equity sources can be tapped for capital projects.

Figure 10–4 Corporate Structure

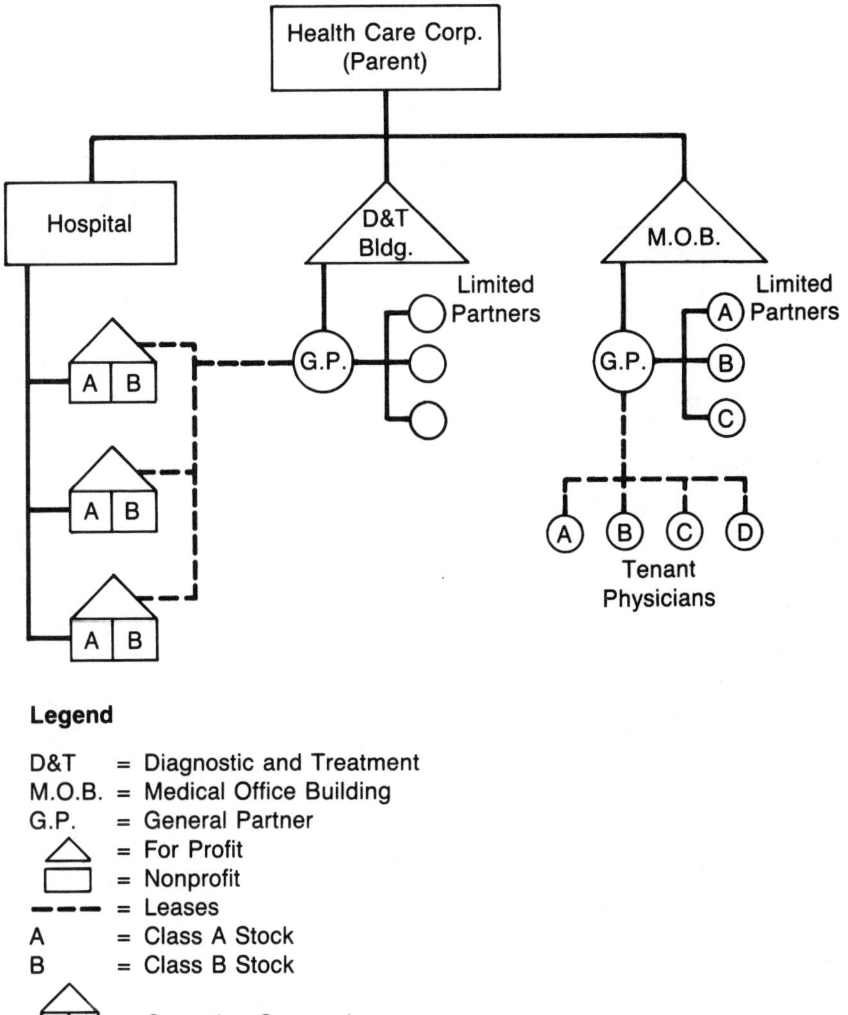

3. The health care organization maintains control of all of its operations.
4. Maximum organizational flexibility is built into the corporate structure.

As the future is surveyed it seems clear that the hospitals that survive and prosper will be those that develop their strategies around these four advantages.

Figure 10–5 Management Structure

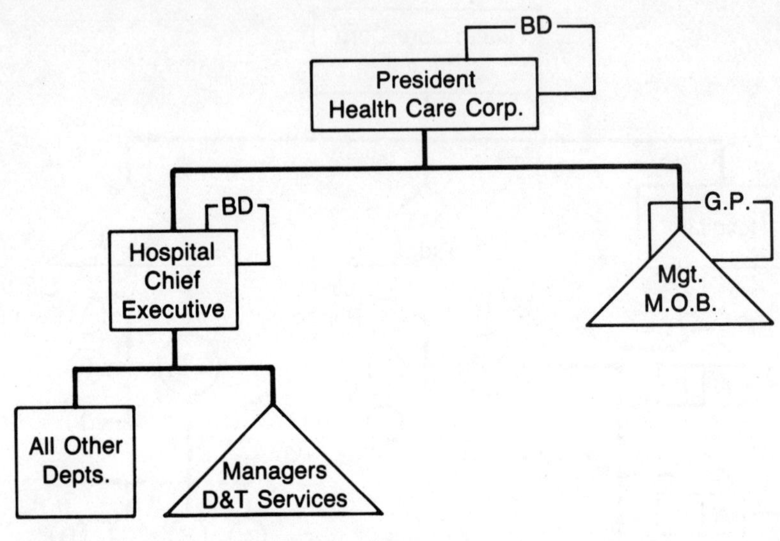

Legend

BD	=	Board
G.P.	=	General Partner
M.O.B.	=	Medical Office Building
D&T	=	Diagnostic and Treatment
△	=	For Profit
☐	=	Nonprofit

Chapter 11

Management Contracts for Hospitals

WHY CONTRACTS?

Since the 1970s there has been interest in the use of management contracts to manage hospitals by multihospital systems, either investor-owned or nonprofit. Multihospital systems are continuing to expand their management contract services for several reasons: the desire to move away from having to use tax money for medical indigency and capital purposes, the spiraling demand for new high-cost technology and the rapidly increasing complexity of hospital operations, and the loss of a sense of accomplishment because of the growing frustration among trustees unable to view their participation in hospital affairs as really making a difference.

Many times hospital chief executives know how to solve a particular issue but the conservatism of governance, the local political environment, and the status quo approach of medicine on broader social and political matters predetermines a lack of support for a workable solution that pushes, even very gently, against these philosophies.

There is wisdom in going slowly when the mission of a hospital needs to change, but a ''sunk-in-concrete'' approach precludes any movement away from the status quo.

When a hospital governing board converts from a nonprofit, freestanding facility to a unit of management within a multihospital system, the unthinkable becomes thinkable. Subsequently, unprofitable hospital services are closed or rates are raised to cover total operating expenses, plus the management contract fee. Physician recruitment activities are started and often an arrangement for a medical office building is developed. One wonders if the hospital's board of trustees would not have succeeded as well, if its members had been able to ignore the repressive restraints they felt obligated to support.

Many times if a hospital had spent the same amount of money for consulting help as it did for the fee for the first year of the management contract, and been willing to put into actions the consultant's recommendations, it would have been able to continue as a freestanding hospital. There are circumstances, however, where a local board of trustees cannot escape the influence of its community and the physicians involved and a management contract is the only practical way to deal with the situation.

What is often overlooked is the fact that trustees and physicians often put far more value on administrative style, how a hospital executive does something rather than what is actually accomplished, or what is possible if the unthinkable is thought about. When a chief executive decides to raise a critical issue with an unacceptable solution (but the only one possible) at a meeting of the board of trustees or of the executive committee of the medical staff, both groups typically sidetrack the matter, appoint a committee, table for later discussion, or ask for more information. Experienced committee members usually act with grace to take the chief executive off the hook because of his lapse in acceptable behavior. Should he fail to get the message, he will sooner or later be dealt with more directly.

Administrative behavior is what it is because it is defined by the power structure of the institution. If the power structure doesn't want to see the real world, those involved have only to wait until outside forces take control or exert major influence.

When a board of trustees has struggled to resolve a major crisis for a long period of time without success the only way out may be to consider a management contract. The hiring of a firm to manage a hospital does not remove the stewardship responsibilities of the board of trustees. It is only replacing a chief executive officer with a management firm. The legal fiduciary and governance functions are still in effect.

While the use of a management firm to operate a hospital is a new experience for most trustee boards, it is not a new experience for most management firms. The deck is stacked in favor of the management company and reliance on the local hospital attorney is not sufficient to offset this advantage. The local attorney may know the essential elements of contract law, but the unique problems of hospitals may lead to a contract that is not balanced.

In reviewing management contracts used by most of the firms offering this service, there was no instance in which there was sufficient contract language to cover all of the essential elements that a board of trustees should want covered. Some companies use more balanced contracts than do other management firms.

ELEMENTS OF A SOUND CONTRACT

Eleven major sections should be included in a management contract. Rather than detail all elements of each major section it is probably more useful to highlight the elements that are often overlooked.

(1) Introduction Section

In addition to the names, dates, general purposes of the contract, and goals, the contract should require both diligence in the contractor's performance and the use of acceptable management techniques.

(2) Term of Contract Section

The term of a contract should be not less than one year and no longer than five years. If the board of trustees plans to use a management firm as a temporary, bailout step, fairness requires that the contractor know up front that this is the intention. When a short time span is involved, the contractor's costs will be higher because there is an initial effort to identify fundamental problems and to put new procedures in place that are needed to improve the hospital. The longer the time span, the greater the opportunity for the contractor to recapture his initial takeover expenses toward the end of the contract.

This section should also define the method for contract extension, and for modification, as well as the proper notice procedure for contract termination.

(3) Hospital Autonomy Section

The contract should clearly state that the hospital corporation retains its status as a separate corporation and the board of trustees retains control of policy matters, along with control of the medical staff. In essence the policy authority of the board of trustees and officers, during the period of the management contract, must be defined.

The hospital should reserve the right to retain an independent financial auditor and outside management consultants and control of the assets of the hospital corporation.

The hospital should retain the right to designate its representatives to deal with the management contractor and should also insist on the right to approve the contractor's permanently assigned personnel to the hospital. Often overlooked is the need for a clause that prohibits the management contractor from allowing the management contract to be assigned to another firm, except with the approval of the hospital's board of trustees.

(4) Management Control Section

The contract delegates management authority to the contractor, but it should also require the contractor to provide a ''most favored corporation'' status to the hospital within the multihospital system.

Positions to be permanently staffed by the management contractor should be defined in the contract and their specific job descriptions subject to approval by the hospital's board of trustees. The minimum qualifications for filling each position of the permanently assigned staff should be stated.

Often ignored is the issue of full- and part-time employment for the contractor's employees. The management contract should explicitly define what is a full and a part-time employee.

In fairness to the contractor, the hospital should disclose fully any union activities in the past three years. In addition, a typical contract authorizes the contractor to control the number of employees, rates of pay, classification system, conditions of employment, job descriptions, and training. It will also authorize the contractor to collect revenues, pay bills, supervise the facility, coordinate personnel, and give the contractor complete access to the facility.

The contractor should be required to comply with all applicable federal, state, and local laws and regulations, and be held accountable for either attaining or maintaining three-year accreditation from the J.C.A.H., a state license, and other accreditation programs designated by the trustees.

Before there are major changes in hospital activities, the trustees should require that they give their approval.

In fiscal matters, the contractor should have control over the rates charged, accounting and control measures, safekeeping of records, preparation of financial reports and cost reports to third-party carriers, along with contracting rights for physician services.

Specialized services required on an ad hoc basis from the contractor should be authorized in the contract, subject to determining a dollar ceiling and a method of substantiating these services by the hospital trustees.

Contracts typically define payments to contractor employees for salary, fringe benefits, payroll taxes, relocation expenses, and workman's compensation as paid by the hospital.

A strong management contract requires the contractor to regularly report to the board of trustees, providing income and expense statements, balance sheets, cash flow statements, an annual budget including capital items, a quality assurance report, a J.C.A.H. compliance report, and a review of the management status of the hospital.

The management control section should define the method by which the trustees will evaluate the contractor's performance at the time of renewal or extension of the contract. The contract should also define to whom the hospital chief executive reports in the multihospital system and require a regional representative to attend quarterly meetings of the board of trustees.

(5) Contractor Compensation Section

The method of computing the contractor's fee and the method of payment should be defined as well as the indirect expenses of the contractor to be paid by the hospital and any specialized services. The contract should retain the hospital's right to review all unplanned contractor expenditures over $1,000 and require a performance bond. In case of mismanagement, the indemnification rights of the hospital from the contractor should be defined. Default conditions for both parties should be defined and their remedies delineated.

(6) Insurance Section

Contracts generally require the hospital to provide comprehensive public and professional liability coverages, with the contractor held harmless and coverage limits defined.

A clause in this section should hold the contractor liable for dishonesty, willful misconduct, and negligence with regard to his employees.

(7) Recruitment Section

A fair contract will prohibit the contractor from recruiting hospital employees during the contract and for one subsequent year. Likewise, the hospital should be prohibited from recruiting the contractor's employees.

(8) Confidentiality Section

The contract should require the contractor to protect the confidentiality of privileged hospital information.

(9) Termination and Arbitration Section

The contract should include a provision that either party may terminate the contract with proper notice. Penalties for termination should be spelled out. Just cause for termination should be defined, and an arbitration method defined in case of dispute.

(10) Conflicts of Interest Section

The contract should include a definition of conflicts of interest and a method for resolving them and prohibit the contractor from purchasing, leasing, or managing any other hospital in the same primary or secondary market area.

(11) General Section

A general section should include a provision for an outside consultant to periodically review the contractor's performance and report to the trustees.

Conclusion

These 11 sections are the essential elements of a sound management contract. There is the additional question of how much a hospital should pay for a management contract. The basic issue is what is a board of trustees willing to pay per occupied bed for these services or as a percentage of total operating expenses. This is a matter of judgment by the trustees and there is no one answer.

To assess a contractor's performance there should be a quarterly calculation of the hospital's departmental productivity trends, which is reported to the board, as well as a written report of the quality assurance indicators for patient care, medical care, overall infection control, and liability claims. A quarterly report of this type, required of the management contractor, will alert a board of trustees to the overall performance on the contract.

There are excellent management companies and there are poor ones. Once a contractor has been selected, the board of trustees' responsibilities are not over. The members are still on hand to see that their hospital does achieve the standards of care that the community expects.

Part III

Restraints and Regulation

97

Chapter 12

Should Hospital Planning Continue To Be Regulated?*

Over the past several years there has been a growing resentment towards health systems agencies by hospitals. Agency staffs have been inadequate in numbers to handle the volume of work and have demonstrated inexperience in hospital matters. The appointment process itself has been political and consequently a number of agency board members have had little understanding or knowledge of the issues that were being decided. Often their decisions have appeared irrational to informed hospital executives and trustees. Some decisions reached at the local level have been overturned at the state level because of what seemed to be political pressure.

The proponents of regulated planning have pointed to the claims of the health systems agencies concerning the amount of construction they had prevented as proof that hospitals were undertaking unnecessary construction. Yet it was well known among hospitals that when submitting a Certificate of Need application, it was prudent to overstate need so that planning agencies would have something to delete that would not interfere with real needs.

Gradually, it became evident that planning, as presently constituted, had failed. But in the process of failing, a pent-up frustration developed with the concept of mandated planning, to the point where there is strong support among hospitals for doing away with it entirely and replacing it with free and unfettered competition. This idea was embodied in the Gephardt-Stockman bill introduced into Congress in 1980. Although it did not pass, it has been reintroduced in every succeeding session and appears to gain more support for its ultimate enactment. It is a natural reaction to what had taken place.

------

*Adapted from *Health Affairs*, published by Project HOPE, © Spring 1983.

ASKING QUESTIONS

The time has now come to pay serious attention to the question of what will work. To what extent can it be assumed that total deregulation will be a satisfactory answer? Can the pendulum swing from total regulation to free-market competition in one step, or is there some middle ground that needs to be reached, at least for an interim period?

In attempting to answer this question, two major factors need to be kept clearly in mind. First, hospitals are a capital-intensive industry. Their greatest need, now and for the forseeable future, is for capital for physical plant and equipment so they can remain current with technological advances. The ability to acquire long-term debt and to repay it is at the heart of the matter. Whatever steps are taken, assurances need to be given to the capital markets that the role of the investor will not be ignored. Second, hospitals are no longer exclusively social agencies but rather social agencies with deep economic overtones, not only for investors, but as major employers that can seriously affect the employment situation in nearly all towns and cities. In terms of the economic needs of a community, the issue for the hospital is its ability to remain financially viable by providing high-grade health care to the public served.

Opting for the full swing of the pendulum in one step depends on an accurate assessment of the prevailing attitudes of the public, and of those who represent them, to determine if problems that can be anticipated are likely to lead to an outcry for the reestablishment of rigid controls, or to a nationalization of hospitals into a federal, centrally controlled system. Several potential difficulties in health care delivery can be identified and need to be assessed for their impact on public attitudes.

A number of communities have hospital facilities that are owned by units of government, but that are operated either by an advisory board appointed by elected officials or by a nonprofit corporation that leases the facility on contract and operates it as if it were a community, nonprofit general hospital. In the latter case the hospital has no taxing authority and is expected to break even in its financial operations. At present, investor-owned (for-profit) hospital companies are seeking to purchase these hospitals from the units of government. Proposals are being made to city and county officials that are considered to be most attractive. If the hospital has been well maintained, kept up-to-date technologically, and is the hospital of choice for residents, the officials may be offered far more money than they had any idea it was worth. Lakeland, Florida, is an example of this kind of situation. One of the largest investor-owned chains offered to buy the modern 900-bed Lakeland General Hospital for $100 million. Since the hospital only had $6 million in long-term debt the city stood to realize a net of $94 million. The offer was attractive to the city for two reasons: (1) the facility would continue to be operated as a general hospital and (2) the amount of money offered could be invested at prevailing interest rates and would produce an annual return that was nearly three times the existing budget of the city.

The fact that the offer was a $111,000 per licensed bed at a time when the cost per bed for construction was running approximately $200,000 meant that both the city and the investor-owned chain would receive a windfall from the sale of the hospital. Once the hospital was sold, the city would no longer be accountable to the citizenry for its operation. Control of the institution would pass to the new owners. If they increased the pricing structure, put tight limits on Medicare and Medicaid patient days, reduced operating expenses, widened the margin between revenues and expenses so that the bottom line would be enhanced, and passed on these benefits to the owners rather than back to the public in terms of services, this would no longer be of concern to city officials. Even if this situation came about, city officials might still view the sale as having been a sound decision because a sizable percentage of patients come to the hospital from outside the city limits. From their perspective, the windfall permits the city to lower taxes, increase services, or do both for the residents of Lakeland, since the monies obtained would annually yield approximately three times the revenues now being obtained through taxes.

This same community example can also demonstrate another kind of problem that is emerging. The Watson Clinic is a large, multispecialty group practice of 76 physicians located about one block from the Lakeland General Hospital, the only hospital in town. Forty-six percent of the total patient days are generated by clinic physicians. Since the clinic is well known and highly regarded, it draws patients from throughout central Florida. The Hospital Corporation of America (HCA) has approached the clinic and offered to build a 250-bed medical and surgical hospital immediately adjacent to it. A Certificate of Need was prepared for submission to the health systems agency for permission to do so. If approved and built there would be a subsequent decline in occupancy at the existing institution. By catering to the clinic physicians, and limiting the beds to 250, the proposed hospital would be able to operate at full capacity, using the Lakeland General Hospital as an overflow facility as well as for pediatric and obstetrical services. It was intended that the clinic physicians would continue to hold membership on the medical staff of the existing institution in order to maintain their access to the beds at Lakeland General Hospital. By operating only those programs and services that are money winners, HCA would be assured of operating a highly successful financial operation. The existing hospital would then be left with 250 excess beds idling a large capital investment. Though the city of Lakeland and the Watson Clinic never completed their negotiations with HCA, it can be anticipated that this approach will be tried in other communities where large multispecialty groups are now in existence.

Whether or not hospital planning should be totally deregulated in favor of free and unrestricted competition in one step is a matter of public policy. If it is not in the public interest to do so, then it is necessary to decide what kind of restraints are needed and how long they should be applied. What alternatives might be considered for the interim period?

ALTERNATIVE MODELS

The field of public education offers one model that might be considered. It would be possible to create geographical boundary lines, similar to school districts, that define the service area of each hospital. In the case of three or four hospitals operating in the same primary service area, each could be allocated a share of the market. In essence each hospital would have a franchise. Since a hospital typically draws 80 percent of its patients from its primary service area, these areas could be determined without much difficulty for most situations. From the standpoint of investors who hold long-term bonds on the hospital, this method would provide assurances that their investment would be protected. Three difficulties are apparent in this model:

1. About 20 percent of the public leave their area of residence for hospitalization and would continue to do so.
2. To be applicable, an assumption would have to be made that there are the right kinds of physicians (in terms of specialties) and that there are the right number of them practicing in the primary service area.
3. Specialty hospitals (for children, eye and ear, and other specialties), specialty services of hospitals, and teaching hospitals do not fit into this scheme.

A second model that might be explored is one drawn from utility companies. They are granted a monopoly position in a given geographical area and, in exchange, their rates are subject to approval by a state authority. Customers who have complaints about service must deal with the utility or, for more serious complaints, with the state agency. Decisions regarding purchasing for plant and equipment are made by the utility and are not subject to review by the state agency at predetermined levels of capital expenditure, unlike the existing restrictions on hospitals. The state commissions that approve rates charged by utility companies have fewer commissioners than planning agencies and often have knowledge in the field in which they are regulating rates. If applied to hospitals, however, the utility model does not fit since the services being rendered can be plotted from an area with geographic boundaries.

The most serious drawback to both models has to do with the role of the physician. In the public school and utility models the recipient of the service can deal directly with the provider of the service. In the health field the recipient of service must deal through an intermediary, the physician, who determines whether or not to hospitalize, where to hospitalize, and what services will be ordered. If the physician holds medical staff membership in more than one hospital, he can, together with the patient, select the institution for hospitalization, which may or may not be in the same service area. For this model to be workable, it would be necessary to franchise physicians, specialty by specialty, as well as hospitals, so that geographical boundaries would be respected.

Franchising physicians would be dependent upon their willingness to practice in areas with open slots. Practice patterns in all of the developed nations suggest that inner cities with large minority populations and rural areas would continue to be underserved. When physicians have the freedom to decide where they wish to practice and are likely to continue to exercise this freedom of choice, the viability of these models in the health field should be questioned. In the public school and utility models, the recipient of service cannot elect to receive the services from another party. He simply uses what is available or goes without the service.

A third approach has already been attempted. Because hospitals represent large capital investments, some hospital chief executives believe that by having their plans for facilities reviewed by disinterested citizens, it would be possible to avoid unnecessary duplication of facilities. This has not worked for several reasons, including the following:

1. Physicians decide for themselves in which hospital they wish to have medical staff membership.
2. Physicians select hospitals for medical staff membership where they feel they will be compatible.
3. Market shares among hospitals shift.
4. The patient age mix changes over time.
5. The financial mix of patients determines fiscal viability of the institution.
6. In-migration and out-migration in a service area cannot be controlled by a hospital.
7. The supply of physicians in an area has traditionally been left in the hands of the medical staff.

Coping with these variables cannot be accomplished at the institutional level. Because of the operation of these factors, hospitals have maintained for years that they are an inappropriate control mechanism in health care planning and it is necessary for regulators to deal directly with physicians. Until the number of physicians and pattern of admissions are geographically controlled, and until the diagnostic and treatment procedures ordered for a patient are restrained by some mechanism external to the institution, all attempts to bring about the desired changes will be ineffective.

The necessity for affecting the way physicians practice led to the enactment of a law establishing the Professional Standards Review Organization (PSRO). This approach failed because it focused on the clinical decisions of attending physicians being reviewed by other practicing physicians for an appropriate length of stay for each diagnosis. The primary motivation behind this program was cost cutting, not an improvement in the quality of care being rendered. As a result, the medical profession felt it was forced into arbitrary standards of length of stay that did not take into account sound clinical judgment acquired through years of experience. Because the practice of medicine is as much an art as it is a science, practicing physicians on PSRO committees found themselves unwilling to second-guess colleagues for whom they had respect as well-trained professionals.

A similar kind of program was developed in New York state for persons needing surgery who were required to secure a second opinion prior to the scheduled operation. This was much more limited in scope than the PSRO program and therefore had little application to the greater needs of hospitals. The program remained outside the institution and affected hospitals only indirectly by restraining the use of operating rooms.

As an alternative to the traditional ways of financing health care, health maintenance organizations (HMOs) have been eyed with favor because they provide physicians with an economic incentive for keeping patients out of the hospitals and treating them on an ambulatory basis. Since the results indicate substantial reductions in admissions, this approach has been receiving attention. In order to encourage this form of financing, the Health Planning Act exempted HMOs from the Certificate of Need process to encourage their development.

While HMOs had economic appeal to third-party payers because of reduced payments to hospitals, neither physicians nor the public responded with enthusiasm for several years, except in California and in Minnesota's Twin Cities. This lack of support lead to the concept of the Preferred Provider Organization (PPO), where an employer provides a benefit package to the employee and his family. The PPO provides a list of physicians and hospitals which, if used, means the PPO will pay first-dollar coverage. However, if the person elects to go to a physician or a hospital not in the PPO, the patient would pay any differences out of his own resources. This approach has the advantage that no restrictions are placed on the patient's choice and thereby avoids one of the major criticisms of the HMO-type plan.

It would seem that no plan has been devised, or any model proposed, to date that offers a way of securing broad support among the public, the medical profession, or hospitals. Under such circumstances it would seem reasonable to believe that restrictions on hospital planning should not be removed until such time as the consequences of doing so are more clearly understood. Separating an episode of illness from immediate economic consequences worked in this country as long as there were ample resources. Now that we are in a period of scarce resources, and likely to be so for the foreseeable future, it is apparent that a way must be found to reintroduce economic decision making into the system. Care must be taken not to do this so quickly that negative public reaction develops and leads to a quick-fix solution of a national health system or a set of rigid, unworkable regulations.

If the hospital industry were suddenly deregulated, it should be expected that some unnecessary duplication of facilities and equipment would develop as hospitals with strong market positions might move to increase what they already have at the expense of other hospitals in the same or adjacent service areas. Market segmentation would occur where investor-owned chains would affiliate with large multispecialty group practices to provide hospitals for the exclusive use of clinic physicians. In both instances, idle hospital facilities would develop in selected areas of the country.

How the public might react is a moot point. Instead of letting market forces take their course knowing that what was happening was only a temporary dislocation, which would not be repeated once the economics of a free marketplace became fully operational, the public might not wait it out and instead might call for the government to step in and stop the duplication. Given existing public sentiment towards hospitals and their costs this might happen even if the public could be shown that what was occurring was only a temporary situation that would eventually lead to a more responsive, cost-efficient system.

Since business coalitions are rapidly forming, and Congress is increasingly concerned about the costs of the Medicare-Medicaid programs for the years ahead, and since commercial insurance carriers are becoming more vociferous about cost shifting, it should be anticipated that the public would react and want a quick-fix solution. For these reasons, the move towards free competition must embody an interim phase that eases regulations but does not do away with them entirely for a period of two to three years.

AN INTERIM PHASE

An interim phase should continue the Certificate of Need process, but should be applied only to big-ticket items such as expenditures over $3 to $5 million to be used for additional beds. A preferable method would be to use a formula that is tailored to the size of the hospitals, such as requiring that any capital expenditure that exceeds one-quarter or one-third of the book value of the institution must be reviewed by the appropriate state authority. Renovations and remodeling of existing space should be excluded from this limitation.

Local health systems agencies should be abandoned and all reviews of applications handled at the state level. The basis of determination should be historical utilization coupled with the projected demographics and utilization rates that apply to the service area for the next ten years. All factors that have been applied to external conditions over which a hospital has no control should be eliminated, since it has never been possible to show a direct relationship between these factors and the way in which inpatient bed usage takes place.

By using utilization trend lines with projections into the future for five and ten years it would be possible to both reduce and increase bed complements as needed. If moving averages over the last five years were applied, it would be possible to deny applications for increasing bed complements in areas with declining populations. Excess beds that might result could be declared to be provisionally delicensed because of a lack of demand, but might be kept in operation by a hospital if it so desired since they would already be in existence.

In an interim period one other step should be included. State rate review programs should remain in place but be modified. Experience to date shows that if prospective rates are left solely in the hands of government, the rates that are approved will reflect the needs of government more nearly than the needs of hospitals for providing care called for under government programs. A check and balance system is required where the rate of inflation and intensity of use factors are impartially determined by a group outside of both government and hospitals.

In the long run the development of free-marketplace economic competition must be based on the recognition of several assumptions:

1. Resources for health care are not unlimited and economic decision making must become part of the health care equation for every episode of illness.
2. Physicians cannot be mandated into a program; it must be in their economic interest to participate.
3. Government should establish a basic set of benefits for all citizens, but permit those who choose to spend monies for additional coverage with taxable dollars to do so at their discretion.
4. Patients should continue to have freedom of choice of physician and hospital if they are willing to pay for that alternative.
5. Hospitals should be paid on a pricing basis, and cost reimbursement should be eliminated.
6. Any program that is adopted should be based on incentives rather than regulation.
7. Quality of care measures are important but are too elusive to be incorporated into a legislative program and are more properly left to the marketplace for determination.

Even though it may not be an appropriate time to seek passage of a federal bill along these lines, a bill should be developed and sponsored so that as congressional priorities change, or when a health crisis occurs in the funding of health care, it will be ready to go.

What is proposed is not new. When analyzed and compared with what has been offered, it closely resembles the Gephardt-Stockman bill. It uses the same set of assumptions. This is important because the assumptions undergird the reasoning that is needed if the health care system is to be changed in a fundamental way.

Tinkering with the existing system will not bring about what is required. It will only lead to more of the same kind of problems already too familiar to the health field. The time has arrived for the industry to take the leadership and not wait for Congress to show the way.

As one looks ahead it is apparent that "allowable costs" are going to get further and further away from full operating costs. Congress is not going to be able to withdraw the Medicare benefits provided the elderly in 1965. This is a reality of political life that must be understood. Given the choice between restricting entitlements or squeezing hospitals and physicians, Congress will continue to find ways to reduce payments to the providers of health care until such time as a major crisis occurs. Until that time, hospital efforts should be directed toward developing a proposal that embodies the assumptions examined above.

Chapter 13

Cost Control Strategies for Hospitals

TWO FORCES SHAPE THE FUTURE

In thinking about cost-control strategies that can be employed by hospitals, one is forced to start at the point of addressing the question "What will be the character of the health care delivery system in the future?" The general hospital will clearly have a major role in the system but it will be shaped by two separate and distinct forces: the role of the federal government and the attitudes of the public. Both will be important, though the ultimate determinant will be public attitudes. These will reflect multiple viewpoints about expectations, depending on a variety of factors related to different economic groups, age categories, and locations. In a general way, government through its legislative branch will be trying to assess and respond to these differing publics.

At the moment, the legislative branch is reading the various publics as saying that hospital costs are too high and apt to keep on increasing at a more rapid rate than that of inflation and this cannot be permitted to continue. With a history of a 14 to 15 percent increase in annual hospital expenditures, the concern is how to lessen the high rate of increase. The point has now been reached where there is unanimity. Most thoughtful hospital executives concede that steps have to be taken. The problem is finding control measures for costs without impairing quality of care. This is an exceedingly difficult balance to achieve because the modern hospital is a large, heavily capitalized, technological enterprise operating in a complex social setting, but with different attitudes on the part of trustees and physicians that do not square with the dynamics and flexibility required for survival.

DIFFERING VIEWPOINTS

One might believe that cost-control strategies should be viewed alike by trustees, hospital executives, and physicians. That is not so; nor is it true that regulatory bodies will see hospital efforts in the same light as hospital representatives. Each group views the scene from its own set of experiences.

Physicians see a hospital as a support system for their own activities of diagnosis and treatment. By the very nature of their profession they are prone to be proponents of the status quo. Physicians have trouble understanding that housekeeping, maintenance, personnel, public relations, and other functions cannot continue to absorb all of the required financial cutbacks as part of a cost-control strategy in order to protect clinical services.

Trustees should be prepared to deal with recommendations from medical staffs that are aimed at protecting clinical freedoms at the expense of a balanced hospital operation. Governing boards need to appreciate that the typical physician, finding himself increasingly threatened, will be determined not to let things escape from his control that now lie within it. Physicians know their role is of considerable economic importance in a hospital and this provides them with the leverage to continue to protect their interests. Since boards recognize physicians as surrogate customers, they will be careful not to adopt policies that alienate a sensitive medical staff climate.

To push for a single, unified, organizational structure with all major functions reporting through the chief executive is not likely to be greeted with enthusiasm by today's medical staff. Chester I. Barnard, writing in 1938 in the *Functions of an Executive,* put his finger on the reason why it cannot be easily accomplished. He pointed out that an executive's authority can be exercised only to the extent that those over whom he is exercising it accept his right to do so.[1] In today's climate, medical staffs vehemently deny this right exists for administrators. In fact, in many hospitals, they deny it exists even for another physician who may be in an administrative position, such as a full-time chief of staff or medical director.

From the standpoint of organizational theory, what seems like a good idea as a response to mandated controls may be just the reverse. The use and application of governance authority is unlikely to lead to anything but medical staff resistance. A need for the foreseeable future is to have serious, sensitive medical staff leadership, rather than to rely on authority to achieve the required balance of fiscal responsibility. Even though a single, unified top-level structure is certainly desirable, it appears to be unachievable for a majority of hospitals because of prevailing physician attitudes.

In essence, the future is limited to involving a physician only along traditional lines, but attempts can and should be made to broaden the base of physician involvement in hospital affairs as much as possible. Even though this strategy requires substantial chunks of administrative time, it is obvious that future change must involve maximum physician participation.

From their standpoint, physicians view acceptable cost-containment strategies as those that shorten the average length of stay and reduce the number of diagnostic procedures ordered for patients as long as the full range of procedures remains available. Average length of stay has decreased because of utilization review and Professional Review Organization (PRO) activities.

As with any change, there have been side effects that have worked in the opposite direction. The average number of laboratory procedures per inpatient admission has continued to rise, as it has been doing for the last two decades. X-ray examinations have also continued to increase per admission. This is to be expected as a hospital becomes more technologically oriented. While average lengths of stay have been declining, the intensity of service has been rising. In addition, the number of admissions per 1,000 population has also steadily increased over the years; or stated in other terms, the demand for hospital services has been going up.

Because intensity and demand factors have continued to rise, a shortened length of stay has not been enough to offset a rise in real cost, even after factoring out inflation. This situation will remain unless ways are found for keeping patients out of hospitals through a greater emphasis on ambulatory medicine.

Cost-control strategies require the application of new managerial or organizational techniques to control the costs of operation. The question that leaps to mind is whether or not tinkering with a management system will bring about the desired results. Is the problem really a more deep-seated, complex issue that involves many other aspects of health care that lie beyond the scope of management? Is it an appropriate analogy to think of the hospital as a sailboat caught at sea in a vicious storm when the skipper can only reef his sails, head into the wind, and hope for the best, knowing that what is occurring is beyond control? In many respects, this seems to be an apt description.

As it now stands, government talks money and is concerned about the increasing dollars being spent for health care, while hospitals talk quality of care. Both are right, but both are wrong since neither party is addressing the real concerns of the other. Like the skipper of the sailboat, the hospital does not control much of the medical activities that go on inside its four walls and the result is that the hospital is simply trying to ride out the storm.

If the rate of increase in total dollars spent in hospitals is to be slowed down, something must be done to control the number of admissions, and hospitals do not control them. Hospitals are only facilitating agents. There are numerous standards of professional performance that members of the medical staff must meet. But hospitals do not control, nor have they ever controlled, admissions. The decision to admit a patient, which services are ordered, and when the patient is discharged are traditionally matters left solely to the discretion of a physician without interference from the hospital.

The real point of control that has to be affected is the relationship between physician and patient. Hospitals have not, and are not likely to, put themselves in the middle of this relationship. As a consequence, costs cannot be substantially affected until programs are devised that directly impinge on the decision making that goes on in the physician/patient equation. Until these steps are taken, the hospital will remain a sailboat riding out a storm that may well be increasing in intensity.

The root of the cost-control issue is not to be found in the management systems or the organizational structures of hospitals. It is possible to suggest a number of ways to improve the operations of a hospital, such as expanding the responsibility and authority of the chief executive, limiting the size of the governing board, developing systems of hospitals, and involving the medical staff more deeply in the development of hospital policies, programs, and services. All of these changes may enhance organizational effectiveness and improve efficiency, but they will not lead to sufficient change to make a real difference.

In order to slow the cost spiral, it is necessary to bring about substantial changes in the way hospitals are used by the public and the physicians. The focus needs to shift to external factors that shape the delivery system of care. To continue to further erode the decision-making authority of governing boards by imposing more and more stringent controls on hospital operations and capital spending and by having these parameters set by rate review commissions and health systems agencies leads away from, not towards, sound decision making.

DEVELOPING STRATEGIES

Trustees, physicians, and executives must join together in developing appropriate strategies for shaping the delivery system, for this is where real strides forward can be made. As a first step in this process, hospitals should seriously question the payment of first-dollar costs for big hospital insurance carriers. Clearly this unhooks the episode of illness from having direct economic consequences at the time a decision is reached about hospitalization. To make matters worse, the insured usually is of the opinion that, if hospitalization is required, an obligation exists to pay for these services since the monthly premium that is paid entitles the patient to collect from the insurance carrier. The fact that Blue Cross and commercial insurance companies offer policies that encourage utilization is justified by this viewpoint since carriers recognize market demands.

In the restructuring of health care financing, a major priority has to be given to forcing third-party carriers away from paying first-dollar costs. Payments to hospitals will decline when this step is taken.

This is no small task since labor unions and employers have fought bruising battles over this issue for years. Both sides have been reluctant to consider deductibles and coinsurance, but have done so when faced with declining sales in their business.

One of the myths that confuses the health delivery picture is that government, insurance carriers, and Blue Cross keep repeating over and over again how upset they are by hospital costs. Their expression "rising hospital costs" is merely a way of reflecting concerns about the rapidly increasing number of dollars paid to hospitals for services received by the insured. Insurance carrier payments to hospitals have two basic parts: days of care paid for on behalf of the insured and the average cost per patient day of care in a hospital. Even though it is a two-part equation, carriers have elected to focus on only the half that is safest from their point of view, cost per patient day. The other half, insurers usage, goes untouched.

Hospitals must move in unison to force the attention of third-party payers on the physician/patient relationship, rather than on the hospital. Past dealings with carriers have involved debate over the adequacy of reimbursement, casting the hospital in the role of being money hungry and unconcerned with public considerations. If hospitals join together in a coordinated stand on eliminating first-dollar coverage, they can reverse existing roles. If these efforts are resisted, they can and should consider threatening to terminate contracts with insurance carriers on the grounds that they are less interested than hospitals in the amount of monthly premiums paid by the insured; otherwise, carriers would make these changes. Unless carriers are put between "a rock and a hard spot," they will probably not seriously look at moving away from first-dollar coverage because of countervailing pressures from labor unions.

A second needed consideration is to deal with the malpractice situation. Given the suing climate that pervades our society, a physician needs to be assured protection against capricious lawsuits. If third-party payers wish physicians to increase the use of ambulatory care in order to reduce inpatient admissions, physicians need protection from malpractice lawsuits. To expect physicians to exploit ambulatory care to the maximum extent may be asking them to incur a lawsuit risk they consider unnecessary. In order to eliminate the risk, the federal government should consider the establishment of a federally created insurance corporation to protect the physician in his exercise of reasonable clinical judgment. Such legislation needs the support of the Social Security Administration in order to assure the public and congressional representatives that this type of legislation is not motivated by the vested interests of physicians, but rather by an agency concerned with the appropriate use of health care resources. In such a program, panels of experts would probably have to be developed to review pending cases and evaluate the merits of the professional judgment used in each situation.

What has been lost sight of is that a fee-for-service is a system of payment in which the patient (or his agent) pays only for services received and is not expected to pay for services not received. The system provides the maximum of flexibility and encourages a physician to spend maximum time on professional activities of direct patient care. If the physician opts to work fewer hours per day or per week, fewer patients are seen, and fewer payments are received. When physicians work harder and see more patients, incomes increase. Incentives for working are automatic under a fee-for-service. It is a highly efficient one. There are no built-in inefficiencies. If a physician stops working, is sued, takes a vacation, falls ill, or retires, no organization is responsible for the associated costs. It is a piecework system that forces efficiency. This must be kept in mind when dealing with proponents of closed-loop systems who advocate salaries for physicians; they are pushing for a more inefficient system.

Because of its flexible nature, fee-for-service can be used to accomplish the objectives of the third-party payers in limiting hospitalization. For example, the professional fee schedule for a cystoscopy could be greater when performed on an outpatient basis rather than with the patient admitted to a hospital. The same could be true for ambulatory surgery; the fee schedule would make it to the surgeon's economic interest to perform procedures where appropriate on an outpatient basis. The procedures to be included should be developed by the recognized specialty groups in organized medicine through intermediaries or Blue Cross/Blue Shield plans. The key to workability lies in cooperation and support of private practitioners and the organized medical group to which they relate. Rather than relying on the American Medical Association as the only point of contact, the representation of physicians interests should be broadened to include the specialty organizations.

ECONOMICS ARE KEY

In the process of restructuring the health delivery system, it is essential that the reasonable cost system of reimbursement be abandoned. Economic forces at work must be allowed to become a major determinant in the use of hospital services. To pay a hospital its costs, no matter what that level may be, is not an incentive to sound management. But neither is it wise to substitute government regulation over all of the managerial and financial decisions of a hospital. Both lead to an increase in costs and politicization of the decision-making process. Little can be accomplished until the incentives and behavior of physicians, patients, hospital management, and governing boards are permitted to contribute to rational economic decisions from each party's respective viewpoints. These decisions must also be compatible with the self-interests of the payers of these services. Ways need to be found for increasing competition between health care providers. Physicians and patients have to have an incentive for selecting an institution on the basis of relative quality and known cost of service.

As part of restructuring the health delivery system, the patient must be brought into the economic decision-making process on a meaningful basis. As things now stand, the typical patient neither knows nor can anticipate either physician fees or hospital charges. Literally, there is no economic stake in paying for the costs of these services, except as it ultimately is reflected in that portion of the monthly premium paid. Since each patient's cost is lumped together with thousands of other insurers payments, there is no direct relationship between each episode of illness and the monthly premium. Nor are there penalties for not following a physician's directions for either improving health or staying out of a hospital.

There is a growing concern that the way to limit health care expenditures is to concentrate on the issue of keeping persons healthy, rather than on the question of returning them to health after they have incurred an illness. Hospitals, by their very nature, are repair oriented; they see patients after a physiological change has taken place. Hospitals have not had a significant role in the prevention of illness. Nor has there been a concerted effort among physicians to prevent illness. Physicians are problem solvers who are concerned with discovering disease and treating it. They, like hospitals, react to what is discovered and do not have a primary concern with human preventive maintenance.

The prepayment plan might offer a variety of premium rates. For persons who have had a heart attack or a stroke, there might be a surcharge on the basic premium rate unless the subscriber could present evidence that:

1. The individual is on a regular exercise program.
2. Weight is controlled.
3. The person has attended a course for victims of heart disease dealing with how to change life style to successfully live with the disability.

An annual certification might be required in order to demonstrate continued adherence to the program. Upon receipt of an attesting statement, the premium would be lowered to the standard rate.

For the subscriber who is healthy, credit might be given for proper diet, exercise, nonsmoking, and other positive indicators. The benefit would be a reduced premium. Where an employer bears the full cost of the premium, it might be required that the uninsured be paid the difference between the regular premium and the reduced premium, or conversely have to pay the difference between a regular premium and the surcharge that might be levied. Such a program would be prevention at the point it would most likely be effective. The role of the hospital would be to provide the training programs that would need to be developed for each specific disease group.

For years, those in the health field have believed that no compromise with quality of care can be permitted to take place. It may just be that the public no longer shares this belief. Many may have undergone a real and permanent shift in attitude and now are concerned more with cost than quality. The focus of effort should now be directed to the demand side of the equation and not on cost containment that cripples the health care industry to the point that it can no longer perform its role. The hospitals of New York and Massachusetts are keenly aware of the disastrous effect of limited reimbursement. They know the importance of affecting the physician/patient relationship so that economics come into play in the system.

The string appears to be running out. With increasing frequency, representatives of the public are raising economic problems they want considered. They are questioning capital costs of hospitals. This appears to hospital professionals as a reaction to what they do not like, rather than a balanced viewpoint. The present status of this relationship cannot continue indefinitely, but must be permitted to evolve into an era where programs, services, and controls square with the forces at work in a free marketplace.

As it now stands, hospitals and, increasingly, physicians are being caught up by arbitrarily imposed standards that require the knuckling under of the private health care sector by government dictates and edicts. The game plan that has been evolving on the part of government has three major thrusts—programs designed to cope with physician activities, programs aimed at reducing inpatient utilization of hospitals, and control of operating and capital funding of hospitals.

To date, the controls being applied to physicians have lagged behind those to hospitals. With encouragement of the development of HMOs, physicians will be forced into HMO medicine as a matter of personal economic necessity.

At the institutional level, controls are exercised in the form of reimbursement, which is manipulated to force conformance with federal standards. Remaining largely outside the sphere of control is the physician/patient relationship. This is the crucial point in the entire health care delivery system. For it to be successful, patients and physicians must be so affected that in acting in their own best economic interests, they are also acting in the best economic interests of the body politic.

As it now stands, government controls are based on taking financially protective measures solely against hospitals for anything having to do directly with patient care. At the level of the institution, the restrictions are twofold: the control over capital expenditures and any substantial change in programs or services, under the threat of losing depreciation and interest expense if not approved. This is cost control, not control of demand. The difference goes unrecognized.

It is these broader issues that are being reflected in what is happening to hospital costs. To concentrate on internal efficiency to the exclusion of the more important forces at work is to ignore the real areas of concern. People who are truly ill are going to go to hospitals for diagnosis and treatment and will pay the costs, high as they will be at that time. But they will also be paying $2 for a loaf of bread. Hopefully, fewer persons per 1,000 population will need such care. Whether or not this will be the case does not lie within the scope of hospital activities to decide. Such decisions turn on:

1. Getting economic decision making back into the physician/patient relationship.

2. Providing financial incentives in premium payments to subscribers for adhering to habits that contribute to their good health.
3. Forcing government to cope with inflation in a meaningful and sustained way.

Those associated with hospitals need to direct their strategies toward these ends and not let themselves be misdirected into looking at matters of secondary concern or be disconcerted by not being able to meet the public's expectations about costs.

NOTE

1. Chester I. Barnard, *Functions of an Executive* (Cambridge, Mass.: Harvard University, 1938), 109.

Chapter 14

The Resurgence of a Two-Tier Health Care System[*]

ENTITLING THE ELDERLY

In today's economy of scarce resources, one of the greatest challenges facing Congress is to deal with the enormous problem of runaway costs in entitlement programs. Senators and Congressmen know the difficulties they face at the polls when benefits to citizens are reduced.

From a societal viewpoint, the passage of Titles XVIII and XIX (Medicare and Medicaid) in 1965 was a major step forward. These laws meant that each person could freely select the physician and hospital of his or her choice. The poor and the elderly could receive personalized medical care and would no longer be destined for a charity hospital and clinics with their long, hard, wooden benches.

With the advent of adequate health care financing, the health care system responded, and a majority of people began receiving care on an equitable basis, regardless of their status as public or private patients. Entitlements that had been promised were being delivered.

As inflation increased and the purchasing power of the dollar decreased, the need for periodic adjustments and the indexing of monies received by government recipients was recognized. Steps were taken by Congress to prevent the erosion of this purchasing power. By the spring of 1981, the federal administration realized that major steps had to be taken to realign the economy. Five steps toward improvement of the economy were proposed by the administration:

1. Reduce personal income taxes 10 percent a year for three years in order to increase savings, which could be made available for capital investment.
2. Increase the defense budget by a substantial amount in order to enhance U.S. military capabilities.

---

*Adapted from *Action-Kit for Hospital Law* with permission, © August 1982.

3. Reduce domestic spending by the government in order to maintain the projected deficits at manageable levels.
4. Shift as many domestic programs as possible from centralized control at the federal level to state or local governments, and/or deregulate industries so that private incentives could become operative.
5. Reduce the rate of inflation by tightening the supply of money.

By the summer of 1981, the outlook for implementing these steps was optimistic. The first round of slashing, eliminating some domestic programs and reducing others, got underway. Early 1982 led to a reassessment of the strategy as the Office of Management and Budget presented estimates that revealed a projected deficit of $98.6 billion in 1982 and $91.5 billion in 1983.[1] In the uproar that followed, the projected deficits came under fire and were thought by some to be too low, with most subsequent estimates placing the deficits in excess of $200 billion. Projections for entitlement payments were scrutinized and a growing number of individuals came to believe that the federal budget could not be balanced, and further, that the cost of the Medicare program would be staggering by the end of the decade.

Congress now has a dilemma on its hands with regard to health care programs. If Medicare entitlements are reduced, the elderly citizens, who are rapidly growing in numbers, will be alienated by a reduction in the existing levels of benefits. On the other hand, to leave the benefits in place courts economic disaster. Complicating the problem for Congress is the knowledge that Professional Standards Review Organizations (PSROs), cost containment, and health planning through health systems agencies has failed.

Putting clamps on the providers of health services clearly has not worked as intended. The difficulty that now remains is how to best choose among the alternatives. This will not be an easy task since the political reality is that Congress is unlikely to adopt a program that will antagonize a substantial number of its constituents by reducing Medicare benefits.

If entitlements are considered sacrosanct, then control of Medicare costs can be achieved in one of two ways: (1) design payment programs that encourage citizens to make economic decisions with respect to health care or (2) control payments to providers of service. The latter approach is more palatable to politicians who must vote on these issues. A look at why this is so may be helpful for understanding why it will be favored.

CONTROLLING COSTS

When Medicare and Medicaid were enacted, both bills embodied the concept of "allowable costs." The intention was that hospitals would recapture revenues equal to their operating costs associated with the appropriate financial categories of their patients. Since 1966, when these two programs became operational, "allowable costs" have constantly diminished as a percentage of total operating costs. The federal government has continuously redefined and reduced "allowable costs" in order to restrict flow of tax dollars into these programs. As a result, a hospital today with a year-round, full house of only Medicare-Medicaid patients and no other sources of revenue would go bankrupt.

As "allowable costs" declined, hospitals shifted costs to other financial categories of patients to collect additional revenues. Over the past years, "allowable costs" have constantly shrunk as a percentage of total operating costs. Patients whose hospital bills are paid according to a pricing schedule (self-pays and commercial insurance) now bear the burden for the cost-reimbursed Medicare-Medicaid patients. In some metropolitan areas the cost shift now reaches 20 to 25 percent of per-patient day cost. Commercial insurance carriers are aware of this practice and are concerned about its implications for the future determination of their premium rates.

Over the past two decades the hospital field has reacted predictably to this situation. With each new restriction placed on reimbursement by the federal government, hospitals have responded with outcries to Congress, claiming that it was not the intent of the law to pay less than full operating costs. After a few months the furor has always died down and things have gone back to business as usual. This cycle has been repeated so often that the reaction of the hospital field has become predictable in the minds of Congress. Congress has viewed it as overreaction, since these adjustments in "allowable costs" have not led to a lessening of care for Medicare recipients as long as cost shifting has taken place within a reasonable range. Of necessity, hospital budgets have been adjusted to accommodate to the needs of government. Hospital leaders are now worried that because of third-party pressure they have run out of room for cost shifting.

The point that needs to be made to the hospital field is that once the federal government was permitted to make a significant distinction between "full operating costs" and "allowable costs" there was no way of preventing the widening of the gap between the two. The only visible guideline was lost. Any strategy employed after that point was doomed to be ineffective.

After seeing hospital executives use the same tactics year after year, Congress has become immune to their pleas. Because of past experience with hospitals, it is unlikely that Congress is going to start listening again; it has heard the same song for too many years. Even if Congress now sees a difference in what is being said, it cannot afford to pay much attention, given the projected federal deficits it faces. Of necessity, it is concentrating on the immediate problem of closing the gap between government spending and revenues. As responsible lawmakers, congressional members can only view the difficulties confronting the hospital industry as part of a much larger economic problem with which they must deal.

Given widespread public opinion that hospitals are inefficient, together with a Congress that may well share this belief, and a history of hospitals crying wolf at every reduction in reimbursement, it seems likely that even deeper cuts will be made by Congress in view of the projected deficits.

At some point, hospitals are going to have to squarely face the issue and determine for themselves the wisest course of action. Trapped by an inability to further cost shift additional cutbacks in Medicare reimbursement, and with no suitable legislative programs in view, hospitals are most likely to respond to the situation in a manner similar to that of nursing homes.

ALTERNATIVE STRATEGIES

In 1965, many of the nursing homes in this country applied to the Social Security Administration to become certified Medicare nursing homes. After two or three years in the program most owners and managers of nursing homes voluntarily decertified their beds because of the inadequacy of the reimbursement received.

This same strategy may be followed by hospitals. When cost shifting can no longer be carried out and Medicare reimbursement is further restricted, hospitals may voluntarily cancel their Medicare/Medicaid contracts in order to remain financially viable. Once one governing board makes such a decision, other hospitals in the service area will make the same decision since financial pressures will be increasing on all of them. Patients will be informed that the hospital will be willing to provide care, but that the patients must assume the primary financial responsibility and seek their own reimbursement directly from the appropriate government office. The effect of this turn of events would be a back-door reduction in benefits to Medicare recipients. A patient would have to bear the difference between what was paid to the hospital and what was received from the government. If a patient could not pay the entire bill the hospital would have to absorb the unpaid balance. The government would not be a party to it. The transaction would be strictly between the hospital and the patient. The irony of such an arrangement would be that entitlements to beneficiaries would be reduced without Congress having to take a stand on the issue.

It can be anticipated that governing boards of hospitals will give the matter serious and prolonged consideration before voluntarily withdrawing from the Medicare-Medicaid programs. While studying the issue, hospitals will likely contact other institutions, local hospital councils, and state hospital associations, to get a sense of how others are likely to act. Because of antitrust concerns there will be no coordination of decision making. Once a leading hospital in a community takes this step, other area hospitals can be expected to quickly follow the lead.

No hospital will follow this course until it views itself as being on the verge of bankruptcy. The deeper the cuts in Medicare payments, and the sooner they come, the sooner hospitals will reach the point of this decision.

When to voluntarily withdraw from Medicare can be easily determined by each hospital. The decision will take place when, on a cash basis, the hospital reaches the point where it can no longer pay its current operating expenses because it will have depleted its depreciation reserves and cannot make up the loss from operations or from nonoperating revenues. Where this point in time lies will differ among hospitals, even those in the same community, because of variations in the amount of outpatient service each provides, the margins between costs and prices on these ambulatory items, and the annual amounts received from philanthropic sources. In the event that there is a high degree of competition from nonhospital sources for outpatient services, there would be no opportunity to raise prices by hospitals in order to continue to cost shift some of the Medicare-Medicaid burden.

Hospitals have been able to delay facing the issue of voluntarily decertifying from Medicare-Medicaid much longer than nursing homes did because the levels of reimbursement have only gradually deteriorated and they have had multiple sources of revenue. Not only did they have differing categories of inpatients that were a mixture of self-pay, commercial, and cost reimbursed, but they were able to charge for a variety of services, such as laboratory, X-ray, and emergency rooms that nursing homes did not offer. Had they relied on room charges and pharmacy items alone, they would have been in the same position as nursing homes and would have had to face up to the issues much earlier.

When a hospital reaches the point that it is seriously considering terminating its contract, it can be anticipated that the governing board will seek a middle ground if at all possible. Rather than take an action to terminate the Medicare-Medicaid contract, the board will likely first want to cap the number of admissions from these sources. This may be set at no more than 50 percent (or some other lower percentage) of inpatient admissions. Should such a decision be implemented, it can be expected that some members of the medical staff will strenuously object.

By and large, the patients of any physician tend to be in the same age category as the physician. A young physician typically has a young patient population. Older physicians typically have patients that are older. Thus, a decision to cap Medicare patients will disproportionately affect some of the older, more established members of the medical staff. They will quickly point out the inequity of such a policy on the premise that it is unfair to them. This will force reconsideration by the board. As the issue is debated around the board table, the new policy will probably be rescinded and the decision made to continue as before. Inevitably, though, it will resurface over the next few months as the financial situation weakens. Finally, a decision will be reached to voluntarily terminate the Medicare and Medicaid contracts.

In hospitals that have a long tradition of providing free care, there may well be an attempt to reinstitute free clinics, where the medical staff is obligated to spend one-half a day a week providing free medical coverage for clinic patients. Such an effort is apt to be unsuccessful since most physicians in private practice today no longer feel they should be forced into such activities and will be unwilling to go along with the board decision citing ''unfair taxation.'' Because of this prevailing attitude such efforts are likely to be aborted at an early stage of planning with the physicians believing that they are being coerced into the program because of a government failure to provide sufficient funds to meet the obligations it accepted when it passed the enabling legislation.

As the above scenario unfolds, it may become more complicated if a cost-containment program is adopted by the Congress in an attempt to stem the outflow of tax dollars to the providers of health care. If such a program comes about, it will prevent hospitals from engaging in more cost shifting and probably lead them to terminate contracts at a faster rate because they will be deprived of an opportunity to pursue a practice that has enabled them to continue to honor their Medicare-Medicaid contracts. In effect, such a program would leave them in a position of accepting less and less while at the same time would take away their ability to shift costs to other third-party carriers. The end result is predictable, a quick termination of contracts because the financial bind will be serious.

TWO-TIER HEALTH CARE

With this point reached, a two-tier health care system will rapidly reemerge. Public hospitals will feel the impact quickly. Admissions will rise dramatically as the elderly and the medically indigent seek care. Since those over 65 years of age use hospitals at a rate that is three times the rate of those under 65, and those over age 75 use them at eight times the rate, the numbers shifting to public hospitals are apt to be more than can be accommodated. Finding the money to provide this care from state and local tax dollars will be a major problem since previously supplied federal dollars will no longer be available.

Indigent and charity hospitals will not be alone in coping with the flood of new patients. All public hospitals will be looked upon as having a responsibility. District hospitals that have traditionally operated as if they were voluntary non-profit institutions will discover that their legal status as public hospitals may require them to accept these patients.

The basis of the present dilemma is not that hospitals are inefficient, but that hospital and medical care are personalized services that are costly to provide. As long as legislators cannot face up to the enormous cost of the entitlements provided the citizenry, the existing situation will continue to worsen. Yet, a political reluctance to do so is understandable. A promise made to the American public in

1965 with the passages of Titles XVIII and XIX must be modified if federal budget requirements are to be satisfied. To permit a reduction in entitlements through the back door is not a stable long-term solution. If voluntary terminations come about, a polarization of public opinion can be expected as the elderly find themselves caught between two opposing forces, hospitals and the federal government. As the elderly find that they must pay hospitals directly for services rendered to them and then seek reimbursement from a federal government that increasingly pays them less and less, they will become increasingly militant. As pressure mounts they will seek redress from the government. Marches and picketing of Congress and the White House will occur. Examples will be forthcoming of elderly couples who had to deplete their life's savings in order to pay for needed hospital services and were left penniless. To avoid such a possibility would seem to be in the public interest.

Time is running out. Short-term and simple solutions cannot be counted on to do the job. Major restructuring of the financing mechanism is required. A first step in this direction has been taken, an abandonment of cost reimbursement as a payment mechanism. What is now needed is to develop a way to encourage the purchase of medical and hospital care as an economic decision. The Gebhardt-Stockman proposal, or something similar to it, fulfills these requirements. To stop short of this innovative and imaginative approach is an open invitation to the perils described.

NOTE

1. "Federal Budget Deficits and Surplus," *Chicago Tribune*, 9 February 1982, 4.

Chapter 15

The Basis of a Medicare Crisis[*]

ROOT CAUSE

Ever since the enactment of Medicare in 1966, new federal regulations restricting the definition of reasonable cost for reimbursement have been issued periodically. As each new federal regulation has been issued, the hospital field has repeatedly voiced the opinion that a financial crisis would follow. Yet hospitals have continued to operate. A few hospitals have closed and some have merged or consolidated into either investor-owned or nonprofit corporate chains. The net result, however, has been a continued service capacity, even though many corporate structures have been altered and cost shifting from government programs to private sources has steadily increased.

With the passage of the Tax Equity and Fiscal Responsibility Act in September 1982 and the Prospective Payment System for Medicare in March 1983, the hospital field again began talking about an impending crisis, including both financial difficulties and organizational problems between hospitals and their medical staff. As in the past, the larger society believes there is a hollow ring to the crisis talk.

Privately, hospital executives view the shift from cost-based reimbursement to a fixed-price-per-case basis for a diagnosis or procedure as a new era of concern. The root cause for this concern is not the fixed-price concept but rather the belief that the price levels established are too low. The prices to be paid by Medicare are based on the median cost of each diagnosis or procedure in 1981 adjusted to a 1983 price level. The use of a median cost roughly means that one-half of the hospitals will be reimbursed at a cost below the then existing reimbursed Medicare cost. The

---

[*]Adapted from *ACHE* with permission of American College of Healthcare Executives, © August 1983.

concern on the part of hospital executives for adequate payment levels was underscored when the report on the future financial stability of the Medicare fund was published in 1983.

Hospital chief executives are deeply concerned about these new laws because of the past practice by the federal administration and Congress of ignoring increasing utilization and of focusing only on limiting Medicare payments to hospitals to balance the Medicare fund. Further restrictions on Medicare funding is anticipated as the federal government faces a major deficit for several years.

The root of the crisis is the general acceptance at the federal level of several beliefs and demands that prevents the development of a consensus for finding a realistic solution to the potential shortage of Medicare funding. These beliefs are in conflict with the economic realities of hospitals. Before a financially sound and acceptable Medicare program can be developed, political demands and economic realities must be faced and resolved. A failure to do so will lead to future Medicare program instabilities that will neither meet the essential care needs of the public nor the financial needs of hospitals.

NINE BELIEFS

Government decisions on the Medicare program are based on nine beliefs, which must be examined in terms of the economic realities hospitals experience.

1. *Hospital care is a right for all Americans.*

Passage of the Medicare Act was the federal government's mechanism for ensuring the provision of medical care to the nation's elderly. The conditions of participation for hospitals in the Medicare program require acceptance of all Medicare patients without discrimination when a physician orders a hospital admission. Since hospitals are also prevented from billing Medicare patients for amounts in excess of the program's limits, hospitals must accept reimbursement payments determined by the federal government as full payment or terminate participation in the program.

In the years since the enactment of Medicare, there has been a steady reduction in the program's definition of the elements of reimbursable costs. By 1982, Medicare was paying 68.7 percent of the billed charges of hospitals and stimulating a practice of excess charging to other paying patients to cover Medicare shortfalls and meet capital needs.

If hospital care is to be maintained as a right, the federal government cannot indefinitely continue to limit Medicare expenditures. Capping prices at a rate determined by the funds available in the Medicare Trust Fund when there is a steady increase in the number and amount of medical care consumed by enrollees will not work.

Hospitals are economic units in our society with the same economic realities as industrial and commercial enterprises. When hospitals leave vendor bills unpaid, supply sources disappear; when hospital employees can find jobs at higher rates of pay in other businesses, they quit. If a product line in business generates losses rather than profits, a company discontinues the line if future profits cannot be anticipated. As losses on Medicare patients increase, hospitals will, sooner or later, either restrict their patient services to the level of available Medicare revenues or discontinue hospital services to these patients.

The usual federal position has been to criticize hospital operations for being inefficient and not for establishing excessive charges. The rationale of the fixed-price program is that establishing a price for each case will motivate hospitals to become more efficient. Such a position is valid only to the extent the hospitals can achieve additional operating efficiencies and is invalid beyond the point at which they cannot achieve efficiencies to deliver their services at a cost lower than Medicare payments. If hospital care is to continue to be generally available to Medicare patients, the federal government, in the long run, will be required to set hospital prices that cover the costs of operation at efficiency levels most hospitals can achieve.

The existing Medicare system does not operate in this fashion. The determination of reasonable operating efficiencies resides in each hospital and not in the federal government. When the Secretary of Health and Human Services has the sole authority for establishing Medicare prices, it is a unilateral decision and non-negotiable. The rates determined in this way are not based on any operating efficiency standards, but rather on the needs of the government to avoid a deficit balance in the Hospital Insurance Trust Fund. This approach minimizes the need for Congress to act to increase the tax rate.

On the other hand, if hospitals are faced with this situation and they respond by reducing services or withdrawing from the Medicare program, a different but equally serious political issue will also be created for Congress. The prevailing desire of hospitals is to continue to serve Medicare patients. They will do so, however, only as long as economic reality allows them to continue to serve these patients.

Hospital care is available to the American elderly only through the participation of physicians. Because the drafters of Medicare legislation recognized the need for physician participation and the widespread use of fee-for-service practice, a fee payment system was established that was not based on cost and was identified as Part B-Medicare. This system provided that a physician can be paid either a fixed fee through patient assignment or by establishing an individual fee and personally collecting from the Medicare patient, who in turn submits the paid physician bill to the program intermediary and receives a fixed fee in return.

This system allows physicians to continue to select the patients they choose to serve and to turn away those they do not choose to serve. The net effect is to provide physician care to Medicare patients, but to limit their choice of physicians when they cannot afford additional physician payments. Part B-Medicare experience has shown a steady decrease in physicians accepting assignment of benefits, which either restricts the patient's choice of a physician or increases his or her personal medical expenditures.

Hospital care as a right for Medicare patients is compromised in another way. Since physicians are part of a free enterprise system in America, they have the freedom to determine where to practice medicine and to determine to which hospitals they will admit their patients. These freedoms generate a drive within hospitals to maintain modern facilities with state-of-the-art technology in order to attract physicians. When hospitals have high volumes of Medicare patients and, therefore, lower operating revenues, they gradually lose their attractiveness to physicians. As a result, Medicare patients are steadily having their right to the same level of hospital and medical care abridged.

2. *Medicare beneficiaries should have free choice of hospitals.*

From its inception, the goal of the Medicare program has been to maintain the general availability of existing sources of hospital and medical services to the elderly, and this has been accomplished.

With the establishment of fixed prices for hospital services, continued free choice is not sustainable when the marginal costs of providing services to Medicare patients exceeds the marginal revenues received. When this occurs, hospitals will terminate their Medicare contracts in situations where they have sufficient marketing strengths to replace Medicare patients with non-Medicare patients. Typically, such hospitals will be located in suburban areas adjacent to large cities. However, rural hospitals with large Medicare volumes will not be able to terminate their contracts.

Because physicians have the option of either accepting Medicare payments as their total fee or billing separately, free choice of physicians is a reality only for Medicare patients with the economic resources to pay additional fees. Should a fixed-fee program for physician services be enacted, and the privilege of additional billing be eliminated, it is predictable that physicians with large practices will begin to turn away Medicare patients if the fixed fees are less than satisfactory.

Continuation of free choice of hospital for Medicare beneficiaries is therefore dependent on the level of payments established by the program. As long as there is a large annual federal budget deficit coupled with a depletion of Medicare funds, the possibility of maintaining adequate reimbursement levels for hospitals is problematical. The continuation of free choice for Medicare enrollees is, therefore, limited to making one of two choices: establishing reimbursement levels acceptable to hospitals and physicians either by raising Medicare taxes or by using general tax monies and increasing the federal deficit, or legislating participation in the Medicare program for hospitals and physicians. Either of these choices will create undesirable consequences with major impact in our society.

3. *Medicare patients should receive the same level of hospital care in quality, quantity, and amenities as other patients.*

A basic motivation of most hospital staffs and physicians is to provide every patient with the best medical care and hospital services that can be provided in the local community. In the last 30 years, hospitals have upgraded their physical facilities to remove differences in amenities in order to provide one class service to all patients. During the same period, physicians urged the rapid adoption of new medical technology and were attracted to hospitals with the most modern equipment.

The desire of the health care community is consistent with the goal of providing the same level of care for Medicare patients that is provided to patients paying the total cost of their services. However, when Medicare funding is inadequate other alternatives are likely to be considered.

Since the establishment of different levels of hospital care in one facility is almost impossible, two alternatives will be considered. One alternative is the development of a second facility in which the quality, quantity, and amenities are reduced to the level that can be provided within the limits of Medicare payments. The other will be a termination of the Medicare contract in situations where hospitals believe they can continue to provide the desired level of care for other patients.

In situations where either choice is unrealistic, hospitals will continue to accept Medicare patients at prices established by the government and reduce the scope of their operation to all patients. Where there are other hospitals in their market area that do not accept Medicare patients, the level of service will deteriorate in the Medicare hospital and two different levels of service will gradually develop. Medicare patients will then experience lower-quality care with fewer amenities than non-Medicare patients. With inadequate Medicare reimbursement, the same level of services cannot be maintained for all patients.

4. *A means test is unacceptable for Medicare patients.*

In the early discussions of the Social Security program, there was general recognition that it would have much greater public acceptance and support if its benefits were characterized as an earned benefit rather than being seen as a government dole. This judgment was correct since no stigma is now attached to receiving Social Security checks by elderly citizens at all economic levels. A similar decision was made during the development of the Medicare program and the benefits are likewise publicly perceived as earned.

Modifications have been proposed that would tax health benefits above specified levels and Social Security payments beyond defined income. These proposals are one step toward compromising the principle of not using a means test to qualify both Social Security and Medicare benefits.

Should a means test be established for Medicare benefits, it is likely that the program will be seen as Medicaid for the elderly. If this happens, its popularity would decrease since the payment of Medicare would not automatically qualify an elderly citizen for its benefits.

5. *Hospitals operate inefficiently because Medicare payments are based on cost and would operate more efficiently if paid on a price basis.*

With the enactment of a prospective payment system for Medicare, a fixed price was established for hospital services. However, the pricing system that has been adopted is not consistent with the concept of price in a system of economic competition. The use of a fixed-price concept is only applicable when the product or service is reasonably standardized.

The use of a fixed price for hospital services assumes that the quality and quantity provided all Medicare patients with the same diagnosis or procedure are reasonably identical and the cost of the resources used is about the same. The validity of this assumption is questionable and difficult to accurately measure. The indirect cost allocations to patient service activities and the direct cost of individual patient services are complex and each patient requires a different range of services. Every patient with the same diagnosis does not receive the same array of services; the problem is compounded when a single patient has multiple diagnoses.

The application of a fixed price to a variable quantity of health services is the same as using one sale price for a specific type of automobile regardless of the number of extras ordered, such as air conditioning and a radio.

The conclusion that the use of a fixed price for hospital services will lead to greater efficiencies implies that a hospital's level of efficiency can be determined. The economic concept of efficiency requires a measurement of inputs in terms of outputs; a satisfactory methodology has not yet been developed for hospitals. Consequently, statements about hospital efficiency are opinion rather than fact, and the reasonableness of relating pricing to efficiency cannot be determined.

6. *Cost shifting to non-Medicare patients for below-cost payments of the Medicare program is an acceptable practice by hospitals.*

Beginning with the early days of the Medicare program, hospitals have gradually increased their rates to non-Medicare patients to offset revenue losses from decreasing per-case Medicare payments. Until the decade of the '80s, there was little market opposition to this practice. In the last few years, market reactions have appeared in the form of business coalitions, preferred provider organizations, and the promotion of independent practice associations and health maintenance organizations.

With the enactment of the prospective payment system for Medicare and its diagnosis related group pricing practices, both hospitals and health insurance companies have started to discuss the necessity of moving to a uniform payment system to prevent further cost shifting. While cost shifting may be an acceptable hospital practice to the federal government, it will only remain a useful strategy for hospitals to the extent that other large insurance carriers are willing to continue to make excess payments.

It is in the interest of the Medicare program to reduce the cost-shifting practices of hospitals. When non-Medicare insurance carriers resist excessive cost shifting, hospital services will still remain available to their patients, while Medicare patients will find access to hospital services gradually restricted.

7. Nationally, hospitals will not withdraw from the Medicare program when reimbursement is reduced because 42 percent of their total patient days are paid by Medicare.

It is a basic business principle to terminate operating losses whenever marginal costs exceed marginal revenues. Determination of this situation in a business is dependent upon a specific set of facts which have a wide degree of variability. Because hospitals operate in a business environment, they face the same economic reality. Those hospitals that could absorb the loss of Medicare revenues are ones with Medicare patient loads of less than 35 percent, and are typically located in an area of increasing population with generous amounts of disposable income. Typically, institutions with these service area characteristics are older suburban institutions with relatively large medical staffs.

The deterrents to termination of a hospital's Medicare contract are a strong community philosophy for serving all classes of patients, a viewpoint that the nature of the losses are a short-term phenomenon, a belief that additional non-Medicare patients would not be attracted, or an inability to understand marginal cost and revenue concepts.

In the long run, hospitals will consider termination when they perceive insolvency is likely to occur.

8. Hospitals should be limited to one major source of payment for Medicare patients.

At the inception of the Medicare program, it was believed desirable, because of the limited financial resources of the elderly, to have a high proportion of their hospital bills paid by Medicare. Subsequently, as cost increases occurred, modest deductibles and coinsurances were increased, along with cost shifting to non-Medicare sources.

Ultimately, the feasibility of maintaining one major source of payment will be determined by the ability of the Medicare program to control both utilization and costs within the limits of acceptable tax levels. Past experience would indicate that this result cannot be achieved, primarily because utilization levels continue to increase, despite the establishment of a utilization review mechanism.

The history of health insurance contracts suggests that the present Medicare system will gradually experience increasing problems. During the past 30 years, there has been a large decrease in the use of Blue Cross contracts that provided a defined number of days of care without limiting the amount of service or hospital charges. At the same time, commercial insurance carriers increased and their contracts defined both dollar amounts and units of service. The Medicare program is essentially a Blue Cross service contract with dollar limits on hospitals and no limits on units of necessary services. The experience of Blue Cross means that Medicare will not be able to successfully control utilization until its enrollees participate in utilization decisions.

9. *Restriction of hospital reimbursement is the primary control on the costs of the Medicare program.*

Until the enactment of a prospective payment system, Medicare relied on progressively narrower definitions of includable costs to control expenditures. With the adoption of a fixed-price arrangement, the Secretary of Health and Human Services can unilaterally establish payment prices to hospitals without any restraints.

Since Congress will not participate in the establishment of hospital rates and the secretary has the unilateral right to establish them, a real crisis will occur. Intense political pressures can be anticipated as some hospitals withdraw from Medicare while others face bankruptcy.

Before a crisis arises, it would be reasonable to reexamine the nine premises on which the Medicare program is structured. As long as all nine premises are adhered to, other Medicare expenditures will continue to escalate at an unacceptable rate and the hospital field will be in a most serious financial crisis. The political consequences will be of major importance.

Until the legislative and executive branches of the federal government recognize that the political premises of the Medicare program have serious economic effects on hospitals, a workable, stable system to provide medical care for the elderly will not be developed. The time to reach new accommodations is in the next few years before the coming crisis arrives.

Since its inception, Medicare has been politically focused and has ignored the economic realities of hospital care. If a major crisis in health care is to be avoided, the economic forces affecting hospitals for each of the nine political foundations of Medicare need to be examined and modifications in these principles made in order to accommodate both political and economic realities.

Chapter 16

A Second Opinion: The Prospects of Medicare's Hospital Insurance Trust Fund[*]

REPORT TO CONGRESS

In March 1983, the Special Committee on Aging of the United States Senate received "an information paper" prepared by the Congressional Budget Office (CBO) (see Table 16–15). This report projected an accumulated deficit by 1995 in the Hospital Insurance Trust Fund of $400.9 billion. The present trends are extrapolated to 1995 in arriving at the accumulated deficit. Should the Congress extend the TEFRA (Tax Equity and Fiscal Responsibility Act) limits beyond the sunset provision in 1985 to the year 1995, the anticipated deficit of $400.9 billion would be reduced to $310.3 billion.

The report is based on the following assumptions:

1. An annual projected growth in hospital costs of 13.2 percent for Medicare patients
2. Covered earnings projected to grow at an annual rate of 6.8 percent
3. An uncovered difference between hospital costs and HI income of 6.4 percent
4. An inpatient utilization rate projected to grow at 1 percent per year for Medicare patients

In order to continue the analysis on a year-by-year basis through 1995, a table was developed on the annual number of patient days for enrollees in the Medicare program.

---

*Adapted from *ACHE*, Vol. 29, No. 3, pp. 7–21, with permission of American College of Healthcare Executives, © May/June 1984.

The growth in patient days covered by Medicare is expected to continue through 1995 as stated in the report. For the years between 1983 and 1995, the patient days are anticipated to increase by 42.4 percent as shown in Table 16–1.

Knowing the number of patient days of care leads to two questions.

1. Are all those days of care necessary?
2. How much money will it take to pay for this care?

The CBO report does not address ways to reduce the number of patient days but instead focuses on the financing aspects, an appropriate approach in dealing with the problem from an economist's viewpoint, but one that does not address the issues of how to cope with increasing inpatient utilization.

The results of concentrating on ways to pay for hospital care and to reduce costs are aptly spelled out in the report, which outlines six approaches to resolving the deficit:

Table 16–1 Projected Medicare Patient Days of Care

Year	Age 65 and Over Population $9ppp$[1]	Inpatient Utilization Rate[2]	Annual Patient Days
1980	25.7 (million)	4,300[3]	110.5 (million)
1981	26.2	4,343	113.8
1982	26.7	4,386	117.1
1983	27.3	4,430	120.9
1984	27.8	4,474	124.4
1985	28.4	4,519	128.3
1986	28.9	4,564	131.9
1987	29.5	4,609	136.0
1988	30.1	4,655	140.1
1989	30.7	4,702	144.4
1990	31.3	4,749	148.6
1991	31.9	4,797	153.0
1992	32.6	4,844	157.9
1993	33.2	4,893	162.4
1994	33.9	4,942	167.5
1995	34.5	4,991	172.2

[1]Annual increase of 2 percent per year.

[2]Annual increase of 1 percent per year, assumes 0.2 percent for aging is included in the 2 percent.

[3]*Source:* National Center For Health Statistics, *Utilization of Short-Stay Hospitals: Annual Summary of The United States, 1980,* DHHS Publ. no. 82-1725, Hyattsville, Md., March 1982.

1. Increasing co-insurance, which would require a co-insurance rate of 36 percent by 1995, or a premium increase to each enrollee of $2,000 per year
2. Prospective reimbursement, which would reduce payments to hospitals by 42 percent by 1995
3. A combination of co-insurance and prospective reimbursement, which, if divided equally, would require by 1995 a co-insurance rate of 18 percent and a prospective reimbursement rate that would annually increase by 6 percent for general inflation, plus 1.6 percent for all other elements
4. Higher payroll taxes that would increase by 2.54 percent by 1995
5. General revenue financing for this program, which would require $73.8 billion by 1995
6. A combination of co-insurances, prospective payment, and higher payroll taxes, which, if followed and divided equally, would require a co-insurance rate of 12 percent by 1995, a prospective rate formula that would increase by 7.4 percent per year, and an HI tax rate increase of 1.76 percent by 1995.

The conclusion reached is that the financing problem requires more restrictive measures than are now being contemplated. Present, but not yet addressed, is the question of inpatient utilization. This is the most significant factor of all and can best be appreciated when related to the availability of dollars.

In the CBO report, it was indicated that hospital costs are expected to increase by 13.2 percent per year. Yet the average increase per patient day from Medicare is 10.18 percent.

Table 16–2 indicates that the gap between what is paid for services to Medicare patients and the cost of providing the services will widen and by 1995, hospitals will be receiving only two-thirds of their incurred costs under the CBO projections. By 1995, the Medicare payment would be $872.82, but the hospital cost would be $1,314.09, or a difference of 34.6 percent between the payment and the cost. If TEFRA is extended, the gap will become even greater.

Using the assumptions of the CBO report, two conclusions can be reached:

1. The HI Trust Fund begins to get into serious financial difficulty by 1987.
2. Hospitals begin to get into serious financial difficulty at about the same time because of the gap between payments and costs.

UTILIZATION RATES ARE KEY

Because inpatient utilization is the key to the Medicare dilemma, other forms of treatment need to be explored so that Medicare patients will seek their care in attractive, convenient ambulatory settings. The decision to be admitted to a hospital is also more traumatic than a visit to a physician's office. Persons 75 years

Table 16–2 Patient Revenues per Patient Day Under the CBO Projection

Year	Anticipated Outlay[1]	Outlay Available to Hospitals[2]	Annual Patient Days[3]	Payment per Hospital Day	HI Year-End Balance
1981	$ 30.7 (billion)	$30.7 (billion)	113.8	$231.98	$ 18.7
1982	36.0	31.0	117.1	264.73	8.3
1983	41.1	35.8	120.9	291.98	8.8
1984	46.2	38.5	124.4	319.13	7.5
1985	51.0	42.6	128.3	342.17	5.9
1986	60.0	48.4	131.9	373.01	2.2
1987	68.5	51.3	136.0	433.09	−6.5
1988	77.0	54.3	140.1	472.52	−20.4
1989	86.6	57.0	144.4	515.93	−40.7
1990	97.4	59.5	148.6	563.93	−68.9
1991	109.5	61.7	153.0	615.69	−106.7
1992	123.0	63.2	157.9	670.04	−156.3
1993	138.2	64.2	162.4	732.14	−219.8
1994	155.4	64.6	167.5	797.61	−300.1
1995	174.8	63.7	172.2	872.82	−400.9

[1]*Source: Prospects for Medicare's Hospital Insurance Trust Fund.* An Information paper prepared for the Special Committee on Aging, United States Senate, March 1983 (Washington, D.C.: Government Printing Office, 1983), 4–5.

[2]A review of the *Statistical Abstract* indicates that hospitals receive 86 percent of the anticipated outlays, the remainder being paid for administrative costs, skilled nursing home care, and end-stage renal dialysis.

[3]See Table 16–1.

of age and over use 2.67 days of care to every one day of care for those in the 65–74-year-old age group. When the two age groups are combined, the appearance is given that the inpatient utilization rate is not nearly as high because the 75-years-and-over age group has been merged with a group (65–74 years of age) that uses only 37.5 percent as many patient days. This is reflected in Table 16–3.

Persons between 65 and 74 years of age use hospitals at a rate three times greater than those under 65 years of age. Those 75 years of age and over use hospitals at a rate that is eight times that for those under 65 years of age. Combined, they use hospitals at a rate five times greater than for those under 65 years of age.

One approach to inpatient utilization is to review the experience of HMOs with persons 65 years of age and older. The results are in marked contrast to that of Medicare, as seen in Table 16–4.

Table 16–3 Utilization Rate 65 to 74, 75 and Over, and Combined 65 and Over

	65–74			75 and Over			Combined 65 and Over		
	Population[1] ×	Utilization Rate =	Patient Days	Population ×	Utilization Rate =	Patient Days	Population ×	Utilization Rate =	Patient Days
1970	12,316	2,760	33,948	7,791	7,360	57,342	20,107	4,540	91,290
1980	15,425	2,580	39,732	10,283	6,880	70,864	25,708	4,302	110,596
1990	18,623	2,520	46,872	12,449	6,720	84,000	31,072	4,213	130,872

[1]Table 16–1.

Source: U.S. Bureau of the Census, Current Population Reports, Series P-25, No. 922 (Washington, D.C.: Government Printing Office, 1982); assumptions made by author for 1985 and 1990.

Table 16–4 Hospital Days per 1,000 Persons Age 65 and Over

	United States	Kaiser-Permanente Medical Care Plan Age/Sex Adjusted
Pre-Medicare	3,449	2,453
After Medicare		
1967	3,698	2,912
1968	3,990	2,552
1969	4,048	2,336
1970	3,904	2,193
1971	3,835	2,190
1972	3,935	2,225
1973	3,853	2,171
1974	3,963	1,918
1975	4,003	2,030
1976	4,121	1,945
1977	4,156	1,906
1978	4,184	1,884
1979	4,182	1,851

Source: Merwyn R. Greenlick et al., "Kaiser-Permanente's Medicare Plus Project: A Successful Prospective Payment Demonstration," *Health Care Financing Review*, 4 (Summer 1983): 87.

An assumption can be made from Table 16–4 that if all Medicare enrollees had joined an HMO by January 1, 1985, the inpatient utilization rate would have become 1,851 per 1,000 population.

The 1,851 patient days per 1,000 population is an outside parameter that has to be regarded as a hypothetical number that is unattainable. It does define the lowest possible point and is useful in thinking about what might be accomplished, even though it has been argued that the persons 65 years of age and over in HMOs are not representative of the degree of illness typically found in that age group.

AN ALTERNATE SCENARIO

If the HMO scenario were followed, the projected $400.9 billion deficit would instead be a surplus of $260.9 billion, a turnaround of $660.9 billion. Instead of an inpatient utilization increase of 16 percent between 1982 and 1995, there would be a decline of 57 percent because of lowered utilization. The HMO scenario, if followed, would have required hospitals to have met the CBO projection of cost per patient day as well as to have reduced sharply the inpatient utilization rate.

To achieve the desired results, doctor office visits would have to be included in the Medicare program as part of the standard benefits. The use rates for visits are shown in Table 16–5.

Table 16–5 Doctor Office Visits per 1,000 Health Plan Members

Year	Under Age 65	Age 65 and Over	Use Rate by Age 65 and Over
1967	3,279	4,769	145.4%
1970	3,280	4,566	139.2
1975	3,043	4,966	163.2
1980	2,546	4,964	195.0
1981	2,559	4,889	191.1
1982	2,555	5,189	203.1

Source: Merwyn R. Greenlick et al., "Kaiser-Permanente's Medicare Plus Project: A Successful Prospective Payment Demonstration," *Health Care Financing Review* 4 (Summer 1983): 87.

Though the office visit rate is twice as great for those 65 years of age and over as compared with those under 65 years of age, the tradeoff of office visits for days in the hospital is financially advantageous to the Medicare program.

Table 16–6 indicates that the Medicare program could offer the enrollees an incentive for switching from the existing benefit package by including physician services under Part A, which would eliminate the need to purchase supplementary insurance or to pay the physician for the difference since the Medicare program would pay for all costs of both the physician and hospital components. The enrollees benefit and the Medicare program annually saves $833,890 for every 1,000 enrollees who switch to this option.

By offering to include office visits as a benefit under Part A if enrollees elect the HMO option, the net savings to the Medicare program is approximately ten times the cost of including it.

Table 16–6 1985 Savings to the Medicare Program per 1,000 Enrollees by Using HMO Approach

	Hospital Care	Office Visits
Medicare Utilization	4,519 (Table 16–1)	2,555 (Table 16–5)
HMO Utilization	1,851	5,189 (Table 16–5)
Difference	2,668	2,634
Cost Per Day/Or Visit	×342.17 (Table 16–2)	× 30.00 (Assumed)
Reduction In Hospital Costs	$912,910	$ 79,020
Net Savings Per 1,000/ Enrollees		$833,890

Source: Tables 16–1, 16–2, and 16–5.

The two scenarios, CBO and HMO, establish the boundaries of the Medicare problem. On the one hand, the year-end fiscal deficits envisioned by the CBO report are not acceptable, while on the other hand, the utilization rates achieved under the HMO approach could not be accomplished in the existing climate of public attitude, nor in terms of the availability of HMOs to cope with the envisioned increase in membership. Like the conclusion reached in the CBO report on the financial alternatives, the conclusion on inpatient utilization is the same: some combination or multiple approach must be sought. To zero balance the HI Trust Fund, ways must be found to decrease the utilization rate by encouraging the use of ambulatory services. In addition, the ceiling on hospital payments must be kept at the level projected by the CBO.

Staying within the CBO limit requires hospitals by 1995 to have an average cost per patient day no greater than $872.82. This can be accomplished if hospitals hold Medicare increases to an average annual amount of 10.18 percent. Since hospital costs are expected to grow at 13.2 percent, the gap between that amount and the available amount of 10.18 percent is 3.02 percent. This gap can be closed by increases in productivity in hospitals. It seems reasonable to expect that under the DRG method of payment, hospitals will respond as they move away from a cost-reimbursement system to one of prospective payments.

NEW PROGRAMS NEEDED

Developing programs that will result in a decline in the utilization rate presents a difficulty but is necessary for balancing expenditures and income. If the outlay of $872.82 per patient day is accepted as a reasonable target for 1995, the ability to zero balance the HI Trust Fund then depends upon the utilization rate that is achieved in each year through 1995. Table 16–7 was constructed to demonstrate the utilization rates that zero balance the fund each year beginning in 1985.

Achieving the projected reductions in the utilization rates can be expected to be difficult because of the mounting pressures leading to an increase in the use of hospitals by those 65 years of age and over. The types of pressures are illustrated in Table 16–8.

From 1975 to 1980 the rates of discharge of a number of clinical categories of illness for Medicare patients increased (see Table 16–9). These pressures reflect two factors:

1. Under the Medicare program, the financial barriers to receiving medical care have been minimized.
2. As a result of advances in technology, medical conditions previously undetected are now being diagnosed and treated.

Table 16–7 Utilization Rates Required To Zero Balance the HI Fund Commencing in 1985

Year	Population[2]	Patient Days	Cost per Day[3]	Annual Cost	Available HI Fund[4]	Year-End Difference	Year-End Balance	Utilization Rate[1]
1981	26.2 (million)	113.8	$231.98	$26.4 (billion)	$30.7 (billion)	$4.3 (billion)	$18.7 (billion)	4,343
1982	26.7	117.1	264.73	31.0	22.0	−9.0	8.3	4,386
1983	27.2	120.8	291.98	35.3	35.8	0.3	8.6	4,440
1984	27.2	120.6	319.13	38.5	38.5	—	8.6	4,354
1985	28.2	124.5	342.17	42.6	42.6	—	8.6	4,415
1986	28.8	129.7	373.01	48.4	48.4	—	8.6	4,503
1987	29.4	118.5	433.09	51.3	51.3	—	8.6	4,031
1988	30.0	114.9	472.52	54.3	54.3	—	8.6	3,967
1989	30.5	110.5	515.93	57.0	57.0	—	8.6	3,622
1990	31.1	105.5	563.93	59.5	59.5	—	8.6	3,393
1991	31.6	100.2	615.69	61.7	61.7	—	8.6	3,171
1992	32.1	94.3	670.04	63.2	63.2	—	8.6	2,938
1993	32.6	87.7	732.14	64.2	64.2	—	8.6	2,690
1994	33.2	81.0	797.61	64.6	64.6	—	8.6	2,440
1995	33.7	73.0	872.82	63.7	63.7	—	8.6	2,166

[1]1981–1983 actual, 1984–1995 anticipated rate in order to zero balance HI Trust Fund at year end.
[2]Table 16–1.
[3]Table 16–2.
[4]Table 16–12.

Source: Tables 16–1, 16–2, and 16–8.

Table 16–8 Key Indicators of Utilization Pressures Age 65 and Over

	1965	1970	1975	1980	Percent Change
Indicator					
Total Patient Days	60.0 (M)	77.2 (M)	88.8 (M)	105.4 (M)	+75.5%
Patient Day Rates—					
1,000/Population	3,443	3,457	3,592	4,051	+17.7
Total Discharges	4.65 (M)	5.88 (M)	7.65 (M)	9.86 (M)	+117.2
Discharge Rates—					
1,000/Population	263.9	306.1	359.3	405.2	+53.5
Average Length of Stay	13.1	13.1	11.6	10.7	−18.3

Source: Utilization of Short-Stay Hospitals, Summary of Nonmedical Statistics, United States, 1965, 1970, 1975, 1980, Department of HEW—Health Resources Administration.

Both of these pressures are desirable social goals and should be continued in the future. How to keep these social goals intact without bankrupting either hospitals or the HI Trust Fund is the essence of the dilemma facing Congress.

When the CBO projected annual patient days are compared with the optimal model, the magnitude of the reductions needed to reach the levels required to zero balance the HI Trust Fund is apparent.

Table 16–10 indicates that the differences through 1986 are minimal but in the succeeding years the gap widens and makes it questionable as to whether the optimal utilization levels can be attained during the 1990s.

Table 16–9 Rates of Discharge for Age 65 and Over, 1975 to 1980

Clinical System	1975	1980	Percent Change
Neoplasms	385.2	425.0	+10.3%
Diabetes Mellitus	122.6	170.7	+39.2
Nervous System and Sensory Organs	196.9	248.7	+26.3
Circulatory System	1,047.1	1,170.4	+11.8
Respiratory System	349.4	406.1	+16.2
Digestive System	490.1	519.0	+5.9
GU System	264.7	284.5	+7.5
Musculoskeletal System	156.8	215.9	+37.7
Fractures	161.0	288.8	+79.4

Source: Utilization of Short-Stay Hospitals, Summary of Nonmedical Statistics, United States, 1965, 1970, 1975, 1980. Department of HEW—Health Resources Administration.

Table 16–10 Comparison of Annual Patient Days for CBO and Optimal Models

Year	CBO[1]	Optimal[2]	Annual Rate Difference	Optimal as a Percent of CBO Rate
1981	113.8	113.8	—	—
1982	117.1	117.1	—	—
1983	120.9	120.8	−0.1	—
1984	124.4	120.6	−3.8	97.0%
1985	128.3	124.5	−3.8	97.0
1986	131.9	129.7	−2.2	98.3
1987	136.0	118.5	−18.5	87.1
1988	140.1	114.9	−25.2	82.0
1989	144.4	110.5	−33.9	76.5
1990	148.6	105.5	−43.1	71.0
1991	153.0	100.2	−52.8	65.5
1992	157.9	94.3	−57.6	59.7
1993	162.4	87.7	−74.7	54.0
1994	167.5	81.0	−86.5	48.4
1995	172.2	73.0	−99.2	42.4

[1]Table 16–1.
[2]Table 16–6.

From the viewpoint of the hospital field, the steps that need to be taken to avoid the projected deficits center on, first of all, keeping Medicare patients out of the hospital and having them receive most of their medical care on an ambulatory basis, and second, on the control of hospital payments.

Permitting the utilization rate to continue to rise and offsetting these increased costs to the HI Trust Fund by reduction in hospital payments is not in the public's best interest because of the ultimate deterioration in the quality of care delivered in hospitals. The application of DRG payments to hospitals is not going to resolve the Medicare HI Trust Fund deficit because it deals only with the amount of payments to hospitals after patients have been admitted. At best, DRGs are a stop-gap measure and are useful to the extent that they delay the deficits in the Trust Fund. This provides a time to put programs into place that will impact the utilization rates.

EVALUATING OPTIONS

The control of payments to hospitals, by itself, will not prevent large deficits from taking place. Nor can utilization be reduced to the point that, by itself, the fund remains solvent. Any plan or program that is proposed must include both if it is to be successful. Proposals that may be put forth for evaluation in the future should first be analyzed by applying two measurements:

1. Determination of the utilization rate of patient days per 1,000 Medicare enrollees
2. Determination of the number of dollars that hospitals will be paid for each day of care

It does not matter whether hospitals are paid on a price, cost, or case basis; it is the adequacy of the payment that is material, not the method of payment. It may be true that the method of payment affects the efficiency of hospital operations, but if the revenues are inadequate, either the quality of care will decline or hospitals will place limitations on the numbers of patients accepted from the source that does not make adequate payments.

The impact of varying utilization rates and varying costs per patient day is summarized in Table 16–11.

The various projections of the 1995 year-end balances (Tables 16–12 to 16–14) raise more problems than they produce possible solutions. As pointed out in the CBO report, hospital costs per patient day cannot be permitted to annually rise by 13.2 percent, or in 1995 the deficit in the HI Trust Fund will reach $651.7 billion. To reach the $400.9 billion deficit level, hospitals must increase productivity by 3.02 percent annually. If additional restraints are placed on Medicare payments to hospitals, the increase in productivity will have to become even greater. Under TEFRA, there is an additional annual loss of revenue of 6.0 percent. Hospitals cannot be expected to achieve an annual improvement in productivity of 9.02 percent.

Table 16–11 1995 Projected Results in the HI Trust Fund

Model	1995 Utilization Rate	Average Daily Hospital Rate	Year-End Balance
CBO	4,991	$1,314.09	$−651.7
CBO	4,991	872.82	−400.9
HMO	1,851	1,314.82	− 15.9
HMO	1,851	872.82	+265.9
Optimal	2,166	872.82	+ 8.6

Source: Tables 16–2 and 16–5.

Table 16–12 HMO Scenario Using CBO Projection of Cost per Patient Day, 1981–1995

Year	KFHP Inpatient Utilization Rate[1]	65 and Over Population[2]	Patient Days	CBO Payment PPD[3]	Paid to Hospitals	Available Income[4]	Year-End Result	Year-End Balance
1981	4,343	26.2 (million)	113.8 (million)	$231.98	$26.4 (billion)	$30.7 (billion)	$ 4.3 (billion)	$ 18.7 (billion)
1982	4,386	26.7	117.1	264.73	31.0	22.0	−9.0	8.3
1983	4,430	27.3	120.9	291.98	35.3	35.8	0.3	8.8
1984	4,474	27.8	124.4	319.13	39.7	38.5	−1.2	7.6
1985	1,851	28.4	52.6	342.17	18.0	42.6	24.6	32.2
1986	1,851	28.9	53.5	373.01	20.0	48.4	28.4	60.6
1987	1,851	29.5	54.6	433.09	23.6	51.3	27.7	88.3
1988	1,851	30.1	55.7	472.52	26.3	54.3	28.0	116.3
1989	1,851	30.7	56.8	515.93	29.3	57.0	27.7	144.0
1990	1,851	31.3	57.9	563.93	32.7	59.5	26.8	170.8
1991	1,851	31.9	59.0	615.69	36.3	61.7	25.4	196.2
1992	1,851	32.6	60.3	670.04	40.4	63.2	22.8	219.0
1993	1,851	33.2	61.4	732.14	44.9	64.2	19.3	238.3
1994	1,851	33.9	62.7	797.61	50.0	64.6	14.6	252.9
1995	1,851	34.5	63.9	872.82	55.7	63.7	8.0	260.9

[1]Reference (census). Extrapolations made by the author.
[2]Table 16–1.
[3]Table 16–2.
[4]Fourteen percent less than income for each year.

Source: U.S. Bureau of Census, Current Population Reports, Series P-25, No. 922 (Washington, D.C.: Government Printing office, 1982).

Table 16–13 Year-End Balance in 1995 Using CBO Projection of Utilization and 13.2 Percent Annual Growth in Hospital Costs

Year	CBO Patient Days[1]	PPD Cost[2]	Annual Outlay	Funds Available[3]	Year-End Difference	Year-End Balance
1981	113.8 (million)	$ 231.62	$ 26.4 (billion)	$30.7 (billion)	$ 4.3 (billion)	$ 18.3 (billion)
1982	117.1	262.19	30.7	22.0	−8.7	8.3
1983	120.9	296.80	35.9	35.8	−0.1	8.2
1984	124.4	335.98	41.8	38.5	−3.3	4.9
1985	128.3	380.33	48.8	38.5	−6.2	−1.3
1986	131.9	430.53	56.8	42.6	−8.4	−9.7
1987	136.0	487.36	66.3	48.4	−15.0	−14.7
1988	140.1	551.70	77.3	51.3	−23.0	−37.7
1989	144.4	624.52	90.2	54.3	−33.2	−70.9
1990	148.6	706.96	105.1	57.0	−45.6	−116.5
1991	153.0	800.28	122.4	61.7	−60.7	−177.2
1992	157.9	905.91	143.0	63.2	−79.8	−257.0
1993	162.4	1,025.49	166.5	64.2	−102.3	−359.3
1994	167.5	1,160.85	194.4	64.6	−129.8	−489.1
1995	172.2	1,314.09	226.3	63.7	−162.6	−651.7

[1]Table 16–2.
[2]1981 cost per patient day annually adjusted by 13.2 percent increase.
[3]Table 16–8.

Source: Tables 16–2 and 16–8.

Table 16–14 Year-End Balance in 1995 Using HMO Projection of Utilization and 13.2 Percent Annual Growth in Hospital Costs

Year	HMO Patient Days[1]	PPD Cost[2]	Annual Outlay	Funds Available[3]	Year-End Difference	Year-End Balance
1981	113.8 (million)	$ 231.62	$26.4 (billion)	$30.7 (billion)	$ +4.3 (billion)	$ 18.3 (billion)
1982	117.1	262.19	30.7	22.0	−8.7	8.3
1983	120.9	296.80	35.9	35.8	−0.1	8.2
1984	124.4	335.98	41.8	38.5	−3.3	4.9
1985	52.6	380.33	20.2	38.5	18.3	23.2
1986	53.5	430.53	23.0	42.6	19.6	42.8
1987	54.6	487.36	26.6	48.4	21.8	64.6
1988	55.7	551.70	30.7	51.3	20.6	85.2
1989	56.8	624.52	35.5	54.3	18.8	104.0
1990	57.9	706.96	40.9	57.0	16.1	120.1
1991	59.0	800.28	47.2	61.7	14.5	134.6
1992	60.3	905.91	54.6	63.2	8.6	143.2
1993	61.4	1,025.49	63.0	64.2	1.2	144.4
1994	62.7	1,160.85	72.8	64.6	−8.2	136.2
1995	63.9	1,314.00	84.0	63.7	−20.3	115.9

[1]Table 16–8.
[2]1981 cost per patient day annually adjusted by 13.2 percent increase.
[3]Table 16–8.

Source: Table 16–8.

While the HMO route is the most desirable from the perspective of reducing utilization to the levels required to zero balance the trust fund, this rate is not likely to be followed since it would have required all Medicare patients to be enrolled in an HMO or PPO by January 1, 1985. To accomplish this would have necessitated mandatory participation, hardly a method in keeping with public attitudes. Yet, the HMO approach could be tailored to encourage enrollment by creating incentives for joining. If an enrollee were given the option of having physician services included for both in- and outpatient services as part of full Medicare benefits, a substantial percentage might wish to enroll. A voluntary program of enrollment would permit HMOs and PPOs to gear up gradually in absorbing the additional members. In those parts of the country where no HMO or PPO coverage is available, the enrollee would continue under existing arrangements.

If such a program were offered, the medical profession could be expected to react negatively and to lobby vigorously against it. On the other hand, even though those 65 years of age and over use office visits at a rate that is slightly more than double that of those under 65 years of age, the net savings that would result would be ten times the cost of hospitalization. Because the hospital utilization rate of those 65 years of age and over is much lower in an HMO or PPO, it would permit the pegging of a utilization rate higher than the level experienced by the HMO (2,166) or the PPO (1,851), thus encouraging prepayment mechanisms to seek to enroll Medicare recipients as desirable members. The advantage to the Medicare enrollee would be a savings in out-of-pocket costs since the need to purchase supplementary coverage would be eliminated. Such a person would also be protected in the event that under the Medicare program in later years it became necessary to institute deductibles or co-insurance for those not in an HMO or PPO in order to zero balance the fund.

ADDITIONAL MODALITIES OF CARE

Another step that could be taken to reduce hospital utilization would be to encourage the development of hospice and home health care programs in a significant number of hospitals. This would provide physicians with two additional modalities of care that are not now available in most hospitals. The extent to which these programs would reduce utilization cannot, as yet, be determined. A way to encourage this development would be to add a small percentage to the rates for those DRGs that typically require the follow-up care available by means of these two modalities.

The control and reduction of hospital utilization is dependent upon clinical and financial programs that are interrelated. Both will be needed in order to bring the rate down to a level that is financially viable under the Medicare program.

If only financial approaches are followed, the desired results will not be achieved. A continual reduction of payments to hospitals would, by 1995, mean that they could be paid only $610 per patient day at the CBO projected usage rate instead of the $873.82 that is now anticipated in order to zero balance the funds. Since Medicare now pays 68.7 percent of hospital charges, further reductions to only 42 percent would be necessary to zero balance the HI Trust Fund in 1995, a solution that would not be appropriate.

UTILIZATION PRESSURES

Neither is an approach based solely on utilization likely to be successful. The elimination of the projected $400.9 billion deficit in 1995 would require that the CBO-projected number of total patient days of 172.2 million be reduced to 73.0 million in that year. Decreasing total patient days to only 42.4 percent of the CBO projection does not seem to be realistic; the gap is too wide to be closed. To attempt to do so would ignore all of the factors that have led to an upward pressure on utilization, including the following:

1. Net additional persons entering the Medicare program each year
2. Increasing length of life with more persons entering the 75-and-over age category each year
3. Willingness of the 65-and-over age group to seek medical care when financial barriers are minimized
4. Growing ability of physicians to detect and treat more illnesses every year
5. Desire of physicians to treat illness once it is discovered in a patient

Reversing these utilization pressures to the levels required for financial solvency of the fund may not be possible. Combining utilization control programs with improved financing through the adoption of some co-insurance and deductible features appears inevitable. It seems safe to predict that by the time the year 1995 comes to pass, Medicare will, out of financial necessity, have to recognize that the dollars spent for Medicare will pay a major part, but not all, of the medical costs of the elderly. At that point, Medicare will be in step with the basic purposes of the Social Security program, a supplemental program designed to assist people in their older years, not total coverage for retirement.

The issues just described are complex and not readily amenable to being solved. Congress is going to be dealing with one or more aspects of this program in nearly every session for the next decade or two. The years ahead are going to include

Table 16–15 Impact of Extending TEFRA to 1995

Year	Patient Days	Outlays to Hospitals	TEFRA Hospital Average Daily Payment	Without TEFRA	Difference	Percent Loss
1985	128.3	$ 43.8	$341.39	$342.17	$ −0.78	—
1986	131.9	49.1	372.25	373.01	−0.76	—
1987	136.0	55.3	406.62	433.09	−26.47	−6.1
1988	140.1	62.2	443.97	472.52	−28.55	−6.0
1989	144.4	69.9	484.07	515.93	−31.86	−6.2
1990	148.6	78.7	529.60	563.93	−34.33	−6.1
1991	153.0	88.5	575.16	615.69	−40.53	−6.5
1992	157.9	99.4	629.51	670.04	−40.53	−6.0
1993	162.4	111.7	687.81	732.14	−44.33	−6.0
1994	167.5	125.6	749.85	797.61	−47.76	−6.0
1995	172.2	141.2	819.98	872.82	−52.84	−6.1

Source: An Information Paper on the Prospects for Medicare Hospital Insurance Trust Fund (Washington, D.C.: Government Printing Office, March 1983), Table II, 4.

increasing challenges and clearly no one-time solution that will be a cure-all for the dilemmas we have examined.

REFERENCES

Prospects for Medicare's Hospital Insurance Trust Fund. An information paper prepared for the Special Committee on Aging, United States Senate, March 1983 (Washington, D.C.: Government Printing Office 1983), 4, 5.

National Center For Health Statistics, "Table 2: Number, Percent Distribution And Rate Of Days Of Care, Average Number Of Hospital Beds Occupied Daily: United States, 1980," *Utilization Of Short-Stay Hospitals: Annual Summary Of The United States, 1980*, DHHS Publ. no. 82-1725, Hyattsville, Md., March 1982.

U.S. Department of Commerce *Statistical Abstract of the United States, 1982–1983*, 103rd ed. (Washington, D.C.: Government Printing Office).

Merwyn Greenlick et al., "Kaiser-Permanente's Medicare Plus Project: A Successful Prospective Payment Demonstration," *Health Care Financing Review* 4 (Summer 1983): 87.

Utilization Of Short Stay Hospitals, Summary of Nonmedical Statistics, United States, 1965, 1970, 1975, 1980. Department of HEW—Health Resources Administration.

U.S. Senate, Special Committee On Aging, *Prospectus For Medicare's Hospital Insurance Trust Fund: An Information Paper* (Washington, D.C.: Government Printing Office, March 1983).

Health Care Financing Administration, Office Of Research and Demonstrations, *Health Care Financing Review*, 3 (March 1982).

U.S. Bureau of the Census, *Current Population Reports*, Series P-25, No. 922 (Washington, D.C.: Government Printing Office, 1982).

Chapter 17

Shooting Oneself in the Foot[*]

AN AGING POPULATION

Writing in the *New England Journal of Medicine* in November, 1982, John K. Iglehart reported on the congressional activities that culminated with the president signing the Tax Equity and Fiscal Responsibility Act (TEFRA) of 1982 on September 3. The act included savings from the Medicare program. Iglehart pointed out that these "savings" were approved with little disagreement among politicians representing a spectrum of views, giving particular credit to Senator Robert Dole (R-Kansas) for leading the attack. Iglehart goes on to state that this "action of Congress represents a clear signal that the federal government is no longer willing to pay the bills that hospitals submit for service to Medicare beneficiaries."

The assumption seems to be that hospitals are going to go along with the government's position. They will simply accept whatever the government decides to pay. If that is the case, Senator Dole and his colleagues in the Congress may discover that Senator Dole has shot himself in the foot. Why this may be so requires an explanation.

The root of the problem rests with the proportion of the population 65 years of age and older, an increasingly larger share of a growing population. The growth rate of the total population is shown in Table 17–1.

Even though the population will increase by slightly less than 20 million people between 1980 and 1990, an 8.5 percent growth in ten years, the graying of America will be occurring at a faster rate (see Table 17–2).

Between 1980 and 1985, a net addition of 2,495,000 persons entered their Medicare years. By 1990, there will be 5,364,000 more persons in this category

---

[*]Adapted from *Hospital Progress* (now *Health Progress*) with permission of The Catholic Health Association of the United States, © December 1983.

Table 17–1 Population of the United States, 1970–1990 (in 000s)

Year	Total Population
1970	205,052
1975	215,973
1980	227,658
1985	237,000
1990	247,000

Source: Table 17–22.

than there were in 1980. The 65-years-of-age-and-over category is increasing at a rate of 21 percent in this decade, approximately two and one-half times the overall growth rate. Those age 65 and over use hospital care at a much higher rate than those under age 65, and those 75 years of age and up exacerbate usage to an alarming extent, as shown in Table 17–3.

Table 17–3 indicates that people between 65 and 74 years of age use hospitals at a rate three times greater than those under 65 years of age. Those age 75 and over use hospital care at a rate that is eight times that of those under 65 years of age. When it is taken into account that the number of persons in the older years category is growing at a rate two and one half times the rate for those under age 65, the consumption of hospital resources is seen as occurring at a rate six times the rate of those under age 65. In the 75-years-of-age-and-over category, resources are consumed at a rate sixteen times greater. If the two older categories are combined, hospital resources are consumed at a rate that is ten times greater than that of those under 65 years of age. Such a rate of consumption clearly presents a real problem in the financing of health care for older citizens. The cost of this care is a legitimate concern of both Congress and the elderly.

Table 17–2 65 and Over Population of the United States, 1970–1990 (in 000s)

Year	65–74 Age Group	75 and Over	Total 65 and Over
1970	12,316	7,791	20,107
1975	13,426	9,270	22,696
1980	15,425	10,283	25,708
1985	16,922	11,281	28,203
1990	18,623	12,449	31,072

Source: Table 17–22.

Table 17–3 Patient Day Utilization for the United States per 1,000 Population, 1970–1990

Year	Under Age 65	65–74	75 and Over
1970	920	2,760	7,360
1975	910	2,730	7,280
1980	860	2,580	6,880
1985[1]	850	2,550	6,800
1990[1]	840	2,520	6,720

[1]Assumptions made by author.

Source: Health Care Financing Administration, Office of Research and Demonstrations, *Health Care Financing Review,* vol. 3, no. 3 (March 1982).

MEDICARE PAYMENTS TO HOSPITALS

Congress has attempted to deal with the problem by adopting programs that reduce the outflow of dollars to hospitals. It has concentrated on payments to health care providers and has been careful to avoid reducing the scope of services to the beneficiaries of the Medicare program. While this approach is politically sound, it will ultimately force hospitals to take an initiative they would prefer not to pursue in order to prevent widespread bankruptcies in the next few years. The passage of the Tax Equity and Fiscal Responsibility Act effectively put hospitals on notice that they may have to act in order to avoid such an outcome. A review of the TEFRA reductions for the first three years of that program indicates the scope of reductions (see Table 17–4).

Table 17–4* Proposed Program and Hospital Medicare Reductions, 1983–1985 (in Millions)

Year	Total Amount	Hospital Portion
1983	$2,867	$1,987
1984	4,423	2,780
1985	5,961	3,939

*See Table 17–23 for details.

Source: Table 17–23.

When the cuts were implemented, the gap between full operating costs and "allowable costs" became even larger. To cover these shortfalls of the Medicare program, hospitals have proportionately increased their billing rates to commercial insurance and self-pay patients. The extent to which this practice can be expanded because of the proposed cutbacks is questionable. Past experience with Medicare shortfalls can be seen in Table 17–5.

The column in Table 17–5 reflecting differences in dollars represents the average amount per day that is cost shifted. The impact on a hospital depends on what the proportion of Medicare patient days to total patient days is in each individual institution. An argument might be made that the "Difference in Dollars" column also includes retained surpluses as well as a Medicare shortfall. While this is true, the bottom line of a community nonprofit hospital rarely exceeds 3 to 4 percent, a factor equivalent to about $10 per day. In states with rate review programs, the retained surplus is close to zero. For all practical purposes, retained surpluses are not a significant item. The importance of Table 17–5 is that in seven years, allowable costs declined by 6.7 percent and paid only slightly more than two-thirds of a patient's bill. To recapture the other one-third, the hospital is forced to play Robin Hood by overbilling other patients since the Medicare contract prevents the hospital from billing Medicare patients for the difference. Because of the TEFRA legislation, the 68.7 percent reimbursement for every one dollar paid out continues to decline. The degree of the inadequacy of Medicare reimbursement is determined by the total number of dollars available for payment to hospitals. Since this is as yet unclear, three possible levels of funding have been used to project how hospitals will be affected. Table 17–6 reflects a liberal set of circumstances. The first column reflects the history of Medicare expenditures and

---

Table 17–5 Hospital Charges and Medicare Payments, 1974–1981

Year	Hospital Charges per Day	Hospital Reimbursement by Medicare	Difference in Dollars	Percent of Total
1974	$120	$ 90.48	$ 29.52	75.4%
1975	145	108.90	36.10	75.1
1976	171	127.40	43.60	74.5
1977	197	144.20	52.80	73.2
1978	225	162.23	62.77	72.1
1979	255	181.56	73.44	71.2
1980	294	204.62	89.38	69.6
1981	334	229.46	104.54	68.7

Source: Health Care Financing Administration, Office of Research and Demonstrations, *Health Care Financing Review,* vol. 4, no. 2 (December 1982): 166.

Table 17–6 Liberal Model of the Availability of Medicare Funds To Pay Hospitals Through 1985 (in Billions)

Year	Set I
1980	$21.9
1981	23.9
1982	25.9
1983	27.9
1984	29.9
1985	31.9

Source: Health Care Financing Administration, Office of Research and Demonstrations, *Health Care Financing Review,* vol. 4, no. 2 (December 1982): 166.

projects the same pattern through 1985. For the past several years payment to hospitals has been increasing by approximately $2 billion per year.

Table 17–7, shows the availability of dollars if payment to hospitals is capped at the 1982 level of expenditures and the TEFRA reductions are imposed.

The other possibility is to continue the pattern of recent years because of the increasing number of persons being covered by Medicare but to deduct the amounts attributable to TEFRA reductions. Based on the information that is available, this is the likely level of funding to hospitals (see Table 17–8).

In order to determine how each of the three possibilities affected hospital reimbursement from Medicare, it was necessary to determine the average level of hospital charges through 1985. Based on Medicare reports (see Table 17–26), hospitals had a daily charge of $294 in 1980 and $334 in 1981. With a modest in-

Table 17–7 Restrictive Model of the Availability of Medicare Funds To Pay Hospitals Through 1983 (in Billions)

Year	Capped	TEFRA	Net to Hospitals
1980	$21.9	—	$21.9
1981	23.9	—	23.9
1982	25.9	—	25.9
1983	25.9	$-2.0	23.9
1984	25.9	-2.8	23.1
1985	25.9	-3.4	22.5

Source: Health Care Financing Administration, Office of Research and Demonstrations, *Health Care Financing Review,* vol. 4, no. 2 (December 1982): 166.

Table 17–8 Likely Model of the Availability of Medicare Funds To Pay Hospitals Through 1985 (in billions)

Year	Table 17–6 Funds	TEFRA	Net Available
1980	$21.9	—	$21.9
1981	23.9	—	23.9
1982	25.9	—	25.9
1983	27.9	$ –2.0	25.9
1984	29.9	–2.8	27.1
1985	31.9	–3.4	28.5

Source: Health Care Financing Administration, Office of Research and Demonstrations, *Health Care Financing Review,* vol. 4, no. 2 (December 1982): 166.

crease of 5 percent annually in the patient day rates, hospital charges reached $406 in 1985, as seen in Table 17–9.

When the amount charged by hospitals is compared with the amount paid by Medicare through 1985 under each set of assumptions, the percent paid by Medicare is obtained as seen in Tables 17–10 and 17–11.

When the third set of assumptions is used, the results are as seen in Table 17–12.

If hospital charges had risen faster than 5 percent per year through 1985, the consequences would have been more severe. The combination of an expanding

Table 17–9 Hospital Charges—Daily and Annual

Year	Hospital Daily Charge	1980–1985 Annual Amount (in Billions)
1980	$294[1]	$31.4
1981	334[1]	32.0
1982	351[1]	38.4
1983	369[2]	41.1
1984	387[2]	44.0
1985	406[2]	46.9[3]

[1]Actual.
[2]Assumed.
[3]Daily charge times patient days (Table 17–25).

Source: Health Care Financing Administration, Office of Research and Demonstrations, *Health Care Financing Review,* vol. 4, no. 2 (December 1982): 166.

Table 17–10 Liberal Assumption (in Billions)

Year	Hospital Charges	Paid by Medicare	Percent Paid by Medicare
1980	$31.4[1]	$21.9[2]	69.6%
1981	32.0	23.9	68.7
1982	38.4	25.9	67.4
1983	41.1	27.9	67.9
1984	44.0	29.9	68.0
1985	46.9	31.9	68.0

[1]Table 17–9.
[2]Table 17–7.

Source: Tables 17–7 and 17–9.

population of 65 years of age and older, TEFRA reductions, and increasing costs of hospital care results in enormous pressure on the financing mechanism and the hospital system.

CHANGING UTILIZATION

The demographic shift to the older age categories continues to be the major factor affecting the financing of Medicare patients. These demographic changes, coupled with the amount of care received by Medicare patients, dramatically re-

Table 17–11 Restrictive Assumption (in Billions)

Year	Hospital Charges	Paid by Medicare	Percent Paid by Medicare
1980	$31.4[1]	$21.9[2]	69.6%
1981	32.0	23.9	68.7
1982	38.4	25.9	67.4
1983	41.1	23.9	58.2
1984	44.0	23.1	52.5
1985	46.9	22.5	48.0

[1]Table 17–9.
[2]Table 17–7.

Source: Tables 17–7 and 17–9.

Table 17–12 Likely Assumption (in Billions)

Year	Hospital Charges	Paid by Medicare	Percent Paid by Medicare
1980	$31.4[1]	$21.9[2]	69.6%
1981	32.0	23.9	68.7
1982	38.4	25.9	67.4
1983	41.1	25.9	63.0
1984	44.0	27.1	61.2
1985	46.9	28.5	60.8

[1]Table 17–9.
[2]Table 17–8.

Source: Tables 17–8 and 17–9.

---

flect the disproportionate growth in use of hospital care by those in the older age categories.

Table 17–13 indicates that in a 20-year period those under age 65 are slowly increasing their use of hospitals, while for those at the oldest level, utilization will increase by 46.5 percent by 1990.

Table 17–14 looks at the shift of patient days in selected years when age cohorts are compared. In 1980, those under 65 years of age used 65.1 percent of all patient days in 1970, but this will be reduced in 1990 to 58.1 percent. Table 17–14 depicts these shifts.

Table 17–14, which extends to the year 1990, indicates that the shortfall will continue to deepen since the demographic forces at work will continue in the same direction. By 1990, nearly all hospitals will be in difficulty. Some hospitals will

---

Table 17–13 Patient Day Growth by Age Categories in Percentages, 1970–1990

Year	Under 65	65–74 Ages	75+ Ages	Total Population
1970	100.0%	100.0%	100.0%	100.0%
1975	103.3	107.8	117.7	107.0
1980	102.1	117.0	123.6	109.0
1985	104.3	126.9	132.8	113.5
1990	106.6	138.1	146.5	119.4

Source: Table 17–24.

Table 17–14 Proportion of Patient Days by Age Cohorts (in 000s)

Year	Total	Under 65	65–74	75 and Over	Total Number of Patient Days
1970	100.0%	65.1%	13.0%	21.9%	261,490
1975	100.0	62.8	13.1	24.1	279,880
1980	100.0	61.1	14.0	24.9	284,316
1985	100.0	59.8	14.5	25.7	296,735
1990	100.0	58.1	15.0	26.9	312,228

Source: Tables 17–22 and 17–24.

feel the pinch earlier than others because of their financial mix of patients and because they have a higher proportion of Medicare days. The greater the proportion of Medicare days, the quicker will come the day of reckoning.

It is obvious that the gap between hospital charges and reimbursement from Medicare will continue to widen in the years ahead. Looked at on a per diem basis, the average daily hospital charge of $406 in 1985 reflects a growing gap as seen in Table 17–15.

From 1980 through 1985, Medicare reimbursement rose 20 percent, while at the same time hospital charges increased 38 percent.

CASE STUDIES

To determine the degree to which cost shifting would have to be used in order to make up for the shortfall from Medicare, two models might be used to demonstrate the probable outcomes. The first model represents a typical 250-bed hospital

Table 17–15 Daily Hospital Charges Compared to Medicare Reimbursement 1980–1985

Year	Average Daily Hospital Charge	Medicare Reimbursement	Difference
1980	$294	$205	$ 89
1981	334	229	105
1982	351	237	114
1983	369	232	137
1984	387	237	150
1985	406	247	159

Source: Tables 17–9 and 17–12.

operating at 80 percent and generating 73,000 patient days of care. The second model, identical in size, has an adverse selection in terms of financial mix because of its location in a mature city with a high proportion of elderly citizens. The first model results are shown in Table 17–16.

To date, this shortfall has been overcome by hospitals overbilling the commercial and self-pay patients. If this practice is continued, hospitals will have to increase their charges to these patients by 41.6 percent, so that the daily charge will come to $575 per day.

In the second model, shown in Table 17–17, with elderly patients constituting the majority of patient days, the results are strikingly different.

Because of a variation in the financial mix, the shortfall is much greater. The overbilling that is needed requires an increase to the commercial and self-pay patients of 139 percent, to $972.31 per patient day.

Those hospitals with very high Medicare loads are going to be at a substantial disadvantage compared with those that have minimal numbers of Medicare patients. Since many hospitals with a high percentage of Medicare patients are in the inner cities of metropolitan areas, further restrictions on Medicare reimbursement will affect them disproportionately. They are not going to be able to cost shift to the extent necessary to survive. Businesses in their areas will be unwilling to see their premium dollars used in this fashion. Hospitals having to charge $972 per day for the same services that can be purchased for $575 per day are increasingly going to discover that patients covered by commercial insurance are going to be steered to the $575 per day hospital. The fact that the price differential is caused by the

---

Table 17–16 Model A Hospital

Financial Mix	Annual Patient Days	Daily Rate	Annual Revenues
40% Medicare	29,200	247[1]	$ 7,212,400
20% Other Cost Reimbursement	14,600	386[2]	5,635,600
40% Commercial-Self-Pay	29,200	406[1]	11,855,200
Total	73,000		$24,703,200
Gross Revenues	73,000 × $406		$29,638,000
Shortfall	(16.7)%		($ 4,934,800)

[1]Table 17–15.
[2]Assumed to be 5 percent less than the full charges.

Source: Tables 17–4 and 17–15.

Table 17–17 Model B Hospital

Financial Mix	Annual Patient Days	Daily Rate	Annual Revenues
70% Medicare	51,100	247[1]	$12,624,417
10% Other Cost			
Reimbursement	7,300	386[2]	2,817,800
20% Commercial-Self-Pay	14,600	406[1]	5,927,600
Total	73,000		$21,369,817
Gross Revenues	73,000 × $406		$29,638,000
Shortfall	(27.9)%		($ 8,268,183)

[1]Table 17–15.
[2]Assumed to be 5 percent less than the full charges.

Source: Table 17–15.

Medicare shortfall is not going to be considered sufficient reason for absorbing a difference of $397 per day. The business community is increasingly demonstrating that it is unwilling to pay excessive amounts to make up for some other party's shortfall. It will increasingly insist of paying the same level of dollars for the same services. When this point is reached, hospitals will have to squarely face up to the issue of Medicare shortfalls and make their own decisions irrespective of whatever federal programs are on the books.

ADDITIONAL FACILITY NEED

The growing number of Medicare enrollees will require the use of additional hospital facilities. At the present time, the cost of capital for buildings and equipment is excluded from the computation of Medicare payments and is a direct passthrough for reimbursement without restrictions. The magnitude of the need for additional facilities is shown in Table 17–18.

In 1982 the TriBrook Group average project cost per bed was approximately $200,000, based on studies of TriBrook. The capital requirement for coping with the Medicare increase is seen in Table 17–19.

Because of the widespread concern about hospital costs, many persons have concluded that the Medicare Hospital Insurance Trust Fund is in danger. Yet, when the operations of this fund are examined, this turns out not to be true, as seen in Table 17–20.

Table 17–18 Additional Bed Requirements for Medicare, 1980–1990

Period	Additional Persons 65 and Over (in 000s)	Additional Patient Days (in 000s)[3]	Additional Beds at 80 Percent Occupancy
1980–1985	2,495[2]	10,229[1]	33,630[1]
1986–1990	2,869	11,763	38,673
1980–1990	5,364	21,992	72,303 Beds

[1] In ending year of period.
[2] Table 17–2.
[3] Table 17–25.

Source: Table 17–2; Table 17–25.

Since the inception of Medicare in 1966, there have been only three years when expenditures were greater than revenues. At the end of 1979, the fund had a surplus in excess of $13 billion and in 1982 funds from this account were transferred to underwrite the monthly checks mailed to Social Security recipients.

PAYMENTS TO PHYSICIANS

There is also misunderstanding about payments to physicians for their services. Under Medicare program Part B, physicians often bill the patient for the dif-

Table 17–19 Capital Requirement for Additional Medicare Beds

Year	Beds	Project Cost per Bed	Additional Capital (in Billions)
1985	33,630[1]	$200,000	$ 6.726
1990	38,673	200,000	7.753
Total	72,303		$14.479

[1] Table 17–18.

Source: Table 17–18.

Table 17–20 Medicare Insurance Trust Fund (in Millions)

Year	Net Change in Fund	Fund at End of Year
1966	+$ 944	$ 944
1967	+ 129	1,073
1968	+ 1,010	2,083
1969	+ 422	2,505
1970	+ 698	3,202
1971	− 168	3,034
1972	− 99	2,935
1973	+ 3,532	6,467
1974	+ 2,652	9,119
1975	+ 1,399	10,517
1976	+ 88	10,605
1977	− 163	10,442
1978	+ 1,035	11,477
1979	+ 1,751	13,228

Source: Table 17–27.

---

ference between what Medicare pays and their fee, unlike hospitals, which can only accept payment from Medicare.

As seen in Table 17–21, in a seven-year period, the percentage received by physicians rose 4.3 percent, while in the same period, hospitals' percentage of allowed charges decreased by 6.7 percent.

Table 17–21 Payments to Physicians Under the Medicare Program

Year	Allowed Charges	Amount Paid	Percent of Allowed Charges
1974	$ 3.6[1]	$2.6[1]	73.8%
1975	4.4	3.3	74.8
1976	4.6	3.5	75.5
1977	6.2	4.8	76.3
1978	6.4	4.9	76.7
1979	8.5	6.6	77.4
1980	9.7	7.6	77.9
1/1–11/28/81	10.1	7.9	78.1

[1]In millions.

Source: Table 17–28.

OUTCOMES

Given the set of circumstances just described, the question is "How will a hospital respond to the anticipated restrictions on income from Medicare sources?" The basic issue is not, as some people think, should hospitals be for or against DRGs, or prospective payments, or cost reimbursement. As we have seen, when it comes to getting paid by Medicare, the issue is not the method of payment; the issue is the amount of money received. If payment is adequate, the method of payment is secondary. Management will adjust and play by all of the rules of the game, so long as the dollars received, by whatever method, are adequate. If the method of payment changes, adaptation will occur. But, if the level of funding is reduced, then steps must be taken to ensure financial viability. If Medicare funding is reduced in the coming years, hospitals will be forced to take steps if they are to remain viable. To believe that the method of payment has first priority is to put the cart before the horse.

In one-hospital towns, the options for offsetting Medicare shortfalls will be very restricted. Because it is the only hospital in the area, the hospital will not be able to place a ceiling on the number of Medicare patients it will accept. If it happens to be a nonprofit hospital, the governing board may attempt to convert it into a public institution under city or county auspices in order to have access to tax funds to cover the revenue shortfalls. In some communities, this will occur; in others, it will fail because tax funds are already stretched to the limit.

In other one-hospital towns where ownership is either nonprofit or public, the hospital may be sold to an investor-owned chain. The proceeds of the sale may then be used to establish a community fund to pay for Medicare shortfalls as well as indigent care.

In larger communities where there are several hospitals, other approaches are open for exploration. Some hospitals may elect to terminate their Medicare contracts. These will be the hospitals that have a low percentage of Medicare patients, or serve an affluent population, or have a reputation as the finest hospital in the area. When considering such a step, they will first undertake a careful financial analysis to determine whether the hospital can survive on a lower occupancy rate immediately following implementation of this action, and if it can wait out a period of time until occupancy rates start rising again. Such a strategy will work for hospitals that are first to take these steps in their communities. Hospitals that delay will not be able to follow this course of action because their Medicare loads will have risen precipitously as a result of the decisions of the hospitals who have elected to terminate. Inevitably, those who wait will become Medicare-Medicaid hospitals providing care at an inferior level because of the limitations of reimbursement for these categories of patients.

In other situations where there are a number of hospitals in the same general area, a different strategy may be employed. When a hospital owns another nearby

Table 17–22 United States Population

Date	All	65 and Over	65 and Over Percent of Total
1970	205,052	20,107	9.8%
1971	207,661	20,561	9.9
1972	209,896	21,020	10.0
1973	211,909	21,525	10.2
1974	213,854	22,061	10.3
1975	215,973	22,696	10.5
1976	218,035	23,278	10.7
1977	220,239	23,892	10.8
1978	222,585	24,502	11.0
1979	225,055	25,134	11.2
1980	227,658	25,708	11.3
1981	229,807	26,253	11.4
1982	231,990	26,678	11.5
1985	237,000	28,203	11.9
1990	247,000	31,122	12.6

Source: U.S. Bureau of the Census, *Current Population Reports*, Series P-25, No. 922, "Projections of the Population of the United States: 1982 to 2050" (Advance Report) (Washington, D.C.: Government Printing Office, 1982).

---

hospital or can buy or merge with a second institution, serious consideration will be given to decertifying one of them by terminating its Medicare contract. The decertified hospital will be operated in traditional ways with respect to patient care. All of the amenities that the American public has come to expect will be continued, as well as state-of-the-art technology. The other hospital in the two-hospital system will become the Medicare hospital. It will serve government-sponsored patients exclusively and will be operated on the premise that the level of reimbursement provided by Medicare dictates the quality of care. Under this approach, management will do whatever is necessary to stay within the dollar level that has been imposed. For example, if nursing care must be held to two hours per patient day, then that is where the staffing pattern will be pegged; if salary increases must be deferred, then they will be put off; if budgeted positions cannot be filled because of lack of money, then they will go unfilled. In short, everything will be done to stay inside the limits established. In a few years, these hospitals will be institutions that are neither desirable places in which to work or to be sick.

Providing two levels of care in the same hospital facility, one geared to the concept of doing whatever is required for patient care, the other controlled by dollars, may be tried but will be found to be unworkable since both physicians and hospital professionals will be reluctant to make such distinctions in the same

Table 17–23 Tax Equity and Fiscal Responsibility Act of 1982, HR 4961 (in Millions)

Item	1983	1984	1985
80 Percent Radiologist/Pathologist	160	210	250
Elimination Of Nursing Differential	95	110	125
Hospital-Based Physicians	63	73	84
Compromise—Hospital Reimbursement	480	1,770	3,770
Elimination of Private Room Subsidy	54	75	80
Temporary Delay In Periodic Interim Payments	750	100	(870)
Percentage Arrangements	15	17	20
Interest On Overpayments	25	25	20
Private Sector Utilization Review	330	385	440
Utilization And Quality Control Peer Review	15	15	20
Subtotal—Hospital	1,987	2,780	3,939
Other			
Medicare Secondary For Older Workers	350	530	600
Part B Premium As A Constant Percentage Of Costs	45	240	480
Single Reimbursement Limit For Skilled Nursing Facilities And Home Health Agencies	18	46	46
Elimination Of Duplicate Payments For Outpatients	160	225	270
Audit And Medical Claims Review	130	300	300
Reimbursement Of Assistants At Surgery	55	130	150
HI Tax For Federal Employees	122	163	176
Subtotal—Other	880	1,634	2,022
Grand Total	2,867	4,423	5,961

Source: U.S. Congress, House Tax Equity and Fiscal Responsibility Act of 1982, Public Law 97-248, 97th Cong., H.R. 4921 (Washington, D.C.: Government Printing Office, 1982).

setting. This can only be accomplished by keeping the two apart and operating them as separate facilities.

What is unrecognized by many in government is that the real issue has been lost sight of in the effort to contain the payment to hospitals by the Medicare program. The issue is the adequacy of payment to hospitals for these patients. The use of DRGs on a case-cost payment basis is workable so long as the method of payment permits hospitals to do their jobs. But, by having the amount to be paid unilaterally determined by the federal government through the Secretary of Health and Human

Table 17–24 Patient Day Projections, 1970–1990

| Year | 65–74 | | | 75 and Over | | | 65 and Over |
	Population[1]	Utilization Rate[2]	Patient Days	Population	Utilization Rate	Patient Days	Total Patient Days
1970	12,316	2,760	33,948	7,791	7,360	57,342	91,290
1975	13,426	2,730	36,582	9,270	7,280	67,486	104,068
1980	15,425	2,580	39,732	10,283	6,880	70,864	110,596
1985	16,922	2,550	43,095	11,281	6,800	76,160	119,255
1990	18,623	2,520	46,872	12,449	6,720	84,000	130,872

[1]Table 17–1.
[2]Table 17–2.

Source: Tables 17–1 and 17–2; TriBrook Group, Inc.

Services, it should be obvious from the above tables that the secretary will encounter serious difficulties in attempting to balance federal needs and hospital reimbursement.

Warnings from hospitals are apt to go unheeded in the next few years. The use of diagnostically related groups as a payment mechanism assumes that hospitals will control the diagnostic and therapeutic decisions of individual physicians through pressure on medical staffs. What is not sufficiently appreciated is that a physician is primarily tied to the patient and only secondarily to the hospital. The physician has a direct accountability to the patient, but only a peripheral concern with the financial health of the hospital. If DRG case-cost limitations get to where they interfere with the physician's clinical judgment, the winner will be clinical judgment, not cost. Since it is physicians who sit on the utilization committees and review clinical activities, they are going to be in sympathy with the exercise of good judgment in the clinical management of a patient's course of treatment. When case costs reach a level where several members of the medical staff are routinely above the target rate, the members of the utilization committee are apt to conclude that they are being asked to perform a role they can no longer in good conscience support. Should that occur, they can be expected to withdraw their participation in this activity.

If physicians reach the point where they become disenchanted with the Medicare program, a two-tier health care system will quickly emerge; hospitals will have no alternative but to accept the collective judgments of their medical staffs. It is difficult to imagine that case-cost levels determined at a central point for all hospitals can be so finely tuned that they do not cross the line of unacceptability to physicians, given the governmental pressure to restrain Medicare expenditures.

What can be done to restrain Medicare expenditures and yet avoid a reduction in the benefits of the program to the beneficiaries? If the government continues to ratchet down hospital payments, the result will be payments so low that they have

---

Table 17–25 Projected Utilization Rates 65 and Over

Year	Patient Days 65 and Over[1]	Population 65 and Over[2]	Utilization Rate
1980	110,596	25,708	4,300
1985	119,255	28,203	4,228
1990	130,872	31,072	4,212

[1]Table 17–24.
[2]Table 17–2.

Source: Table 17–2; Table 17–24; TriBrook Group, Inc.

Table 17–26 Medicare Hospital Insurance: Number of Bills for Inpatient Short-stay Hospital[1] Care Approved for Payment, Covered Days, Total Charges and Amount Reimbursed, by Type of Beneficiary and Period Approved as of September 26, 1981

| | Approved Bills | | | Hospital Charges | | | | |
| | | Covered Days of Care | | | | | Amount Reimbursed | |
Period Approved	Number (in Thousands)	Total (in Thousands)	Average Per Bill	Total (in Thousands)	Per Bill	Per Day	Total (in Thousands)	Percent of Total
				Total				
1974	8,073	87,925	10.9	$10,524,686	$1,304	$120	$ 7,936,618	75.4
1975	8,542	90,292	10.6	13,104,395	1,534	145	9,835,732	75.1
1976	9,084	95,060	10.5	16,215,493	1,785	171	12,074,678	74.5
1977	9,421	96,409	10.2	19,014,392	2,018	197	13,914,134	73.2
1978	9,779	98,497	10.1	22,149,690	2,265	225	15,958,917	72.1
1979	10,149	100,744	9.9	25,706,488	2,533	255	18,305,228	71.2
1980	10,856	106,880	9.8	31,417,258	2,894	294	21,859,378	69.6
Jan.-Sept. 1981	7,275	70,834	9.8	23,981,203	3,278	334	16,475,333	68.7
				Persons Age 65 and Over				
1980	9,565	94,746	9.9	27,627,033	2,888	292	19,257,789	69.7
Jan.-Sept. 1981	6,420	62,849	9.8	21,126,110	3,291	336	14,535,529	68.8
				Disability Beneficiaries				
1980	1,291	12,134	9.4	3,790,225	2,936	312	2,601,589	68.6
Jan.-Sept. 1981	855	7,985	9.3	2,855,093	3,339	358	1,939,804	67.9

[1]General and special hospitals reporting average stays of less than 30 days.

Source: Office of Statistics and Data Management, Bureau of Data Management and Strategy, Health Care Financing Administration.

forced the country back to two tiers. The mere fact that Medicare now accounts for 42 percent of all patient days, and this will soon be 45 percent, indicates that adequacy of payment to hospitals is the crucial question to be addressed. Medicare has become such a large part of every hospital's annual number of patient days that to receive inadequate payment can only lead to unfortunate results. The continuing rise in Medicare patient days will not change just because of the introduction of a DRG method of payment.

The use of diagnostically related groups and case prices for each Medicare patient's stay may seem to be satisfactory. It should be remembered that these case costs are based on medians for each DRG category. This means that nearly half of all physicians are exercising clinical judgments that are now in excess of target rates. If case costs turn out to be more responsive to the needs of the federal budget than to the clinical needs of patients, the result will be a two-tier hospital system. Such an outcome can be avoided, but it will require some modifications in the proposals now being considered by Congress.

The use of DRGs is a move away from cost reimbursement and is in the right direction. However, since it applies to only 42 percent of a typical hospital's inpatient workload, the two-tier system will quickly develop if inadequate payments result, one designed for the 58 percent, the other geared to the level of payments made on behalf of the other 42 percent. By empowering the Secretary of Health and Human Services with total authority in the setting of case costs for Medicare patients, the government becomes the sole arbiter of the adequacy of payments. No room is provided for competition to enter the arena.

The likelihood of further reductions in payments to hospitals is going to compel hospitals to make the unthinkable alternatives become thinkable: a two-tier system that was abandoned in 1965 (when the Medicare program was enacted). If hospitals are not permitted to respond to patient needs as determined by physicians but are instead forced to respond to government, their recourse will be to limit Medicare admissions, withdraw from the program entirely, or create two levels of care. It would seem appropriate to avoid this outcome by earnestly examining alternatives to such a conclusion.

Table 17–27 Table 3.22, Operations of the Medicare Hospital Insurance Trust Fund, Calendar Years 1966–1979 (millions)

| | | | Income | | | | | | Disbursements | | | Trust Fund | |
| | | Transfers From RR Retirement Account | Reimbursement for Uninsured Persons | Premiums from Voluntary Enrollees | Reimbursement for Military Wage Credits | Reimbursement for PSRO Review | Interest on Investment | Total Disbursements | Benefit Payments | Administrative Expenses | Net Change in Fund | Fund at End of Year |
Year	Total Income	Payroll Taxes											
1966	$ 1,943	$ 1,858	$ 16	$ 26	—	$ 11	—	$ 32	$ 999	$ 891	$108	+$ 944	$ 944
1967	3,559	3,152	44	301	—	11	—	51	3,430	3,353	77	+ 129	1,073
1968	5,287	4,116	54	1,022	—	22	—	74	4,277	4,179	99	+ 1,010	2,083
1969	5,279	4,473	64	617	—	11	—	113	4,857	4,739	118	+ 422	2,505
1970	5,979	4,881	66	863	—	11	—	158	5,281	5,124	157	+ 698	3,202
1971	5,732	4,921	66	503	—	48	—	193	5,900	5,751	150	− 168	3,034
1972	6,403	5,731	63	381	—	48	—	180	6,505	6,318	185	− 99	2,935
1973	10,821	9,944	99	451	$ 2	48	—	278	7,289	7,057	232	+ 3,532	6,467
1974	12,024	10,844	132	471	5	48	—	523	9,372	9,099	272	+ 2,652	9,119
1975	12,980	11,502	138	621	7	48	—	664	11,581	11,315	266	+ 1,399	10,517
1976	13,766	12,727	143	0[2]	9	141	—	746	13,679	13,340	339	+ 88	10,605
1977	15,856	14,114	0[1]	803[2]	12	143[3]	—	784	16,019	15,737	283	− 163	10,442
1978	19,213	17,324	214	688	13	141	$29	805	18,178	17,682	496	+ 1,035	11,477
1979	22,825	20,768	191	734	16	141	33	942	21,073	20,623	450	+ 1,751	13,228

[1]No transfer was made in 1977 because of a change in the transfer date from August to June. The 1978 transfer is for contributions during the quarter period covering the transition quarter and fiscal year 1977.

[2]No transfer was made for 1976 because of the change in transfer date from December to March. The 1977 transfer was for benefits and administrative expenses during the 15-month period beginning July 1976 and ending September 1977.

[3]Includes $2 million in reimbursements from general revenues for costs arising from the granting of noncontributory wage credits to persons of Japanese ancestry who were interned during World War II.

Source: The Board of Trustees, Federal Hospital Insurance Trust Fund, *1980 Annual Report of the Board of Trustees of the Federal Hospital Insurance Trust Fund*, June 17, 1980, p. 27.

Table 17–28 Medicare Supplementary Medical Insurance: Number of Physicians' Bills Paid, Total Charges, and Amount Reimbursed, by Type of Bill, Type of Beneficiary, and Period Recorded as of November 28, 1981[1]

(All Numbers in Thousands, Except Percents)

Calendar Year Recorded*	Total Physicians' Bills				Surgical Bills				Medical Bills			
			Amount Reimbursed				Amount Reimbursed				Amount Reimbursed	
	Number	Allowed Charges[1]	Total	Percent of Allowed Charges	Number	Allowed Charges[2]	Total	Percent of Allowed Charges	Number	Allowed Charges[3]	Total	Percent of Allowed Charges
					Total[5]							
1974	54,190	$ 3,626,579	$2,675,850	73.8	8,265	$1,523,903	$1,158,036	76.0	45,926	$2,102,675	$1,517,814	72.2
1975	64,505	4,367,672	3,269,126	74.8	9,357	1,815,784	1,392,595	76.7	55,148	2,551,891	1,876,532	73.5
1976	66,598	4,630,124	3,496,957	75.5	9,004	1,867,424	1,440,561	77.1	57,594	2,762,701	2,056,396	74.4
1978	85,294	6,427,211	4,931,792	76.7	10,597	2,554,245	1,990,518	77.9	74,699	3,872,967	2,941,276	75.9
1979	109,645	8,482,230	6,569,097	77.4	13,256	3,377,687	2,645,098	78.3	96,389	5,104,543	3,923,999	76.9
1980	117,487	9,711,949	7,561,652	77.9	14,342	3,925,041	3,082,750	78.5	103,046	5,786,909	4,478,873	77.4
Jan. 1–Nov. 28, 1981	113,750	10,144,109	7,923,141	78.1	13,808	4,112,092	3,236,445	78.7	99,942	6,032,016	4,686,696	77.7
					Persons Age 65 and Over							
1980	105,143	8,645,961	6,724,177	77.8	13,033	3,527,380	2,769,036	78.5	92,011	5,118,581	3,955,132	77.3
Jan. 1–Nov. 28, 1981	101,682	9,021,014	7,038,985	78.0	12,540	3,696,038	2,907,626	78.7	89,142	5,324,975	4,131,359	77.6
					Disability Beneficiaries							
1980	12,344	1,065,988	837,475	78.6	1,309	397,661	313,714	78.9	11,035	668,328	523,741	78.4
Jan. 1–Nov. 28, 1981	12,068	1,123,095	884,156	78.7	1,268	416,054	328,819	79.0	10,800	707,041	555,337	78.5

[1]Includes only those bills for which reimbursements were made by carriers and that were recorded in the Social Security Administration central records before November 28, 1981.

[2]See Table 3, footnote 2.

[3]Represents allowed charges as determined by the carriers on the basis of customary charges for similar services generally made by the physician or supplier of covered services and also on prevailing charges in the locality for similar services.

Source: Office of Statistics and Data Management, Bureau of Data Management and Strategy, Health Care Financing Administration.

REFERENCES

John K. Iglehart, *New England Journal of Medicine* 307 (1982): 1288–1292.

U.S. Bureau of the Census, *Current Population Reports*, Series P-25, No. 922 (Washington, D.C.: Government Printing Office, 1982).

Health Care Financing Administration, Office of Research and Demonstrations, *Health Care Financing Review*, vol. 3, no. 3 (March 1982).

U.S. Congress, House, Tax Equity and Fiscal Responsibility Act of 1982, Public Law 97-248, 97th Cong., H.R. 4961 (Washington, D.C.: Government Printing Office, 1982).

Health Care Financing Administration, Office of Research and Demonstrations, *Health Care Financing Review*, vol. 4, no. 2 (December 1982): 166.

Board of Trustees, Federal Hospital Insurance Trust Fund, *1980 Annual Report of the Board of Trustees of the Federal Hospital Insurance Trust Fund*, June 17, 1980, 27.

Health Care Financing Administration, Office of Research and Demonstrations, *Health Care Financing Review*, vol. 4, no. 2 (December 1982): 167.

Chapter 18

Hospital CEOs and Economic Competition

SPEEDING UP DECISION MAKING

As interest in economic competition has grown in the hospital field, chief executives have become intrigued with the notion that their role will finally be more fully appreciated by both governing boards and medical staffs. They recognize that future institutional risks will be economic in nature and fall within the purview of management. Thus far, little thought has been given to how competition will impact the role of a chief executive and bring about changes in administrative behavior. Traditional characteristics, traits, and attitudes of trustees and physicians will undergo a shift as they, too, recognize the impacts of competition.

Hospitals have engaged in competition with one another for a long time, but only in noneconomic arenas of hospital operation. They have competed for patients by improving the quality of care and increasing the range of comprehensiveness of services in order to attract physicians and encourage them to admit patients to their hospitals. Competent and capable physicians have understood the quid pro quo between themselves and a hospital; they admitted patients as long as a hospital offered the most up-to-date technology, adequate numbers of nursing personnel, and a cheerful environment that catered to the needs of physicians. In a multihospital community this type of institution was the most respected and popular one in town. Because hospitals received payment for patient services from insurance carriers, neither patients nor attending physicians concerned themselves with cost.

Economic competition will bring about a significant change in attitudes. The role of a third-party payer is no longer to passively pay the hospital bills of the insured, but is shifting to negotiating with both physicians and hospitals for their services, offering a guaranteed volume of work for a predetermined price. Third-party payers will not pay hospitals for the costs of providing the services rendered, but only the agreed-upon price. Hospitals increasingly are bidding for contracts. If an institution is inefficient and is high-cost, its bids reflect this fact in the proposals made to carriers. If it is efficient and low-cost, it can bid lower and win the contract. In turn, patients who have health insurance are restricted to receiving care from physicians and hospitals with whom the carrier has contracts. Free choice of physician and hospital by the patient is limited to those with whom the carrier has contracts. Economic competition has arrived.

In a present-day hospital, the successful CEO needs a well-developed set of political skills. An ability to negotiate and compromise between differing viewpoints, while at the same time keeping a hospital moving ahead, is a prized commodity. Finding the greatest amount of common ground between internal factions with different goals requires a good deal of patience and often protracted periods of time in order to reach a consensus. This set of skills is based on knowing whom to involve, when to involve them, and how much to expect of them. Years of experience in negotiating health care contracts are essential.

The criteria by which a management team is evaluated is undergoing a change. Dollars of revenue and costs of operation become more important as price increases are publicly resisted. As a result, a CEO now looks for associates who carefully watch operational statistics and take appropriate corrective action on their own initiative to keep costs in line without reducing the level of the quality of services. Administrative staffs are developing a growing appreciation that their CEO views being tough-minded as a necessary ingredient to successful performance. They are also learning that being tough-minded must be coupled with real leadership skills to maintain acceptable standards of departmental performance. These skills cannot be learned in a short period of time, but come as a result of many years of well-rounded experience in succeedingly difficult assignments. Junior members of an administrative team will recognize that any one of the senior members could probably step into the role of the CEO and be effective. They will not see the CEO as being head and shoulders above immediate subordinates, but rather as the senior member of a team of competent executives.

REGULATION MAY BE FAVORED

When the public recognizes that many trustees favor cooperation rather than an unregulated competitive environment, there is bound to be considerable support at the grass roots for continuing to regulate the hospital industry. A highly structured environment sits more easily on the conscience of trustees because it is less risky since competition tends to destabilize traditional practices. Trustees of community resources are uncomfortable in risking a substantial percentage of resources in programs and projects where there is a degree of uncertainty about outcome. From personal business experiences, trustees know that a competitive environment often involves taking steps that they would prefer not to take. However, trustees understand that to remain competitive additional resources must be pumped into the enterprise. They know that the specter of failure is always the companion of success.

CEOs need to have a sensitivity to the reluctance of trustees to develop aggressive marketing programs and to make expenditures solely aimed at competitors. Since governing boards have a preference for regulation, cooperation between institutions, and an orderly environment in the industry, a CEO of the nonprofit hospital is apt to be in a lonely position when it comes to risk taking. CEOs in the nonprofit sector will learn to their dismay that the rewards for successful risk taking will be different from those of their colleagues in the for-profit sector. The not-for-profits will take risks to protect or strengthen market share, or assure fiscal viability, but not to put as many surplus dollars as possible on the bottom line. Stated another way, nonprofit hospitals will take risks to avoid failure, while for-profit hospitals will take risks to achieve greater financial success. The difference may be subtle but will profoundly affect the way a CEO is regarded by the governing body.

CEOs IN NONPROFIT HOSPITALS

When risk taking is a failure for a nonprofit hospital, board members will put some distance between themselves and the CEO. On the other hand, if successful, the CEO will be regarded as simply doing the job for which he was employed. Those who philosophically see themselves as conservators of community funds are apt to look for a scapegoat if a risk turns out badly. But success is apt to be buried since the rewards of the risk taking become part of the stream of revenues required to keep a hospital up-to-date in new technology or to offset bad debts and charity allowances.

In economic competition CEOs of nonprofit hospitals will find their judgments on the line. No longer will they be able to hide behind decisions of governing boards. The fact that a governing board may have approved a risk-taking activity will not let a CEO off the hook; accountability for performance and good judgment will rise to greater heights in the coming era.

Relationships between the medical staff and the CEO will also undergo change. Difficulties will be encountered by a CEO when a move away from the status quo is made. The compelling reasons will be economic, but physicians will be hard put to think in these terms as having equal priority with patient care and comprehensiveness of services. Physicians are accustomed to their role as the initiator of important hospital changes, deciding on new procedures or new clinical equipment and new programs. From their viewpoint the role of a CEO is to provide the support systems needed to respond to diagnostic and therapeutic orders of attending physicians. This should be expected since physicians see hospitals as patient care institutions where all other concerns are secondary in importance.

In a period of ample resources, with noneconomic competition and a rapid expansion of clinical technology, the existing physician attitude was reasonable. Physicians were not only the gatekeepers to a hospital but enjoyed an advantage over the institution since economics was not a major concern. In this environment there was no abridgement of a physician's decision to admit a patient to a hospital; the institution was a bystander as were insurance carriers to this decision. Regular payment for hospital services was fast and would automatically occur after care was rendered.

NEW RULES FOR ECONOMIC COMPETITION

Under economic competition the terms of reference will be drastically altered and, in turn, substantially affect a hospital CEO relationship with the medical staff. When economic competition is in full force, a hospital can look forward to receiving a request for a proposal (RFP) from an insurance carrier for a quotation on providing services for "x" numbers of days of inpatient care. If a hospital CEO is entrepreneurially-oriented, the quotation submitted will be the result of a collaborative effort with the medical staff. The hospital response will likely be a combination of hospital services and the professional component with both parties discounting their usual prices, hoping that by doing so the result will be the low bid received by the insurance carrier. The first time a CEO proposes a combined bid physicians may react negatively, since they believe that hospitals should have no say in the level of their professional fees. However, when physicians go along with this proposal and the result is successful in winning new business, other hospitals and medical staffs can be expected to follow suit. Should medical staffs cling to traditional attitudes, they can look forward to a continued loss of business. Insurance carriers are concerned with total hospital bills for each case, not with component parts and can be expected to award contracts on this basis. A few rounds of lost bids will lead medical staffs to conclude that a hospital CEO has an important role in securing contracts for both hospital and professional services. No longer will physicians attempt to keep a hospital economically neutral to protect their incomes, but will realize that a CEO is an important ally in winning contracts.

During the early stage of economic competition, CEOs are not likely to use a combined bid approach on a medical staff. The first skirmish inside a hospital is more apt to be with hospital-based physicians who will be asked, as part of the hospital bid, to accept 75 to 80 percent of their usual, customary, and reasonable fees. Their reaction is predictable. When broached, hospital-based physicians can be expected to marshall support among private practitioners on the medical staff to prevent an intrusion into their professional prerogatives. Their argument will be that if a CEO is successful the next step may include private practitioners, and the general medical staff will rally to the support of the hospital-based specialists.

Some CEOs will not survive this internal battle. Other CEOs will recognize that this approach endangers their position and will not pursue this approach. Only those who are risk takers will proceed.

In hospitals that have undergone corporate restructuring and created a parent-subsidiary model (i.e., where the hospital is a subsidiary of a health care corporation operating several subsidiary corporations), the perils of dealing with a medical staff will be lessened for the CEO of the parent organization. Being removed from daily operations of the hospital, the parent CEO is not easily accessible to members of the medical staff. Since the CEO's interests of necessity involve other subsidiaries in the health care corporation, as well as the hospital, the CEO will have a more detached and objective perspective of the need for a combined bid to successfully obtain a contract. Given the importance of such a contract to the total corporation, a parent CEO can push harder against medical staff attitudes without fear of retaliation, knowing the governing board of the parent organization will probably have a similar viewpoint to that of the CEO.

Risk taking by a CEO of a parent corporation in a health care multicorporate organization will be a well-traveled route by the time economic competition matures. As the number of subsidiary corporations increase, and as more and more health-related activities are spread to multiple sites, the CEO will think and behave as an entrepreneur. The challenge of developing new programs and services in a risk-filled environment will be appealing and satisfying to a CEO. Previously, challenges encountered in traditional organizations included testing CEO's administrative ability to reconcile differences between key figures in the medical staff and the governing board, and resulted in making progress on programs, inch by inch.

DEVELOPING THE ENTREPRENEUR

As entrepreneurial instincts develop, a CEO will slide into the role of leader of the total organization, rather than remain the servant of the governing board. As a CEO gains confidence as an entrepreneur, earlier anxiety that might be felt in tackling board or medical staff problems will be minimized. Gradually a CEO will come to appreciate a risk-taking environment as one which provides more real satisfaction than previously experienced as a hospital administrator. In turn, there will be less and less reverting to consensus decision making and more and more reliance on hard data and objective thinking. In the event a CEO leaves a health care corporation it is predictable that many will remain in their community, where roots have been established, to locate some kind of business enterprise where their skills honed in the hospital administrator position can be utilized in a business form. Within the field of hospital administration, there will be an increase in the number of CEOs learning their profession to develop businesses of their own.

There will also be an attitude change among nonprofit hospital CEOs under economic competition toward investor-owned hospital chains. They will increasingly come to understand that for-profit hospitals make substantial net profits by carefully segmenting a marketplace and filling service gaps by providing new programs of high quality care at economically attractive prices. As nonprofit CEOs see their investor-owned CEO colleagues receive substantial bonuses and equity positions in these companies for outstanding managerial performance, talented administrators will desert the nonprofit sector for the greater rewards that will be theirs in for-profit hospitals. Because they are capable executives, they will seek tangible recognition of their abilities.

From a management standpoint, economic competition will force nonprofit hospitals to adopt management information and reporting systems that are carbon copies of those in use in for-profit hospitals. Interpretations of reports received and the actions that follow will parallel those found in investor-owned hospitals. Instead of casually reviewing ratios (such as employees per occupied beds on a monthly basis), under the new game plan, CEOs are apt to call for this report on a daily or weekly basis and follow-up adverse reports with corrective action on the same day.

The budgeting process of hospitals can be expected to be tightened. Instead of slotting new vacancies at the beginning of a fiscal year and leaving it up to the discretion of department directors to fill vacancies at their leisure, a CEO will adopt a two-step procedure. The slotting of the new positions, or the filling of vacancies at budget time, will be dependent upon demonstrating increased work-loads that are expected to occur. When the date arrives to fill a position the second step will be invoked: a review of workloads to date to be sure that what was expected has, in fact, occurred. Only then will the position be filled.

IMPACT ON TEACHING HOSPITALS

Teaching hospitals, under economic competition, will be particularly hard hit. CEOs in these hospitals will face the most severe problems. Their dilemma will be to compete successfully on an economic basis for patient care contracts and at the same time continue to provide residency and postgraduate education for large house staffs. If they continue to lump together patient care and education, the teaching hospital will be able to attract only those patients requiring unique hospital services unavailable elsewhere in the community. Since tertiary level care demand is limited, other steps will be necessary.

As economic competition increases, teaching institutions will probably have to separately identify patient care costs from educational costs in their accounting system. This may turn out to be a difficult task, but one that will be accomplished because of the necessity for doing so. Once achieved, it will still leave unsolved the problem of funding educational programs. Teaching hospital executives will be hard pressed. If no financial responsibility is accepted for education programs, they will be confronted by a hostile teaching faculty. If, on the other hand, they acquiesce to the educational commitments of the institution, they risk pricing patient care services above the going marketplace—with dire financial consequences. Leaning too far in either direction, or hanging on to the status quo, may lead to unfavorable results.

Given existing constraints, the first responses of teaching hospitals under economic competition are predictable. Insurance carriers will be asked to accept bids that are higher than bids of community hospitals because of the superior patient care nature of teaching hospitals due to its educational component. This argument has been effectively used since the early days of third-party coverage.

In university hospitals a CEO will have an especially difficult situation. When a hospital is part of the university and the CEO reports to an academic dean or vice president educators dominate the decision-making apparatus. The necessity for competing on a price basis in a marketplace may not be squarely faced until the medical center is faced with the very real prospect of bankruptcy. Should this occur, there will be an organizational wrenching, in which administratively-oriented executives are replaced with educational administrator types. As the results of this change become clear, the conclusion will be reached that the basic problem was not management but the pricing of services at a level that is noncompetitive. Once that point is driven home to medical school faculties, the next step will be to seek funding for education from alternative sources. Since tax monies are most likely to be used for new support, they will be sought after at all levels of government. When tax funds are made available, there is likely to be a quid pro quo involved; a university medical center will get tax dollars in return for providing patient care services for welfare and indigent patients. The wear and tear on university hospital CEOs in making this kind of transition will be the most difficult experienced by any chief executive in the field of hospital administration.

Economic competition will markedly affect CEOs but will also cause structural changes in the organization of a hospital. Hospitals will grow in size and complexity, with many turning into health care corporations operating multiple kinds of health services at multiple locations. The hospital/health care corporation will have annual revenues many times larger than at present.

CHANGING BOARD FUNCTIONS

As the pace of competition increases, CEOs will have to be granted wider decision-making authority by transfers from the governing board to the chief executive. Making the hard decisions that balance quality of care, comprehensiveness, and price will become administrative decisions because of the complexity involved. Ultimately, this will lead to a reduction in the number of governing board committees and ultimately in the size of the board. Because of the increasing necessity for rapid decisions most matters will move directly to a governing board for action instead of going through committees and then to the board. Trustee decisions will be based on recommendations of a CEO rather than from a committee. As these changes become standard operating practice in a hospital, governing boards will seek to put into place improved and expanded evaluation techniques to prevent becoming captives of a CEO, hearing and acting only on matters brought to them through administrative channels. Feedback mechanisms will increase in sophistication and will lead to improved and strengthened accountability of a CEO to the governing board.

Economic competition will separate the daring from the timid in hospital management. Survivors will be seasoned, tough-minded hospital executives who thoroughly enjoy taking risks in an environment where winners and losers can easily be identified. It will be a high stake game where balanced judgment, experience, ability, and courage will be needed in large measure.

Part IV

Executive Roles in Hospitals

Chapter 19

Retaining Executive Talent in Nonprofit Hospitals

Until the early 1980s the prevalent method of paying for hospital care was cost reimbursement. There was little reason for hospital governing boards to be concerned about the finances of the institution. A medical staff requested, the governing board approved, and the management implemented the decision. The hospital chief executive was a facilitator. As long as any additional costs were included in the cost report, income rose to meet the new levels of expense.

Concerns about serving the public, charity, philanthropy, tender loving care, humanitarism, and dedication were the philosophical underpinnings of the hospital field. As economic competition stiffened and the marketplace for health services contracted, greater and greater attention had to be paid to business activities that were common to the management of for-profit enterprises. Hospital chief executives increasingly had to deal with problems of market share, profitability, productivity, bond ratings, debt-to-equity ratios, fair employment practices, business plans, profit centers, and lines of business.

NEW WAYS OF THINKING

These new ways of thinking came suddenly and were an abrupt departure from previous times. Governing boards had historically taken pride in their hospital as a nonprofit corporation that plowed back any year-end surplus into new equipment and services. Whether the program paid its own way or not was not a serious matter as long as the expenses and income zero balanced at the end of a fiscal year. The satisfaction of knowing that the public interest was being well served was a trustee's compensation. A chief executive, though salaried, was expected to share in the fundamental belief of the value of a nonprofit hospital; no one received a dividend, but the public received more comprehensive care year after year.

In the expansionist period since the end of World War II, spanning several decades when hospital care was underwritten by cost-reimbursement systems, little attention was paid to the level of management skills of the administrative team. Whether it was superior or mediocre was of little importance because hospitals were nonprofit and reimbursed all of their costs, whatever they might be, high or low. The performance of a chief executive was as apt to be criticized by governing board members for achieving too high a year-end financial surplus as for a major loss being sustained in the fiscal operation. Performance was measured more on how the chief executive got along with key physicians on the medical staff and key board members. Such measurements could be applied only in a hospital economy of ample resources, a riskless environment.

MEASURES OF PERFORMANCE

The major reason that the performance of hospital chief executives was judged by how well they got along with the key players on the board and medical staff was, in large measure, due to the lack of measurements of hospital operation that could be quantified. As concerns grew about the business aspects of hospital care, more attention was given to developing quantifiable indicators of performance. These included:

1. Full-time equivalents (FTEs) per occupied bed
2. Ratio of debt to equity
3. Percentage share of the market
4. Number of days of accounts receivable
5. Net profit as a percent of operating expense
6. Contractual allowances as a percent of gross revenues
7. Occupancy as a percent of available beds

In the future, as more importance is attached to measures of performance, as reflective of executive performance, less and less attention will be devoted to subjective factors that once dominated the evaluation process. There will be a growing appreciation that a top-flight hospital executive is a prized asset.

As the health care marketplace has become increasingly competitive, a chief executive can no longer function as a facilitator. Stressful situations can no longer be avoided when revenues decline. Operating problems must be squarely met and best judgments exercised, and these must be based less on knowledge of patient care and more on financial expertise. In the future the abilities of hospital chief executives and the members of senior management are going to determine the success or failure of our institutions. Future emphasis will more and more be on solid planning and flawless execution.

A realization of the value of a chief executive in this new environment is not apt to come about rapidly among governing board members of nonprofit hospitals.

Trustees are likely to continue to view a chief executive from a traditional perspective and to determine salary and perquisites in traditional ways.

The procedure historically followed by trustees was to review published salary surveys in trade journals to determine what other hospitals of similar size were paying in order to establish salary parameters. Then a percentage increase was applied to existing salaries based on the latest obtainable figures for the effects of inflation. When performance was judged to be above average, a few percentage points were tacked on to the rate of inflation; if performance was judged to be less than desired, a percentage or two might be deducted from the rate of inflation. This result was then compared with the information obtained from outside sources to be sure that the parameters were not exceeded. This method and its results were usually considered by either governing board members or chief executives to be less than entirely satisfactory, but they were utilized because no other approach to determining salary levels was known.

As long as the hospital was philosophically deeply rooted in the nonprofit concept and conducted all of its activities on one site, under one corporate structure, this system continued to function without change. However, during the 1970s nonprofit hospital executives became increasingly restless as they saw former classmates and colleagues move from senior positions in nonprofit hospitals to executive positions in investor-owned chains of hospitals. Nonprofit hospital executives that made this transition in the early years of the 1970s found that they were no longer considered by fellow administrators as peers, because the investor-owned hospitals they joined placed a high value on economic returns from operations.

As investor-owned chains grew in numbers, more and more senior executives were being joined by many of the best and brightest graduates from programs in health care administration who deliberately chose careers in for-profit hospitals. As investor-owned ranks increased, executives in nonprofit hospitals began to change their attitudes about employment in for-profit hospitals. From informal chats with their colleagues who had shifted allegiances to the for-profit sector they learned that salaries were comparable, that promotions to divisional and regional positions were part of the scheme of things, that quantitative measures of performance were utilized in judging executives, and that opportunities for stock ownership were considered to be important motivators of performance. They also learned that a chief executive of a hospital in a chain had his performance appraised by a person equally knowledgeable about the health field; a professional judged another professional. This was important because it meant that if a chief executive in a for-profit hospital in a chain made a correct, but unpopular, decision with a local board or medical staff, the chain would provide protection if pressures built up to hire a replacement. Rather than termination, which would occur in a sole hospital situation, the executive under pressure would be moved to another hospital in the chain.

ALTERNATIVE CAREER ROUTES

In many respects, a nonprofit hospital executive came to view the for-profit field as a viable alternative, one that might offer greater long-term financial rewards, greater authority to do a job, and greater safety if performance was satisfactory. Those just entering the hospital administration field, upon completion of their graduate studies, also read these signs as positive. From their perspective, the for-profit field represented freedom to exercise managerial skills and greater opportunity for rewards and advancements. They and other more experienced hospital administration colleagues are now acting on these perceptions and moving into for-profit firms in the health field. Unless nonprofit governing boards change traditional salary programs, the ultimate result will be a dearth of first-rate executive talent in nonprofit hospitals.

Nonprofit hospitals are going to have to find ways to permit senior management to participate in equity situations to be able to acquire assets subject to capital gains taxes rather than salaries subject to income taxes. If nonprofit hospitals do not face up to this change, top executive talent is ultimately going to move to investor-owned chains where such possibilities already exist. Some nonprofit hospital organizations are already experimenting in this direction by creating for-profit contract management firms owned by their own senior management. Under a parent-subsidiary organizational model this can be accomplished without jeopardizing the nonprofit status of a nonprofit hospital corporation.

AN EXPANDED CEO ROLE

In a hospital today, it is necessary to have a full-time leader with broad authority in the organization if it is to survive. It is no longer a question of whether it is desirable, or whether a medical staff likes the idea or not; the economics of the external environment require a clear-cut identifiable leader. It will occur however only after trustees appreciate that a formal leader in an organization has to, in fact, be where the buck stops; there must also be an awareness recognized throughout the hospital organization that there are no avenues around the chief executive. As long as there is a belief, in any part of the organization, that the authoritative person at the top of the structure can be circumvented the coordination of the major activities will be delayed or interferred with to the detriment of meeting organizational objectives.

Hospital executives recognize that the organizational structures of their institutions are not suitable to withstand the societal pressures now being focused on the health care field. They are also aware that most governing boards wait too long before making decisions and are apt to delay decisions until a consensus develops.

The traditional wobbly three-legged stool is not an appropriate structure for coping with the increased internal stress which is created by current issues. The three legs of hospital organization must be unified. Unification is necessary even though it will probably meet with internal resistance, much of it coming from a medical staff. Deciding to create a strong central authority position in a hospital organization in the chief executive is a necessity. Making a decision to shore up the existing traditional organizational structure by centralizing authority largely in the hands of a single individual is not in keeping with the tradition of the nonprofit hospital. It will likely be misunderstood and needs to be buttressed by a governing board entering into a contract with the chief executive, one that prevents hasty decisions in the event of serious disagreements over the authorities of the chief executive.

The survival of a hospital is a board responsibility that cannot be shared with others. Trustees represent ownership, and ownership carries with it an obligation to decide how best to survive. Given the conditions that now exist, governing boards when they search for an appropriate organizational mechanism to ensure survival will eventually reach a conclusion in most hospitals that the chief executive position is the appropriate location to become the leader of a hospital and a coordinator of all its aspects: governance, management, and medical staff. The major value of a contract in reaching this decision is that the contract defines authorities and is a clear indication to all parties that the chief executive officer is their leader.

When the future of nonprofit hospitals is examined, it is clear that the traditional relationship of a chief executive and governing board needs to be buttressed in three ways:

1. By providing opportunities for participation in related equity opportunities for senior management personnel
2. By providing a chief executive with greater freedom in decision making over all parts of the hospital organization
3. By certifying the defined relationship between governing board and chief executive by contract.

These new pathways will be accepted only reluctantly, but those who attempt to maintain the status quo in terms of philosophy and organizational structure, in the face of what is now happening, will only be ignoring reality.

Chapter 20

The Changing of the Guard[*]

The role of the chief executive has undergone a gradual, steady change because of its growing complexity since the close of World War II. However, the present change now underway is an abrupt departure from the traditional role of a CEO. The contrast between what was and what will be clearly demonstrates a difference in the types of leadership needed for these two periods of time.

During this century, the role of the hospital CEO had approximately the same dimensions from 1900 until 1945. This role was typified by the title of superintendent. Emphasis was on solving day-to-day operational problems: five minutes here, five minutes there. Reaching back into a hip pocket of experience to answer questions, listening to complaints, seeing salesmen—these were the activities of importance. Once a month the superintendent would meet with the governing board to review accounts receivable and approve accounts payable.

Beginning in 1945 the pace of hospital activities began to accelerate and the superintendent became the administrator. The executive's role no longer focused only on internal operating problems. Instead, the CEO administrator frequently left the premises to attend meetings. The role of the state hospital association emerged. The state association's rapidly growing activities were staffed by volunteer administrators who began to deal directly with state legislators and their committees, as well as the bureaucracy of state government. Cooperative and concerted effort was the theme of the day in confronting the increasing rules and regulations promulgated by all levels of government. The involvement of administrators in these outside activities was aimed at protecting the internal operations of the hospitals so that they could continue to function as they had in the past.

By the early part of the 1960s the administrator had become the executive director, reflecting the continuing drift into more complexity. New departments

---

*Adapted by permission from *Hospitals*, Vol. 58, No. 23, December 1, 1984. Copyright 1984, American Hospital Publishing, Inc.

were being added, diagnostic and treatment procedures were becoming more comprehensive, costs were rising, and physical plants were being expanded—the climate was one of unbridled growth. Cost reimbursement was the dominant form of payment to hospitals and became even more important as the Medicare legislation, which adopted a cost-reimbursement system, passed Congress in 1965. The CEO experienced even more demands on his time; not only were internal operations continuing to grow and require attention, but the cost of new equipment, driven by technology developments, outstripped philanthropy. Thereupon, the debt market was entered.

The CEO's attention was now centered on unfolding developments, and in order to manage the internal operations while staying abreast of the external problems, his working day lengthened. The executive's job requirements did not change, but grew. As long as the CEO had the constitution of a bull moose, he survived.

By 1970 the executive director had become the executive vice-president. The governing board's role remained largely unchanged through these decades. The board remained as demanding of the CEO's time as it had been in the past and expected the CEO to be knowledgeable on all matters brought to its attention. From the board's viewpoint the CEO was still a facilitator, taking care of the physical plant, coordinating hospital activities with the medical staff, and increasingly representing the institution to outside agencies and organizations. This often meant that 50 percent of his time was spent outside of the hospital. The work day, as well as the work week, continued to lengthen. As the decade of the 1980s began, the title of the CEO again changed with president becoming popular and widely used.

Throughout all of the periods of management shifts the structure of governing boards in nonprofit and public hospitals remained unchanged. The size of most governing boards continued to be too large with too many board committees. With increasing frequency, marketplace opportunities were lost because of a lengthy approval process. Competitors in the marketplace were often able to take advantage of the slow decision-making process of the nonprofit hospitals.

Aware of this constraint, chief executives of nonprofit hospitals recognized the necessity for overcoming slow decision making by governance. Even though the corporate restructuring of the parent-subsidiary organization model had originally found its supporters among those CEOs looking for a way around the Certificate of Need process, it quickly became obvious to thoughtful CEOs that it could also be used as a means of getting around a cumbersome board structure. The size and composition of the hospital board could be left in place, but any activity not directly related to inpatient care could be handled more expeditiously through another route. Because these other corporate boards are much smaller in size and have senior management executives as part of the governance structure, the slowness in decision making could be avoided.

Since some of the nonpatient care activities are organized into for-profit corporations, the measuring of management performance includes criteria normally applied in business. The entrepreneurial spirit was propagated among the ranks of CEOs in nonprofit hospitals as they have watched many of their professional colleagues move into for-profit health care organizations. The attractiveness of the for-profit sector to those in the nonprofit arena is related not solely to personal economics but also to the expanded responsibilities and authorities of the CEOs in the for-profits, particularly with respect to a governing board. How to deal with an outdated and old-fashioned governing board structure has become a matter of growing importance.

The role of the chief executive is no longer that of a facilitator, but rather is closely akin to that of a corporate president with two exceptions. Most governing boards in nonprofit hospitals possess a stewardship mentality, where the trustees exercise prudence and caution so as not to dissipate the monies and assets entrusted to their responsibility. This philosophy is no longer viable in the new economic risk-taking environment of the hospital. The CEO now has to be acknowledged by trustees as the head of the organization that includes the governing board as well as of internal operations. In a very real sense the CEO has to become the formally acknowledged leader of the entire organization, not just operations. The shift must now be made from production manager to corporation president.

The other exception is the relationship to a medical staff. This is unique, with no parallels in other industries, although it is sometimes compared to faculties in university organizations. Physicians, however, are not beholden to a hospital and have a strong sense of self-independence. This results in a loose link to the organizational setting that is not apt to change in the foreseeable future. Medical staffs are unlikely to acknowledge that they are part and parcel of a hospital organization, except in a peripheral manner. Their role through an organized medical staff will remain the same to assure patient safety.

At the core of the change now underway is a shift in the relationship of governing board and chief executive. Instead of a chief executive being thought of by board members as an agent for carrying out their decisions, the chief executive will be viewed as the leader of an organization that includes the governing board. The extent of the authorities exercised and the degree of influence wielded by an executive will be considerably greater. This response will be necessary in an economically dominated environment where the decision-making process of governance must be greatly speeded up in order to successfully compete. Executive skills will be increasingly recognized by governing boards as a prized commodity that can spell the difference between success and failure of an institution. The board will see its role change from making the decisions that were implemented by a chief executive to assisting a chief executive in the decision-making process.

Those chief executives accustomed to the role of facilitator will have a difficult time in shifting to the new role of organization leader. Those who make this transition will be joined by a younger generation of executives who are unimpaired by the constraints of tradition. A decade from now health care executives will look back and clearly recognize that the 1980s was a time when there was a changing of the guard in the ranks of hospital professionals.

Chapter 21

The Day After*

Charlie Jones opened his eyes, looked at the clock, which read 7:40 a.m., and then gazed up at the ceiling asking himself if he had just had a nightmare or if he really had been—terminated—let go—fired—relieved of his administrative responsibilities—whatever it was that Russell Adams, the board chairman, had said to him at 8:13 p.m. last night when he was informed that his services as the chief executive of Riley Memorial Hospital were no longer needed.

Automatically, after 23 years as a chief executive, his thoughts turned to the hospital. For the first time in over two decades he realized that his day's activities no longer included the hospital, but were concerned with what he wanted to do for Charlie Jones. Getting out of bed he realized that he could dress leisurely this morning and didn't have to hurry to get to work—there was, for him, no work to go to.

As he adjusted the hot water faucet in the shower he began to ask himself why this had happened. Mentally reviewing various aspects of the hospital operation, he knew that the cost per patient day was next to the lowest of the seven hospitals in the area, so that productivity was not a factor. The physical plant certainly was in A-1 condition. Over the past four years 3 ½ million dollars had been spent to bring mechanical and electrical systems up-to-date and he had paid for these improvements out of operating surpluses. No board member, that he could recall, had taken exception to that activity.

Certainly, he and the board had been concerned that the average occupancy had fallen to the mid-60s in the last 18 months. This decrease in occupancy had forced the hospital to lay off 134 personnel, in order to keep the hospital from going in the red. That had caused some problems with a few trustees because several physicians had gone to them and complained about the closing of two specialized

---

*Adapted from *ACHE* with permission of American College of Healthcare Executives, © November/ December 1985.

nursing units and the commingling of their patients with patients on the general medical and surgical floors. On balance, he concluded that the board had understood the necessity for taking these steps and that there had been general support for doing so.

Stepping out of the shower he directed his thoughts toward his relationships with the board and the medical staff and asked himself how they had changed. What immediately came to mind was his inability to control the number of matters of importance that he had to increasingly bring to the board. Because of the speed with which conditions were changing in the external environment, he was no longer able to control the rate at which he had to bring them up. He had lost the ability to time decision making to the pace at which the board could comfortably handle the items.

As he was getting dressed he realized that his area of greatest concern about the governing board was its understanding of the medical staff and individual physician relationships to the hospital; or, as he often had said to himself, their lack of understanding. He had known for more than a year that this lack of understanding was the most likely area to give him problems. As the surplus of physicians had grown, coupled with the downturn in the use of physicians and hospitals by the public, he had watched the medical staff become fearful of its economic security in the future.

He had been particularly surprised by some of the older, well-established practitioners who had been telling him that they had been experiencing a downturn in the number of patients they were seeing. Instinctively he had known that this would inevitably lead to difficulties with them, as the hospital would be economically forced to compete for revenues on the same turf as physicians on the medical staff. What bothered him the most was that he had seen this conflict coming, had tried to prepare the governing board for dealing with this kind of situation, but had had little success because of the four physicians on the governing board.

Pausing to look out the window, he let his eyes follow the path of the youngsters on their way to school as he recalled the difficulties he had encountered in a recent board meeting when he had attempted to review a proposed contract submitted by a health maintenance organization. Rather than going over the contract, as he had expected, the physicians had taken the position that the hospital's responsibility was to be supportive of private practitioners engaged in fee-for-service medicine and that the hospital should not be a party to any payment scheme that deviated from what was already in place. He remembered thinking, at the time, that the four board member physicians probably regarded his actions as being the first step in an attempt to take over the medical staff.

After the board meeting he had walked out to the parking lot with the board chairman where they had conversed for almost an hour about what had happened, and the chairman had assured him that he knew those physicians and that they could be counted on to keep the hospital's needs and interests above those of the medical staff. While he only half-believed what Russell Adams said he mentally conceded to himself that this might indeed be true, given time and the changing events going on in the hospital field.

As he sat down to breakfast he stared out of the window lost in thought. Thinking back over the last six months he began to appreciate that his naming Bill Handy chief operating officer and turning over all of the internal operations to him, which had been fully endorsed by the board, had really never been understood or accepted by many of the physicians who considered his role to consist primarily of serving the interests of the medical staff. The fact that he had little familiarity with the parking problem of physicians, which had surfaced at a general medical staff meeting, had led to comments being made in the corridors by physicians that Charlie Jones really didn't care whether Riley Memorial had a medical staff or not.

Finishing his cup of coffee he thought about the straw that broke the camel's back. All too vividly the events of the last three weeks rushed through his mind. On Monday, three weeks ago, Bill Handy told him that he had received a telephone call from a local real estate broker, with whom he was friendly, indicating that the hospital's three radiologists had purchased a 2½-acre site across the street from the hospital and were planning on building an ambulatory imaging center. Hearing this, he had reached into a file drawer in his desk and quickly scanned the hospital's contract with the radiologists. While there was no provision preventing them from investing in this kind of activity, the contract did specify that their full-time professional services were to be devoted to the hospital. The contract further specified that any exceptions could only be made by the chief executive of the hospital.

Armed with the contract, he had gone to the radiology department and looked up Dr. Ralph Kemper, the chief, whom he had known for the last 15 years. Sitting in Ralph's office drinking coffee together he had asked him about the broker's information. Dr. Kemper, without hesitation, said that it was true, that they had the schematics in hand from the architect and had a preliminary understanding with the largest local bank about a loan. When asked about the hospital's contract, Ralph had indicated that the three radiologists had agreed that they would not divert ambulatory patients from using the hospital and went on to add that the three planned to staff it on their days off and bring in one additional radiologist, who would be completing his residency in three months. They did not plan on bringing him into their partnership that served the hospital but planned to employ him by the new company, "Imaging Center, Inc.," which was the vehicle they had created to undertake this venture.

Finishing his cup of coffee, Charlie had left Ralph's office with a sinking feeling in the pit of his stomach that the wheels were now set in motion for a confrontation that could not be avoided. He knew that the three radiologists were regarded by their colleagues as the best in the city and that any attempt made by the hospital to enforce its contract with them would create a real storm with the entire medical staff. Yet to do nothing would lead to a significant loss of revenues. In spite of the assurances of the radiologists it was clear that the building of an imaging center across the street from the hospital was no coincidence. Charlie knew he was caught in the middle without any workable alternatives. He remembered he had listed possibilities in his mind:

- Go along and do nothing.
- Threaten to terminate their contract.
- Have the board hold a session with them.
- Bring it up at the Joint Conference Committee meeting.
- Find an alternative radiology group and give notice of cancellation of contract.

As he had mulled over the list, he realized that the board would be willing to hold a meeting with them, but when the chips were down they would not force the issue, but somehow would expect the hospital management to develop a program that would compensate for lost revenues. At that point Charlie smiled to himself, the safest way out for him would be to make no waves and get along by going along. If he followed that course it would be about three years before the impact would be felt in the financial statement of the hospital and in the meantime he could leisurely look around for another CEO position and be out long before the hospital faced serious financial problems. He quickly rejected this notion saying to himself that this was not in the hospital's best interests, yet he knew that he would be exposed if he took any other course. While he hadn't anticipated what had taken place, when it had happened he had known that something like this had been bound to arise, sooner or later, and had raised the question with the executive committee of the governing board six months earlier about a long-term contract for his services.

He had made the point at the meeting where he brought up the subject that the hospital field was undergoing rapid change which was adversely affecting the financial picture and that he could foresee the time when he would be coming to the board with recommendations that would be highly unpopular with the medical staff but would be necessary in order to maintain the financial viability of the hospital. His comments were politely received by those present and it was indicated that this would be studied. He had heard nothing further on the subject and had found himself reluctant to raise the issue again with them.

As he looked back from his perspective of this morning, he realized that he should have been much more forceful about a contract. He had been afraid that if he had brought up the subject a second time he would have been turned down and then would have been forced to decide whether to stay or to seriously look for another hospital. Had he looked around and received an offer from another hospital, he had known that one of the conditions of employment would have been a contract. He knew that this was becoming routine in CEO positions being filled in the last couple of years. He also knew that CEOs with long tenure, such as he had, were seldom able to achieve the same results. Boards usually had to go through replacing one CEO with another in order to learn that competent executives were no longer willing to take chances with boards seeing issues realistically and were therefore seeking to protect themselves financially when taking on a job that had become increasingly risky in the last few years.

As he reviewed the contract situation, he recalled two other instances in the past three years where he had thought about the desirability of having a contract. The first had taken place over the hospital constructing a medical office building five miles away in a newly developing area of the city. At that time he had discussed the idea with the Medical Executive Committee, whose members had agreed with him about the timing and the location of such a facility, but had taken the position that this was a physician activity and the hospital should not be involved. They had been so adamant that Charlie had backed off without pursuing it further. To this day he regretted not having gone ahead with the project.

The other incident had occurred about a year ago when he had wanted to develop three off-site primary care centers. Again he had discussed it with the Medical Executive Committee, as well as the Executive Committee of the governing board. Both groups had seen the desirability of this program, but as before, the physicians had taken the position that the hospital should not be involved, and had added a wrinkle to their argument that had led the board to agree with their position. The physicians had claimed that if the hospital went ahead this would be the corporate practice of medicine. Charlie thought to himself, if I had a contract I would have pushed harder in both of those situations. Thinking back over those two instances he realized that physicians desire to keep the hospital as an economic neutral in the health field and certainly do not want competition from hospitals in addition to what they already encounter from their own colleagues.

The difference between those two situations and this last problem with radiologists was that this latest incident no longer kept the hospital neutral. As Charlie saw it, it would lead to a significant drop in radiology revenue, and therefore was a step beyond what had previously been the case. If he had had a contract he would not have been forced to so readily accept the political aspects, but would have had more organizational flexibility to protect the best interests of the hospital. Looking to the future he knew that his successor, whoever it might be, would need a contract if the hospital was going to remain financially viable.

Grudgingly Charlie had to admit to himself that on The Day After he sure wished he had had a contract. Knowing the board members as he did he figured that they probably would give him three months' severance pay, the title to the hospital car he drove, and wish him well.

At 54 years of age he knew he had to find a position. He didn't have enough saved so that he could retire, nor did he want to, but he was concerned that his age would be a barrier to employment. Thinking about retirement he suddenly realized that when the hospital had altered its pension plan six years before, vesting had been an important issue but had ultimately been resolved by establishing a ten-year period and that prior employment in the hospital would not be counted. Thinking back to those discussions he knew that as of today he would receive no pension benefits even though he had been at the hospital for 23 years. Ruefully he admitted to himself that he had looked out for the interests of the hospital for a long time, but he sure had ignored his own interests.

As he thought about the radiology problem that had brought everything to a head, he realized that physicians today were concerned with the growing surplus of physicians and the decline in the use of medical services by the public. They would take whatever steps they could to protect their incomes, even at the expense of the hospital. He admitted to himself that if he was in their shoes he would do the same.

Finishing breakfast Charlie decided to go for a walk and think about his own future. As he put on his jacket he couldn't help but wonder what lay ahead for him and Myra, his wife. At his age he speculated that he might not be too salable in the marketplace and, given the difficulties of managing a hospital in the last few years, he wasn't too sure that he wanted to go back to a hospital. He had been thinking for the last year or so that he ought to go into some kind of business for himself. As he thought about that possibility, he knew that any step in that direction would require remortgaging his house and at his age, with one son still in college, he wasn't sure that taking such a risk was advisable. If the business failed he would have nothing for the rest of his life.

Turning the corner and starting to walk down the next block he wondered what other kinds of work he might consider. Given his knowledge of a hospital he wondered if he should go into consulting. This would be a field where he would be able to help others gain from his experiences and at the same time earn an excellent livelihood. He thought he might look into that possibility even though he wasn't sure how one goes about getting clients.

Another idea occurred to him—what about becoming the president of an HMO—it certainly is a growing field that will be needing leadership. He knew the health field, had served for six years on the board of the Blue Cross plan, and always had an interest in prepayment. As he continued in thought he concluded that claims management wouldn't be much different from the way you handle accounts receivable in the hospital, and marketing should be easy if the plan had a good package of benefits to offer.

Suddenly his thoughts turned back to the events of the last few days. He knew that what had taken placed was not a reflection on his administrative skills; he ran a good hospital and he knew it, but he had just been trapped by a set of circumstances. When he recommended to the board that they terminate the radiologists' contract by giving the required 90-day notice, since they were dead set on moving ahead, the board had assured him that they were all in accord that this was the proper course to follow. He remembered that he had carefully drafted the letter to the radiologists clearly indicating that this was a board decision and that, acting as its agent, he was transmitting the action to them by letter. As a courtesy he had sent a copy of the letter to the president of the medical staff. While he knew the letter would create a problem he had not been prepared for the storm that ensued. For the three days following the receipt of the letter the radiologists had spent the majority of each day buttonholing as many members of the medical staff as possible, telling the physicians that Charlie Jones was taking steps to move them out of their percentage arrangement with the hospital to a salary basis and that this was the reason behind his opposition to their building a new facility across the street.

By the end of the week the president of the medical staff decided to call a special meeting of that body to discuss the hospital's intrusion into the private practice of medicine. The meeting was held the following Wednesday evening in the hospital's cafeteria. Charlie recalled the meeting vividly—it was one of the worst he had ever attended. It had started off with the president reading a copy of the letter to the entire medical staff. Charlie remembered looking around the room and thinking to himself that this was the largest turnout in the history of the hospital. When the president finished, a dozen hands shot up in the audience. The first one to his feet was a physician who seldom admitted a patient but was an outspoken critic of the administration. He quickly pointed out that the radiologists had as much right as others on the staff to go into another business for themselves, even if it was the same one they practiced in the hospital, and that he, for one, would refer all of his ambulatory patients to the Imaging Center for diagnosis.

From the other side of the room another physician stood up, was recognized by the chair, and said that the real trouble with the hospital was not the medical staff but the administration. He indicated that the physicians had been asking for a private dining room for three years and it still was only a hope; that enough parking spaces were not provided for doctors; and that in his eyes Charlie Jones wanted to run the medical staff just like he did the rest of the hospital and that what was really needed was a motion to terminate the administrator. This was immediately seconded, passed by a substantial majority with only a scattering of nays, and the meeting was adjourned shortly thereafter.

At the next meeting of the board Charlie had been excused after the routine matters had been disposed of and he had gone back to his office knowing that the physician board members were going to present the staff recommendation. While he had mentally counted heads during the time between the special medical staff meeting and this board meeting, he had made no attempt to meet individually with selected board members because he had told himself that after 23 years of service the board had long ago come to a decision about his abilities and that the members would therefore vote accordingly, if the question of his continued employment came to a vote. Insofar as he could tell, of the thirteen board members, the four physician board members would vote in accordance with the wishes of the staff, two lay board members would automatically vote with them as they always did, and the others would be in Charlie's corner. He thought it would be tight, but that he would win. When at 8:13 p.m. Russell Adams had come to his office and informed him that he had been terminated, he had been shocked. He thought he had heard incorrectly, but Russ had repeated the statement when he had asked him again.

Returning from his walk he slowly hung up his jacket and began to recount the board vote of the previous evening. Russ Adams had told him that the vote had been close and he had only lost by the narrowest of margins, which he took to mean the vote had been seven to six for terminating his services. That meant that one vote he had counted on had swung against him. As he reviewed the possible swing votes he realized that it really didn't matter, but what he hadn't fully appreciated up to now was that a bloc of votes, even if less than a majority, can be effective in swaying a group decision.

When the governing board had decided to include four physicians of the medical staff in its group some eight years ago, he had not objected because the size of the board had been increased from nine to thirteen at the same time and he had concluded that since the physicians would only be one-third of the votes he really didn't have to be concerned. Now, in retrospect, he acknowledged to himself that it really did make a major difference, as he had witnessed on innumerable occasions when the four had voted together. He could recall no instance where the board vote had been against the position of the physicians when they all voted alike. When the physicians had voted three to one on issues, he remembered several times when the board would vote with the one and not the three. But when the physicians all stood together the rest of the governing board had always gone along with their thinking.

Having picked up the daily newspaper on his way into the house from his walk, he sat down in his rocking chair in the living room determined to take his mind off of the events of the previous day. Finishing the sports section he casually turned to the Help Wanted pages and scanned the columns wondering if he would shortly be reading them carefully every day. His thoughts were interrupted by the ringing of the phone. Answering it he found himself talking with an old friend, the chief executive of a large hospital in an adjoining state, who had just heard about his termination from Bill Handy, the CEO at Riley Memorial. His friend said that he had gone through a similar experience not too many years before and had found it to be traumatic. Like Charlie, on the day after, he had wished he had a contract. When he took his present position he had been firm on the necessity for one and looking back he told him that as the CEO of a hospital he thought it to be the only prudent course to follow. He told Charlie that before he had a contract he never had realized the advantages of having one. He indicated that he considered the recommendations he now made to his board to be more open and frank, but that he was comfortable in doing so because of the economic safeguards that protected him in the event he had to make a choice between telling it like it is versus providing the politically palatable answer or recommendation. He then asked Charlie if he was going to retain an attorney.

Charlie admitted that the thought had crossed his mind and he was considering calling the hospital attorney because they had worked together for over 15 years and had a warm, personal relationship. Charlie's friend immediately reacted to this comment by pointing out that he should not do that because the attorney represents the hospital as his client and Charlie had to appreciate the fact that he may well become an adversary of the hospital. Charlie needed to discuss the matter with an attorney not associated with the hospital or any of its governing board members. Charlie acknowledged this made sense and thanked his friend for calling him.

As he put down the phone he began to consider more seriously the question of whether or not to discuss what had happened with an outside attorney. He recalled hearing in corridor conversations at the last meeting of the state hospital association that three chief executives had, in the recent few months, reached settlements of several hundreds of thousands of dollars each, after encountering similar situations with similar results. He wondered if they had experienced any difficulties in finding a new position because they had sought legal remedies. Charlie thought about how he would answer the question "Have you taken, or are you contemplating, any legal action against your former employer?" and would such an admission rule him out of further consideration. On the other hand, he wasn't sure that he was still marketable, having crossed the 50-year mark a while back, in which case he wouldn't have to worry about answering such a question.

Then there was the question of whether or not it was ethical to sue the institution. Not long ago he had terminated 134 employees because of the decline in census and not one of them had threatened to take the hospital to court. Was his situation that much different? Yet, didn't his 23 years count for something? The more he thought about it the more he came to feel that he should at least sit down with an attorney experienced in this field and get an opinion as to what course he should follow. Having dealt with attorneys for years he appreciated that seeking counsel didn't mean he would sue the board, but that he really needed to understand his current situation. Never having been here before he thought he might benefit from such a conversation.

With that he began considering calling Russ Adams and suggesting that the board may have overreacted the previous evening and might want to reconsider the action it had taken. Since the vote had been so close one person changing positions would be enough to reverse the decision. Yet, the more he considered doing this the more he realized that neither he nor the board members would forget what had taken place and that it would color any situation that might be encountered in the future. Furthermore, suppose no one did change his vote in Charlie's favor but instead one or more of those who had voted for him elected to change their votes. All things considered, Charlie concluded, the best for all concerned would not be to contact Russ Adams with this idea. For better or worse, what was done was done and he realized he needed to get on with his life. But, he vowed, I am not going to make the same mistakes in the future that I have in the past.

TO THE READER

What happened to Charlie Jones in the months following his sudden departure from Riley Memorial Hospital? Did he move on to another hospital as its CEO? Did he leave the field and start a new career? Did he stay in town and establish his own business? Did he sue the hospital?

To all of these questions there is only one answer—we don't know what happened to Charlie. We hope for the best for him, but what really came to pass we will never know. If he was lucky, the dark cloud of misfortune had a silver lining. If he was unlucky, he found out how tough a place the world can be for an unemployed executive.

One thing Charlie did learn from his experience: The hospital of today is a risky place for a chief executive. It will become more so in the years just ahead, no matter how capable the CEO might be. When a field is in transition, events occur that are beyond the control of the organization because the environment in which it operates is no longer stable and predictable. Under such circumstances the CEO needs to protect himself, as well as maintaining a deep concern for the hospital and its role in our society.

Chapter 22

The Compleat Executive

In the present-day world of excessive government regulation, performance expectations for hospital executives have risen to new heights. When federal expectations are coupled with patient, trustee, physician, employee, and community pressures for administrative performance, a need for the ''compleat executive'' is created.

A hospital executive who is truly a professional generalist manager is capable of meeting these new expectations. A master executive technician is certain to fail.

What is a compleat executive? What characteristics separate the professional administrator from the bureaucratic technician when each practices in the same environment and with the same basic knowledge?

A graduate student enters into a profession through the study of a specialized curriculum. The student is selected by teacher members of the profession who believe they can identify basic individual characteristics necessary to the later emergence of a competent practitioner. This selection does not guarantee the ultimate development of a true professional; rather it is an optimum choice of a combination of characteristics possessed by prospective students, reviewed and selected in a limited period of time.

CHARACTER, PERSONALITY, AND STYLE

Ultimately, three levels of individual characteristics determine which students will continue to develop professional excellence. In an emerging profession, such as hospital administration, these characteristics are uniquely important for success because much of the knowledge of the field has not yet been rigorously tested in a theoretical way but rests on generalizations derived from institutional work situations.

The three levels central to all professions are character, personality, and style. The most basic requirement of a compleat executive is character, or those individual mental and ethical traits that are demonstrated in administrative practice through moral excellence and firmness. A person's character underpins his personality; which is a complex of individual characteristics that are exhibited through emotional and behavioral tendencies. At the outer edges of personality a person acquires a style, the skill and grace by which an individual expresses himself.

A compleat executive is highly developed and mature in character, personality, and style. The world external to an individual experiences these characteristics in reverse order, by first noting a person's style, later experiencing his personality, and after time learning about his character.

The style of a hospital executive must be appropriate to a specific institution, its patients, trustees, physicians, employees, and the community leadership. Appropriate skill and grace are defined differently by each group and by individual members within each group. Executive sensitivity is needed to identify the criteria used by members of each group in reaching their judgments about an individual's style. Some criteria, such as always being prepared with the right information and data for every meeting, is used by all groups, since some standards are commonly accepted in all groups and most individuals within each group. Other criteria are specific to a particular group; the businessman trustee expects business skills in the hospital executive, while a physician expects a comprehension of clinical problems and an ability to converse easily on medical matters. Likewise, the cook, yardman, intensive care nurse, plant superintendent, fiscal officer, chaplain, maid, and nurse's aide each expect understanding and clear communication in their terms.

EXECUTIVE CLASS

A professional hospital executive knows how to converse in the language of each group and understands each value system and the operational concepts used by both internal and external groups interacting with the hospital and the executive.

To a compleat executive each group, and subgroup, is a challenge. To become indoctrinated with their mores, habits, and customs, to stay current, to catch the shifting trends in each group, to share respect and ideas in a variegated pattern of thought, cross-purposes, and mixed emotions is on the daily agenda of a professional hospital executive.

The ultimate compliment regarding an executive's style is to say the individual has class. This means that each group recognizes the professional executive as being in touch with the group and therefore is accorded a high social rank. Such a person embodies the group's definition of elegance. A plant engineer's definition of elegance and that of the chairman of the board are different, but the compliment of each is an accolade.

Conversely, a bureaucratic executive has little elegance, or presence, and lacks an understanding of group values and expectations. Sensitivities are limited, are unidirectional, and not omnidirectional. Such an executive has no worries about being a chameleon, or a tiger changing stripes. This blindness to other personal and group needs ultimately leads to an opinion that the individual is banal and ordinary. The penalty paid is positional. A bureaucratic executive is not given an opportunity to lead in a crisis because there is no personal respect from employees, physicians, trustees, and community.

The compleat executive does not lose the common touch.

Administrative style blends imperceptibly into an individual executive's personality. Emotional and behavioral traits inexorably intertwine with the individual's ego. The professional administrator cannot afford the luxury of an unbridled ego. However, there must be an ego strong enough to believe in the capacity to lead and steady enough not to need adoration and acquiescence endlessly. There must be a confidence without a cockiness. A professional administrator must honestly believe that every man is as good as he is, and that he is as good as every other man. The true executive must know how to walk equally with presidents, physicians, orderlies, and technicians.

Emotional security means being flexible, in believing that one's personal way is not always the best way. Delegation is one of the most difficult of administrative skills to acquire and practice. An executive must not be afraid to share authority, responsibility, and knowledge because not to share is to lose in many ways. To avoid risk taking to help another person's growth and development is to stunt both an individual and the hospital. The professional administrator's best role is to set standards of performance for others in the hospital organization and to always expect the best from other persons, to lead by example, and to stay out of another's way as that individual strives to meet expressed expectations.

The personality of an executive must be sufficiently mature to encourage personal development in other people. Despite limited time and energy, an executive must be accessible to all parts of the hospital and to patients, curious about their problems, desires, and motivations. There must be a persistent belief and practice that there is a higher potential in every person who is willing to strive and the administration must be a part of supporting the opportunity to do so.

An effective hospital organization requires predictable behavior in its leaders. A compleat executive must be predictable to the organization under all conditions. Consistency and fair play are the hallmarks of the professional.

The personality of a bureaucratic executive is notable for apathy toward other people, unevenness in equitable treatment, and silence where the need for leadership is obvious. Straightforwardness is often lost in a jungle of indecision and indirect orders. Maddening blind spots about the value of the work of others are commonplace. Personal public accolades are often sought at the expense of others in the hospital organization. Personal failures and inadequacies are hidden behind glowing public utterances. The hospital organization is bent and twisted into a vehicle to flatter a personal ego.

The professional executive strives to react to the feelings of others without losing control of personal emotions and is someone who can find a way to express sympathy and feelings and to maintain a sense of humor.

Underpinning the personality and style is an executive's character. Moral firmness is obvious in times of organizational crisis. Individuals in a hospital experience administrative character quietly. A person of strong character is generally recognized as one who walks with the crowd but keeps his own virtue.

THE EXECUTIVE AS GENERALIST

A professional with character has the firmness of a teacher, yet is recognized as a broad-gauged generalist who always keeps a sense of balance and perspective. Through experience the true executive learns to be a sensitive listener and does not stop discourse by flaunting technical knowledge. There is an awareness that as much can be learned from other people as can be learned from him. Effective writing and speaking is the handmaiden of personal skills.

Professional executives of excellence march to their own drummer because they don't compromise principles, because they are more attuned to inner satisfactions than to fame and fortune. Theirs is the courage to pursue their own dream.

The sine quo non of a compleat executive's character is a general acceptance by others of a personal loyalty, honesty, and caring. Such an executive is known for a breadth of experience, for thinking broadly, as well as being well read in more fields than one's own area of expertise. A sense of adventure is always present and personal fears are unknown to others. There is a personal understanding about individual happiness, contentment, fulfillment, and service. Personal agonies and ecstasies are totally private.

THE DREAM AND THE REALITY

The genius of the professional executive's character is a personal, persistent desire to make the world a shade better for all those who will follow, so that other people won't face the same disappointments and frustrations that may have been lived through earlier. The goal is to bequeath a situation that is manageable and does not require excessive effort on the part of a successor. Fulfillment for the compleat executive is knowing that at the end of a career one has lived and served as he had wished to do so throughout a lifetime of work. The individual will have pursued a dream with pragmatism, recognizing throughout the difference between moonbeams and reality.

A professional executive gradually recognizes through experience that nearly all people are caught up in myths, which they deeply believe, and seldom see true facts and real issues. There is an awareness that the world is not perfect, equitable, or fair, that beyond a certain distant point, time and energy are wasted trying to focus reality for believers in myths.

Reality means that petty criticism and bad motives are often ascribed to the best of personal motives and skilled accomplishments. One learns to rise above pettiness. And also one learns privately that understanding, dedication, and intelligence are no substitute for experience, specific knowledge, and appropriate behavior. The true professional will learn that frustration is a frequent companion.

Reality is learning that fame and respect are two quite separate choices. That the professional hospital executive is in a stewardship role where the expected standard of performance is much beyond the standards of those who do the expecting.

The compleat hospital executive will have learned the reasons for respecting older people, and physicians, whatever their idiosyncrasies. Because the world is constantly changing and people typically resist change, the model executive will often find rationalization and incompetence when rationality and competence are needed.

In the past decade the professional executive's role has been expanded into the local, state, and federal political arena. Because of the variety of issues, obfuscation of motives, and competing pressures, character, personality, and style will acquire greater depth and polish.

The compleat hospital executive will find happiness in having more work to do than time to do it in, greater demands upon resources than ability to meet the demands, and an ongoing sense of continually helping people through working in a profession characterized by constant challenge.

Chapter 23

The Hidden Side of Hospital Productivity*

FRAYING OF THE SOCIAL ETHIC

The social ethic that drove hospitals for decades began to fray around the edges at the time the present decade was entered. Truisms like ''the best possible quality of care at the lowest possible cost'' turned out to be less than total truth. The fraying became an unraveling when the hospital world fell apart around 1983 as admissions declined, average lengths of stay shortened, equipment became even more complex and costly, government ratcheted down its payments or froze them, business and industry took a ''get tough'' stance, and outpatient procedures became more commonplace. In a nutshell, economic competition arrived on the hospital scene. The social ethic now no longer dominates but shares primacy with economic concerns. The hospital is now being economically driven as cost reimbursement departs the scene and is replaced with prospective pricing.

The hospital field has been impacted by two major events that took place about ten years apart. The most significant one occurred in the early '70s when the price of a barrel of oil rose to $36 and the U.S. economy was hard hit, shifting from one of ample resources to one of scarce resources. This started the chain of events that finally caught up to the hospital field in 1983-84. A number of separate trends all came together at that point in time.

The second major event was when the federal government adopted DRGs. This was a public signal that cost reimbursement was dead and that pricing was the wave of the future. As a result of the recession in the early part of the decade, business and industry realized that they had to control their labor costs more carefully and took a hard look at the health insurance premiums they were paying. As labor contracts were renegotiated, co-insurance and larger front-end deduct-

---

*Adapted from *Health Progress*, Vol. 66, pp. 24–27 and 56, with permission of The Catholic Health Association of the United States, © November 1985.

ibles started to reappear. Business executives began to appreciate that they could affect what they spent for health care. In casting around for other mechanisms that would control premium costs, capitation plans moved from the back burner up to the front burner, with both government and business favorably disposed toward them.

As first-dollar coverage declined and capitation plans gained support, hospitals felt both effects. Looking back to the early '70s, were the Arabs responsible for what has been happening to hospitals? It would seem as if they were partially responsible, though they didn't have this in mind.

Other events took place that created the present climate in the hospital field. Knowing that hospital costs were suspect in the public's mind, the American Hospital Association developed a voluntary cost-containment program in the mid-1970s that had a modest impact on rising hospital costs, but after two years it ran out of steam and was quietly buried. In early 1983 the Congressional Budget Office issued a report on the prospects for the Medicare Hospital Insurance Trust Fund and predicted that it would run out of funds by 1988 or 1989. From the viewpoint of the administration and of Congress, this would be intolerable since they are preoccupied with trying to keep the annual federal deficit below 200 billion dollars per year. Knowing that the minorities would not look favorably on a means test, or on increased deductibles, or increased co-insurance, the government had to look for a safer target. The prospective payment mechanism of DRGs filled the bill.

The results of the Medicare Hospital Insurance Trust Fund expenditures for hospitals for 1984 were gratifying. The dollars had been budgeted at $41 billion, but when the figures all came in, the expenditures turned out to be $38 billion. Was the shift from cost reimbursement to prospective pricing responsible for what had taken place? To what extent had the efforts of employers in restructuring their employee benefit programs played a role in stemming the rise in hospital costs and the decline in patient days? Did the shift from the social ethic to economic competition lead to substantial improvements in hospital productivity because it became fashionable for hospital executives to manage their institutions under these circumstances?

A MULTIFACETED CONCEPT

Given all of the cross currents of events and trends that have been at work on hospitals, it is appropriate to review the meaning of productivity, a multifaceted concept. Productivity is not a synonym for efficiency, though efficiency is a factor that needs consideration. Efficiency is concerned with getting more bang for the buck. Productivity deals with the results obtained—did the bigger bang do the job for which it was intended? Part of the equation becomes one of understanding what is society's expectation of hospitals in satisfying wants or needs. For instance, hospitals can claim that they are partially responsible for the results summarized in Table 23–1, that took place between 1972 and 1982 per 100,000 population.

These results indicate that somewhere along the line improvements in productivity took place. Some of what was obtained by society was related to what goes on in a hospital, some was unrelated. To the extent hospitals contributed, they improved productivity. The public probably is aware of this, but the more basic public question of concern is the degree to which hospitals are inefficient and spending money that is wasteful or are making unconscionable profits.

LESSONS ABOUT HOSPITAL PRODUCTIVITY

The public probably would be surprised by the answer that would be given by most hospital chief executives if asked "How did it go at your hospital last year?" Almost always the answer is along the lines of "Well, the census dropped 10 to 20 percent but the hospital had the largest bottom line in its history." If pursued, it turns out that admissions were down slightly, the average length of stay declined from one-half to one full day, and a substantial layoff of employees occurred for

Table 23–1 Selected Causes of Death, 1972–1982 Per 100,000

	1972	1982	
Death Rate	940	852	9.4%
Life Expectancy	71.3	74.6	+4.6%

Causes of Death	Per 100,000		Percent Change
All Causes	940	852	−9.4%
(1) Diseases of Heart	360.8	326	−9.6
(2) Malignant Neoplasms	167.3	187	+11.9
(3) Cerebrovascular Disease	102.1	68.0	−33.0
(4) Accidents	55.2	40.6	−26.4
(5) Chronic Pulmonary Disease	14.2	25.8	+81.7
(6) Pneumonia and Influenza	29.8	21.1	−29.2
(7) Diabetes Mellitus	18.2	14.9	−18.1
(8) Suicide	18.8	12.2	−35.1
(9) Chronic Liver Disease	15.9	11.9	−25.2
(10) Atherosclerosis	15.5	11.6	−25.2

Source: Advance Report of Final Mortality Statistics, *1982 Monthly Vital Statistics Report,* Vol. 33, Number 9, Supplement, U.S. Department of Health and Human Services, December 20, 1984; Monthly Vital Statistics Report, *Final Mortality Statistics, 1973,* Vol. 23, Number 11, Supplement 2, December 10, 1975.

the first time. A belt tightening took place. When it became necessary, the chief executive took the required steps to prevent a sharp decline in productivity. The lesson is clear—hospitals, like other enterprises, are as productive as they have to be, and no more.

In determining how far is far enough, the initial reaction of the chief executive is often one of over-reaction because of not being sure of where or when the organization may hit bottom. A preferred course is to play it safe in order to avoid serious financial difficulties. This same phenomenon is observable in other industries. When the automative industry had a lock on the domestic market, it behaved in the same way as hospitals. When foreign imports became a serious threat that jeopardized the financial viability of the Big Three, they moved with speed and determination to correct their shortcomings. The same behavior patterns are observable in banks, trucking, and airlines, which have responded vigorously when faced with economic competition under deregulation.

The second lesson about productivity is equally clear—organizations (including hospitals) that become fiscally imperiled move rapidly to improve productivity once they recognize the economic dangers.

Hospital executives, like those in other industries, are not apt to seek to improve productivity if there is no organizational threat at hand, and if the actions to be taken require terminating employees. In this urbanized society in which we live, organizational decision makers appreciate that losing one's job is a serious matter that is not to be taken lightly. Decisions cannot be made merely to satisfy an abstract notion about being as efficient as possible. No one wants to be regarded by employees as cruel or inhuman.

If a chief executive believes he is the only person associated with the organization who foresees financial difficulty he is unlikely to take steps to improve productivity until such time as other key persons are reading the same signs and seeing the need for action. Lee Iacocca would not have been successful at the Chrysler Corporation if he had been the only person who knew that the company was in deep difficulty. Key people have to be in agreement about the need to improve productivity before a program can be implemented.

When there is a gradual erosion in the financial situation of a hospital, there is a general acceptance of conditions as they are and there is little organizational interest in bringing about change. Fifteen years ago contractual adjustments and bad debts amounted to about a 5 percent difference between gross revenues and net revenues. Each succeeding year the gap widened slightly until the present, when the gap is often 20 to 25 percent. Though the problem has progressively grown, it was ignored until there was a sharp decline in patient days within a short period of time. It is the hospital version of the farmer who had to hit the mule on the head with a two-by-four in order to get his attention. So long as it is "business as usual," the focus of a manager's attention is on his own day-to-day routine problems, protecting his own turf, and making sure he is being fairly treated by the organization. It takes a crisis that threatens the entire institution in order to overcome the inertia that ignores the other than day-to-day concerns.

Since it takes a crisis to legitimatize the necessity for improving productivity, the best kind of crisis is one that is external to the organization. For example, the shift from inpatient to outpatient procedures for a number of procedures and services led to a downturn in hospital admissions. As admissions fell, nursing units were closed. An empty nursing unit is a stark reminder that the flow of patients is drying up and that some kind of shift has taken place in the market.

When a hospital decides to improve productivity by reducing its labor costs through layoffs, the first cut is always the easiest to do. Each succeeding effort becomes more difficult and very quickly reaches a point where concerns are raised about patient safety and the quality of care. So long as employee reductions are made in nonpatient care areas, a medical staff remains unconcerned, but it will strongly react if the cuts involve those in direct patient care.

Keeping quality of care standards up and at the same time reducing labor costs is a new dimension for most hospitals. The macho executive who strives for a "lean and mean" organization can experience difficulty in a hospital where any errors in managerial judgment must, of necessity, be conservative and protect patient safety. This unique requirement may not be appreciated at the federal level where the initial success of the DRGs may lead to a belief that turning down the revenue screws another notch or two will yield further success. A first-time success always leads to thinking that it can be repeated again with the same kinds of results.

The results obtained through DRGs are going make other third-party payers believe they should do the same and adopt a price-per-case mechanism. As each year goes by, the payers are all apt to assume that they can negotiate an even better price for the following year and will put pressure on the hospital. At some point in time, the hospital executive is going to become steadfast and take a position that to make further concessions will jeopardize patient safety. The payer organizations are likely to view this as a negotiating ploy and keep up the pressure, particularly since this point may be reached as early as the third or fourth round of negotiations. Hospitals have only a limited potential for improving productivity and when that is exhausted they will opt for patient safety and run the risk of bankruptcy. Given a choice between jeopardizing patient care or bankruptcy, hospitals will choose bankruptcy.

Often quoted and widely believed is the statement that the purpose of an organization is the maximization of profits. In other words, productivity should be pushed to its theoretical limits and indefinitely maintained at that level. Such a belief is without foundation. All enterprises are managed to a level of organizational comfort. Organizational comfort can be defined as the point at which the dollars on the bottom line are satisfying to the board and chief executive and, at the same time, represent the least amount of resentment among employees toward their working conditions.

Persons who have direct patient care responsibilities are less motivated by productivity goals than by the reactions of patients and the need to assure their safety. Patients are often unaware that a nurse standing at the bedside chatting and exchanging pleasantries is really looking for signs of improvement in the patient or is concerned about a deterioration and is looking for telltale symptoms. Much of what passes for pleasantries between a patient and a hospital employee has more significance than that; what is taking place is a monitoring process on the progress of the patient. This becomes second nature and automatic for nurses, to the point that they may not seem to be working but rather taking a respite from the daily activities of the nursing unit. In such a setting it is to be expected that productivity goals are secondary to the patient care objectives.

Leadership is of considerable importance in the setting and enforcing of productivity standards in hospitals. When a large number of employees are professionals and have direct patient care responsibilities, they have to be in agreement on established productivity levels to be effective. Standards cannot be imposed. There must be a consensus that standards are realistic and adequately provide for patient care. The role of a leader is to instill a pride in employees so that they strive for productivity standards that have been set while maintaining the quality of the service.

In hospitals, where large numbers of professionals are employed, there may be conflicting loyalties that interfere with the established level of institutional productivity. Nurses who are in hospital supervisory and management positions often consider themselves to be nurses first and managers second. They, like other professionals, relate to their own societies, as well as to the local corporate culture. In the event the two come into conflict, a preferred course of action is to look to one's own professional group for guidance. During times when there is a shortage of nurses, nurses are apt to be strongly supportive of their professional society. However, when times have changed and there is a surplus of trained professionals in the market, economics tends to be given far more weight and easier standards of patient safety may be rationalized as satisfactory. The degree of flexibility is, however, sharply limited and stops short of the point where patient safety may be jeopardized.

The concept of maintaining an average level of productivity for a given period of time is not a useful tool in direct patient care services since an average is someplace close to halfway between those that exceed the average and those that fall below it. What is crucial is the low point of productivity, not an average. If, for example, a nursing unit is above the average for 15 days and then is below the average by the same amount for the next 15 days, the monthly statistics on productivity for that unit would show up as being right on the mark. Yet, the month-end number does not red flag those low days where patient care might have been jeopardized. In a setting where safety is a paramount concern, averages have to be applied with caution.

IMPROVED PRODUCTIVITY WON'T OFFSET SHORTFALLS

Having reviewed a series of constraints and limitations on productivity and its application in the hospital industry (see Exhibit 23–1), what can be said about the future? Two trends appear to be likely in the foreseeable future: payments to hospitals will continue to be reduced and economic competition will continue to grow. The availability of operating funds will be steadily eroded in the next few years through a combination of separate, but related, trends. Medicare, which is now 42 percent of a typical hospital's business, will be geared down through the continued application of a payment formula and a freeze on annual adjustments. The revenue picture becomes even more grim when the other 58 percent of the hospital business is examined. Between HMOs, PPOs, and insurance carriers, all seeking larger and larger discounts from hospitals, financial pressure will more than offset any gains in productivity that may be achieved. All general hospitals,

Exhibit 23–1 Lessons about Hospital Productivity

1. Hospitals, like other enterprises, are as productive as they have to be, and no more.
2. Organizations, including hospitals, that become fiscally imperiled move rapidly to improve productivity once they recognize the economic dangers.
3. Unless threatened by a financial crisis, executives are reluctant to terminate employees in order to improve productivity.
4. Key people associated with the organization have to be in agreement about the need for improving productivity before a program can be implemented.
5. Improvements in productivity do not take place when there is a gradual erosion in the finances of the hospital.
6. Improving productivity occurs as a response to a major shift in the marketplace.
7. Reducing labor costs as a means of improving productivity has limited application in a hospital.
8. Executives do not believe that the purpose of an organization is to maximize profits by improving productivity to its theoretical limits, but rather to levels of organizational comfort.
9. Productivity goals are of secondary importance in those hospital departments that have direct patient care responsibilities.
10. In patient care, effective productivity standards are not unilaterally determined and enforced by management but result from understandings mutually arrived at between management and those providing the direct care to patients.
11. Among professionals they have an allegiance to their profession as well as to the organization that employs them. Institutional productivity norms must lie within the generally acceptable standards of the profession.
12. For services provided directly to individuals, average productivity, over time, has limited application since a minimum level is the crucial factor, not the average.

not just public or nonprofit hospitals, will be affected. The price/earnings ratios of the for-profit hospital chains will suffer as well, and will be eased only to the extent that the hospitals are involved in capitation plans and the selling of hospital products. The revenue shortfalls, for all hospitals, will not be covered by improved productivity.

One of the myths that is making the rounds in the health field is that hospitals must be making significant gains in efficiency since they have lower occupancies but stronger bottom lines. The conclusion seems to be that hospital executives have trimmed payrolls and sharpened purchasing practices to the extent that productivity has been considerably improved. It is true that this has taken place, but not at a rate that enhances efficiency; rather there has been a decline. The number of full-time equivalent personnel per adjusted occupied bed was 4.23 in 1984, an increase of .59 or 16.2 percent since 1980. In each year there have been increases, as follows:

1980	3.64
1981	3.76
1982	4.01
1983	4.19
1984	4.23

These results are from a private survey of 78 hospitals that belong to the National Council of Community Hospitals. Its purpose was to determine the extent to which intensity of illness has been rising. A number of factors were studied, all of which tend to reinforce the belief of hospital executives that intensity has increased. Two questions on this survey answered by nursing executives are instructive on this point. When asked "To what extent has the hospital experienced a change in the intensity of patient illness in the last year?" 92 percent indicated it was increased. When asked "To what extent do you agree with the statement that hardly any inpatient can get out of bed without assistance any more?" 70 percent agreed that this is now the situation.

While there has been a reduction in the number of employees in many hospitals as a result of a declining census, terminations did not keep pace with the downward trend in patients, but lagged behind it, leading to a higher number of FTEs per occupied bed. In 1984 there was a 13.3 percent increase in RNs and a 6.7 percent decrease in LPNs over 1983, while aides decreased 18.5 percent. The distribution shift was as follows:

Year	RN	LPN	Aide	Total
1983	58.6%	23.0	18.4	100.0%
1984	64.6	20.9	14.5	100.0%

In total numbers, nursing departments grew 3 percent and, to a significant degree, shifted to a higher skill level while at the same time the number of patient days fell 6.2 percent.

It might be argued that seeking the opinions of knowledgeable persons about nursing is not a sound way of measuring changes that are going on in hospitals and that asking opinions of nursing executives is hardly a respectable methodology for arriving at conclusions. Yet, when the subject is one where meaningful numbers cannot be developed in order to quantify results, the next best thing is to find out what experienced professional judgment thinks about a subject. Since these persons are reliable observers, the conclusions reached are generally valid.

IMPLICATIONS

What does all this mean? In general, a conclusion can be reached that there is disagreement about what hospitals are doing. The insured who are paying premiums for hospitalization want higher levels of efficiency, a viewpoint shared with the carriers who sell prepaid hospitalization plans. On the part of government, when paying for the Medicare population, there is a concern for holding the line on expenditures to providers so that senior citizens remain satisfied with the benefits they receive. If push comes to shove, past experience indicates that hospitals will continue to be short-changed by the government.

While these concerns for efficiency seem to have widespread support in the public sector, hospitals have been marching to a different drummer. Hospitals have been less concerned with efficiency and much more concerned with productivity and patient care. They have responded magnificently. Hospitals have taken the public's desire to heart, average lengths of stay are down, and there is a shift from inpatient to outpatient procedures. The result is a changed patient population, one that is much sicker and treated more intensively.

In coping with this shift, hospital executives have maintained a delicate balance by responding to patient care concerns and the need for patient safety, but also heeding, to the greatest extent possible, the public's desires about increased efficiency. As one views the modern hospital, it is obvious that people are receiving more and more treatment out of the hospital, but once in it they are receiving care that is costly, but necessary.

Greater amounts of resources are being expended on inpatients because they are sicker. This is the hidden side of productivity, the one that cannot be seen from the outside. It reflects a combination of events that have taken place and demands a sophisticated understanding and balancing of factors to achieve the results that are being obtained. Outsiders need to appreciate that though resources may be from government, prepayment, or business and industry, they can have only a limited impact on hospitals and their costs. Insiders will continue to give first priority to patient care. They will listen to the outsiders but, when the time comes to make decisions, the American public can be assured that patient safety will not be jeopardized.

Thinking Conceptually about Hospital Efficiency

What do critics mean by hospital inefficiency? The chaos caused by the indiscriminate use of the concept of efficiency has made today's national hospital scene appear more like someone out in a field trying to net elusive butterflies than an organized, thoughtful effort reflecting an industry's acceptance of responsibility.

If the hospital field at large is to successfully thwart the stigma of inefficiency it is necessary to promote a common concept of efficiency and its general acceptance.

To find a working definition of hospital efficiency that applies to the hospital as a whole, and not only to separate programs and departments, is difficult.

The unique purpose of a hospital is to provide clinical services to patients as directed by physicians. Efficiency of the whole hospital, therefore, means developing a measure that reasonably reflects the totality of clinical services provided by a hospital to all of its patients, both in- and out-patients.

Effectiveness is frequently carelessly used interchangeably with the word efficiency. There meanings, however, are quite distinct. Effectiveness is concerned with the degree of medical benefits patients receive from the rendering of clinical services. How the services controlled by the physician benefit the physical and mental conditions of patients is a medical judgment and does not relate to the efficiency with which a hospital delivers these services. Appropriate measures of effectiveness for a hospital as a whole would be the number of patients admitted or the amount of clinical services ordered by physicians.

This confusion is not uncommon, because concepts of efficiency and effectiveness between hospitals and physicians are not generally separated; yet, in fact, each has a unique, but articulated role in medical care. Often overlooked is the fact that patients contract with attending physicians, pay a fee for these services, and the physician acts as the patient's agent in ordering a hospital's clinical services for his patient. This relationship is similar to the one that exists between an attorney and his client in the courtroom.

MEASURES OF EFFICIENCY

Literature in the field of management is typically generalized and vague about the meaning of efficiency. In management books several different ideas are often used to define efficiency. Some of these are:

- Progress toward organizational objectives at the least possible cost
- Personal efficiency in individual performance
- Work output above normal expectations
- Doing work right
- Satisfaction of individual motives when operating jointly toward a common goal
- Productivity
- Reduction in unit cost of output

In the hospital field, the idea of a reduction in cost is often used two ways: to mean a slowing in the rate of increases in hospital charges, such as a decrease in the annual rate of increase from 14 percent to 12 percent from one year to the next, or to mean an absolute lowering of hospital charges, such as decreasing patient day charges from $300 to $275 per day.

Both of these ideas have a ring of rightness in expressing the meaning of efficiency, but they are, likewise, less than a total meaning.

The use of the concept of productivity, as a measure of efficiency, is more sophisticated than merely cost reduction. Productivity is generally used as a ratio measurement to compare inputs with outputs, or as a measurement between input costs and required productivity for a given level of output. Expenditures can be measured over time by a summing of inputs and outputs.

Productivity is, however, less than a whole concept of efficiency, except for one firm producing one product. In this situation productivity and efficiency are identical. However, in one firm with many different outputs of products and services productivity is meaningful for one product, while efficiency is related to the total outputs of the firm.

Two difficulties are encountered when productivity and efficiency are used as synonymous terms. One difficulty is that the input elements of capital, labor, and plant are diverse and must be reduced to a common measurement to be additive. The unit commonly used to make these elements additive is a measure of each in terms of cost, or in dollars. Multiproduct or service firms, however, require a distribution of dollar costs for the indirect and overhead costs of the output for each product or by service to determine the total cost for each specific product or service. To accomplish this distribution requires the use of reasonable, but artificial rules of indirect and overhead cost distributions. Thus, there often is less than, or more than, an equitable distribution of input costs to each item of output. In addition, the time period used can unevenly affect the distribution of these costs. Parsimonious decisions of the day often increase productivity in the short range for a firm and sacrifice long-range productivity increases.

The other difficulty with using productivity and efficiency terms interchangeably involves the problem of output definition for hospitals. A diagnostic patient is a different output than a gall bladder patient, while an appendectomy in a six-year-old is a different case than one in a 68-year-old. The work on diagnostic related groups is only a first step in developing the kind of knowledge needed to group hospital outputs into standardized units of output.

If the concept of efficiency is more than cost reduction, productivity, satisfaction of individual motives, personal efficiency, or doing work right, then what is hospital efficiency?

COMPARING HOSPITAL EFFICIENCIES

The inherent difficulties of finding a commonly accepted definition of hospital efficiency can be visualized by contrasting two different hospitals operating in circumstances at opposite extremes in their institutional characteristics and local environment.

For example, one hospital might be a 400-bed suburban hospital with comprehensive medical services, a physical plant five years old, high occupancy levels throughout the year, and no indigent patients. Professional personnel are in adequate supply and there is an abundance of specialized physicians. Patient day charges are $500 per day and patient day costs are $400 per day. Its annual revenue and expense surplus is $4,000,000.

The other hospital might be a 400-bed inner-city hospital with comprehensive medical services, a 35-year-old physical plant, and an average occupancy of 60 percent. Professional staff are chronically in short supply, and the medical staff membership is steadily decreasing in numbers and increasing in age. There is a 30 percent contractual allowance and bad debt writeoff rate. Patient day charges are $500 per day and patient day costs are $580 per day. The hospital is losing approximately $4,000,000 annually because of below-cost Medicaid reimbursement, and caps on revenue increases.

Which hospital is more efficient, or more inefficient?

Management activities in these two hospitals are quite different. The suburban hospital administration is busy planning additional programs of care and introducing new technologies and has an expansionist frame of mind. The inner-city administration is actively retrenching programs, increasing security, jerry-rigging major repairs, juggling accounts payable, and is reductionist in thinking.

The board of trustees in the suburban hospital is busily reviewing ways to finance the next building program, buying all major capital equipment recommended by the medical staff, and increasing executive salaries to assure a stable management. The inner-city board of trustees is continually hearing complaints from the public and medical staff members about hospital operation, wondering what is wrong with its chief executive officer, and resisting every effort to raise any salaries.

The medical staff of the suburban hospital is regularly developing new recommendations for expansion of services and equipment, complaining about HSA restraints, and pleasing the PRO with a low average length of stay. At the inner-city hospital, members of the medical staff are always threatening to transfer their appointments to other hospitals because of old equipment, outmoded facilities, inadequate nursing staff, reductions in programs of care; they are unaware of the HSA, and fighting with the PRO because of the above average length of stay.

Which hospital is more efficient in the short run and in the long run?

The way things are today there is no way to identify quantitatively either hospital as efficient or inefficient. To compare these two hospitals a common criteria must be used to make judgments about their efficiency.

LIMITATIONS OF THE CONCEPT

A workable application of the concept of efficiency requires one to focus only on the organizational resources under the control of the hospital. To achieve such a focus three limitations must be recognized and accommodated in the definition of hospital efficiency.

The first limitation is a recognition that a hospital is a firm with multiple outputs, and not a simple organizational entity producing one standardized product or service. A hospital provides nursing services to surgical, medical, and obstetrical patients, plus laboratory tests, and operating rooms, and many other functions, over a wide range of services. Each completed test and clinical procedure is an output of hospital services. Conversely, dietary services, medical records, business office, administration, and other activities are supportive of clinical services, but not of the essence for medical services to patients. The only hospital services that really count are the clinical services. Therefore, all clinical tests and procedures are part of a hospital's output.

A second limitation is the fact that hospitals do not control proscriptive medical practice, except at the outer edges, of a range of tests and procedures. The control of the number and scope of diagnostic and therapeutic measures, and their mix, is determined by the physician, and not by a hospital. Therefore, the efficiency of a hospital does not encompass decisions by attending physicians. This means that the concept of hospital efficiency is limited to whatever type of patient is admitted and to all specific tests and clinical procedures under the control and direction of the medical staff and its members. If the scope of services to a patient, for example, the appropriateness of admission or length of stay, is to be evaluated, it is properly a question of the effectiveness and efficiency of physicians, and not that of hospital operation. In essence a physician is the customer and the patient a consumer of hospital services. It must be assumed that the customer, the physician, is always right, and if he isn't, then the organized processes of the medical profession must deal with the problem since it is not a matter of hospital efficiency.

A third limitation arises out of the necessity to measure hospital inputs, or dollar costs, in different ways, because a hospital uses a variety of pricing mechanisms. Hospitals set rates for services on both a specific test and clinical procedure basis, such as $17 for an A.P. and lateral chest film, and also a collective basis, such as a daily service charge of $210 for a two-bed accommodation.

As all hospital executives know, rates charged for any particular service are adjusted annually with two criteria in mind: how departmental costs have shifted since the last budget period and what difficulty would be faced in collecting the adjusted departmental rates in the next budget period. In essence, hospitals try to maximize reimbursement and minimize difficulties in the collection of revenues.

An ultimate restraint on hospital operations are the total dollars of revenue anticipated for services provided to patients. This means that forces external to a hospital, in the final analysis, control the dollars needed for hospital operations and affect any given level and scope of service. This may appear to be an overestimate of the actual situation, but in fact, if hospitals do not perceive any ultimate income restraint, both formal and internal hospital prices would be higher than their present levels.

A dilemma exists. In a free-market economy, a firm may be highly efficient, but if the market does not buy its output, the firm will fail. Hospital services do not face this restraint. Until recently, the market need for medical services exceeded an ability to produce and finance these services. Because of the existence of third-party cost reimbursement, critics of the hospital field argue that issues of efficiency do not motivate hospital executives.

Lost in the debate of "yes, it does" and "no, it doesn't matter" is the understanding that hospital productivity is only measurable at the department level, and that statements about its efficiency are in the last analysis value judgments, or personal opinion, not sustainable by a rational, organized set of data.

HOSPITAL OUTPUTS ARE NOT ADDITIVE

Efficiency is only personal opinion because the many different clinical service outputs of a hospital are not additive. The present state of knowledge provides no methodology for measuring the efficiency of a single hospital. Output measures for a physical therapy department, such as modalities per man-hour, cannot be added to nursing man-hours per patient day, plus laboratory tests per man-hour, and on and on, to reach any sensible conclusion. Technologies and processes of each clinical department in a hospital are unique and nonadditive.

Also ignored is the issue of levels of quality of service. Measures of quality of care in hospitals have been steadily developed by the Joint Commission on Accreditation of Hospitals, state boards of health, the Commission on Professional and Hospital Activities, various specialty boards in medicine, and individual hospitals. Because quality of care is a most fundamental matter in hospitals, and medical care is generally understood to mean diagnosis and treatment, as well as asceptic concepts, separate and minimum acceptable standards are established by each procedure. Because quality of care is the heart of the matter there are many vigilant enforcers in each hospital. This persistent concern for quality of care is further reinforced by medical malpractice concerns, so that a pursuit of efficiency, which forces quality of care below levels acceptable to either the medical or nursing staffs, will not long be tolerated. This means that every hospital is restrained in its administrative ability to lower quality standards to a much larger extent than in other industries, or than is generally understood, even by health professionals.

On every nursing station in a hospital, be it medicine, surgery, obstetrics, or any other specialty service, the internists, surgeons, obstetricians, and pediatricians establish a hospital's quality level, not the administrative staff. The quality of care in all hospitals varies by the quality of its medical staff, and not the impact of its administrative staff.

Concerns about the quality of hospital care are reflected not only by adherence to a variety of medically developed criteria, but also by the scope of service available in a hospital. This fact is demonstrated by a general awareness among health professionals that two hospitals of the same bed size may have significantly different clinical services. One hospital may treat patients mostly at a secondary-care level and have few clinical services beyond nursing services, laboratory, radiology, operating rooms, and an emergency service. Another hospital may have dialysis, several specialty intensive care units, stress and gastrointestinal laboratories, and a whole host of other special services aimed at patients needing tertiary levels of care.

These differences are frequently accommodated by reimbursement plans through categorization of hospitals by the number of clinical services operated, with each service equally counted. Such a practice is a crude method for identifying differences in hospitals, but a step in the right direction.

No generally accepted reimbursement program has, as yet, recognized the differences inherent in specific clinical services. For example, a clinical laboratory in one hospital may routinely offer 200 different kinds of tests, while a second hospital's laboratory may offer 400 separate tests. This same situation applies to every clinical department and service operated by a hospital. To compare hospitals without identifying the total range of services routinely available in each clinical department is to count a Piper Cub and a Boeing 747 as equivalent because each one is an airplane and can fly.

PROFESSIONAL JUDGMENT ENTERS THE EQUATION

Often overlooked by critics of hospitals is the fact that attending physicians must have sufficient freedom in diagnosis and treatment decisions to use their professional judgment in the care of patients. Such legitimate freedoms mean that hospitals can control the number of tests and clinical procedures ordered by attending physicians only at the outer margins of medical care. Consequently, whatever is ordered by a medical staff should be included as an output measure for hospital efficiency purposes, which will also be reflective of the differences in the range of tests and procedures for every clinical department in a hospital.

Hospitals have organizational arrangements and processes that are significantly different from organizations typically used to demonstrate an accepted economic concept of efficiency, where long-run equilibrium of price through pure and perfect competition is assumed. The past practice of economists has usually been to ignore any differences and proceed with a traditional economic analysis. The hospital field has typically ignored economic analysis and concentrated on productivity analysis at the department level, on the theory that all savings are worthwhile. In both instances efficiency opinions remain only as value judgments of the individual expressing a view.

However, despite current practice it is desirable to try to find a way of gradually moving toward a more workable criteria for hospital efficiency. At the present time productivity measures of hospital performance cannot be added together to reach a meaningful conclusion because the units of measurement are different and therefore not additive. To the degree that different departmental units of measurement can be made additive there will be a more accurate approximation of a measurement of hospital efficiency. If the output of all clinical departmental units could be calculated in standard terms and added together, the result would be a reasonable estimate of the efficiency of a hospital.

FINDING A COMMON UNIT OF MEASUREMENT

In thinking about finding a common unit of measurement for all clinical tests and procedures through an examination of departmental productivities, it should be possible to find a consumer unit of measurement. The basic ratio used to express clinical departmental productivity is outputs divided by inputs. For the total hospital, where there is a common unit of output measure for every clinical department, an approximate measure of efficiency would be:

$$\text{Hospital Efficiency} = \frac{\text{Nursing Output}}{\text{Nursing Input}} + \frac{\text{Lab Output}}{\text{Lab Input}} + \frac{\text{X-Ray Output}}{\text{X-Ray Input}} + \text{etc.}$$

By separately considering the various elements in each departmental numerator and denominator it may be possible to find ways to improve present-day practices.

In thinking about a numerator for the total hospital, and ways of measuring departmental outputs in a standardized way, a count of the total number of physician orders for each patient has been used as an estimate of total hospital services to a given patient. This is a step in the direction of developing a total hospital measure, but it is limited by the fact that with this approach a laboratory white count, for example, would have the same weight as a radiological gastrointestinal series; two entirely different procedures in terms of hospital resources. Furthermore, this type of measurement does not include standing orders and routine procedures in a hospital that trigger many patient services without any entry by a physician on the order sheet.

Because the meaningful workload of a hospital is its total output of clinical services to patients, a useful efficiency measure should include as many clinical services as possible, and on a basis that reflects as many differences in resource use as are in reality consumed.

A way to develop a unit of measurement for hospital operations, which would allow different clinical services to be additive, and also measure total usage, would be to calculate an average for the number of manpower minutes needed to perform each specific clinical procedure. For example, pathologists directing hospital clinical laboratories have separated all laboratory functions into detailed, discrete items, such as specimen collecting or performing a white count, and assigned relative values to each activity. By knowing the total number of functions performed, a total output measure for laboratory services can be accurately estimated. Whether it is done manually or automatically, the workload unit value remains the same.

The kind of approach used to estimate clinical laboratory output can also be used as a model for other professional groups to develop similar workload units. By using the lowest possible whole number, one, or multiples of one, for procedures that take longer than one minute, a series of values can be developed for each test and clinical procedure in every clinical department.

To calculate clinical service units (CSUs) for a hospital the total CSU units of every clinical department can be obtained by multiplying the annual volume of output for each test and procedure by their estimated value and adding them all together to give total CSUs for the department. For example, a laboratory white count might have a CSU value of 4 and a radiological gastrointestinal series a CSU value of 50. If there were 10,000 white counts done in a year, the CSU value would be 40,000 and for the G.I. series, where 500 procedures were completed, the CSU value would be 25,000.

The total CSUs for all hospital clinical departments could then be added together, because there is a common unit of measurement, minutes of time. The total CSUs for a hospital would then be a reasonable estimate of its total clinical effort for a given period of time. Further than that, a standard unit of measure common to all hospitals would be established, and thereby provide a basis for comparison of institutional clinical outputs among all sizes and types of hospitals.

Accumulation of this kind of data can easily be accomplished since all clinical departments routinely maintain these types of service statistics. By multiplying each service statistic by its CSU value, the total clinical effort could be rather closely approximated.

The one clinical service in a hospital that would require a new service statistics system would be the nursing department. However, a few hospitals are using service statistics generally similar to the categories of analysis used in nursing audits.

A CSU system of this kind should be focused on departments because the goal is to arrive at an estimate of total hospital clinical output. For research purposes, a CSU system could be used on a patient-by-patient basis to obtain a measure of individual service requirements or on a diagnosis-by-diagnosis basis similar to a diagnostic related grouping.

A CSU system could also help resolve the age-old problem of combining in- and outpatient volumes for the same test or procedure. For example, the workload value for a white count would be the same for the actual performance of the test, such as a value of 4; however, the additional value of 3 would be added for inpatient white counts because of the need for a phlebotomist to travel from the laboratory to the patient and return. Therefore, the CSU value for an inpatient white count would be 7 and for an outpatient 4.

The use of CSU values also provides a way to account for the differences between hospitals in departmental range of services, since the hospital with a more elaborate service would generate a higher total CSU value. A hospital with a clinical laboratory offering 200 different tests might have an inpatient annual CSU volume of 4,000,000 CSUs, while another hospital with 400 different tests, including some exotic types, might have an annual CSU volume of 9,000,000.

Another way to demonstrate the difference between these two different types of laboratories would be to calculate an intensity ratio for laboratory services. If each hospital annually had 10,000 inpatient admissions, the CSU values of 9,000,000 and 4,000,000 could be divided by 10,000 and the intensity index would be 900 for one hospital and 400 for the other hospital.

By repeating this logic for each department and then adding the CSU outputs together of all clinical departments a total CSU for a hospital could be found. Even if the CSU value for any specific test or procedure was not entirely accurate, it would still provide a general index of the clinical outputs of a hospital, because all hospitals would be applying the same CSU value to each clinical output.

The total CSUs for a hospital would be in the range of a million, or multiples of a million. A 400-bed hospital would probably have between 60,000,000 and 150,000,000. This number could be reduced in different ways to make it easier to understand. One simple way would be to divide the total CSUs by 1,440 for minutes per 24 hours, so that the result would be average CSU units per patient day.

The elements used in the denominator of an efficiency ratio are the input measures for the use of capital, labor, and plant expressed as dollars for a specified period of time identical to the numerator.

The elements of inputs to be used in the denominator should be determined by the kind of efficiency index desired. Depending on the particular purpose, three different input measures might be selected: total revenue, net operating revenue, or total operating expenses.

From a third-party reimbursement point of view, total revenue would be the choice for a denominator. Hospital rates charged for clinical services to patients when billed to third-party carriers become a cost to the carrier and are of primary concern to them. However, hospital rates are a function of the total monies received from all third-party carriers. Whenever a third-party carrier, such as Medicare and Medicaid, has a reimbursement formula that covers less than total cost plus a reasonable surplus, a hospital increases rates to other carriers to offset this below-cost reimbursement and total revenue is overstated.

From a hospital perspective, net operating revenue as a denominator is a more reasonable choice. Contractual allowances and bad debts, which are deductions from total revenue, are not within the control of the hospital and are properly excluded if a concept of efficiency is to be a measure of management's judgment and skill in the use of its resources.

Another way to look at hospital efficiency would be to use total operating expenses as a denominator, which would most accurately reflect the operating judgments of management. This would be a more direct comparison of resource use and output measures. Capital expenses would be included to the extent of depreciation charges. Since the basic goal of management is to create the lowest possible cost mix between capital and labor, depreciation is properly included.

The argument would soon be raised that a new hospital would have much higher depreciation charges than an old hospital and would therefore have a lower efficiency. This is, of course, what would happen, but the rational economic argument would be that the departmental productivity of a new hospital would be higher and should offset the increased depreciation costs. If it does not occur, then to the extent of the difference, the new hospital is inefficient.

Total operating expenses would include all of the service and administrative functions of a hospital, because institutional efficiency is achieved by the way management rations total dollars to specific departments through the budgeting process.

The following example illustrates the application of CSUs in the measurement of hospital efficiency between the old and new 400-bed hospitals previously described.

	Old Hospital	*New Hospital*
Total Beds	400	400
Annual patient days	87,000 (60%)	130,000 (90%)
Annual operating expenses	$27,400,000	$36,400,000
Average CSUs per patient day	920	740
Annual hospital CSUs	80,040,000	96,200,000
	(920 × 87,000)	(740 × 130,000)
Hospital efficiency	$\frac{80,040,000 \text{ CSUs}}{\$27,400,000}$	$\frac{96,200,000 \text{ CSUs}}{\$36,400,000}$
	2.92	2.64

The number 2.92 is an index of the efficiency of the old hospital and 2.64 of the new hospital. This says that on a relative basis the old hospital is 10.6 percent more efficient than the new hospital in the way it uses its input resources (dollars) to deliver clinical services to patients.

No absolute scale of efficiency for hospitals can be achieved, because maximum hospital efficiency is unknown. Efficiency is therefore relative between hospitals. However, the efficiency number of many hospitals could be arranged in rank order and their range efficiencies related to operating conditions for new insights into management decisions and hospital characteristics that improve efficiency.

One adjustment would be required for use of any of the three suggested denominators. The economic concept of efficiency is based on an equilibrium model which assumes that the price of inputs is the same for all firms in an industry. Since this is not a real-world fact, a price adjustment would be required for different regions of the country, through the use of a consumer price index, the wholesale price index, or some other appropriate index. Within the same city in most instances, no price adjustment would be needed.

Another major use of total CSUs would be the computation of an intensity of service index for hospitals. This could be done by, as in the example, computing the average patient day CSUs by dividing either total patient days or number of admissions into total inpatient CSUs.

If the development of an overall efficiency index were to be explored and developed by the hospital field there would be a new way to respond more clearly to persistent criticism. Hospitals would benefit in three ways from the development of an efficiency index. The first would be the separation of hospital efficiency from that of the efficiency of physician responsibilities in hospitals. Second, by focusing on the use of either net operating revenues or total operating expenses to measure inputs, the impact of below-full-cost reimbursement from third-party reimbursers could be highlighted and used to respond intelligently to criticism. Last, such an index would provide a better way to make more reasonable comparisons of efficiency between hospitals because uniform criteria for efficiency would be used in the same way by all hospitals.

Chapter 25

The Hospital CEO in Transition

Like all other bosses the chief executive of a hospital lives in two worlds, an organizational one and a personal one. When one is disrupted repercussions are felt in the other. The two roles are separated at times, commingled at times, or blurred into one occasionally, depending upon the pressures being exerted by a combination of the organizational and personal sides of the individual's life. Typically, a hospital chief executive has had little difficulty keeping them separate and neatly compartmentalized, until recent years, by adhering to a daily schedule that allocated time between the two roles. In general, the work schedule could be predicted one week, one month, or six months in the future with a fair degree of accuracy. But then the world began to change and the CEO's organizational role began to shift as the institution and the professional role became more uncertain and stress became a way of life.

Because a chief executive occupies a unique position at the apex of an operating structure, this person's feelings, attitudes, and values are important. It is the weaving together of an individual's traits and characteristics with those of the corporate role that is in transition. There may well be a spillover effect from one role to the other. When one side or the other becomes so demanding as to upset the equilibrium that the executive has established it may adversely affect performance at either the office or at home or in both places. Because a hospital executive is a human being first and an executive second what happens personally often affects the corporate role. Since the executive is pivotal in organizational workings of the institution, it may also affect a hospital.

A hospital chief executive lives in an organizational climate that has both stabilizing and upsetting factors and the challenge is to find bridges between the two. In the personal world there are stabilizing factors and upsetting ones. The difference is that on the organizational side the use of resources can be varied in a way that cannot be done on the personal side of the equation.

INCREASING STRESS

In days past CEO stresses encountered in the corporate role could satisfactorily be reduced by developing different organizational patterns. This did not impact the private side either mentally or physically. Whatever happened could be accommodated in a reasonably short period of time. Conventional wisdom suggests that when there are upsetting organizational factors they should be stabilized as quickly as possible by objective methods; carefully reviewing information obtained from various management information systems, on-site evaluations, analyzing problems, rearranging priorities, shifting resources, changing procedures, and modifying policies—the assumption being that resources are available to bring about the desired results.

But when resources are too little to cope with problems as they develop, and when time is so limited and circumscribed that an executive is prevented from tackling problems, or they lie outside the control of the hospital, not only is the institution affected, but then a spillover effect may occur.

Since human factors dominate and determine the way the organizational role is handled, how an executive feels about himself and his role is important, far more important than past education, experience, or training. An ability to handle conceptual problems easily, to understand statistical information readily, to be knowledgeable about hospital operations previously were the basic ingredients needed to reach a chief executive's position, but these are now only part of the backdrop for daily activities. Trying to survive in an organizational jungle with a large governing board, a suspicious medical staff, restrictive third-party reimbursement, inappropriate decisions from the local HSA now requires the hide of a rhinoceros and the single-minded determination of a bulldog. Intellectual skills need to be blended with emotional maturity. Working in an environment filled with uncertainty, increasingly unreasonable demands from a variety of sources, bureaucratic double-talk, arbitrarily imposed rules and regulations from outside agencies, and a growing list of unresolved problems and issues requires a level of internal stability not previously needed. Analytical abilities are superseded in importance by a necessity to maintain a sense of humor, a state of optimism, an ability to absorb unwarranted criticism, and an understanding of group dynamics, by stubbornness and perseverance in the face of unreasonable odds with an ability to anticipate questions and answer them before they are even asked. Obviously, this is a set of performance requirements that will be difficult to fulfill.

Where a chief executive used to spend most of a workday having individual conferences with departmental directors, reviewing progress on assigned projects, and mapping out changes in detailed procedures and reviewing reports, the day is now most often a steady round of conferences and committee meetings, disrupted by frequent full-day absences from the hospital to participate in coping with external forces affecting the operation of the hospital. The executive's loss of control of time may well be the single most important change that has occurred for a hospital chief executive in the last two decades.

Caught up in a daily web of meetings that demand substantial chunks of available time a CEO finds that the ongoing activities of the hospital increasingly leave him isolated. Even though not much of importance may be going on in a meeting, a chief executive is acutely aware that entering and leaving the meeting room is not appropriate. While in a meeting, phone messages are piling up, reports, memoranda, and letters are doing the same, and the list of people wanting face-to-face conversations continues to grow. One of the frustrations when returning to the office at the end of such a day of meetings is finding that the pile of things to do has grown substantially even though the CEO has been at work all day.

RUNNING OUT OF TIME

Feelings of frustration are reinforced when an executive looks at the calendar for the next day and sees a day similar to the one just experienced. This is particularly annoying to a successful chief executive because it does not square with work habits developed over the years. In the course of a career, executives internalize a sense of urgency about work. They are always anxious to get finished with whatever is going on in order to begin to tackle the next problem. Executives become impatient if meetings with subordinates take too long. They want to get to the bottom line and skip the details. This drive to continually resolve the unresolved makes a CEO a restless person, a skimmer of information and one who concentrates not on what has been accomplished but on those matters yet to be dealt with as soon as possible. To be stuck in meetings day in and day out with no relief in sight leads to problems on three levels that a chief executive must face: (1) the CEO role in the institution, (2) his own feelings about his role, and (3) the growing imbalance between corporate and personal life.

The hospital chief executive comes to understand that the position is in transition and is now different from what it was in the past. The members of the immediate office staff often recognize this change before the CEO does and they set up barriers that make it difficult for anyone but an immediate subordinate to penetrate the organizational wall. This brings about isolation and leads to the need for an associate to head up the internal operations of the hospital.

This is a double-edged sword since, on the one hand, it is a way to reduce the number of troublesome problems, but on the other hand it leads to an even greater feeling of being alone and, hence, less satisfaction. No longer is there the opportunity of wrestling with a clear-cut problem in a one-on-one relationship; these are now the province of subordinates. Instead, the CEO is left with the indecisiveness of group meetings, timetables that keep slipping, an inability to exercise accustomed authority, and a feeling of being responsible for matters over which control is no longer possible. A CEO becomes only a participant in this setting, with his thoughts and opinions received with less warmth and appreciation than was the case when he was dealing directly with department directors.

The shift in the way time is spent is particularly difficult. Even though a CEO may have been in the same position for two decades or more, performance requirements are no longer the same. Over the years CEOs attempted to reduce organizational uncertainty and to continually seek to ensure predictability in every phase of the operation—organizational uncertainty is to an executive what a missed diagnosis is to a physician. Through the development of more sophisticated management information systems and the employment of an experienced executive as an associate a CEO is able to cope with the problem solving of the internal operations. However, the rest of the workload may still add up to more time than is available. The typical response is to lengthen the workday.

More often than not, the day commences with a 7:00 a.m. meeting with a medical staff group, proceeds to a mid-morning administrative staff meeting followed by a noon luncheon meeting, either in or out of the hospital, succeeded by mid- and late-afternoon appointments with key subordinates, culminating in a dinner meeting that may not adjourn until 9:00 p.m. Such a schedule requires the stamina of a bull. If a CEO tends to overeat and shuns regular exercise, this kind of routine leads to excess poundage, slack muscles, and a loss of mental agility. This is a brutal schedule when kept up month after month, year after year. Too much pressure constantly applied from too many directions leads to a decreasing ability to cope with the demands of an organization. It may reach a point where a CEO has a loss of humor, becomes preoccupied, lacks enthusiasm, suffers anxiety, has feelings of depression, seeks relief in alcohol, loses a sense of personal worth, and in extreme situations undergoes a personality shift.

How one thinks about himself impacts his role as an executive. An executive may not be aware of the continual pressure, but others not knowing the full extent of the pressure may be less than charitable about personal behavior traits they see exhibited in dealings with a CEO.

Feelings of stress gradually develop out of a sense that one is trapped by his environment. Throughout one's work life there is the feeling that organizational momentum needs to be sustained and that it is up to a chief executive to make this happen. A feeling of helplessness often occurs as a CEO repeatedly rediscovers that nothing is clear, that accomplishments take too long to occur for even minimal problems. Without realizing how it happened, a CEO winds up on a treadmill running faster and faster and yet unable still to get on top of all of the problems. This is particularly burdensome because past performance in a managerial role forced an executive to concentrate on unresolved matters. Years of focusing on open issues developed a habit of keeping in the forefront of one's mind those items that need to be settled, not those that are resolved.

Persistent job-related frustration often leads an executive to consider taking his talents and applying them in another industry. A hospital CEO may go as far as to have confidential interviews with corporate executives in the community. From them a CEO may ultimately conclude that the idea of transferability of executive skills from one industry to another, which one has been led to believe is true, is really not a viable alternative. Lack of experience usually becomes an insurmountable barrier in moving out of one industry and into another.

The next step may be to consider a business venture. A chief executive is typically older than 40 years of age. With the prospect that a business may not be successful this approach is too risky and thus the only option remaining is to continue in an existing career in the same industry.

In an institution where the operations are managed by a number two executive, a chief executive may have too little time for handling those matters that require detailed attention because of the role as institutional spokesperson that must be performed. In large measure a hospital CEO has become a key trustee without portfolio or title. This is a role that only a CEO can perform since it often requires in-depth knowledge of operations as well as an understanding of the general attitudes of those involved in the governance structure of the board.

A gnawing problem to a hospital chief executive is recognizing a role change but finding it is neither understood nor accepted by members of the governing board or medical staff. This dichotomy of role perception leads to misunderstandings, a spreading thin of CEO time, and ultimately may include the development of deleterious social habits.

The obvious solution to a lack of time is to delegate additional responsibilities to other members of the administrative team. This is not easy to do in a voluntary nonprofit hospital. Lacking end-product measurements on hospital activities where no neat and tidy assessment of performance can be obtained, only limited justification for additional administrative positions can be used to explain the need to a nonprofit board of trustees.

Even though it is often suggested that the chief executive take control of his environment, establish priorities, learn to say no, follow a regular exercise program, provide intervals during the workday for brief relaxation, avoid working weekends, and find a set of management techniques, this is the kind of advice akin to that of a physician telling a mother of three young children to stay off her feet for six weeks. It is sensible but not very practical.

The problem for a hospital CEO is to be able to cope in situations where only limited application can be made of these techniques. It is not a ''cop-out'' to suggest that a hospital CEO is subject to unusual conditions.

Even though a CEO has no direct control over the medical staff, the governing board, and the external factors that operate on a hospital, a CEO recognizes that, in the board's mind, the CEO remains fully accountable for the total hospital, in every dimension. This attitude severely restricts coping abilities even when a CEO is a competent, secure executive and a participating family member.

This situation is not due to other people caring little about a CEO's hospital or family responsibilities, or to a callous attitude by individual board members, or the vindictiveness of a medical staff, but rather it is related to the competition for a CEO's time. Groups dealing with serious matters require time and attention. The fact that a CEO knows that attendance at a Little League game is a family must, the game almost always loses out to a need to attend a meeting of the governing board. And, even when a CEO really desires to go to the game, this reason for absence from a board meeting can't be cited for fear of criticism.

Seldom addressed in the literature is the problem of the chief executive who needs help to cope, but must respond to the needs, desires, and demands of groups to whom he is accountable, both formally or informally. In a hospital, this difficulty is heightened because the end-product measurement is an intangible: quality patient care. Lacking measurements, a hospital chief executive instinctively recognizes that governing boards are going to judge performance by paying more attention to form than to substance.

ORGANIZATIONAL AMBIGUITY

A chief executive of a hospital lives with a great deal of organizational ambiguity because of the peculiar relationship of a medical staff in the organization structure. A dilemma often arises for a CEO when a governing board expects vigilance about the quality of patient care, but at the same time expects administrative cooperation with the medical staff.

When administrative steps need to be taken which impact physicians, a hospital CEO accepts the fact that a stressful situation is created. A CEO is aware that physicians regard a lack of clinical training as a barrier to a CEO from reaching valid conclusions about quality of care issues. Even though a hospital CEO does what senior executives in other industries do, operating on second- and third-hand information and statistical reports, these sources are not often regarded as valid by physicians.

Because a hospital CEO can neither claim clinical competence nor direct authority over a medical staff, a series of maneuvers are required to bring about the needed results. If in this process a CEO becomes suspect to some physicians, they will scurry around the hospital searching for evidence that the CEO is not doing the job properly, or that departments are not operating satisfactorily. As all executives know, there are always examples to be found. As a list of dirty linen is compiled a CEO may be increasingly boxed in, without any way out. Lacking end-product measurements that reflect overall results of organizational performance, there are no easy responses.

Mounting frustrations caused by a variety of factors over which a CEO has no effective organizational control means vulnerability to stress more than in any other position in a hospital. This is so for three reasons:

1. At the apex of an operating organization, there are socially important responsibilities to perform as the major representative of a hospital and these cannot be delegated to other positions. Stated differently, the ability to manage one's own time is severely restricted because of the demands of outside groups.
2. A CEO is accountable to a governing board that cannot meaningfully measure performance except by unstated norms.
3. A CEO's organizational relationship to a medical staff is clouded in ambiguity.

SIZING UP THE SITUATION

These three reasons severely restrict the ability of a hospital CEO to exercise a full range of coping mechanisms that are usually available. Administrative effectiveness is determined by an ability and willingness to put oneself in the other person's shoes, whether of a board member, a physician, an agency official, or a consumer. Both administrative behavior and availability of time are largely controlled by what others expect of a CEO. These expectations may be unrealistic on an individual basis but may be even more unrealistic from the viewpoint of a group relationship. The problem is not that a hospital executive fails to recognize group pressures, but rather that he lacks an ability to extricate himself from the organizational restraints. The same restraints carry over into personal life. The needs of family members are secondary when job demands are excessive. Both situations lead to imbalances in living that must be adjusted. When stabilizing and upsetting factors are listed for both the organizational and personal sides of a CEO's life, the difficulties are readily apparent.

Among hospital organizational factors are the following upsetting factors:

1. Inadequate operating revenues
2. Lack of adequate capital
3. Inability to maintain technological innovation
4. Lack of adequate authority
5. Inexperienced subordinates
6. Conflicts between governing board members
7. Ill-defined end-result measurements of hospital performance
8. Loss of organizational momentum
9. Anti-administrator attitude by medical staff

10. Hostile public climate toward hospital
11. A governing board more concerned with procedures than substantive issues
12. Lack of sufficient knowledge of hospital operations by governing board members
13. The need to learn to live with decisions made by outside groups that have no accountability for the results of hospital operation

At the same time the stabilizing forces include:

1. Setting and following schedules
2. A financially sound bottom line
3. Competent subordinates
4. Predictability in the operations of the hospital
5. Adherence to valid precedents
6. Institutional goals clearly articulated and followed
7. Annual growth in units of services
8. Acknowledged value of hospital to the life of the community
9. Up-to-date physical plant and equipment
10. Well-developed management information systems
11. Efficient internal operations
12. Continuity of governing board membership
13. Governing board leadership that is responsive and sensitive to competent management

In the same vein there are both upsetting and stabilizing factors at work in a chief executive's personal life. Among the upsetting factors are:

1. Poor health
2. Compulsiveness
3. Poor work habits
4. Inadequate salary
5. Inadequate fringe benefits
6. Social snubs
7. Intense preoccupation with job
8. Unbalanced work-to-play relationship
9. Feeling of job insecurity
10. Emotional problems with other family members
11. Sustained criticism from family members
12. Lack of appreciation of job pressure

Stabilizing factors include:

1. Self-discipline
2. Stamina

3. Realism
4. Strong survival instincts
5. Discretionary income
6. Satisfaction with position
7. Good family relationships
8. Job security
9. Good health
10. Adequate time for nonjob-related activities
11. On schedule with career growth plan

The fact that both roles of a chief executive are separate, but related, requires an understanding of ways to keep a hospital CEO in the saddle and performing at a high level under growing pressures. Though they are limited, options for maintaining personal stability are available to a CEO.

Personal options include:

1. A sustained and adequate exercise program
2. An avocation that has the potential for a second career
3. Outside income
4. Breadth of perspective
5. A sense of self-worth

Organizational options include:

1. A sophisticated budgeting process
2. An employment contract
3. Sophisticated management information systems
4. Strong, competent key executives
5. Performance-oriented review of personnel at all levels
6. An entrepreneurial view of responsibilities

In essence, an organizational load can be lightened by shifting some responsibilities, strengthening the management systems by providing built-in job security, and maintaining a physique that can meet a rigorous schedule.

The essential issues causing stress are clear. Stress on a chief executive is here, is growing, and is not going to go away, no matter what techniques are employed, since this role is going to continue to evolve. If a CEO is married to a saint, has angels for children, and the good luck to have inherited a fortune, the changing nature of the professional role will not throw him into a tailspin. But for the less fortunate CEO, one should bear in mind the findings of Hans Selye, who after years of study of human stress summed it up as follows, ''Don't be afraid to enjoy the stress of a full life, nor too naive to think you can do so without some intelligent thinking and planning. Man should not try to avoid stress any more than he would shun food, love or exercise.''[1]

NOTE

1. Hans Selye, *The International Dictionary of Thoughts* (Chicago: J.G. Ferguson Publishing Co., 1975), 692.

Part V

Managing Physicians

245

Chapter 26

Changing Characteristics of a Medical Practice[*]

Over the next generation the context in which a physician practices medicine will be undergoing change as will all other segments of the health field. Physician changes will be minimal when compared with those that other major providers, hospitals, and nursing homes will experience. The doctor-patient dyad will remain intact, since it is a personal, hands-on service involving a one-to-one relationship. This will not alter, no matter what new technologies are introduced or what takes place in the way in which medical practice is organized. Surgeons will still operate on patients, orthopedists will still handle fractures, and internists will still diagnose and treat patients requiring hospitalization. Then, as now, the practice of medicine will be a blend of art and science. Medical judgment will remain the basic ingredient of a physician's service and of value to society as a whole.

ENVIRONMENTAL CHANGES

The changes that will take place will have more to do with the environment in which a physician practices, not with the practice of medicine, even though diagnostic and treatment capabilities will be enhanced by continuing improvements in technology. The role of a physician as a clinician will remain the same, but the role of a physician as an organizer of medical care and as an entrepreneur will probably be different.

The altered role that physicians will play will require a set of skills and knowledge that traditionally have not been part of medical practice. For decades physicians have concentrated on developing and maintaining their clinical expertise, believing that their colleagues and the public would recognize their

---

*Adapted from *Hospital Progress* (now *Health Progress*), Vol. 64, pp. 37–41, with permission of The Catholic Health Association of the United States, © March 1983.

247

professional abilities and that this would lead to large and successful fee-for-service practices as long as the patient had an unrestricted right to select a physician of choice. This traditional outlook has led to the characterization of the physician's practice as a reflection of rugged individualism and independence. When the future is examined in terms of developing trends, it appears that a crucial concern of physicians centers around the constraints that are apt to occur with respect to the nonclinical aspects of the practice of medicine.

The distinction between clinical and nonclinical elements is likely to become blurred in the minds of physicians as these new constraints develop. The issue of quality of care may become confused with economic and organizational concerns. Nonphysicians are more likely to clearly see the distinctions because they are not as intimately involved in the actual practice of medicine. The result will be heightened tensions between physicians and hospitals, third-party payers and government.

ECONOMIC FACTORS AT WORK

Two reasons, both economic in nature, lie behind current developments. The first is readily understood by physicians and makes them apprehensive about the future, while the second seems more remote. On the one hand physicians are aware that the supply of doctors is growing at a faster rate than the population so that by 1990 there will be a 50 percent increase in the number of physicians in practice. From approximately 400,000 in 1980 there will be an increase to almost 600,000 by 1990. Instead of 1.7 physicians per 1,000 population, a ratio that has existed for nearly a century, there will be 2.45 physicians per 1,000 population. Physicians recognize that this means increased competition for them, and they are unsure of how to meet it.

This concern is real, particularly when it is noted that many have never before faced competition. Getting into practice has been nearly a riskless proposition for most physicians. In the past, they simply finished their residencies, selected a community or a group they felt comfortable with, hung up their shingles, and their appointment books began to fill. If they had chosen wisely they often had full calendars at the end of their first or second year in practice and would be considering not taking any new patients. Within a short period of time new physicians would be as busy as they wanted to be. In their offices no one looked over their shoulders to check on their quality of care and in the hospital they knew that they would encounter no difficulty if they practiced at the prevailing standards of the institution. They enjoyed both professional and economic freedom and expected it to continue as long as they maintained professional competence.

On the other hand, the shift from a national economy of ample resources to one of scarce resources has had an impact on individual practices that is indirect and more difficult to deal with because it involves federal-level government decisions. At this level, the voice of organized medicine is often pitted against the interests of the elderly, unions, the needs of the military, and a host of other interests, all competing for the same dollars.

Restrictions on expenditures for medical care are something most physicians previously experienced while serving residencies, but something that they thought they had left behind when they entered private practice. Until the early years of the '80s this was the case. Physicians applied their clinical judgments, ordered the appropriate procedures, and were unconcerned about the costs, knowing that third-party payers would pick up the tab for medical care of their patients. In a sense patient care outranked economics.

Many physicians came to believe that if a procedure was clinically justified that was the end of the line for their responsibility. In some measure this is still true, though there is growing interest in requiring physicians to justify procedures and have patients repeat procedures that fall outside the range of the expected cost.

The combination of a growing surplus of physicians and an economy of scarce resources caused the changes that are now taking place. External forces, government, insurance carriers, and hospitals are exerting pressures that will eventually lead to reactive postures by the medical profession, not only toward these forces, but also among physicians themselves, as each attempts to protect his personal economic turf.

Like any other group in society, physicians can be expected to resist efforts to restrict their clinical practices. The fact that they may enjoy an unusual degree of freedom as compared with people in other fields and professions has little meaning to them. From the physician's perspective, additional constraints represent an abridgement of the conditions that traditionally existed and they will be resented. Any program that interferes with a physician's right to establish his own fee schedule for services is one example. Thus, most private practitioners look unfavorably on insurance carriers, government agencies, and health maintenance organizations where standard fees are used.

As fixed-fee systems grow in number, physicians will grudgingly agree to established rates, but only when their number of patient appointments begins to decline. If their patient loads remain high they will not participate. Since there will be a growing number of physicians in practice it is likely that even well-established ones will face this problem. When physicians have a large practice, they are more concerned about life style than maximizing incomes and will opt for reducing their workday to have more time for personal pursuits. Physicians with other value systems will refill their appointment books by joining programs that have standardized and controlled fees.

As the supply of physicians increases there will be an effort made by physicians with established practices to prevent the newcomers in practice from joining medical staffs, particularly in the Sun Belt regions of the United States. The arguments that will be used for closing medical staffs will center around appropriate use of hospital facilities and the need to maintain professional skills by having an adequate number of patients to ensure that acquired skills are used frequently and not lost through lack of practice. In communities experiencing rapid growth the closed staff option will be a powerful argument because of the cost of adding additional hospital facilities. In areas where out-migration results in a declining population base these arguments will have less validity because of an excess of hospital beds.

Another development will be an increased segmentation of the medical marketplace. Given a choice between referring a patient to a hospital for a service or to a practicing physician who offers a similar service, the decision will usually be made to send a patient to a colleague in practice. This is due to the referring physician's preference for supporting the private practice system, knowledge that the charge for these services may be lower since the burden of indirect costs is less than in a hospital, and also because a patient will receive more personal attention.

PHYSICIAN-HOSPITAL TENSIONS

As economic pressure grows, physicians will become more acutely concerned about hospital activities that overlap into areas where private practitioners could provide the same service. Hospitals that develop primary care centers in outlying areas and contract with physicians for their services can expect to receive petitions from their medical staffs alleging that the hospital is involved in the corporate practice of medicine. In these instances, hospital governing boards may find themselves between a rock and a hard spot. They will recognize that medical staffs bring patients to their hospitals, but they will also feel a counter-pressure of knowing that they have to protect their market shares, particularly if they have incurred substantial long-term debt, whose repayment depends on protecting their market share. They may appreciate a physician's desire to keep the hospital as an economic neutral, but may not be able to go along with it when they view the mortgage repayment schedule of a hospital. Under these circumstances tensions will mount between hospitals and physicians.

The upcoming changes are seen as threats to the practice of medicine when viewed from the perspective of a physician. In the past, competition has been between physicians. Those practicing in a specialty could easily identify their competition—it was not all physicians in the area, only physicians in the same specialty.

The process of developing insight and understanding of what happened economically was easily accomplished through informal conversations at meetings of a specialty society. The gathering of this information required no particular skill, analytical ability, or judgment in determining what course to follow. A physician did not need a marketing plan. An attractive office, a good location, responsiveness to patients' concerns, and respect from colleagues based on professional competence sufficed; a riskless environment. The concern now is whether these elements are enough. All of them may be present and a physician may still not have a full calendar, a situation due to competition from other physicians.

The perceptions of physicians about hospitals are likely to continue, but they will change in focus. There are differences between hospital executives and physicians. In large part, this is due to the differences in their roles. Each has been shaped and molded by legal requirements, economics, training, organizational structures, and self-perceptions. The stresses and strains that have developed are the result of the tugging and hauling of these forces on the participants. They are not, except in a few instances, the result of excessive egos, meanness, or psychotic personalities of either physicians or executives. The lack of accord arises out of ignorance, or lack of understanding, of each other and the different pressures under which each operates.

Since the publication of the Flexner report in 1910, which identified gross inadequacies in patient care and medical procedures, hospitals have developed into technologically sophisticated institutions by responding to one question, "Does the program or service that is proposed enhance patient care?" If affirmatively answered, the second, and always second, consideration was to find ways to finance the activity.

In general, governing boards believed that they could always secure the necessary funds. This belief was justified during a period of ample resources. It is now clear that this belief is no longer valid. As resources have become scarce, the question to be answered is "Does the proposed activity enhance patient care at a cost that enables a hospital to remain competitive in the marketplace?" This is a different question and markedly alters relationships. When economic competition increases there will be more and more decisions made that will lead to new tensions between hospitals and physicians. These will occur because physicians typically view the management team of a hospital as being in charge of the support system that carries out patient orders for diagnostic and therapeutic services. They do not see management as being in charge of the total operation of a hospital. Physicians do not believe that a hospital CEO is the leader of the entire organization, rather than only the part that does not include physicians. It is for this reason that physicians do not look favorably upon hospitals paying salaries to physicians, which would clearly bring them within the domain of administration. As long as they are private practitioners and members of the medical staff, physicians are accountable only to other physicians.

The existing physician's perspective will change because economics have now become the first priority. Physicians will likely persist in the view that patient care has the highest priority and will therefore probably neither understand nor appreciate competition. A physician should always be an advocate of a patient and his safety in the hospital environment. This is the primary role of a physician now and in the future. Yet the structure that has encouraged this attitude will be drastically altered.

DIFFERING PERSPECTIVES

The new emphasis of financial affairs as a prime factor in the health care equation creates considerable distance between physicians and hospital executives. In the past, executives often felt at a disadvantage in the patient care arena. They lacked an intimate knowledge of medical jargon and often did not take the time to learn and appreciate the significance of a new clinical procedure or technique. At times executives seemed, from the physicians' standpoint, to be real detriments or barriers to clinical progress because of their lack of medical and nursing knowledge.

On the other hand, physicians often held simplistic views about what makes an organization run, the fact that executives could not reasonably discuss problems with them, except as it related to clinical matters. This gap has widened in the last few years and can be expected to continue to widen as hospitals unbundle into multiple corporations and convert themselves into health care corporations that ultimately will operate multiple operations at many sites. As this shift occurs a physician's voice in corporate affairs will be muted, but will continue to be heard in the hospital subsidiary.

Because of the organizational distance between a parent and subsidiary corporation, the CEO of the entire organization will be less subject to medical staff influence and will rely more on objective and analytical data for decision making. Physicians will increasingly understand less and less about the corporate organization as its complexity is magnified. Physicians' interests are clinical and patient-oriented; executives', organizational and financial. There will always be differences because the two groups are focused on different objectives, but both objectives are necessary for success.

Developments in the next two decades in the health field will not revolve around the physician and patient care. These elements will continue to be important and basic to the functioning of a delivery system, but the central focus will shift to organizational structure and finance. Membership on medical staffs of institutions that convert to either vertically or horizontally integrated health care corporations during the next several years will be sought by physicians because these institutions will have kept up-to-date with technology. This will result from positioning these corporations in marketplaces that have favorable reimbursement, unique services to offer, and attractive facilities for patients and physicians—all of which generate higher revenues to bring about its preferred status as a place to practice. Hospitals that appreciate the opinion of Wall Street as being as important as the opinion of the medical staff will be the survivors. Institutions that listen only to medical staffs and their interests will find that ten years from now those medical staffs will have disappeared, only to reappear in the institutions that have sustained an A or better rating from Standard & Poor's or Moody's over the years.

The issue of physician-hospital management relationships will be increasingly of less concern in the years ahead. The extent of change now underway in the hospital field is going to significantly realign the relationships and problems that have traditionally existed between the two groups, irrespective of the feelings that may be involved on either side.

Physicians who wish to teach will be in the publicly financed sector; physicians who want to be in the private practice will be in the private health care sector where health care corporations will be the most significant force controlling the delivery of health care.

MEDICAL PRACTICE CHARACTERISTICS

Given a changed health care environment, how are the characteristics of a medical practice apt to be different in the decade ahead? Clearly, with the growth of economic competition and third-party payers bargaining over prices rather than reimbursing on costs, there will be a restriction of free choice by physicians. This may be stringent under a typical health maintenance organization format, but somewhat less restrictive in a preferred provider organization approach. Both place restrictions on the services and ordering of physicians and hospitals, or provide a financial penalty on the patient if a service is used that is not under contract. In the future, practitioners can be expected to provide their services on both a fee-for-service and a contract basis to patients in their practice. The proportion of each will depend on local circumstances.

The same requirements will dictate the use of physician specialists. To the extent contractual relationships are in place there will be a shift in referral patterns as well. The collegial pattern of referrals will be replaced with contractual obligations to contract physicians for subscribers in these plans, which will force a shift of referrals.

Also, as a result of subscriber contracts physicians who have been accustomed to fee-for-service and charging on a per-unit of service basis will be put at risk by the terms of the contract for providing care to a number of patients at a negotiated fee that may well be less than the "usual, customary, and reasonable fee" they charge on fee-for-service. The ability of an insurance carrier to negotiate these terms will be enhanced because of the oversupply of practicing physicians expected by the latter part of the decade. Because of this surplus a physician will come to learn that competition will not be on service alone, but rather will be based on a combination of price and service, particularly among specialists where board certification can be used by the providers as a yardstick for determining those with whom they wish to contract.

With a contract approach the patient is no longer a purchaser of services in the same way that he has been under existing conditions. Most individuals at the present time are either enrolled as part of a group selected by the employer or are purchasers of an individual policy, neither of which restricts the choice of physician or hospital. When contract purchasing enters the situation both hospitals and physicians will be screened from approved lists provided to an insured. This screening on behalf of the insured will consist of two parts, the cost and charges and the quality of care. The first element is easier to pin down since prices can be locked in by contract. The other element is more difficult to control because it is judgmental and must be determined by agents of the third-party carrier. In all likelihood they will seek some arbitrary measure, such as Joint Commission accreditation in the case of a hospital and board certification for physicians.

As a business venture the establishment of a new medical practice will be more risky in the future because of the great increase in the supply of physicians. Now the required capital investment is relatively small and will not increase substantially in the years ahead. These front-end costs are modest, probably running less than one-half of the first year's billing. To date, the downside risk of getting into practice has approached zero. This is not likely to continue because a physician is going to have to consider how much competition he will have for the same kinds of services. Though it may lengthen the time needed for repayment of loans, this is not apt to be a significant factor.

In the future the number of employees on the payroll of a physician (office personnel) will not change and will remain small.

The fear of not making it in solo practice will cause many physicians newly in practice to join groups where they are assured of an agreed-upon income level, with the group assuming the cost of space, equipment, and malpractice insurance. Because clinical practice will not change, the inventory of items kept on hand will remain at present levels. Cash flow and accounts receivable seem likely to be extended as third-party payers attempt to hang on to cash as long as possible in order to maximize their return on the float in their cash management programs.

One of the major changes that can be anticipated is for physicians to resort to advertising in order to gain a competitive edge over their colleagues. Initially, this will be carried out by entrepreneurial physicians and will be resented by the rest of the medical profession. However, as advertising becomes successful, the remaining physicians will feel threatened by this approach and reach a conclusion that they must also engage in advertising in self-defense. Eventually, advertising will become widespread and will become accepted as a cost of doing business.

When all of these factors are summarized the results are as shown in Table 26–1. When these characteristics are studied it is evident that not only will the practice of medicine change in response to technological innovation, but the

Table 26–1 Changing Characteristics of a Medical Practice

Item	Now	Later
Choice of Physician	Unrestricted	Semirestricted
Referral Patterns	Collegial	Dictated and Collegial
Pricing of Services	Per Unit	Bulk Beds and Per Unit
	Free To Set	Restricted
Competition	On Service	On Price and Service
Supply of Physicians	Moderate	Oversupply
Entry into Practice	Easy	Moderate
Method of Payment	Fee-for-Service	Contract/Fee-for-Service
Purchaser of Service	Uninformed	Informed
	Patient	Third Party
Capital Investment	Low	Low
Number of Employees	Few	Few
Cash Flow	High	Moderate
Risk	Nil	Moderate
Inventory	Low	Low
Accounts Receivable	Low	Moderate
Advertising Costs	None	Moderate

way in which medical practices are organized and run will be even more severely affected. Expenses will be somewhat higher, competition will markedly increase, and income will probably be more restrictive under the contractual arrangements. The freedoms now enjoyed by the medical profession will have new constraints on the way in which physicians practice, with higher risks being run in establishing and maintaining practices.

When the upcoming changes are looked at through the eyes of a practicing physician they may seem to be monumental because they are a departure from a tradition that extends back for nearly one hundred years. When viewed from the perspective of society physicians do not appear to have a tough row to hoe since the problems they are now going to face are similar to those that have been experienced by other professional groups for years. In a sense, physicians are now about to enter the mainstream of life and to experience both the joys and frustrations of a profession.

Chapter 27

Self-Governance of a Medical Staff*

For a number of years the Joint Commission on Accreditation of Hospitals (JCAH) has included in its standards the idea that the medical staff of a hospital would be self-governing. Interpretations of what this means have varied considerably depending upon the viewpoint of the interpreter.

The problem arises in the organizational context when a subordinate post of the organization, the medical staff, can be subordinate to a governing authority in a hospital and at the same time be self-governing—a contradiction in terms. To an organizational purist, it is either subject to a governing board or it is not. If it is subject to a board, then the subordinate body is responsible for meeting and carrying out the dictates of a superior body in the organization, and there is no room for a concept such as self-governance.

On the other hand, when it is appreciated that the clinical decisions of individual physicians are best judged by other physicians and that trustees do not have the necessary knowledge to decide such matters, it seems evident that the review of clinical performance must be left in the hands of those who are competent to render judgments: the medical staff. In this sense, the medical staff is self-governing.

Yet, there exists an interdependence between a governing authority and a medical staff that does not permit unilateral action by either party.

PATIENT SAFETY IS PRIMARY

The ultimate purpose of an organized medical staff is to assure patient safety. A governing authority and a medical staff both have responsibilities in this regard. The appropriate conduct for carrying out this responsibility is the key to self-

---

governance. A governing authority must see to it that there is a defined process in place for reviewing the clinical performance of each member of the medical staff and that the process is regularly and continuously being used. The governing authority has a responsibility to know that medical staff evaluation is working.

It is the evaluation process that is of interest to trustees. A medical staff is accountable for using a medical care evaluation system to review the clinical judgments of individual practitioners. Judgments made by medical staff committees to review the clinical work of a hospital medical staff must be on a regular basis. The basis of self-governance is rooted in a belief that physicians, as professionals, will honestly review each other's work in order to protect patients.

In the event decisions reached by the medical staff become suspect, the governing authority may temporarily suspend its delegation of the clinical review to a medical staff, and at its discretion, seek outside, competent clinical judgment to verify the decisions reached by its own medical staff.

Self-governance is not granted to a medical staff to enable its members to ''circle the wagons'' and to protect all medical staff colleagues in a free and unabridged exercise of clinical judgment. Nor does it include a right to be accountable only to a medical staff. Self-governance is a contingent delegation of responsibility, accompanied by appropriate accountability, to assure patient safety. At any time it may be withdrawn if the superior body in an organization believes that the process that has been agreed to is being abused by a subordinate group.

The use of the words ''self-governance'' to describe the way in which peer review of physicians' clinical activities is carried out has led to numerous misunderstandings. Some physicians have chosen to interpret self-governance to mean that the medical staff could decide on its own bylaws, rules and regulations, departmental chiefs, and staff officers free and independent of either hospital management or governing authority. It is often argued that since the medical staff is ''self-governing,'' like any other governing body, there is an embodiment of authorities as part of its role in governance. In all likelihood, this peculiar interpretation has been fostered by using the word ''governance.''

DIFFERING VIEWPOINTS ON SELF-GOVERNANCE

Self-governance is frequently misunderstood, in different ways, by both trustees and physicians. Trustees recognize that they lack competence to judge the work of individual physicians and that a medical staff organization is an anomaly that does not fit with any of their prior experiences. Trustees may be intimidated by the language of physicians and by the concept of self-governance, which is widely accepted as meaning ''keep your hands off of medical staff activities.'' Unless the relationship between a governing authority and the medical staff is clearly understood, as well as the way the various aspects of this delegation are woven together, trustees will tend to avoid control of a medical staff because they do not know the intricacies of clinical medicine. Some trustees are aware that a medical staff is accountable to the governing authority, but only understand the concept and do not know how to bring it into a viable, dynamic, working relationship. It has no meaning to trustees in an operational sense.

On the other hand, physicians are not apt to encourage better understanding by trustees. Physicians often believe the interests of a medical staff are better served by keeping the governing authority at arm's length and off balance with respect to legitimate medical staff prerogatives. Physicians may believe that the less the governing board knows about their activities, the safer physicians are in their own practice of medicine within a hospital setting. This viewpoint can only lead to the erection of barriers, loss of communication between these two groups, and further intimidations of trustees.

With the advent of the use of mandated diagnostically related groups (DRGs) for the payment of hospital care, the existing relationships between governing authorities and medical staffs have come under increasing strain. Though physicians' services are not included in the DRG payment to a hospital, the physician is the person who triggers the use of the diagnostic and treatment procedures received by a patient. As payments are tightened on DRG reimbursement by the Medicare program, more and more physicians are going to discover that their clinical decisions result in a patient's hospital bill that is more costly than that permitted by a DRG. They are going to be faced increasingly with defending their decisions to a utilization review committee. This will occur with more frequency in the years ahead since DRGs are based on the median of hospital costs. This means that nearly half of the physicians will be faced with such a situation, since the median implies that half of the physicians, by definition, will fall outside allowable limits.

The reaction of a medical staff is predictable. Physicians will attempt to limit a hospital's ability to dictate their clinical decisions. One reaction will be for a medical staff to seek to incorporate as an independent organization and contract with a hospital for physician services and patients. From their perspective, this may seem to be a reasonable approach when they believe themselves to be separate and apart from the hospital corporation.

Self-governance, as a concept, implies independence. In their minds physicians may believe they have the leverage to bring about self-governance since only members of a medical staff can admit patients to a hospital. A threat is usually made when a hospital board insists on maintaining control and physicians respond by planning to admit patients to other nearby hospitals.

While such a prospect may give a hospital board pause for concern, upon reflection, trustees will recognize that a corporation legally accountable for all activities in its facilities cannot enter into such an arrangement without assuming a considerable exposure of corporate assets. When this kind of agreement is proposed, it is essentially a formal recognition of a medical staff "circling the wagons." Under such conditions, a hospital board can never be sure that the process of peer review is functioning, since the board would have no right to intrude in another corporate body or interfere in the internal workings of an outside corporation. Only when a medical staff is an integral part of the hospital corporation can the governing authority assure itself that the process they approved to review medical care is not only working, but working well.

Such a threat also overlooks the fact that all hospitals are operating under the same DRG program and that moving patients from one hospital to another by physicians does not alter the basic problem; it remains in both institutions.

A major difficulty stemming from the use of "self-governance" is that community hospital medical staffs assume this prerogative includes the right to elect departmental chiefs and the chief of staff without any approval by a governing authority. Quite often trustees share this opinion because they see this as part of the responsibility of self-governance. What they overlook is that an election process implies that elected leaders owe their positions to their constituents who elected them, not primarily to the governing authority. Who then represents the governing authority in assuring that the quality of medical care is reviewed in accordance with the bylaws of the medical staff?

WHO REPRESENTS THE TRUSTEES?

When trustees are asked "Who represents the trustees" their typical response is that it is the medical staff. Such a reply is difficult to understand since many medical staffs number in excess of 100. If staff leadership is primarily accountable to the medical staff, who is looking out for the interest of the governing authority? Does this answer mean that each physician is accountable only for his own actions? Obviously, this is not the case, and the governing authority, when cornered logically, usually concludes that there is joint accountability, to both the medical staff and themselves. This conclusion would be acceptable if both parties saw it that way, not when a medical staff leadership sees it differently.

The results of a questionnaire given to 34 physicians in medical staff leadership positions showed that 30 out of 34 (88 percent) believed that the Medical Executive Committee is primarily accountable to the medical staff, not to the governing authority. If this finding represents the way most physicians view the role of the Medical Executive Committee, then a governing authority really has no organizational component to turn to for carrying out the process of peer review. The review process may be in place, but whether it is effective remains totally in the hands of physicians and at a level of effectiveness decided by a medical staff, not the governing authority.

Over the last decade there has been a trend toward placing senior physicians of a medical staff on boards of the governing authority. Often that person is the president or chief of staff, and in some cases a president-elect or incoming chief of staff is included as well. From the perspective of the community, nonmedical board members view physicians as part of the governance structure that deliberates around a board table. Board-member physicians are expected to provide insights about how decisions are reached that will impact the practice of medicine in a hospital. Physicians are considered by other trustees to be equals who have a valuable contribution to make to board discussions. Again, this is not how physicians typically view their roles as trustees. Physicians see themselves as representing the medical staff and safeguarding its prerogatives from any encroachment by a governing authority or management. The questionnaire mentioned above was equally revealing on this point; 24 of the 34 physicians (71 percent) saw themselves as being representatives of medical staff interests when sitting as trustees. They are primarily present at board meetings as physicians and only secondarily as trustees, not the reverse.

Again, in the questionnaire, when asked if members of the governing authority had an unabridged right to attend committee meetings of the medical staff (if this was the wish of the board), 24 out of 34 (71 percent) believed that this is not the case; the governing board members can attend only if requested to do so by the medical staff.

When asked in the questionnaire if the election of a clinical chief requires board approval or concurrence, 19 out of 34 (56 percent) indicated that this is a matter solely to be determined by the medical staff and does not require any action by the governing authority.

On the matter of securing governing authority approval of the adoption of medical staff bylaws or changes in them, 14 out of the 34 (41 percent) believed that this is not necessary, that the medical staff may decide for itself how its members are to be organized and how they shall conduct their affairs.

These points, taken collectively, appear to indicate that many physicians view a medical staff as separate and apart from the rest of the hospital organization, as an autonomous body that decides for itself how it will conduct its business. Self-governance is viewed as just that, the ability to decide for itself without direction or interference from a governing authority.

The question again arises as to who represents the interests of the governing authority. The third part of the leadership of a hospital has to be examined. What is the role of management? Answers vary, depending on the perspective of the respondent. To a physician, management is not in charge of medical staff activities, though management may coordinate its activities. If desired by physicians, hospital administration may perform the mechanical functions of sending out notices, preparing minutes, scheduling facilities, but it may not participate in medical staff decision making. A chief executive is not the head of the medical staff; that authority belongs to the chief of staff and/or president. A CEO may be seen as the agent of the governing authority, but since physicians see the medical staff as a self-governing body, this agent is as restricted as the governing authority with respect to the medical staff. Generally, physicians will acknowledge that a CEO heads the support systems that process the diagnostic and therapeutic decisions of attending physicians with regard to their clinical orders.

THE ROLE OF THE CEO

How does a governing authority view the role of a CEO with regard to the medical staff? Since trustees are not accustomed from their own experiences to dealing with an organizational anomaly like a medical staff, they often have a blurred concept of the role of a CEO vis-à-vis the medical staff. In hospital areas such as finance, physical plant, nonclinical departmental operations, marketing, planning, and personnel management, there is no ambiguity. But in the areas of direct patient care where the activities of physicians impinge on and use hospital services, lines of authority are not clear and physicians are less sure how to proceed. For example, if the director of clinical laboratories is violating the terms of his contract with a hospital, trustees would quickly conclude that a CEO should correct the matter, but would be unsure whether or not the corrective action would include terminating his contract, even if the hospital's attorney concurred. Trustees would recognize a pathologist as a member of the medical staff as well as a member of the administrative staff in the position of director of clinical laboratory. This relationship becomes even less clear if a problem leads physicians on a medical staff to mistrust laboratory results that involve clinical interpretations of laboratory results. This is the kind of organizational problem trustees would prefer not to have occur since they do not have a clear understanding of how far the authority of a CEO extends. Given a choice, many trustees would like to have a CEO handle this problem to avoid reaching the governing authority for a decision.

This same situation occurs when unnecessary deaths take place. Since deaths are typically reported through nursing department channels to a CEO, the problem lands on a CEO's desk and there is no clear organizational understanding of how to proceed. In terms of authority, a CEO recognizes that deaths are a medical staff affair and should be dealt with through its organization structure. However, experienced judgment will motivate a decision to take up the matter with the departmental chief and/or the chief of staff to secure the proper review and restriction of an errant physician. In some cases, a CEO is confident that a medical staff will take the proper steps. In other situations, a CEO will be concerned that the only action will be inaction. Even in the same hospital where a CEO has had long tenure, the reporting of such an incident to medical staff authorities may have varying results because of the annual rotation of staff officers. In some years, a death review process would function as intended. In other years, there would be inaction, depending upon the quality of staff leadership.

These vagaries of staff leadership are largely unseen by members of a governing authority who lack daily contact with medical staff officers. To put it in other terms, the process of review will work better in some years than in others. In either case, a CEO usually has serious reservations about taking up the incident with the governing authority because the CEO may be fearful that the trustees will over-react through lack of familiarity with this type of problem. The usual course of action is to keep the matter away from the governing authority and to handle it directly.

Knowing that medical staff leadership may be prone to overlook a death case and not take the required steps, a CEO may first seek to arrive at a satisfactory conclusion by meeting with the physician involved to secure the desired results. A CEO, if this course is elected, recognizes that he is on shaky organizational grounds, but will be convinced that this is the wisest course of action given the cast of characters. It is only when the needed results are not obtained that the matter will be brought to the attention of the governing authority.

If a hospital is a public institution that is required to hold board meetings open to the public (to operate "in the sunshine"), the disclosure of an unanticipated death by a CEO to a governing board presents a serious problem. Knowing that a medical staff has not acted, and not being in a position to decide whether the clinical decisions leading up to an unnecessary death were appropriate, a CEO is caught on the horns of a dilemma. To report the matter and run the risk of public disclosure before a competent medical review of the case has occurred is to jeopardize the reputation of an attending physician; not to report it and delay a reviewing process permits a reoccurrence to take place by not enforcing patient safety concerns.

In addition, a nursing staff becomes uneasy when there is failure to act on a serious matter. Nurses come to the conclusion that the hospital's standards of patient care are not being enforced, which tends to restrict communications to a CEO about the single most important concern of a hospital. Neither risk is acceptable. Yet hospitals required to operate in the sunshine have not directly faced up to this issue, nor have state hospital associations taken a vigorous stance to modify existing conditions. When this situation obtains, the modus operandi is to look the other way because the avenues for seeking remedial action are not satisfactory. Often the result is a level of patient safety that is inadequate.

FEARS OF PHYSICIANS

Today, physicians are fearful. They are afraid that a growing surplus of physicians is going to reduce the number of patients using their services. They are also afraid that hospital corporations are becoming so large that they will ignore physician interests. Physicians are concerned that the growth of HMOs, IPAs, and PPOs will decrease the size of their practices. They know the world of the health field is changing more rapidly than ever before and believe these changes can only adversely affect physicians. Given these fears and apprehensions, physicians retreat behind the protective arm of the medical profession, where these same concerns are a common concern. As a result, physicians seek leverage to protect their profession from further erosion. Then self-governance becomes a rallying point as a legitimate barrier to prevent further intrusion on, at least, one front.

Carried to an extreme, which has occurred, a medical staff may believe that self-governance gives physicians the right to employ legal counsel to protect their interests, as well as the prerogative to have a medical staff office with employees in order to prevent governing board members of management from obtaining access to individual credential files, minutes of medical staff committees, and records pertaining to medical staff activities. Medical staffs may even pay the president/chief of staff an annual salary to ensure actions on behalf of the medical staff.

An interesting phenomenon among some organized medical staffs is the lack of discipline on matters of organizational policy. When a medical executive committee makes decisions, there is no assurance to the governing authority or hospital management that a necessary course of action toward individual staff members will occur. Each physician then is likely to decide for himself whether or not to comply with directives from trustees or CEOs.

On the other hand, when a medical staff makes decisions affecting clinical activities such as adopting regulations concerning consultations or establishing restrictions on drug therapy, or other activities that directly impact patient care, these decisions are accepted by individual practitioners and followed. It is in the arena of nonpatient care activities that physicians are reluctant to acknowledge any authority, including those of other physicians.

Trustees accept the concept of self-governance because they recognize that a medical staff is composed of individuals who are not hospital employees, but rather are the customers of the hospital since physicians independently decide for themselves the extent to which they will use a hospital. Because of this unique relationship, trustees are unsure how far their authority can be exercised, either directly or through a chief executive officer. The result is that most medical staffs in community hospitals are granted an unusual degree of freedom and only gross violations of ethics or clinical competence are questioned by trustees. In many instances, an unnecessary death or two must occur before a governing authority will involve itself with the quality of medical care in a hospital.

Short of unnecessary deaths, trustees are not likely to take any steps to improve the quality of medical care. This places a chief executive in a difficult position since reports are forwarded through nursing or from hospital-based specialists. In effect, physicians may be walking time bombs for malpractice proceedings involving the hospital. On the other hand, a CEO is concerned about the possibility of an unnecessary death, yet well aware that not enough solid information is available to take necessary steps. The self-governance concept tips the balance towards doing nothing until a tragedy takes place.

As a result, self-governance, rather than contributing to patient safety, works in a reverse manner, leading to unfortunate incidents before corrective steps are invoked. There is no question that most medical staffs will act after the fact, but all too often any steps taken prior to an event are construed to be interference, particularly if initiated by a senior member of management.

In the winter of 1982-83, the J C A H revised its accreditation standards and widely distributed them for review purposes. In the course of the ensuing revisions, a number of attorneys argued for changing the traditional title of Medical Staff Organization to a new title, the Organized Staff. Their argument for making this change was the fact that medical staffs now include non-M.D.s, such as podiatrists, optometrists, clinical psychologists, and chiropodists as members. The lawyers were concerned that this trend would result in a growing number of lawsuits by nonphysicians to obtain staff privileges and hospitals would be found to be in restraint of trade if they did not grant the requested privileges to individuals found competent in these allied medical fields. To head off this possibility the attorneys recommended that the medical staff organization should be renamed the Organized Staff. The uproar that followed forced the JCAH to reverse itself and to continue to use the traditional title of Medical Staff.

CHARACTERISTICS OF A MEDICAL STAFF

When one steps back and attempts to understand the meaning of governance for a medical staff, several points emerge:

1. A medical staff organization is designed to provide an organizational framework to physicians and allied health professionals who have been extended privileges to use a hospital, but who are not, in the main, employed by a hospital.
2. Members of a medical staff are not accountable to hospital management for the way in which they spend their time.
3. Members of a medical staff bill patients directly for their professional services and decide the amount of the fee.
4. Medical staff members individually decide the diagnostic and treatment procedures ordered for patients.

These characteristics determine the medical staff organization structure that has developed. They permit an interface to occur in an organized and responsible way between the individual practitioner and hospital resources.

In essence, the relationship between a member of a medical staff and a hospital is one that says:

1. Doctor, you are responsible for your own livelihood.
2. Doctor, you may use our hospital resources under the rules we prescribe.

A problem arises when a physician believes that hospital rules and bylaws, which are determined through a process of self-governance, do not apply to individual physicians who have a right to decide these matters for themselves. The test of whether rules and regulations are reasonable or not from the perspective of a hospital is usually not given consideration by a medical staff as they are developed. As might be expected, a medical staff considers self-governance to include every aspect of medical staff activities, unless it is specifically reserved by the governing authority and clearly states that activities are to remain directly controllable by the trustees.

SELF-GOVERNANCE HAS FAILED

Because of the lack of understanding that exists of the concept of self-governance, the use of this term should be abandoned since the words do not accurately describe the relationship of a medical staff to the other components of a hospital. It might be more useful to substitute the words "delegated governance." These words would clearly indicate that a governing authority has delegated selected functions to a medical staff, but like all delegations it is a contingent delegation that may be withdrawn at any time accountability is ignored. In order to clarify authorized delegations, the concept of "reserved rights of the governing authority" needs to be included. The reserved rights of the governing authority should be spelled out and include the following:

1. The governing authority maintains the ultimate responsibility, authority, and accountability for all activities of the hospital.
2. The medical staff bylaws and rules and regulations are subsidiary to the governing authority and may be withdrawn, if in the opinion of the governing authority, the agreed upon process of peer review is not being conducted in a manner considered appropriate by the governing authority.
3. The officers of the medical staff are recommended by that body to the governing authority for confirmation.
4. The appointment of a physician to the medical staff is a governing authority decision with the medical staff certifying the applicant's clinical skills.
5. The governing authority holds the Medical Executive Committee accountable for the activities of the medical staff.

Given the reluctance of a chief executive officer to bring to the attention of the governing authority matters involving members of a medical staff until a tragedy or near tragedy has taken place, a governing authority may wish to put an additional safeguard in place. Since nurses have increasingly stressed their clinical responsibilities as separate and apart from physicians, a governing authority might consider adopting a policy requiring nursing, through appropriate organizational channels, to report all incidents involving potential medical and nursing clinical mismanagement to the governing authority. Such a policy, if implemented, would make the governing authority aware of the walking time bombs within the medical staff and nursing department, and would put in place an early warning system about potential difficulties. This practice would enhance the governing authority's ability to take corrective action before a serious incident occurs rather than having to cope with a situation on an after-the-fact basis.

The danger of this policy is the potential for it to become a punitive organizational tool used by nursing to get even with physicians that they dislike. On the other hand, if properly used and if each incident is carefully reviewed by the chief executive, before submission to the governing authority, it will strengthen the ability of the hospital to ensure patient safety.

In retrospect, self-governance has failed as an instrument for warning governing authorities of impending disasters. Delegated governance, reserved rights of a governing authority, and a requirement that nursing report all clinical incidents to the governing board would be important steps to take in enhancing patient safety.

Chapter 28

Perceptions of a Medical Staff Organization

Joining the medical staff of a community hospital is an eye opener for physicians just entering private practice. With their initial medical care experience in a teaching environment, where the attending physician always had the final say on patient care, it is exhilarating to write patient orders in a community hospital knowing that one's decisions are where the buck stops. Being one's own boss is something looked forward to from the early days in medical school. As clinical experience was gained self-confidence grew as a fledgling physician came more and more to rely on his individual evaluation of a patient's condition.

LEARNING CLINICAL SKILLS

During his years of medical training the physician learned that there was a large body of knowledge he needed to know in order to competently diagnose and treat patients. In addition to the scientific aspects, he quickly learned that he also was called upon to handle the emotional aspects of illness, that patients were often fearful or afraid of what he had to say.

How to manage a practice, how to market one's medical services, and how to behave in a medical staff organization of a hospital were not part of this training. During a residency the new physician has only peripheral contact with these concepts. This to be expected since it is a full-time activity just to develop the required clinical skills. Had an attempt been made to acquaint the physician with managing, marketing, and organization during training he probably would not have given them priority because of the need to round out his clinical knowledge. Time spent on nonclinical activities, from the standpoint of a resident, is time that could better be spent in adding to the store of expertise needed to competently care for patients.

ENTERING PRIVATE PRACTICE

It is only after a transition has been made to private practice that the nonclinical concepts become important. The lowest priority in nonclinical understanding is medical staff organization. Getting an office going and building a medical practice is an activity of overriding importance. A part of this process requires establishing a hospital connection for medical staff privileges. When an application for membership is completed the applying physician receives a copy of the medical staff bylaws. As this document is perused the physician discovers that a medical staff is self-governing. From his individual perspective this is as it should be since it is his patients who are admitted to a hospital where he decides on the diagnostic and therapeutic procedures to be followed by hospital personnel.

Clearly, if he is in control of a patient then collectively all physicians should be in control of the medical staff. The stated purpose in medical staff bylaws authenticates this line of reasoning when the physician reads that he is a member of a group that is self-governing. Because he has had no previous experience as a medical staff member, he remains unaware of the limitations of this concept when it applies to an organization within an organization.

At about this time the new private practitioner is also undergoing a shift with regard to his role models. During training, most often in a large urban hospital, a respected professor or chairman of a clinical department in the university filled this role, a paragon of clinical excellence. In the community hospital setting, where he now finds himself, the role model is more apt to shift to a highly successful practitioner on the medical staff. The one-dimensional role model of clinical perfection is replaced with a multidimensional model who is clinically excellent, has succeeded economically, is influential in the community, is clearly a leader among his peers, and enjoys the fruits of his labors.

As the new practitioner participates in medical staff activities and joins other physicians in informal conversations in the hospital on rounds, he begins to tap in on the grapevine of both the hospital and the medical staff. The hospital grapevine he soon discovers is similar to the ones he previously knew, but the medical staff one is different. Instead of an exclusive focus on patient care he hears a number of other topics being discussed. Sometimes the conversation is about fees, salaries for office staff, fringe benefits for office staff, problems with nursing, closing the medical staff, or new programs being planned by administration that may cut into the economic territory of some medical staff members.

On balance, less than one-half of the informal conversations among attending physicians may center on clinical matters. When the new practitioner raises a question about self-governance with his colleagues he is informed that the medical staff annually elects its own officers and departmental chairmen, the Medical Executive Committee is accountable to the general medical staff, and the physicians who serve on the hospital governing board are there to represent the interests of the medical staff. Since there seems to be general agreement about these matters the new medical staff member believes these statements to be true and adopts them as the basis of his relationship with the hospital.

In due time the new staff member becomes involved in organizational activities of the medical staff, serving on committees, and eventually may be elected an officer of the medical staff. As he accepts more and more responsibility and moves into a staff leadership role he has increasing contact with the senior members of the administration of the hospital. He becomes involved in solving problems that develop between physicians and the hospital. In the course of doing so one or more of these problems is going to involve a decision as to what is hospital turf and what is medical staff turf. When a particular problem under discussion begins to unfold, the physician viewpoint is most likely to reflect his concept of self-governance. If the issue pertains to patient care and the remedies suggested by the physicians are in keeping with quality of care standards, no jurisdictional questions will arise. Even when the suggested solution is less than desirable from an administrative viewpoint, the solution will probably be accepted unless it involves a serious hazard to a patient.

On the other hand, if the medical staff leadership is concerned about an economic issue, such as the hospital undertaking a program that is directly competitive with selected members of the medical staff, the issue of organizational relationships may be brought to the forefront. When it surfaces the set of attitudes about the independence of the medical staff that were formed at the time private practice was entered will be the basis for the new practitioner's position in the ensuing discussion.

Should the chief executive comment on the relationship of a medical staff to the hospital as being one in which the hospital bylaws are controlling over the medical staff bylaws, this is apt to be disbelieved by physicians. Because they have taken the concept of self-governance in a literal sense for a number of years, such a statement by management may be regarded as self-serving.

Looked at from the physicians' perspective it is understandable why they view the medical staff as an organizational body that is separate and apart from the hospital.

As an organizational entity within the corporate structure, the medical staff is responsible for the quality of medical care in the hospital. However, it is delegated responsibility, from the governing board to the medical staff. Since the governing authority is a collective body that exists to establish institutional policies and derives its authority from the Corporate Act of the state, trustees delegate the responsibility for medical care to those who are competent to carry it out and provide them with an organizational mechanism for doing so. But, in doing so, trustees cannot disassociate themselves from public accountability for the quality of medical care provided in the hospital.

A governing authority creates a medical staff for only one purpose, to assure patient safety. This is a contingent delegation that may be withdrawn if the governing authority comes to the conclusion that patient safety is endangercd. The organized medical staff is not created to protect the interests, economic or otherwise, of the medical staff. Its sole purpose is to protect patients while in the hospital. This is why emphasis is placed on reviewing the clinical performance of individual staff members through a clinical department structure and the various medical staff committees.

The use of the words self-governance by the Joint Commission on Accreditation of Hospitals has not been helpful in clarifying this important matter. The term is too encompassing and has led physicians to an erroneous conclusion. Many physicians have come to believe that a medical staff is not a subordinate body to the governing authority but rather is a body that is on the same organizational plane as the governing authority.

The result of this misinterpretation has fostered organizational problems, since both parties involved operate from differing sets of assumptions about organizational structure. In fairness to physicians it should be pointed out that governing authority members have also lacked clarity on this point. All too often they have viewed the medical staff as an entity over which they have no control. In the event of a serious clinical mistake trustees realize that the hospital is involved but are unsure of what steps can and should be taken, given the precedent of a hands-off policy towards the medical staff.

JOINT VENTURES

With the current interest in developing joint ventures between hospitals and physicians these existing relationships are likely to become more confusing unless care is taken to develop realistic understandings of the purpose of a medical staff and its true functions. Joint ventures need to be separated out and kept apart from medical staff activities. When a joint venture is contemplated it should be developed with selected physicians who may be members of the medical staff but are considered for participation because it is in the mutual economic interest of both participants.

When joint ventures are considered a hospital needs to work with individual physicians and should not deal with the medical staff as whole, since economic ventures lie outside the reason for which a medical staff was created. Likewise, when a hospital becomes involved in developing a capitation plan, the matter should not be brought before the medical staff but should be open only to those physicians who desire to participate in this activity under the prescribed rules of operation.

In both of these programs, the hospital needs freedom to enter into economic relationships that benefit the institution to maintain its own economic viability. In doing so a hospital needs to be mindful that where it can advantageously join with interested physicians on the medical staff a joint venture should be encouraged, but this is not an activity of a medical staff per se.

Self-governance has been misinterpreted for so long a period of time that it is easy, as far as physicians are concerned, to include economic issues as well as patient safety. Changing this mind set cannot be rapidly accomplished because physicians have come to believe that the hospital should treat all members of the medical staff equally. Physicians will be slow to recognize that being equal applies to clinical care and clinical review and does not include joint economic enterprises.

An example may be helpful to illustrate this point. Assume that a hospital has built a health care facility in another part of town and is in the process of determining the extent and number of clinical specialists needed. The hospital then decides that only one general surgeon is required. However, two leading surgeons on the medical staff both express interest in the new facility. One is needed, but two have applied. In terms of the way a medical staff views this issue, both surgeons would be seen as having an equal right and it is up to the hospital to change its position.

The hospital, however, should make it clear that this decision does not involve the medical staff because it has nothing to do with patient safety. This is a business venture that is being developed. The appropriate approach is to ask each of the two surgeons to bid on the opportunity for appointment with an understanding that the hospital will accept the best offer.

Governing boards are going to have to keep reinforcing the idea that a medical staff organization is solely for the purpose of protecting patients. It is important to establish these boundaries since not all joint ventures will be equally successful. When a failure occurs it needs to be crystal clear in the minds of everybody involved that the venture was strictly a business affair.

As more and more physicians enter into joint ventures with hospitals, it will become increasingly important to protect professional interests from commercial interests to ensure that an organized medical staff continues to function in an appropriate manner and not become embroiled in economic matters.

With a growing surplus of physicians in this country self-governance, as it is now understood, will be seen by many physicians as a way for members of a medical staff to protect their economic interests by not permitting additional physicians to join the staff. In the future, the decision to close a medical staff may become more commonplace in community general hospitals but it cannot be carried out to protect the economic interests of physicians; rather it must be based only on ensuring that physicians are treating significantly large enough numbers of patients to maintain their clinical skills. The result may be of economic benefit to members of the medical staff but the action taken by a governing authority is based on its concerns with the quality of medical care rendered in the hospital.

Self-governance is a flawed concept because it should apply only to a review of clinical competence and establish the organizational structure needed to assure the governing authority that it is being appropriately conducted.

The starting point for this understanding is to clarify the purpose of a medical staff in order for individual physicians to understand why it exists. If joint ventures with physicians are to become successful, the concept of self-governance needs to be redefined as delegated governance that is limited to ensuring patient safety.

Chapter 29

Contracts for Hospital-Based Specialists

Historically, medical care for hospitalized patients was provided solely by independent, private practicing physicians. In 1918, the American College of Surgeons accreditation program first required that activities of physicians be organized in a formal way through a medical staff organization.

At about the same time, the state of medical knowledge and technology reached a point where laboratory medicine and diagnostic radiology were beginning to develop as institutional specialties of medicine. This change was quickly followed by the development of an organized, specialized anesthesia service in larger teaching institutions.

For the next three decades, 1920 to 1950, these hospital-based physician activities gradually spread to all but the smallest hospitals in the United States.

Since the early 1950s, both expanding medical technology and the development of new subspecialties in medicine have rapidly increased the number of hospital-based medical specialties. Today these specialties include emergency services, medical education, electrocardiology, electroencephalology, electromyography, nuclear medicine, administrative medicine, physical medicine, pulmonary medicine, nephrology, neonatology, house physicians, psychiatry, therapeutic radiology, and primary care ambulatory medicine.

The addition of these medical specialties in the hospital setting increased complexity and raised new questions about hospital-to-physician, and physician-to-physician, relationships. These relationships were further complicated in the 1970s by a large upswing in medical malpractice issues.

The increased number of hospital-based medical specialties with several physicians providing these services in the same specialty has raised problems about the application of the concepts of private practice in medicine to their specialty.

PRIVATE PRACTICE OF MEDICINE

Traditionally, a physician practiced medicine as an independent contractor, free to choose whom he served, with complete freedom to diagnose and treat patients and to render or not render a bill to patients for his professional services. Except for laboratory medicine and diagnostic radiology, this was the customary practice of almost all physicians until the 1950s.

When physicians hospitalized patients, they totally controlled medical care as the attending physician. They were accountable for the patient's medical outcome. If consultants were used, the attending physician selected the consultant physician and they generally did not stray from the consultant's sheet on the medical record to make entries on an attending physician's order sheet. In essence, the attending physician controlled continuity of patient care.

The attending physicians were free to bill for their services and collect as they saw fit. The patient received one bill, or occasionally an additional consultant's bill. With the development of multiple hospital-based medical specialties, the situation changed for both the attending physician and the patient.

Private medical practice meant the right to admit a patient to a hospital of the attending physician's choice, an appointment to the medical staff of a hospital with a delineation of privileges, freedom to use diagnostic and therapeutic modalities, and an obligation to participate in general staff, departmental, and committee meetings.

In the past several years, these professional freedoms have gradually been circumscribed by governmental and insurance carrier regulation. Usual and customary fee structures, P R O reviews, tighter hospital regulations, reviews mandated by external agencies, and cost-containment efforts have reduced medical freedom.

The attending physician's role has been altered by these changes, as well as by the development of hospital-based medical specialties. Likewise, the appropriate role of hospital-based physicians has gradually been differentiated from that of the attending physician.

CHARACTERISTICS OF HOSPITAL-BASED MEDICINE

Probably the greatest difference in clinical practice between hospital-based physicians and attending physicians is the privilege of admitting patients. In most instances, the hospital-based physician has either limited or no admitting privileges. In general, the attending physician is the source of all patients admitted, while a hospital-based physician is a provider of specialized medical services on the orders of the attending physician.

Institutional medical practice developed because of a need to use highly expensive instrumentation, sophisticated facilities, and specifically skilled ancillary medical personnel. The population base required to cost-justify institutional medicine is typically much larger than one required to sustain a general surgeon, internist, or family practitioner in private practice.

Patient services provided by hospital-based physicians are frequently not visible to the hospitalized patient, or if a hospital-based physician visits a patient, the importance of his medical judgment remains unknown to the patient.

In complicated diagnostic and therapeutic cases, or in the case of seriously ill patients, five, six, or more physicians may be involved. If each involved physician renders a separate bill for professional service, the patient becomes confused and payment problems frequently arise. With greater and greater frequency, hospitals and physicians have recognized the difficulties inherent in multiple professional bills and have moved to arrangements that allow the hospital to bill and collect for their individual professional services.

To provide efficient and effective medical services hospital-based physicians must achieve a higher level of organizational integration than attending physicians. Since many hospital-based physicians' services are carried out through their direction of ancillary personnel, institutional objectives and needs must transcend their personal goals. This is an infrequent experience for attending physicians, but often a daily occurrence for hospital-based physicians. Their efforts must support and coordinate with the needs of the attending physician.

In addition, the use of ancillary personnel requires a hospital-based physician's integration into the management structure of the hospital to achieve cost-effectiveness. This means that hospital-based physicians must be authorized to use the management tools of the organization to achieve efficient use of ancillary manpower. They are expected to recommend budgets, to hire and fire, to discipline personnel, and to coordinate their activities with the support services of the hospital. Without this kind of participation in hospital affairs, the diagnostic and treatment goals of attending physicians will not be met, and articulation of the necessary elements of medical care will not be accomplished.

To achieve this level of integration, a hospital-based physician is given two hospital appointments. One appointment is a clinical appointment as a member of the medical staff and the other is an administrative appointment, as a part of the management structure of a hospital. For example, a chief of the pathology service and director of laboratories holds the appointment of a chief of service as a member of the medical staff and as a member of the administrative staff of the hospital as a director.

A chief pathologist's accountability is to both the medical staff for clinical services and to the hospital administration for the management of the laboratory department.

MEDICAL MALPRACTICE ISSUES

In the past decade both federal and state courts have participated in more clearly establishing hospital accountability and responsibility for the acts of hospital-based physicians.

Some of these recently emphasized legal trends can be summarized as follows:

- When an institution has the right to direct the time of service, the manner, methods, and execution of work, a hospital-based physician's legal position as an independent contractor is questionable.
- Hospital accountability must be established for malfunctioning equipment, accuracy of results, failure to notify attending physician of results, and failure to note clinical signs.
- Responsibility must be established for the anticipation of untoward events in the diagnosis and treatment of patients.
- Establishment of clear and enforceable standards of care is essential.
- A legal responsibility must be established by the courts for patients who come to a hospital for emergency services on their own, rather than at the direction of a physician, are hospital's patients.

Because of the legal concept of proximate cause and the increasing complexity of medical services provided by hospital-based physician specialists and their ancillary staffs, liability for medical malpractice by hospitals has significantly increased. Courts now hold hospitals responsible for maintaining organizational coordination and the integrity of both hospital-based physicians and hospital personnel.

Essentially these legal points of view have changed the role of a hospital from that of a place for physicians to work in to more and more that of directly providing care to those in need. The other side of that coin is the way in which the various hospital-based medical specialty societies have responded to these pressures from hospitals and judicial decisions.

STATEMENTS OF MEDICAL SPECIALTY SOCIETIES

Codes of medical ethics for several different hospital-based medical specialty societies are similar. In no instance do they make a statement affirming or prohibiting a physician from entering into a contract with a hospital.

The various codes of ethics have a general thrust that it is unethical for a physician to dispose of his services to a third party who has an opportunity to profit from the sale of these services. They include statements about a variety of reimbursement and billing arrangements with the recommendation that separate billing components for physician and hospital are preferred.

The literature of specialty societies includes model contracts, typically published in the late 1960s, which reflect the concerns of that time when Parts A and B of the Medicare Law were major issues. These codes typically recognized that their members held two hospital appointments, one as a physician and the other as a departmental administrator. In most cases, they have a statement on the society's stance that a physician is free to engage in outside work, provided he does not neglect professional responsibilities to the department.

By the 1970s, this literature was replete with legal citations of court cases testing the right of a hospital to enter into exclusive contracts with physicians. In summary, these cases concluded that hospital privileges are not a vested right of physicians, and they give hospitals a clear precedent to negotiate contracts to provide for the operation of specialized departments, and as a part of the contract, to vest an exclusive right in a physician or group of physicians.

IMPLICATIONS

In the previous discussion of the history and current status of hospital-based physicians their differences from private practice were described. The typical characteristics for hospital-based practice can be summarized as follows:

- No authority to admit patients
- Financial stability provided by an institutional basis of practice
- Ease of establishing a practice, because the clinical base is provided by attending physicians
- Fees for professional services often included in the hospital bill
- Responsibility and accountability for directing hospital staff, calibration and operation of instrumentation, and control of the schedule
- Two appointments in a hospital, one clinical and the other administrative

A hospital-based physician provides services to the patients of attending physicians, either on a standing order basis or as a specifically ordered test or procedure. To carry out these tests and procedures, a hospital-based physician integrates and coordinates the activities of a medically directed hospital service to meet the needs of an attending physician and his patient.

Because a hospital is a complex organization with hundreds of procedures and a large number of departments, the efficient and effective delivery of services must be accomplished within a highly structured environment.

Efficient and effective hospital-based practice requires an intimate understanding and knowledge of organizational processes and a willingness to become part of a larger organization that has established practices and procedures. In addition, hospital-based physicians are frequently required to provide medical services that are institutional in nature and not direct service to patients. For example, anesthesiologists typically direct medical care in a surgical recovery room, rather than requiring the operating surgeon to remain available until a patient is returned to a nursing station. There is also a responsibility to daily schedule all anesthesia service, make preoperative rounds, and supervise the services of certified registered nurse anesthetists (CRNAs).

If the traditional concepts of private practice are applied without modification, and an anesthesiologist retains a right to accept or decline service to a particular patient, an operating surgeon cannot easily schedule cases. The use of CRNAs under anesthesiology supervision, with anesthesiologists working independently, usually creates a work environment of low morale and scheduling difficulties.

Each hospital-based medical specialty has a similar set of problems, particularly if there is more than one physician practicing in a specialty.

It is not happenstance that hospital-based physicians have dual appointments. Because their services are available to all hospitalized patients on either an on-call basis or as a routine service, demands are created that can be accommodated only by establishing a hospital department or program. To provide prompt service on demand, a hospital must be assured that there is a functioning chain of command that will implement around-the-clock coverage.

Because of the need to maintain an up-to-date quality service, there must be a physician-leader with authority and responsibility to achieve and maintain standards of care. To carry out departmental functions, control of professional, technical, and clerical personnel is required.

When leadership of a physician-directed department is not clearly established in one position because there are multiple medical inputs, a department's functioning typically deteriorates. At best, an informal leader may arise, but this person will be attempting to provide leadership under the handicap of not having the management tools necessary to control and direct departmental activities. From an organizational point of view, it is more effective to have a designated departmental director with authority and accountability for performance.

CONCLUSION

There are advantages and disadvantages to maintaining a physician-directed hospital department on an organized basis with a designated director. They are as follows:

Advantages

- Personal accountability for the effectiveness and efficiency of the service
- Assurance of continuity of coverage
- Concern for the quality of care and continual updating of medical technology
- Direct supervision of all personnel of the department

- Ability to interact and coordinate with other hospital departments and activities
- An identifiable position to other members of the medical staff
- Better continuity of care to patients using departmental services
- Responsibility for recruitment of medical and hospital staff to meet manpower needs
- Centralized scheduling of activities

Disadvantages

- Professional fees earned by the department are limited to one designated physician or group of physicians.
- Subspecialty medical knowledge or expertise may not be available in the department to assist an attending physician.
- The use of specialized knowledge may be made more difficult for a member of the medical staff not holding a departmental appointment.

Part VI

Dealing with Hospital-Based Physicians

Chapter 30

The Supply and Income of Hospital-Based Physicians

The trend toward closer ties between hospitals and their medical staffs has gradually evolved throughout this century. Three key factors have served as the principal stimuli:

1. The expansion of the traditional hospital-based specialties of anesthesiology, radiology, and pathology and the later development of subspecialties such as neonatology, nuclear medicine, and radiation therapy due to the rapid growth in medical knowledge.
2. Changes in graduate medical education and training requirements that have encouraged hospitals to add hospital-based physician-directors to coordinate sophisticated patient care programs.
3. The need to effectively manage issues that were traditionally controlled by the voluntary compliance of the medical staff, which has led to the hiring of chiefs of staff, clinical department heads, and other physician-administrators. Typically, these physicians are employed by the hospital to provide a strong interface with the medical staff for quality assurance, accreditation standards compliance, physician recruitment, and other sensitive hospital-medical staff relations issues.

FUTURE TRENDS

While these forces have promoted the expansion of hospital-based physician practices, current emerging trends will have a profound effect on these arrangements in the future. There are several reasons. First, reductions in inpatient use rates will significantly affect the incomes of hospital-based physicians involved in fee-for-service arrangements. As hospitals gain experience under the new Medicare DRG-based payment system, they will encourage physician restraint in the ordering of diagnostic procedures. These reductions will include ancillary medical services and will reduce hospital-based physician practice incomes as departmental service volumes decrease.

While average physician income of attending physicians has fallen in the past several years, the incomes of physicians in hospital-based specialties have continued to rise. When hospital-based physicians begin to experience financial setbacks, they will seek relief from the hospital in the form of salaries or minimum guarantees.

Second, the growing problem of restricted financing of health care will cause hospitals to cut back on the procurement and implementation of costly new technologies and equipment. This slowdown in medical science tertiary-care advances will also result in a similar slowdown in the growth of hospital-based physician arrangements.

Third, as the supply of physicians increases and they become more concerned with their collective financial well-being, economic partnerships between hospitals and medical staffs will become increasingly important. These partnerships will likely take the form of joint ventures where the amount of patient care activity and their operating profits will benefit physicians directly. In the past, incentives for inpatient services have been common among those physicians who are traditionally hospital-based through lease and percentage arrangements. Now, with a redirection in incentives by the DRG-based payment system, economic partnership arrangements will focus more on ambulatory service activities. A premium will be paid to those hospital-based physicians that offer a management acumen to help control costs, market services, and provide general departmental leadership in addition to their clinical expertise. These direct incentives will become standard fare for most physicians, particularly those with practices that have a significant impact on hospital revenues. Members of a hospital's medical staff will be brokers for the hospital's services and will be rewarded proportionately.

These changing market conditions will increase the income ties between a hospital and its medical staff and have major implications for hospital-based physicians. As physician supply increases and as the acquisition of technological advances slows, the services offered by any single physician or group of physicians will be viewed as a commodity driven by the DRG approval. As this occurs hospitals will need to maximize the value received for dollars spent. Sound business practice will dictate that the hospital will continually review the value received for resources spent to assure optimal performance.

In the past, hospital-based physicians could rely on strong support from the medical staff to enhance their negotiating position vis-à-vis hospital management. However, other members of the medical staff will also be forming economic partnerships with the hospital and competing for the same limited resources.

The relative income levels of physician specialists have previously been determined by market conditions. This is now rapidly changing. Should Medicare payments to physicians come under the DRG payment program, significant variations in referral patterns and ancillary service utilization may develop.

Although limitations in health care expenditures will be experienced by both physicians and hospitals, it will be hospital-based physicians who are most affected by these cutbacks. The incomes of hospital-based physicians rose dramatically during the past two decades but now will begin to decline. New market forces will decrease utilization and provide new and different incentives for hospital resource allocation. Hospital-based physicians offering a specialized service will either adjust their income expectations to market conditions or be in constant conflict with management and other members of the medical staff. The relative bargaining strength of hospital-based physicians in such conflicts will be directly proportional to their value to a hospital and the availability of similar alternate talent in the marketplace.

When hospitals renew agreements with their hospital-based physicians, a key factor will be a recognition of these changing trends and will require that flexibility be negotiated into their contracts. The ongoing success of a hospital will, in part, be dependent on management's willingness and ability to aggressively manage its hospital-based physician resources in anticipation of ever-changing market conditions.

Chapter 31

The Role of the Hospital-Based Physician

The number of hospital-based physician positions has expanded as the rate of new medical knowledge and technology has increased. Today, a typical acute care general hospital will staff approximately seven physician positions for each 25,000 patient days. Some positions will be staffed by full-time physicians, while other physicians will be part-time and spend from one to several hours a day on their hospital activities.

These physician positions blend the use of expensive technology with highly specialized knowledge. A hospital is required to have these specialized medical services available on demand for attending physicians.

THE DUAL POSITION OF HOSPITAL-BASED PHYSICIANS

Hospital-based physician positions are a unique organizational arrangement. The two major elements for delivering patient care in a hospital are a medical staff and hospital personnel. Medical staff members are appointed for limited periods of time, have few organizational restraints on the fulfillment of their responsibilities, and have control over their time in the hospital. Conversely, hospital personnel have an employer-employee relationship with only limited discretion with regard to their duties. Hospital-based physician positions are both a medical staff appointment and a management position in the administrative structure.

The dual position of hospital-based physicians creates an organizational environment that restricts the authority and control of a chief executive. Unless a chief executive adjusts a hospital's management strategies to be consistent with this dual relationship of hospital-based physicians, difficulties may result.

Authority, responsibility, and accountability are typical concepts used to describe the major elements of organizational control. Because of the dual nature of hospital-based physician positions, a chief executive's organizational role with respect to them is unclear.

It is obvious to administrative staff members that there is a difference in authority between hospital-based physician departmental directors and nonphysician directors. These differences result from four factors:

1. The appointment of hospital-based physicians customarily is codified by a written contract that explicitly defines their scope of authority to direct and participate in the management of a medically directed hospital service.
2. Autonomy for professional decisions in clinical matters is assured through a medical staff appointment by a board of trustees.
3. Typically, hospital-based physicians are certified by a specialty board in medicine, which adds influence and prestige to their opinions and judgment in both medical and management decisions.
4. With the enactment of a prospective payment system for Medicare, the majority of hospital-based physicians are now paid through fee-for-service arrangements and have either total authority to establish their fee structure or at least the right to recommend it.

These four differences in formal and informal organizational authority create a relationship between a hospital administrative staff and hospital-based physicians that is less direct than it is for the remainder of the management and professional staff. When a chief executive fails to recognize the significance of this difference, a situation of continuing confrontation with members of the medical staff can be created.

In addition to the differences in authority relationships, hospital responsibilities are not the same for hospital-based physicians as they are for nonphysician management and professional staff. In the area of responsibilities there are also four differences:

1. A requirement for state licensure and a need for specialty training with American Board Certification establishes a personal responsibility for a hospital-based physician to maintain ethical and clinical professional standards. Quality of patient care is defined more specifically for them than for hospital personnel.
2. A higher standard of management performance is required because statutory and common law judicial decisions establish greater responsibilities for physicians for administrative negligence.
3. The growing complexity of procedures and systems required to operate them increases the scope of responsibilities of hospital-based specialists because of the unique technical knowledge required.
4. In turn the skill levels required of a technical staff increase in a medically directed department, creating a need for closer supervision by the department director.

When a physician-director of a medical service department does not perform his management responsibilities as completely as is administratively necessary or desirable, a chief executive has substantial difficulty in identifying the cause of the management problem as well as finding an appropriate remedy. The unique authority relationship maintained by the physician-director often obscures internal departmental operations by precluding the issuance of a direct order by the chief executive to change operating procedures or practices.

If physician-directors are inadequate managers they may attempt to shift responsibility for departmental operations to the hospital administration. This is accomplished by alleging that technical staff salaries are too low, instrumentation is inadequate in terms of sophistication or amount, or there is an insufficient number of technical personnel. Such a tactic may gain the support of the general medical staff whether it is true or not.

With the advent of new complex technology, which increases the number of hospital-based physician positions, organizational accountability becomes even more obscure. From experience, hospital-based physicians learn that there is a shared accountability with the medical staff and the management of a hospital. They are aware that modern medical care is a continuum of functions with no totally separate and distinct parts.

A medical service department must integrate its operations with the flow of patients and the operation of other hospital departments if quality medical care, efficiency of operation, and cost-containment objectives are to be optimized. The establishment of totally independent departmental operations increases operating costs to a level higher than the mutual sharing of support services. Hospital-based physicians are likely to emphasize patient care concerns to the detriment of operating costs. Differing perspectives is a common experience between these physicians and the administrative staff.

Hospital-based physicians have another reason for a lack of concern about hospital costs. They are aware that the general medical staff expects accuracy, reliability, rapid reporting of results, and comprehensive clinical and support activities. Because of these expectations, some attending physicians are aware that their own mistakes in patient diagnosis and treatment can be masked. They attempt to shift responsibility to the hospital-based physician. Recognizing this possibility, hospital-based physicians may over-staff to avoid unjustified criticism from attending physicians.

Because of patient, family, and visitor contacts, hospital-based physicians emphasize patient concerns. With sensitivities to patient concerns, physicians strive to increase convenience and ensure a pleasant and attractive environment. Cost considerations are of secondary importance.

The gap between hospital-based physicians and the management staffs is widened when support is sought from the general medical staff, who typically react on an emotional, rather than a rational basis. Such tactics are employed to obscure the lack of management skills of hospital-based physicians. They may infer that cost control concerns are an administrative desire to control or reduce the quality of medicine practiced. In order to make this point, they may attempt to deal directly with members of a governing board and thereby compromise the chief executive.

MANAGEMENT CONCERNS

To cope with the uniqueness of hospital-based physician positions, a chief executive needs to carefully detail in a written contract the authority, responsibility, and accountability of each of these positions. The time has passed when a handshake or a limited contract with generalized statements is adequate. The relationship between a physician and a hospital is complex. A detailed statement of the responsibilities and authorities of each contracting party is necessary if future misunderstandings are to be avoided. Today's circumstances require clearer understanding of the duties, relationships, and roles. In order to maintain and encourage high-quality performance by these physicians, all elements of this relationship need to be defined and evenly balanced.

The role of a hospital-based physician includes organizational elements found in both the medical staff and the hospital management. A mutually satisfying relationship is the goal of a good contract. This can only be accomplished through a comprehensive analysis of the realistic needs of both parties. However, each party's expectations must be tempered to achieve a workable relationship.

A hospital-based physician can neither insist on the same degree of freedom from the hospital organization as a private practice physician nor have the same prerogatives that hospitals grant to attending physicians. Conversely, a governing board or a chief executive cannot insist that hospital-based physicians are no different from other hospital employees. Stubbornness on the part of either party only creates an organizational climate that can lead to major confrontations. Should this occur, patients, physicians, and management all pay an unnecessary price, either through increased costs, litigations, adverse public relations, a decrease in quality of medical practice, or additional pain and suffering of patients. In a larger sense, the public may lose confidence in the medical care establishment.

Capably managing hospital-based physicians is a challenge for medical staff leaders, governing boards, and management staffs. Successfully integrating these positions into a hospital organization requires a thorough understanding of the hospital-based physician's unique organizational role and an ability to express complex issues in straightforward terms. It requires skill to negotiate differing value systems into a workable relationship. Failure to do so eventually generates a state of affairs that leads to poor clinical performance and inadequate management practices.

Chapter 32

Structuring the Contract Negotiation Process

To achieve a satisfactory contract between a hospital-based physician and a hospital, the perspectives of both negotiating parties need to be understood. The process used to establish the contractual elements and the contract's specific language should be clear and understandable to both parties.

The goal of a negotiation is a final contract that is fair to all parties involved. It should promote excellence in medical care as well as protect the interests of patients and community. However, there may be differing opinions about the best way to reach these goals.

Typically, the starting position of a full-time hospital-based physician is that he is in the private practice of medicine and therefore the hospital cannot determine his fee structure, nor should the management be concerned about hours of attendance, participation in outside practice activities, or other aspects of working conditions so long as the clinical service is performed competently and in a reasonable timeframe.

On the other hand, management may believe that the hospital-based physician has been given an established practice with no office expense and a monopoly position. In addition, he has more reasonable work hours than private practice physicians and an income usually in excess of other physicians.

The purpose of the negotiating process is to adjust both perspectives into a more realistic position. Structuring the process begins by creating an awareness in hospital trustees that the authority to control the medical staff is vested in the governing board and not in the chief executive. In negotiations, a hospital-based physician typically tends to emphasize his medical staff status and deemphasize his management position as a department director or a deputy department director. This strategy recognizes that a governing board cannot expect a chief executive to conduct contract negotiations if the basic control of a medical staff is an authority reserved to the governing board.

In the last two decades hospital-based physicians, by and large, have been able to capitalize on a governing board's involvement in negotiations. The result has been to raise the income levels of pathologists, radiologists, and anesthesiologists from minimum specialty income levels to the maximum levels of neurosurgeons and orthopedic surgeons.

When a hospital governing board elects to have the chief executive conduct its negotiations and then alters his recommendations, either to avoid a confrontation with hospital-based physicians or to insist on a contract similar to the standard hospital personnel employment agreement, the result is an unbalanced contract. Such a contract will either permit the hospital-based physician to take advantage of the hospital or the hospital to take advantage of the physician. It is not unusual to find both types of unbalanced contracts in the same hospital.

An imbalance can also occur within the same contract. The scope of professional freedom and responsibility, fairness in pricing, adherence to quality levels, and efficient delivery of services may be unbalanced. This occurs when there has been no meeting of minds between trustees, physicians, and chief executives prior to the actual negotiation process. As a consequence, a common philosophy on the role and management of medically directed hospital services is undetermined.

There are four basic organizational activities common to medically directed hospital services: professional services to individual patients, management activities of the service, educational responsibilities, and in some hospitals, research programs. Because of the commonalities among all medically directed services, it is a good negotiating strategy to treat all hospital-based specialties as alike as possible in their contracts. Where there are differing responsibilities and authorities there should be separate items detailing these differences. Thus, a standard contract should be developed that is applicable to all hospital-based physician specialties and this should be supplemented with additional exhibits and schedules enumerating specific authorities, responsibilities, professional fees, and other elements unique to each specialty.

Because hospital-based physicians are members of both the medical and management staffs, it is desirable to have representatives of management, governance, and general medical staffs participate in appointment and standards of performance decisions. This can be accomplished by appointing a committee with representation from each interest. This committee, either on a standing or ad hoc basis, should be a committee of the governing board and should report its final recommendations to that body. In order to provide objectivity to the process, an outside consultant experienced in negotiating physician contracts and the hospital attorney should also be members of the committee.

The criteria for establishing this committee have been developed from experience. Limiting the number of committee members will allow for adequate discussion time and encourage frank expressions of opinions. A workable size is six to eight members. For a seven-member committee, a desirable composition would be four attending physicians, two trustees, and one senior member of the management staff. Hospital-based physicians should not be appointed, nor should the chief executive be included.

Because the work of this committee is sensitive and has serious internal political implications, it is important to carefully select its membership. Useful criteria for selecting its members are: broad experience in the hospital organization, respect of the other members, an ability to remain objective in analyzing complex issues, a willingness to deal only with major issues, a desire for high-quality medical care, an understanding of the administrative process, and the ability to avoid discussions outside of committee meetings.

Once the committee has been appointed, an initial meeting should be conducted by the hospital consultant. In the meeting, the purpose and functions, as well as other factors, are discussed. These factors include: the unique characteristics of hospital-based physician positions in the organization structure, the medical requirements for competent performance by these physicians, requirements for satisfactory management performance, and the organizational limits to be established for practicing while in these positions.

The recording of these decisions is the responsibility of the hospital consultant. An assessment of the current characteristics of departmental operation, in terms of the expected workloads of the hospital-based physicians, recent financial experience of the department, and the per-unit expense of physician services should be detailed. In addition, all existing physician contracts should be analyzed to evaluate completeness, appropriateness, and equity for both contracting parties. The next step is to interview physician-directors to determine existing problems and to assess the degree of flexibility they are willing to accept in their hospital relationship. At that same meeting, the accuracy of the data provided should be reviewed and the physician-director informed about the current legal and regulatory environment that affects hospital-based practice. When concluded, these findings are reported to the committee as necessary background for making hospital-based physician contractual agreement decisions.

At this point, a decision is needed: should the hospital contract solely with a physician-director of a medical service with several full-time associates (such as radiology, anesthesiology, and pathology) or should it contract separately with each physician? In addition, the insurance limits required, length of the contract, renewal provisions, and how a contract may be terminated should be decided.

In the financial sections of the contract, whether or not the physician will do independent billing and collecting of professional fees, who will approve fee schedules, and whether an annual audit will be required should be considered.

In the operations section of the contract, decisions are needed on the extent of outside professional activities, whether or not approvals are required, the extent of teaching and committee activities, duty hours, substitute coverage, and any special requirements considered necessary by the hospital.

Once these steps are accomplished, the next phase is to prepare instructions to guide the hospital attorney in the drafting of the contract. When completed, the document should be reviewed by the consultant to identify obscure or unbalanced contract language.

A frequent difficulty in contract drafting is the lack of knowledge by the hospital attorney about the unique characteristics of the medical specialty. The various aspects of the authority and responsibilities of hospital-based physicians need to be carefully defined. While hospital attorneys are experienced in drafting contracts, they are inexperienced in the operating characteristics of a medical service. For example, an attorney may not know the technical difference between the use of the words "clinical service" and "department" and may inadvertently select an inappropriate term.

Once these steps have been completed, negotiations with physicians can commence. After the preliminary contract has been developed, a copy of the document should be given to each hospital-based physician. Sufficient time should be provided for them to discuss it with their attorneys and financial advisers. Any questions should be answered and contract language modified, as necessary. Finally, verbal consent should be obtained from the hospital-based physicians for the new contracts.

The results of the individual negotiating sessions between the consultant and contracting physician specialists should then be reported to the committee. Any residual issues should be decided and the hospital attorney asked to prepare a final contract document.

In the negotiating process, there is a significant difference in preparing a contract for a new or replacement hospital-based physician and the updating of a previous contract. With the increasing supply of physician specialists for full-time hospital positions, the recruited physician has substantially less opportunity to make contract demands on a hospital. These situations quickly come down to a take it or leave it attitude by the hospital representatives.

On the other hand, renegotiating a contract with a hospital-based physician can be a different matter. Because of the changing environment, these physicians may be unaware that the legal basis for the hospital-physician relationship, as well as the applicable hospital regulations, have substantially changed in the last decade. As a consequence, an updated contract is often significantly different from contracts written several years ago.

If a long-term physician specialist is insistent about specific items in negotiations, the committee will have to struggle with the issue of this physician's value to the hospital. Committee members would prefer not to face this issue, and their inclination is to accept the demands. Unless committee members are willing to take a position and support it, the negotiating process is not worthwhile. The committee needs to decide what matters are negotiable and non-negotiable ahead of time. If this situation should arise, the consultant's role is to clarify the issue for the committee. The chief executive should not do this because of his continuing need to work cooperatively with all of the medical staff members. However, the consultant is not limited by this need.

The inclusion of a consultant to objectively guide the negotiating process is valuable to both the hospital and the physician. The consultant's experience can bring the contract in step with a changing environment.

Chapter 33

Elements of Incumbent Physician Contracts

In the same hospital there are often a variety of different clauses in incumbent physician contracts. Contracts are written over several years as new specialties are added or replaced. Updating of original contracts is a rarity. Usually, the latest contract is the most inclusive contract.

It is appropriate to propose a standard basic contract applicable to all hospital-based physician specialties. The basic contract could be supplemented with additional exhibits and schedules enumerating specific authorities, responsibilities, approved professional fees, and other items particular to that specialty. In the future when a change is needed, such as compensation, a particular addendum can be renegotiated without involving the entire contract.

There are seven major sections and four addenda in a typical contract.

The first identifies the parties of the contract, their state of incorporation, the date of entering into the agreement, general purpose, and whether there is one or multiple physicians as parties to the contract. In the preliminary drafting stage, the hospital must decide with whom it will contract if there is more than one physician in a medically directed department. There are four choices: a joint professional corporation, an individual, a partnership, or to have all departmental physicians sign one contract. Both the management philosophy of the hospital and the prevailing tax code will influence this decision. In some hospitals, existing arrangements among departmental physicians vary from one department to another and must be taken into consideration.

The second section defines the responsibilities of hospital-based physicians and covers a variety of substantive organizational and legal issues. Assuming that departmental physicians are on a fee-for-service arrangement, the contract should define their status as independent contractors, even though state courts have held hospital-based physicians to be employees or servants for liability purposes. To protect against this contingency, the contract should include a hold harmless clause and require medical malpractice insurance coverage at hospital-specified limits. A current certificate of insurance on file with the hospital should be required.

The contract should require these physicians to accept all referrals for service within the limits of acceptable medical risks. Their fee structure should be subject to hospital approval along with a method for auditing compliance and defining the criteria and procedures for making future rate adjustments.

The method of selecting a physician-director should be consistent with the medical staff bylaws. Typically, many hospitals rotate this position annually among the departmental physicians. This is consistent with the practice of other clinical departments. However, it is inconsistent with good management practice. It is similar to having the house supervisors in nursing annually vote on which nurse will be the director of nursing for the next year.

In this same section, there should be a general definition of responsibilities. An exhibit listing the details of the responsibilities should be attached to the contract. Since these responsibilities change from time to time, they are best defined in an addendum for ease of modification.

Additional clauses in this section should require participation in the educational programs of the medical and hospital staffs and attendant committee work. These physicians should also be required to be members of the medical staff and to assist in the recruitment of professional and technical staff for their departments.

An important requirement is that departmental physicians shall not direct or compete for patients from the hospital. They may engage in outside practice only with the written permission of the hospital management. They should also be required to comply with all applicable regulations and laws and to maintain the ethical standards of the hospital. In addition, diligent performance of their duties shall be required.

Departmental management should be required to obtain prior administrative approval for major changes in operations, services, and activities, and to recommend a source of services when one is not available in their department. Participation in the development of short- and long-range plans should be required, as well as the maintenance of adequate service statistics and daily reports. Physician-directors should participate in personnel evaluations and coordinate their departmental personnel in the care and treatment of patients.

The third major section includes the representations of the physician, which cover completion of an approved residency program, state license, narcotics license, and which attest that information reported on the medical staff application form is correct and no material information has been withheld. Disclosure of any suspension or restriction of state licensure, medical staff appointments, and any malpractice claim, action, or judgment in the past five years should be required. The physician-director should be required to provide for continuity of physician coverage. As a final point, a physician should agree to a physical and/or mental examination if requested by a responsible officer of the hospital.

The fourth section covers the responsibilities of the hospital. Here, the hospital delegates the clinical management decisions to the departmental physicians. Responsibility for paying the expenses of departmental operation, providing qualified personnel, furnishing equipment and supplies, and space should be held by the hospital. This section should also reserve to the chief executive the determination of the number of departmental positions, job specifications, salary, wage scales, and fringe benefits, but require recommendations on these matters from the physician-directors.

The fifth section deals with financial arrangements and the degree of fiscal control exercised by the hospital. Similar financial arrangements should apply to all contracts, with the necessary variations for unique specialty practices, such as anesthesiology. However, the same general degree of freedom or control over professional fees should be consistent.

Some hospitals do not participate in the determination of professional fees charged by hospital-based physicians, while other hospitals require either administrative or governing board approval. When hospital approval is required, a decision must be made as to what criterion is to be used. Usually, it is either the community standard for the same services in other hospitals in the metropolitan area or a regional basis if there are only one or two other local hospitals. In other instances, the criterion is related to shifts in the consumer price index. Whenever hospital approval is required, the committee or the position with approval authority should be identified in the contract.

With the enactment of federal legislation to unbundle professional fees from the hospital bill for Medicare patients, two other contract decisions are needed. One involves the payment of an administrative service fee for activities that benefit patients in general, such as supervising an infection control program, and the other involves separate billing fees for personal services to patients. Payments for administrative services, however, are included in the prospective payment system of Medicare and are not separately reimbursable to the hospital.

The financial section should also define any fringe benefits included and indicate if the hospital is to be the billing and collecting agent. Charges for these services, how and when they are to be paid, and the handling of contractual allowances, bad debts, and charity need to be defined. It is also desirable to define the hospital-based physician's admitting privileges, if any, and what type of consultations will be considered billable.

The sixth section contains the termination clauses. The term of the contract should be specified, along with the manner in which it can be extended and the mechanism for notification of termination. Provision for immediate termination should be included by defining what is a breach of contract by each party.

An important issue to define in the contract is the mechanism for terminating the management appointment of the hospital-based physician and its effect on the medical staff appointment. In some contracts, termination of the agreement will likewise terminate a medical staff appointment, while in other contracts, a physician can continue as a medical staff member. Typically, a hospital that does not provide for termination of a medical staff appointment has not thought through the implications of an open versus closed staff and the resultant impact on departmental operation.

When a hospital selects the closed staff option, it is, in effect, offering an exclusive practice contract. This is a valuable consideration for a hospital-based physician and should not be ignored during contract negotiations by the hospital.

The seventh and last part of the contract is a general section that is a catchall for separate issues that need to be defined. For example, specific approvals should be required for each research activity of a hospital-based physician occurring in the hospital. There should also be a requirement to make the physician liable to the hospital for dishonest and willful misconduct. Such items include requiring hospital approval when a physician enters into a purchase or lease agreement for professional services with any other health care organization in the same primary or secondary service area.

Other issues usually included are a definition of normal working hours, a requirement of physicians to protect the confidentiality of hospital information, and the names and addresses for notices such as for vacations, temporary coverage, etc. From a legal point of view, this section should provide that in the case of a conflict between the contract and medical staff bylaws the contract provisions shall prevail. In addition, it should be stated that interpretations of the contract shall be governed by state law, that contract provisions are severable, and, in compliance with the recent requirement of Medicare, reasonable access shall be available to the physician's books and records.

In the addendum, four exhibits and schedules are usually included. One exhibit should be a detailed list of professional responsibilities and the second a listing of all professional fees. The two attached schedules should record any limitations of appointment or clinical privileges and record claims and litigations occurring in the last five years.

Additional addenda may be included when previous experience with a hospital-based physician has shown a need to define more closely specific issues. For example, the bulk of a cardiologist's income is typically earned from cardiac catheterization, electrocardiogram testing, and a stress laboratory. In addition, the hospital usually requires a director for the coronary care unit, for which an annual salary is paid. An addendum will be needed to clarify the limits of each cardiologist's clinical responsibilities and right to bill for these services. Another example is a department such as radiology, where some physicians are full-time and other physicians part-time, and an agreement is necessary to delineate which physicians are in each category.

Even though the necessary elements of a modern-day hospital-based physician contract may have been defined, they need to be expressed in a written document.

While this is the work of the hospital attorney, great care must be taken to select the appropriate language. Because physicians are highly educated and accustomed to reading technical language, they will carefully review a draft contract and raise questions either about the specific meaning of words or why certain issues are handled in a given way. These concerns must be addressed on an individual basis and resolved if a negotiation is to succeed. A way to limit some of this questioning is to have the consultant review the contract draft as prepared by the attorney and to suggest alternative wording that will be less offensive or will express more clearly an element in the contract.

A meeting with a hospital-based physician should be conducted by the consultant to explain and elaborate current legal and regulatory issues that affect the contract. Physician specialists are aware of regulatory issues because their professional societies circulate this information, but they may not be aware of the legal issues involved. Conversely, if hospital executives conduct negotiations, they may be unaware of the current positions of the professional societies but they do know the legal issues. A consultant brings to the negotiation a knowledge of both issues.

When individual meetings have been completed, the results are reported to the committee and final decisions made with respect to the contract. If a major issue remains, the committee may elect, after a thorough discussion, to interview this physician and then arrive at a final contract stipulation.

In all likelihood the final form of a hospital-based physician contract is neither what the hospital nor the physician would prefer if each had its own way. In the rapidly changing health care environment both parties are best served when a carefully structured relationship is developed. In the end both the physician and the hospital need a contract that is equitable and fair to both parties.

Chapter 34

Negotiating the Contract

When a hospital's chief executive negotiates a professional services contract with a physician to direct a medical care service in a hospital, it is typically a "no-win" situation.

On the one hand, the chief executive's negotiating position is blunted by pressure from medical staff members who accept the premise that hospital-based physicians should have the same organizational freedoms as attending physicians. On the other hand, hospital trustees view hospital-based physicians as an integral part of the organization structure and ignore the fact that authority to control the medical staff is reserved to the board of trustees, not the chief executive.

This organizational arrangement places the chief executive in a weakened negotiating position since a hospital-based physician can elect to emphasize his medical staff status and deemphasize his administrative role as a departmental director. This strategy opens the negotiating process to the participation of trustees, unless they are willing to accept the chief executive's recommended decision, no matter what the degree of reaction from the members and committees of the medical staff.

Imbalance in hospital-physician contracts can occur in various contractual elements: the scope of professional freedom and responsibility, fairness in pricing, adherence to quality levels, and efficient delivery of services. Such imbalances occur because there has been no meeting of the minds between trustees, physicians, and chief executives regarding the philosophy of the role and management of medically directed hospital services.

Unless a particular physician presents a unique set of circumstances justifying otherwise, a hospital should strive for parity and uniformity in developing each hospital-based physician contract. There are three policy areas in a hospital-based physician contract that require discussion and decision in order to assure uniformity.

The first of these policy areas has to do with the general terms of a contract. Before negotiating contracts a hospital should determine whether the contracting entity should be an individual physician or a professional corporation or partnership. A related decision is whether there will be a physician-director contract and authorization for subcontracts with associate physicians by the physician-director or if separate contracts between the hospital and each associated physician will be used. The management philosophy of the hospital will determine which form of contracting will be used.

Other considerations under the general terms are the length of a contract and the notification period required for termination as well as the conditions under which a contract may be terminated by either party. It is not unusual to find contracts in the same hospital with termination clauses requiring as few as 30 days notification and other contracts with no termination clause at all.

The general terms section of the contract should state whether or not professional liability insurance coverage (malpractice) should be carried by the physician, and if so, the minimum required limits of the policy. When malpractice coverage is required, a current certificate of insurance should be on file and the physician should be required to inform the hospital of any practice limitations or of termination by the insurance carrier.

A second area in which similar ground rules should be applied in all contracts has to do with financial elements. There are some necessary variations such as in anesthesiology, but the general degree of freedom or control over professional fees should be consistent. Most physician-hospital disagreements are usually caused by the degree of control exercised by the hospital over professional fees.

Another contract decision required is whether or not the hospital-based physician will be required to accept the assignment of benefits for Medicare patients. These new laws require separate billing for all personal physician services to Part B Medicare except for clinical laboratory services, which remain in the Part A payment. The amount of fee to be paid from Part B to physicians is controlled through the use of a usual, customary, and reasonable (UCR) fee screen. However, the payment screen only applies to the physician when a Medicare assignment of benefits has been accepted. When a physician does not accept an assignment the patient may be billed the physician's established fee and the patient in turn submits the paid bill to Medicare and receives the authorized screen payment.

Under previous Part B regulations physicians may decide on a patient-by-patient basis whether or not to accept assignment. The hospital has no such option and must accept the Part A payment as payment in full. A decision to either decide on no assignment or to require acceptance of Medicare Part B assignments should be uniform for all hospital-based physicians and incorporated in the contract. Recently, some hospitals that require acceptance of assignment have exempted surgical pathology because clinical laboratory payments were retained in Part A. Again, this choice should reflect the hospital philosophy in patient relations.

When a professional fee system is the desired one, the issue of the billing and collection of physician fees arises. Most hospitals prefer to perform this service because it is usually less expensive than using a commercial service and a small profit can be made. On the other hand, many physicians are willing to use a commercial service to keep a hospital from knowing their professional incomes. If the hospital operates a billing and collection service for physicians the contract should provide a way to audit the agreed-upon procedure, and when an outside agency is used the hospital should provide a method for auditing compliance with the fee structure if adjustment approvals by the hospital are required.

The third policy area covers the operations of a department and any limits on outside activities. A hospital-based physician contract should define the coverage required of physicians during the work week as well as on weekends and holidays. In one- and two-physician departments the method of approving substitute coverage by the hospital should be defined in the contract.

When specific teaching assignments and committee participation are required of a position, these requirements should be made part of the contract. If clinical research is to be done by a hospital-based physician, specific approach on a project-by-project basis should be required along with a clear delineation of expenses agreed upon prior to its undertaking. When human subjects are involved, the standard protocol of the medical staff must be followed for this approval.

Control of nonhospital professional activities of hospital-based physicians is typically an issue of importance. In departments where only part-time services are required, such as pulmonary functions or urodynamics, serious problems do not occur since these services provide only a small portion of the physician's income. In other departments, such as radiology and pathology, limitation on nonhospital professional services can generate major issues.

It is a common practice for some radiologists and pathologists to have private offices near hospitals for outpatient work. As pricing becomes an increasingly important aspect of competition, a greater emphasis will be placed on the hospital providing lower-cost services on an outpatient basis. Hospitals will of economic necessity have to place more and more restrictions on the development of competitive enterprises owned by hospital-based physicians. The time to deal with this issue is in contract negotiations before an outside office is in place. There are a variety of strategies that can be considered in dealing with this issue.

Negotiations of hospital-based physician contracts must take into consideration the hospital's philosophy about its role and responsibility for the quality of care, the regulation of fees, and the individual performance of physician-directed patient services. This must be balanced by physician understanding and acceptance.

Typically, physicians are unaware that the law and the legal interpretation of the hospital-physician relationship have substantially changed in the last decade as a result of regulation. Consequently, an up-to-date hospital-physician contract will be significantly different from contracts of several years ago.

The time has arrived when a handshake or a contract limited to enumerating generalized statements is no longer adequate. Today, the relationship between a physician and a hospital is so complex that it requires a detailed statement of the responsibilities and authorities of each party to avoid misunderstandings. A hospital needs to clearly understand and define the scope of duties, relationships, and circumstances under which it desires to contract with a physician. In order to maintain and encourage high-quality performance by its hospital-based physicians, all elements of the relationship should be well balanced. To achieve this goal and be fair to both parties and to remain in step with current legal opinion and regulation, the approach to the negotiation of physician contracts must be comprehensive, deliberative, and objective.

Once the decisions affecting all hospital-based physicians are made, there are three steps in the process of negotiating the contracts.

1. The first step is an assessment of the current characteristics of departmental operation in terms of the workload of the physician-director, the recent financial experience of the department, and the per-unit expense of physician services. In addition, the physician-director should be interviewed to determine existing problems and to assess the degree of flexibility in the desired hospital relationship. At the same time the accuracy of the data provided should be checked and the physician informed about the current legal and regulatory environment.

2. The second step is to prepare instructions to guide the hospital attorney in the drafting of a new contract. Once the hospital attorney has completed the draft of a new contract, the document should be reviewed to identify contract language that may be obscure or unbalanced for either party. A frequent problem in drafting contracts is the hospital attorney's lack of knowledge about the unique characteristics of the medical specialty covered by the particular contract leading to an inability to carefully define the various aspects of the authority and responsibility of the physician-director's position. Hospital attorneys are experienced in drafting contracts, but inexperienced in the operating characteristics of a physician-directed service. For example, an attorney may not know the technical difference between a clinical service and a department in a medical staff organization structure and will inadvertently select an inappropriate word in terms of the bylaws of the medical staff.

3. The last step is to negotiate the contract. Prior to doing this the hospital-based physician should receive a copy of the proposed document with sufficient time provided for him to discuss it with his attorney and financial adviser. A meeting should then be held with the hospital-based physician and any adviser to answer any questions, modify contract language, if necessary, and obtain verbal consent to the new contract.

Figure 34–1 The Physician Contract Process

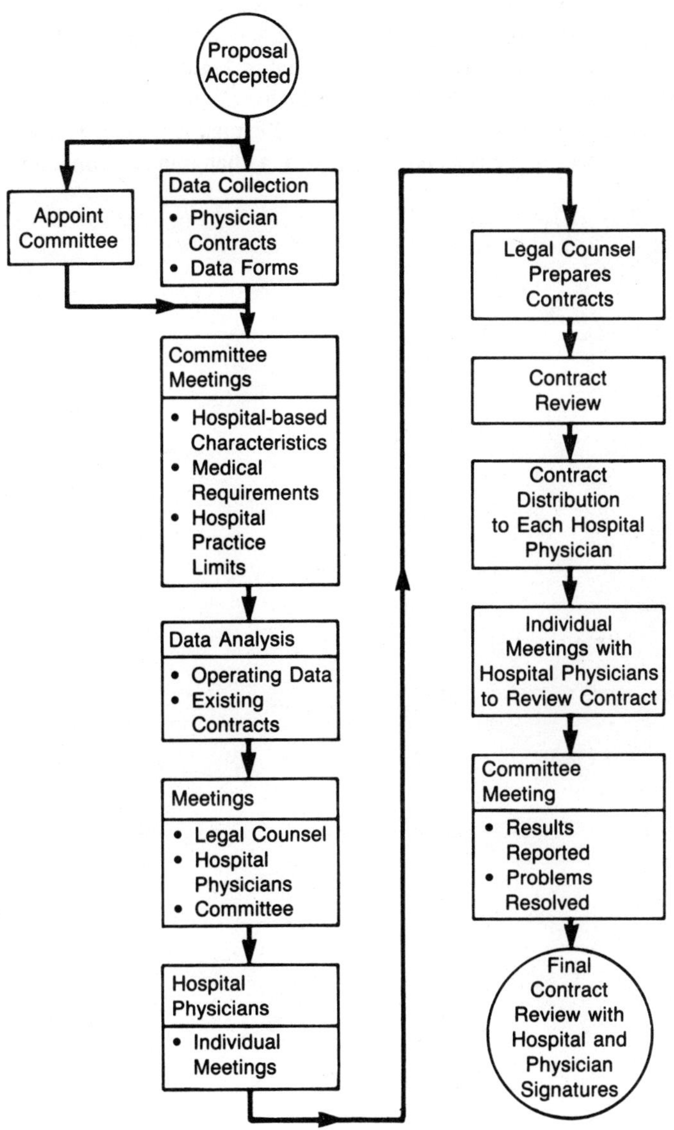

The results of the negotiating session should be reported back to the committee that established the basic elements of the contract for treating all hospital-based physicians equitably. This committee should then resolve any residual issues and instruct the hospital attorney to prepare the final contract document.

The physician contract process is illustrated in Figure 34–1.

Experience has demonstrated that the inclusion of an "honest broker" to guide the negotiating process is valuable to both the hospital and the physician as a way to keep the process objective and in step with a changing environment.

Chapter 35

Medicare Regulations for Hospital-Based Physicians

For a number of years, concerns about Medicare payments to hospital-based physicians have been expressed in Congress and by the administration. From the commencement of the initial Medicare program in 1966 until September 1982, hospital payments by Medicare were based on the reasonable costs of operation and included the services of hospital-based physicians.

On October 1, 1982, the Tax Equity and Fiscal Responsibility Act became operational and provided for the establishment of reasonable compensation equivalents, or ceilings, for payments to hospital-based physicians. Because the implementing regulations were delayed and amendments to the Social Security Act were not signed until April 1983, the 1982 changes did not go into effect pending the introduction of the diagnosis related groups payment system.

Implementation began on January 3, 1984. The effect of the new payment system was to restructure the financial operations of hospitals and their relationships with hospital-based physicians. This was a significant change from the original program where hospital-based physicians were paid under Part B and hospitals under Part A, with one exception, the services of pathologists.

With 40 percent of all hospitalized patients now Medicare beneficiaries and this portion expected to exceed 50 percent by the early 1990s, Medicare payment schemes become the driving force affecting the relationship among hospitals and hospital-based physicians.

Even though Medicare is the largest single source of hospital-based physician income nationally, it does not necessarily follow that this is true in a specific hospital or for all of the specialties in that hospital. Even in a hospital that currently has a majority of Medicare patients, some hospital-based specialties, such as emergency medicine, may derive only 20 to 30 percent of revenue from Medicare sources.

Traditionally, Part B Medicare services have been reimbursed on a charge basis that has been defined as usual customary and reasonable, or the "UCR" basis. A physician's fee meets the usual criterion for payment if it does not exceed the fee customarily charged by a physician for a period of time. The customary criterion is defined as the seventy-fifth percentile of the fee charged for the same procedure by other physicians in a locality. When both criteria are met, the fee is deemed to be reasonable. Under Medicare, payments to the physician on a UCR basis are made at the 80 percent level of reasonable charges and have a deductible provision paid by the patient.

For hospital-based physicians the new requirements are significantly different. Under Part A, coinsurance and deductibles did not apply because the hospital-based physicians' fees were combined with the hospital bills. The new prospective payment system now requires all physician services to be billed to Part B if an assignment of benefits is accepted. To be paid, these services must be personally furnished, must contribute directly to the diagnosis or treatment of an individual patient, and must be services that ordinarily require performance by a physician.

A critical issue for hospital policy is whether or not hospital-based physicians will be required to accept assignments of benefits for Medicare patients. Private practice physicians have the option to make that decision for their Medicare patients. The majority of private practice physicians do not routinely accept assignments. This requires that the patient pay the physician's bill, at whatever rate the physician charges, and then submit the paid bill to Social Security for reimbursement at the UCR rate. The patient absorbs any remaining difference. Hospitals may not bill patients for any differences between what is paid by Medicare and the costs of providing the services. They must accept Medicare reimbursement as full payment.

A private practice physician has the discretion to accept or not accept patients in his medical practice. Hospitals, universally, require hospital-based physicians to diagnose and treat all hospital patients who are an acceptable medical risk. From time to time, hospitals have been faced with a hospital-based physician refusing service when the physician knows the bill is uncollectable. For example, inner-city hospitals that may have a large number of gunshot and stabbing cases sustain large financial losses from such patients. Knowing this, a fee-for-service hospital-based physician administering anesthesia may occasionally refuse to provide this service if it occurs in the middle of the night.

When, by contract the hospital-based specialist is required to provide a medical service without an expectation of payment, the question arises as to whether or not the hospital will guarantee the payment to the physician.

The difficulty with requiring physicians to accept Medicare assignments is that the UCR payments from Part B may be significantly lower than the established fee structure. If there is a potential for a large number of unpaid physician bills, assignments are the only method of securing any payment to hospital-based physicians.

If a hospital does not require the acceptance of Medicare assignments, its elderly patients may receive five, six, or more hospital-based physician bills under the new system. This they will not understand. In addition, the attending physicians wish to limit competition from hospital-based physicians for the available dollars.

Under the new Part B Medicare regulations, both hospital-based and private practice physicians are free to decide whether or not to accept assignments unless the hospital has a contract requiring the hospital-based physicians to accept assignments.

A decision on Medicare Part B assignments should be uniform for all hospital-based physicians. Recently, some hospitals that routinely required acceptance of assignments have exempted surgical pathology because clinical laboratory payments were retained in Part A. If assignments are required, the hospital needs a method of assuring routine compliance by physicians.

Another complication of benefit assignments is the limited payment rate authorized by a UCR screen for hospital-based physicians. This is set at the 60 percent UCR rate of an office-based physician, except for radiologists, for whom the rate is 40 percent. This adjustment assumes that the cost of operating a radiology practice in the hospital is 40 percent of the physician's fee. The same applies to the other hospital-based specialists, except the amount is 60 percent. Radiology uses expensive equipment paid for by a hospital, and radiology fees are reduced because of this factor.

With the adoption of split-billing for Medicare patients, there is a requirement for personal hands-on service to patients. The fact that hospital-based physicians also provide services of a general administrative nature by supervising departmental operations is still covered under Part A. Should a hospital elect to pay a hospital-based physician for departmental supervision, this cost is part of the DRG payment to the hospital. To the extent that a hospital can avoid paying the physician for this service, greater funds will be available to the hospital since the DRG is a fixed price for the total period of hospitalization.

There are two important variations from the standard Part B reasonable charge requirement. In the case of pathologists, their ability to bill under Part B is limited to the services of anatomical pathology, consultations requested by an attending physician, and personally administered tests such as isotope studies.

In anesthesia, it is common practice for anesthesiologists to employ certified registered nurse anesthesiologists and bill for these services. Under the new regulations, anesthesiologists cannot bill for anesthetist services if they were concurrently supervising more than four anesthetists. The regulation also stipulated that the continuation of billing for anesthetists would be limited to a four-year period ending October 1, 1987.

A hospital-based physician under Medicare reimbursement usually has some practice expenses, unless the hospital has agreed to include these costs in the contract. Typically, a hospital negotiates a contract that requires a physician to pay for medical malpractice insurance and the costs of billing and collecting fees, and to separately arrange his own fringe-benefit package.

In most cases, a hospital prefers to do the billing and collection of Medicare fees on behalf of the physician because it is less expensive than using a commercial service and a small profit can be made from this service. On the other hand, hospital-based physicians often prefer to use a commercial service to prevent the hospital from knowing the amount of their professional incomes or because a hospital may not meet their expectations on collection. When a hospital performs the Medicare billing and collection services for hospital-based physicians, the charge for this service should be set high enough to avoid subsidizing the fee-for-service practice of those physicians.

At various times bills requiring mandatory physician assignments have been discussed in Congress. In September 1983, a bill was introduced into the Senate and later enacted that would amend the Medicare law to make it mandatory that payment for a physician's services be made only to a Medicare participating physician. The definition of a participating physician is one who enters into an agreement with the Department of Health and Human Services. The physician agrees to be paid only on the basis of the assignment for services rendered so long as these services are ones commonly rendered to patients by physicians.

As part of the Medicare amendments of March 1983, the Secretary of Health and Human Services was instructed to report to Congress on the feasibility of using a diagnosis related group payment system for physician fees.

In February 1984, an all-payer system was introduced by Senator Edward Kennedy (D-Mass.) and Representative Richard Gebhardt (D-Mo.) which requires that Medicare payments for both hospital and physician services be paid to the hospital. The hospital, in turn, would pay the physician.

These congressional proposals are aimed at reducing the physician costs to the Medicare program. Even though the exact amendments to Medicare are still unknown, additional limitations on physician fees can be anticipated. When this occurs, hospital-based physician contracts will again need to be reviewed in order to make them consistent with new federal laws and regulations.

In the past, many hospitals opposed separate billing by hospital-based physicians because of the anticipated criticisms from patients. By Congress adopting a prospective payment system, with mandated split-billing, the payment mechanism has been moved into a fee-for-service system. From a hospital's perspective the decision to authorize physician billing depends on the decision of the Medicare program. If assignments are mandated, UCR screens will operate to restrict fees to the hospital-based physicians. If not required, medical care expenses to patients will rise. Either way, the hospital faces a difficult decision.

Part VII

The Chaining of Hospitals

Chapter 36

Old Memories and New Dreams[*]

Dreams are made up of what we expect in the future, while memories are the results of experiences we have encountered in the past. To live solely in the past is to deny the future, while to live solely in the future is to deny the lessons and experiences gained from the past. At a time when the health field is being shaken with change rapidly following change, a strong temptation exists to forget the past and to concentrate on the future. A sorting out is needed. What past values should be retained? What should be discarded? What new ideas and concepts should be adopted? These are the elements that make for successful adaptation to a changed environment.

FORCES AT WORK

Before beginning this process an understanding of the forces at work and where they lead has to be developed. It is the backdrop against which decisions are made. By and large there is agreement in the health field on these trends. Those that are clear cut include:

1. Cost-reimbursement as the major method of payment to hospitals will die out.
2. Pricing systems, in a variety of forms, are rapidly coming to the forefront.
3. Competition among hospitals is no longer on quality and comprehensiveness of service, but also now includes economics as well.
4. Cooperation between friendly rivals in the same community is a thing of the past.

*Adapted from *Health Progress,* Vol. 65, pp. 31–35 and 60, with permission of The Catholic Health Association of the United States, © November 1984.

5. Productivity will become increasingly important.
6. Profit margins will be adversely affected.
7. Alternative sources of revenue are needed.
8. Medicare payments will continue to erode.
9. Finances have now joined patient care as a primary concern in a hospital.
10. Freestanding hospitals will be replaced by health care corporations operating multiple activities on multiple sites.

Behind all of these reasons lies the cause, a shift from a national economy of ample resources to one of scarce resources, which is expected to continue for many years into the future. Compounding these factors are the advances being made in medical technology, which are costly and once available, desired by the public as it continues to insist upon being treated at the level of state-of-the-art technology.

Out of this milieu of change has grown the chaining and networking of hospitals, the for-profits or investor-owned and the nonprofits. By the end of 1982 the number of systems was as shown in Table 36–1.

Chains have expanded rapidly and are expected to continue to grow in the immediate years ahead as hospitals recognize they need both diversity in services and a stronger balance sheet. The hospitals of the 1970s are becoming the health care corporations of the 1980s. Those that have moved into these new corporate models are finding additional advantages that had not been anticipated in the planning stages, greater flexibility in responding to changes in the external environment, and a speeded up decision-making process. The latter has developed because corporate management now makes many of the decisions formally reserved to the governing board, and the board itself is typically smaller in number than a hospital board and operates with much fewer board committees, transferring these functions to corporate management. These advantages permit chains and networks to make decisions much more rapidly than freestanding hospitals.

Table 36–1 United States Multihospital Systems by Type of Ownership

| | Owned, Leased and Managed | |
	Hospitals	Beds
Investor-Owned	762	38,651
Catholic	515	139,939
Other Religions	150	26,467
Other Not-For-Profit	497	95,561
Total	1,924	360,618
Percent	33.2%	35.6%

Source: Hospital Statistics, 1983 edition, © 1983 by the American Hospital Association.

At the present stage of development investor-owned (for-profit) hospitals have a decided advantage that is likely to continue for the next few years. Leaders of for-profit chains have broken with the traditions of the past. Historically, most of the hospitals in the United States had their roots in the public or nonprofit sector where any financial gain at year-end was plowed back into the institution in one form or another and where board members regarded the time spent on hospital matters as community service.

Trustees readily accepted their role and their responsibility to protect the interests of the community when deciding hospital policies. Trustees believed in the concept of the best possible care at the lowest possible cost, a goal that was easy for them to subscribe to since it aligned the hospital with the public good of the community. Adherence to these values over the past half century contributed to American hospitals becoming recognized as the best in the world, where patient care was unparalleled in quality. Trustees took justifiable pride in serving as board members of nonprofit hospitals.

As part of a community-sponsored organization, it was natural for the nonprofit hospital value system to view relationships with other nearby hospitals as serving the community more effectively if they cooperated by sharing managerial and marketing information, exchanging salary scales, and by trading off clinical services. The prevailing attitude was that when all hospitals worked together they could better serve the community than if they were competitive with each other.

This, of course, was a myth because nonprofit hospitals vigorously competed with each other, but the competition was on quality and comprehensiveness of service, not on economics. This was understandable since the bulk of the payments for hospital services was based on cost reimbursement; if a new service was added, or an existing one expanded, revenues increased right along with the costs.

The controlling element in the decision of a board to permit costs to rise was whether or not the outcome would enhance patient care. Community need was the determining factor, not economics. In a real sense this was Utopia because dollars were always forthcoming under cost reimbursement.

Over the past five decades traditions in nonprofit hospitals have developed and become ingrained in the value systems of board members when making policy decisions: patient care came first, community need second, and economics was a distant third. Given ample resources in the country there was no need to think seriously about the financing aspects of the decisions reached; they took care of themselves.

At the start of the '80s the economy turned to one of scarcity and it was recognized that there were only finite resources to cover infinite demands. Health care quickly came to be publicly viewed as having an insatiable demand for resources and, therefore, needed to be controlled.

SORTING OUT OF VALUES

As the economic climate changed, traditions were still very much in place in nonprofit hospitals. Giving up, modifying, or altering these philosophical underpinnings is not an easy task.

Because of the reluctance to move away from a set of values that has proven over the years to be successful, the nonprofit field can be expected to move more slowly in adapting to a changed environment than those hospitals in the for-profit field. The for-profit sector does not have to rethink its values and is free of the traditions that still bind the nonprofits. The investor-owned have already reached a point where their ideas have moved to a different philosophy. They see patient care as important, but economics is viewed with equal concern, in recognition that in an economy of scarce resources financial viability and a healthy bottom line is a matter of utmost importance.

This reordering of priorities in value systems enables the for-profits to adapt to a changed environment more quickly than can the nonprofits, because they need to reexamine their values and decide which ones to keep, which to modify, and which to discard. In a very real sense, the hospital field is moving away from a social and charitable activity to a capitalistic industry.

In the process of sorting out values by the nonprofits there is going to be strong resistance to letting go of what was and a desire to keep things as they are at present. As other health care organizations move into a nonprofit hospital's service area their first reaction is predictable, one of anger, followed by a desire to close ranks and keep newcomers out because the newcomers will only go after a segment of the market that is profitable. This anger usually arises out of a feeling that the hospital has served the community well and, therefore, has earned the right to be protected. A nonprofit hospital tends to see competitors as being unfair, even though the result might be lower costs to the public for the services offered. The focus of this effort is to reestablish existing balances, rather than deal with the new realities when they appear on the local scene. Such hospitals fail to appreciate that trying to turn the clock back only delays but does not change the inevitable.

Chains, be they for-profit or nonprofit or networks, view economic competition differently from freestanding hospitals. Because they are involved with a number of hospitals, corporate management has passed the stage of closing ranks. Having already encountered similar situations in other communities they are much more likely to work out a strategy that enables them to successfully compete with the new threat. This may require the infusion of new capital to start up new services. In a chain, dollars are more readily available than in a freestanding hospital and provide a flexibility needed to compete in a risk-taking environment.

SIMILARITIES

In this new hospital world of risk taking the question no longer centers on the viability of the freestanding hospital. Being part of a system is the prudent course to follow when finances are a major concern. Dollars provide the flexibility required to meet the unknowns of the future. Rather, the contest is now between nonprofit chains and networks and the for-profits. Who will be the winners in the years ahead?

The answer is not easy to discern, since both types have advantages and disadvantages, but they also have much in common. In fact the commonalities are much greater than the differences. In a study comparing the two types of chains the percentage of standardization found is shown in Table 36–2.

What this table shows is that health care organizations operating multiple activities at multiple sites have the same kinds of organizational needs in order to hold their systems together. Management information systems are becoming almost identical. Concerns with overtime, flexible staffing patterns, routine information about billings, collections, and methods of payment are standard data. As DRGs take hold, the meshing of clinical information and financial data will also lead to standardization.

The differences lie not in the type of information received but the way in which it affects executive behavior and decision making. At present for-profit executives receive management data on a much more frequent basis, often daily, and make immediate adjustments in operations. Nonprofit executives are more apt to react on a weekly or monthly basis. As the financial noose tightens, this process will speed up and executives will be responding within the same timeframes in both settings.

As to what executives do with the information they receive there will be differences. During the next couple of years nonprofit executives may be slower in reducing payroll costs in the event of occupancy declines, but this won't last long. The primary difference will lie in patient care programs. Patients in financial categories that do not adequately pay the cost of their care will find only limited

---

Table 36–2 Percentage of Standardization Comparing Investor-Owned and Secular Not-for-profit Chains

	Investor-Owned	Secular NFP
Management Procedures	82%	80%
Uniform Accounting	89	85
Uniform Reporting	98	89
Management Information Systems	78	77
Personnel Performance Measures	62	80
Staffing Guidelines	75	65

admissions in for-profit chains. Nonprofit chains will attempt to avoid establishing such restrictions and will be more willing to erode the bottom line in an effort to continue to serve all financial categories of patients.

As operating data are accumulated under DRGs each hospital will view program groupings as profit centers. For those groups that repeatedly result in losses, the for-profits can be expected to move more quickly to either limit or eliminate these services from those offered by the hospital or to aggressively seek a way to provide them in a configuration that enables them to do so at a profit. The nonprofits will be slower in seeking such alternatives, as they search for ways to continue to serve all financial categories of patients.

DIFFERENCES BETWEEN FOR-PROFITS AND NONPROFITS

For the moment, the for-profit chains are riding the crest of a wave of public acceptability. They are viewed as being more efficient than nonprofits because they respond to the economic imperatives of the marketplace, which is in keeping with the American ideas about free enterprise. The question of efficiency was examined in the August 11, 1983, issue of the *New England Journal of Medicine*[1] where a number of studies dealing with investor-owned hospitals and health care costs were reviewed.

It was found that the charges per admission were 17 percent higher, largely from substantially higher charges for ancillary services, and resulted in a greater net income than the nonprofits because of these higher charges. This was reported by Levin et al.[2] In a similar study in California total charges per admission were found to be 24 percent higher in the for-profits.

Interestingly, the categories of fiscal services and administrative services were 32 percent higher in the investor-owned. This fact has profound implications for the future of chained and network hospitals. Before drawing a conclusion it needs to be pointed out that for 1982 the American Hospital Association data show the for-profits had an average cost per day of $340.03, while the nonprofits had an average cost of $330.40, a difference of $9.63. When full-time equivalent person-nel are compared, the for-profits had 3.38 per occupied bed and the nonprofits 3.80, a difference of 0.42 per occupied bed. In terms of operating costs both are about the same, but the larger bottom line of the for-profits from operations is achieved by raising charges substantially above those of nonprofit hospitals. To date, this has been favorable for the for-profit hospitals.

With the advent of a pricing system this will change. All corporate overhead will have to be included in the price charged to the admitted patient and cannot be recaptured by increasing prices on the ancillary services. As this occurs the difference between the for-profits and the nonprofits will become apparent.

Since many of the nonprofit chains are really networks made up of independent hospitals, they have a built-in brake on expanding corporate costs, which will be to their advantage when pricing programs are fully developed. As corporate services are expanded or added at the corporate office, the decision on whether to participate or not will rest with individual member hospitals. If a service is needed by an individual hospital and is economically competitive, the hospital will add this service. In for-profit chains when the corporate office decides to add personnel or new programs, the corporate allocation to each hospital is increased without being subject to approval at the hospital level. This difference in corporate organizational structure and philosophy is seen in the 32 percent higher cost for administrative and fiscal services in the for-profits and in the slightly higher cost per patient day.

The way in which nonprofit chains have been organized requires a corporate staff to remain lean since any hospital can either enter or withdraw from the whole series of services provided by the corporate staff. The structure itself enforces economic discipline in a way that cannot be achieved in for-profit chains where decisions about corporate services are exclusively the province of the corporate staff. As pricing systems take hold, the value of the organizational structure of the nonprofits will be more readily recognized and appreciated.

The exercise of corporate responsibilities reflects the traditions and roots of chains that have developed from nonprofit backgrounds. The divisions among what a local board, the corporate board, and corporate management are responsible for are different, as seen in Table 36–3.

NONPROFIT CHARACTERISTICS

The major difference between for-profit and nonprofit is in the underlying philosophy, not the management techniques. In philosophy there is a wide gap. Nonprofits are committed to serving all financial categories of patients. This will remain. They will, to the greatest extent possible, strive to serve all patients, so long as they can remain solvent. Nonprofits recognize an obligation to the elderly, to the poor, and to medical necessity. Nonprofit chains and networks have an opportunity to use this philosophy to their advantage if they choose to do so.

As new systems grow and increase in numbers they can, if they wish, commence advertising programs directly to the public citing this unique aspect of their philosophy by telling the public that their costs are comparable with for-profits even though they serve all patients, that they are, and intend to remain, medically concerned about all persons, not just those patients that fit into the right financial categories. This is an important distinction, which can only be brought to the attention of the public through a well-orchestrated advertising program. These

Table 36–3 Responsibility by Type of System

Approvals by:	Local Board		Corporate Board		Corporate Management	
	FP*	NP**	FP	NP	FP	NP
Board Appointments	30%	50%	44%	25%	26%	25%
CEO Appointments	22	22	3	59	75	18
Hospital Budget	26	23	20	61	54	16
Capital Expansion	21	20	41	64	38	16
Service Deletions	27	24	15	50	58	26
Service Additions	27	25	12	46	61	29
Sharing Services	29	46	6	31	65	23

*FP = For-Profit
**NP = Nonprofit

programs should stress to the public that nonprofits retain their social commitment in spite of the difficult economic conditions under which they now operate.

CAPITATION OFFERS AN OPPORTUNITY

In the future an opportunity exists that should be taken advantage of by nonprofit chains and networks. Since many of their activities are concerned with unbundled services that are part of the indirect costs of a hospital, these activities provide only limited opportunities for improving efficiency. Financing various kinds of activities is one of the primary reasons for chaining in the investor-owned field and is not yet a major activity in a nonprofit chain or network. By developing a capitation plan, financing in new ways can become a major arm of a nonprofit chain or network that will greatly enhance both corporate fiscal strength and participating hospitals.

Capitation plans have now outgrown their infancy and are beginning to grow rapidly. Elements of successful plans are now known and understood. It seems evident that capitation will become dominant in the health field within the next decade. Should Medicare adopt an elective capitation alternative the growth rate will be even faster than is now projected because it will be available to approximately 22 to 23 million additional people in this country. With continuing higher and higher costs of hospitalization, the solution lies in keeping people out of hospitals and treating more and more patients on an ambulatory basis. Capitation plans have successfully demonstrated how this can be accomplished for patients both in their work years as well as for the elderly. As plans increase, they will become dominant in the health field and the financing mechanism for health care will determine how dollars are spent.

Since capitation plans neither own nor operate hospitals, their primary interest is in establishing and maintaining a premium rate that is competitive in the marketplace; the more competitive the better. Given an opportunity to increase a discount from a hospital, the plans will take the discount since the operation of hospitals is not their responsibility. Profits that accrue from a successful operation of a capitation plan will remain with the plan.

As opportunities for hospital chains and networks are surveyed, it seems that establishing one or more capitation plans to operate in areas where a chain manages hospitals, or has affiliates, is the most significant program that could be developed. Their net profits can be substantial and provide a mutual interest for the chain and the individual hospitals. Since subscribers, under the terms of a capitation plan, use contract hospitals and physicians, it is a way to influence the marketplace to support chain or network affiliates. By using medical staffs of affiliated hospitals as physicians of choice, it can become a meaningful joint venture between the plan and hospitals.

To be effective a capitation plan needs to provide economic incentives for all the providers who participate. Therefore, it should be organized as a for-profit subsidiary of a nonprofit chain in which hospitals own one-third of the stock, physicians one-third, and the chain or network one-third. Net profits then accrue proportionately to all participants. In this scheme of things hospitals provide inpatient care, physicians medical care, and the plan provides marketing, actuarial, and claims services. The result will be a nonprofit chain or network that not only has philosophical appeal to affiliates but also provides strong economic reasons to both hospitals and physicians to join and support it to the maximum extent.

If such a concept is established, it provides an avenue for direct advertising to the public that emphasizes not only the value of the plan to the public but the reputations of participating hospitals that have been earned over years of outstanding service. To date, nonprofit hospitals have failed to effectively communicate the financial benefits the public has enjoyed because of an underlying philosophy that has guided nonprofit institutions. If the public is to appreciate them, nonprofit hospitals are going to have to take an aggressive posture in communicating these values to potential patients.

It needs to be recognized that this kind of proposal is full of risks and difficulties. This strategy requires a thoughtful articulation between the hospital affiliates and sound location selections for capitation expansion. The plan needs able management well grounded in the capitation field and a capitalization which anticipates that mistakes will be made in a start-up phase that may necessitate unexpected outlays. Overall, such a venture is expensive, with an initial capitalization of between $3 million and $4 million, a significant hurdle, but in the new health field environment the stakes are becoming higher and higher and are being met only by the investor-owned field. The challenge is the same for the nonprofit chains and networks.

RETAINING TOP-MANAGEMENT TALENT

As economic competition deepens, the hospital field will encounter a shortage of top-management talent. For many past decades a hospital chief executive was a facilitator; the medical staff requested, the governing board approved, and the management implemented their decision. With an economy of ample resources the system worked well, but it is no longer working because resources are now scarce.

There is a premium on sound managerial judgment. This is recognized by some governing boards who are offering prime candidates for CEO positions increases of 50 percent or more and bonuses for signing. Increasingly, the question will have to be faced whether or not to lock in an executive with outstanding ability so that he is not attracted to another hospital organization. It seems that nonprofit chains and networks are going to have to find ways that permit members of senior management to participate in equity situations where they are able to acquire assets subject to capital gains rather than just salaries subject to income taxes. If hospitals do not face up to this issue the top talent is ultimately going to be in the investor-owned chains where such possibilities already exist. Some nonprofit hospital organizations are already experimenting by creating for-profit contract management firms owned by their own senior management. Under a parent-subsidiary organizational model this can be accomplished while at the same time not jeopardizing the nonprofit status of a corporation.

LOOKING TO THE FUTURE

While for-profits and nonprofits are economically driven, the essence of their difference is that for-profits opt for profitability when hard choices have to be made, while nonprofits opt for responsiveness to community needs. Both will continue to strive for clinical excellence but the for-profits are likely to be more selective in the choices they make, being guided by the profitability factor. Services that are low volume, inadequately reimbursed, or require equipment that is costly to purchase and operate are apt to be avoided. Table 36–4 reflects the kinds of choices that are made.

When more traditional services are compared the differences are not as significant in most of these categories. This can be seen in Table 36–5.

Table 36–4 Percentage of Services Offered in Community Hospitals by Type of Ownership—1982

Service	For-Profit	Nonprofit	Percent Difference
Speech Pathology	20.6%	45.9%	−25.3%
Occupational Therapy	21.5	45.2	−23.7
Premature Nursery	11.8	35.1	−23.3
Dental	33.1	52.7	−19.6
Radioisotope Therapy	12.3	30.9	−18.6
Radiation Therapy	7.4	25.8	−18.4
Mega Voltage	5.4	21.7	−16.3
Hemodialysis	16.7	29.0	−12.3
Hospice	0.7	12.0	−11.3
Cardiac Catheterization	10.0	21.1	−11.1
Home Care Department	5.7	15.8	−10.1
Open-Heart	5.8	14.8	− 9.0
CT Scanner	29.7	38.3	− 8.6
Genetic Counseling	1.0	9.0	− 8.0
Organ Transplant	1.9	5.1	− 3.2

Source: Hospital Statistics, 1983 edition, © 1983 by the American Hospital Association.

Table 36–5 Percentage of Traditional Services Offered in Community Hospitals by Type of Ownership—1982

Traditional Service	For-Profit	Nonprofit	Percent Difference
Histopathology Lab	67.1%	74.0%	−6.9%
Blood Bank	69.9	75.6	−5.7
Postoperative Recovery Room	94.1	92.9	+1.2
Ultrasound	76.2	78.2	−2.0
Respiratory Service	92.4	93.2	−0.8
Pharmacy	94.9	96.3	−1.4
Podiatry	34.6	36.4	−1.8
Radioisotope Diagnostic	66.6	70.5	−3.9
Physical Therapy	84.6	92.2	−7.6
Emergency Room	86.0	94.1	−8.1
Social Work	75.7	85.5	−9.8

Source: Hospital Statistics, 1983 edition, © 1983 by the American Hospital Association.

As a result of the adoption of diagnostic related groups by the Medicare program, a problem has been introduced to hospitals that will be more severe for the for-profit hospital chains than for the nonprofits. Governing boards of investor-owned hospitals usually have several physicians on their boards who typically outnumber the remainder of the board.

Investor-owned hospitals are going to be faced with difficult decisions by the late '80s when DRGs are based on a national rate. Governing boards will be confronted with trying to live with DRG rates that are set at a point that places half of the physicians in the zone of practicing medicine in excess of payable limits. When governing boards attempt to solve this problem, physician-board members are going to be in very uncomfortable positions. As trustees they must ensure fiscal viability of the institution and take steps that lead to this result, even though it may adversely impact some, or all, physicians on the medical staff.

On the other hand, physician-dominated boards will be reluctant to vote in favor of any program that may have this result, because their own feelings are tied to the rest of the medical profession. Trying to decide whether they are physicians first and trustees second, or vice versa, is going to become a serious matter in chains where local boards have physician-trustees that outnumber other trustees.

In the past, the rationale for predominance of physicians on local boards was to assure the medical staff that a hospital was responsive to their views. The quid pro quo, though often unspoken, was that physicians are expected to use a hospital for inpatient services. Looking ahead, it can be anticipated that having several physician-trustees as a strategy, which worked well in the past, will be troublesome to investor-owned chains that have followed this pattern. Since nonprofit chains and networks have appointed only one or two physician-trustees, they will be able to reach consensus more quickly on deciding courses of action that protect the financial viability of their institutions.

At the stage of development that now engulfs the hospital field it is apparent that the day of the stand-alone hospital is past. Nearly all hospitals will enter into some type of arrangement with other institutions. In some cases ownership changes will take place, in others management contracts will be signed, and in still others selected services will be shared.

These arrangements, whatever they may be, are not tests of the future because they are not high-stakes games that are just beginning. The nonprofits were nearly ten years behind the for-profits in commencing the chain movement but have been moving swiftly into a wide variety of collective arrangements to compete with the for-profits. Economic competition between the two types has occurred only at the local level where the stakes have been rather modest. There has not been a showdown with head-to-head competition between them. As a result, it would be difficult to determine which form of corporate ownership and operation will best serve the public's interest.

The test will be decided by the public in the long run. As the future unfolds, both types and systems are apt to underestimate the worth of the adversary system. For-profits are likely to believe that nonprofits will remain slow in decision making, not responsive to changing economic conditions, and lacking in entrepreneurial spirit. On the other hand, nonprofits are likely to see for-profits as predatory, corner cutters, and unconcerned with community health needs. Should either of these two systems come to believe myths about the other system and develop strategic plans based on these assumptions they will make a mistake. The test will be found in the public's decision as to the type of system that is more responsive to its needs, attitudes, and pocketbooks.

Both systems are now at a starting gate and not at the finish line. The race is just beginning. The winner will be determined by paying attention to which system better serves the public interest, not by any other standard. The system that gains the most public support and confidence will ultimately dominate the hospital scene. This should be the goal, to serve the public as it desires to be served, not what a hospital's agents believe the public should expect. Those that seek this goal will:

1. Have the best management talent available
2. Own and operate the best financing mechanisms that the public can purchase
3. Regularly and convincingly tell the public of the philosophy that undergirds every decision of the system
4. Continue to offer the best health care available
5. Be continuously responsive and sensitive to public perceptions rather than provider perceptions

Those that do this most successfully would do well to heed the words of that baseball philosopher, Satchel Paige, who said, "Never look back over your shoulder, someone may be gaining on you."

NOTES

1. Arnold S. Relman, "Investor-Owned Hospitals and Health Care Costs," *New England Journal of Medicine* 309, no. 6 (August 11, 1983): 370.

2. L.S. Levin, R.A. Derzon, R. Margulies, "Investor-owned and Nonprofits Differ in Economic Performance," *Hospitals* 55, no. 13 (1981): 52–58.

3. "Trends in Utilization, Personnel and Finances for Selected Years from 1946 through 1982," in *Hospital Statistics*, 1983 Edition (Chicago: American Hospital Association), Table 1, 6.

REFERENCES

"Hospitals and Beds in Multihospital Systems," in *Directory of Multihospital Systems,* Volume 3 (Chicago: American Hospital Association, 1983), Table 3, 86.

"Do Hospitals in Your System Have Standardized Procedures?" *Modern Healthcare*, April 1981, 89.

"Who Has Decision Making Responsibility?" *Modern Healthcare*, April 1981, 88.

"Facilities and Services in the United States," in *Hospital Statistics*, 1983 Edition (Chicago: American Hospital Association), Table 12A, 193–196.

Chapter 37

Going It Alone May Mean Going Broke

REASONS FOR GROWTH OF SYSTEMS

The reasons put forward for the future growth of multihospital systems are that they have easier access to capital funding, are more efficient in operation, and can bring expertise to hospital matters when needed. Of the three benefits, access to capital is predominant. The other two are the economic equivalent of being in favor of motherhood and apple pie.

The reasons multihospital systems rapidly expand are due to several forces: a desire to move away from the necessity to use tax money for medical indigency and capital purposes; the spiraling demand for new high-cost technology and rapidly increasing complexity of hospital operations; the loss of a sense of accomplishment or, said in a reverse way, the growing frustration of trustees in not seeing that their participation really makes a difference.

In most instances, hospital executives know how to solve a particular issue, but the conservatism of governance, the local political environment, and the status quo approach of medicine on broader social and political matters predetermines a lack of support for a reasonable administrative solution that pushes, even very gently, against these philosophies.

There is wisdom in going slowly when the mission of a hospital needs to change, but a ''sunk-in-concrete'' approach that any variation from the status quo is unacceptable as a consideration, and will not even be discussed, is deadly.

It is always interesting to watch a public hospital convert from hospital authority ownership to being a unit in an investor-owned system and observe the unthinkable becoming thinkable. Unprofitable hospital services are either closed or rates raised to cover operating expenses, medical office buildings and physician recruitment activities are started, and the physical plant is redecorated and new equipment added. One often wonders if the old hospital ownership would not have succeeded as well if it had been able to ignore the repressive restraints they felt obliged to support.

GOING IT ALONE

If this strategy is realistic, then there are ways for a go-it-alone hospital to succeed. One of the ways not to succeed is to attempt to emulate the success stories reported in hospital journals. Vigorously plunging into real estate development, shopping center ownership, and health food stores is not an area of expertise of either hospital boards or hospital executives. Even many of the health-related shared services programs may not turn a decent profit, but instead sap administrative time and effort and divert attention from daily operations of the institution.

An attempt to avoid going it alone without going broke can be successful if a hospital has developed a well-thought-out strategic marketing plan and stays with it.

In these days of restrictive reimbursement, the threat of price competition between hospitals, and the rapidly increasing cost of medical technology, the institutional successes of yesterday are no promise of the same for the future. A hospital can no longer be all things to everyone in a community for health care. What will be needed is a recognition of the specific market niche for a hospital and the services needed to appropriately serve it.

Yesterday's ''shoot-from-the-hip'' gun-slinging trustee, physician, and executive will be gunned down tomorrow by the planning, deliberate ''show-me'' leader. Future successes will be based on cool and rational analysis and program development. A quick promise to appease an irate physician, a compromise decision by the trustees that solves a tough problem with more money rather than facing an issue, or an executive who rationalizes below-average employee performance will create a future where past indiscriminate decisionmaking means thwarted development and implementation of a strategic marketing plan.

Why do hospital governance and medical staffs still sit and do little when it is clear that continued acceptance of the status quo will bring disaster?

A preponderance of hospital executives are knowledgeable about issues that lead to deterioration in the existing state of affairs of their institution, want to make changes to head off trouble, and often have a reasonably workable idea of what to do. If this is so, why do hospitals go broke, or sell out, or buy a management service, or expect to have to do one or the other at some future time?

What is often overlooked is that trustees and physicians put far more value on how an executive does something rather than what is actually accomplished. Even when their hospital record is one of 25 years of continually adding new programs and services and by any reasonable measure would be considered to be a successful institution, judgments are still made on form rather than substance. In the business world, what would be acknowledged as a star performance is regarded simply as doing one's job.

HURDLES TO GOING IT ALONE

The existing value placed on administrative style is to conform with local norms, no matter what the circumstances. This prevents a hospital executive from openly and frankly telling it like it is as well as what is needed. The best that can be done is to send a few trustees and medical staff leaders to a health care seminar such as an Estes Park conference or discuss the heart of the matter with very carefully selected trustees and physicians (of course, on a one-to-one basis, beyond the earshot of others). Too often the leadership is composed of good listeners but poor performers.

When an executive decides to bite the bullet and raises a critical issue that may only have an unacceptable outcome, but the only one possible, both trustees and medical staff typically sidetrack the matter, appoint a committee, table for later discussion, or ask for more information. Experienced committee members do this gracefully in order to take the CEO off the hook due to his lapse of acceptable behavior. Should the CEO fail to get the message, sooner or later a silver bullet will be the reward.

Administrative behavior is what it is because of the power structure of the institution. If the leadership does not want to face the real world with its changing conditions, the result is delayed until organizational walls begin to crack ominously and outside forces take control.

A strategic marketing plan is of no value unless it is actively supported by actions of the board of trustees to make it a reality. Administrative motivation, farsighted anticipation of coming events, and local initiative will not stem the tide of multihospital system takeovers unless a strategic marketing plan is supported by physicians and trustees. It is missing the boat to believe that the superior qualities of a hospital executive can single-handedly maintain a future for a freestanding hospital. Conversely, having a below-average, go-it-alone hospital CEO is a certain way to ensure that a hospital will, sooner or later, become one more facility in a multihospital corporation.

DEVELOPING RESPONSIVE BOARDS

The basic issue has been around the hospital field for 50 years. How do you develop a board of trustees that is deliberative, objective, rational, and sensitive to the larger forces operating in health care? The ability to develop a board with these characteristics is the determining factor in whether a hospital remains freestanding and stable or whether it can't make it on its own.

What then can a hospital CEO do to influence a board of trustees to ensure that there is careful selection of replacement trustees with appropriate characteristics of mind and motivation that lead to a cohesive, analytical body that demonstrates farsightedness in its decisions? The most obvious risk for a hospital CEO is that he will be perceived by the trustees as seeking to put persons on the board who are sympathetic to his position. This thought will be present in many trustees' minds. Awareness of this kind of hazard means that a hospital executive can accomplish this objective only indirectly, with patience, and over a long period of time.

The best way to attain a well-balanced board of trustees is to review its performance and use the findings as the basis for suggesting change to improve its operation. As a starting place, one might broadly categorize the types of decisions a board is making and compare it with those of five years ago. If there are no identifiable shifts toward more informational and evaluative activities, and fewer procedural ones, it is a sign the board is not keeping up with the times. Since CEOs have input into the preparation of a board agenda, they have an opportunity to gradually influence how a meeting will be structured. By better use of acceptable parliamentary procedures, the procedural agenda items can be quickly handled and the recaptured time used to present broader issues with a more complete analysis and discussion. Too often, 30 to 40 percent of the time of a board meeting can be frittered away on minutes, routine medical staff changes, financial reviews, and incidental board activities.

When boards hold meetings during the workday hours, there is often a continuous drive to get out of the meeting, If the meetings are held in the evening hours, the only apparent drive for efficiently disposing of the agenda is on Monday night to tune in the kickoff for Monday Night Football.

In a review of a board of trustees' decisions, timeliness, appropriateness, and quality of thinking should be evaluated. If major issues are left undecided too long, if one board member dominates the outcome, and if possible alternatives of an issue are not discussed, a hospital is steadily heading into an uncontrollable situation.

A second possibility is a periodic evaluation of trustee performance. This activity needs to be carefully introduced. When a medical staff annually reviews the performance of its members, hospital employees have periodical performance evaluations, and the CEO is annually reviewed, it is logical to suggest the same procedure for trustees. How best to do a trustee review is a sensitive issue because of the trustees' reputations and community status.

Probably the best approach is to ask the nominating committee to periodically discuss and evaluate trustee performance and record its conclusions in a memorandum. How much beyond this step such a procedure can be taken must be based on a judgment of the board's reactions. At the same time, criteria should be set up for the selection of new trustees. Considerations of religion, race, and economic status do not measure the qualities of mind and viewpoint needed for a quality trustee. The idea of selecting a trustee because of a particular skill, such as an insurance broker, contractor, lawyer, or banker, to provide expertise in these areas is an out-of-date notion. The skills available today in hospital administration and the full-time staff, plus outside consultants, provide more expert institutional assistance than the talents of a typical trustee.

The rock-bottom criterion for a potential trustee is his philosophy and values and the degree to which they coincide with the prevailing ones of the board or the philosophy that is desired. These are reflected by their concerns about broader health and social issues in our society. A board of trustees with widely divergent viewpoints is guaranteed to have deadlocked discussions. A hospital board meeting is no place to reconcile community differences. Before a trustee is elected, there needs to be a commitment to the mission of the hospital. A hospital is not a primary community vehicle for social change.

Another major responsibility of a designated board of trustees' committee is to police potential and actual conflict of interest issues. This responsibility could be vested in the nominating committee along with trustee evaluation.

The current practice of annually having trustees sign a conflict of interest statement is more of a charade than a serious concern: the most obvious conflicts of interest are now typically under reasonable control; these include the sale of supplies to hospitals, buying insurance coverages, and direct transactions between the hospital corporation and the businessman/hospital trustee. What is still ignored are the bankshots, matters where other outside interests of trustees indirectly impact a trustee's hospital board decisions. For example, a banker has a loan with a nursing home and later votes to keep the hospital out of this business. His superficial motivation can be based on the fear of hospital losses due to existing competition, while his real motive is to protect the safety of an existing loan. Another often unexpressed motive is for a trustee to hold down hospital rate increases because it will later impact the premiums of his company's health insurance coverage.

Any number of examples of hidden conflicts of interest can be described and practically all hospital executives have their own set of experiences. Because a hospital executive discussing this problem is biting the hand that feeds him, it is never mentioned in hospital journals or in a hospital. However, among colleagues it is a frequent topic.

Until a board of trustees can come to grips with hidden conflicts of interest, it will continue to jeopardize the long-run future of hospitals and create acquisition opportunities for multihospital systems.

Another practical dilemma for hospital executives is the usual assumption on the part of the board of trustees that their administrative staff has a limitless amount of time to spend on governance activities. What is unappreciated is that the more administrative effort spent on their affairs means the less time there is for daily operations, medical staff, and community affairs.

How often does a board use a committee to handle a particular problem and then rehash the whole affair when the total board meets? Or how frequently is an executive in a quandary as to whether or not to take a problem to the board of trustees even though it is within his scope of authority knowing that the board really wants to make the decision. Typically, these are issues of lesser concern. Trustees don't really want to face major issues that they know will disturb traditional practices or are at variance with the opinions of some important personages in the community.

This litany of existing governance shortcomings varies from one hospital to another throughout the country. While there are examples of competent, able boards of trustees, they are not the rule, but rather an exception. Hospitals with this kind of outstanding board leadership will insist on capable, motivated chief executives who steadily pursue institutional excellence.

Hospital CEOs can encourage excellence in governance and provide ideas and ways of bettering the performance of trustees, but these affairs are beyond their direct control. To fail to try to improve the decision-making process of a board of trustees is a failure of hospital administration. To fail to accomplish this goal is a failure of governance.

It is worthwhile remembering that the successes of multihospital systems are, in the last analysis, created out of the failures of hospital governance. With a hospital governance of excellence, going it alone will not mean going broke. Status quo "we like things as they are" leadership will result in going it alone and going broke.

Chapter 38

The Hospital in Chains[*]

FORMS OF INTEGRATION

By 1990, the general freestanding community hospital will no longer be the keystone of the health field, but will have been replaced with either a vertically or horizontally integrated health delivery system. The vertical system will evolve out of the community hospital and will continue to have a primary service area orientation but will bring together, into one organizational structure, diverse types of health facilities including several nursing homes, primary care centers, professional office buildings, fitness and wellness programs, and perhaps a second or third hospital. In addition, it may have for-profit activities such as a contract management service and a real estate arm. In time, a health care corporation may have a long list of additional health-related activities where opportunities for either service or profit, or both, exist. All units of this system will probably be within one hour's driving time of each other.

On the other hand, horizontal systems will stem from two sources: investor-owned hospitals and religious institutions. Both are already in place and rapidly growing. This trend can be expected to vigorously continue throughout the decade of the '80s. By the turn of the twenty-first century, the health care corporation will have emerged as a sophisticated corporation requiring managerial skills that were not even envisioned in the health field in the decades of the '60s and '70s.

INTERNAL STRAIN

These drastic shifts are rooted in events of the last 15 years. A number of factors, both internal and external to hospitals, were converging throughout this period and came together in the latter years of the '70s.

---

[*]*Source:* Adapted with permission from the April 1981 issue of *Modern Healthcare Magazine*. Copyright Crain Communications, Inc., 740 N. Rush, Chicago, Ill. 60611. All rights reserved.

One of the first harbingers of things to come occurred in 1965 when Medicare/ Medicaid legislation was enacted. These laws provided that hospitals be paid "allowable costs," which was assumed by many executives to mean their institutions would be reimbursed full operating costs. Fifteen years later it had been learned that these definitions were not identical and had, in fact, grown further apart. By 1980, hospital executives were aware that if all beds were filled with categorical patients the inevitable result would be bankruptcy, since allowable costs paid approximately 80 percent of the costs of operation.

While this erosion of revenue was taking place, there was also a greater pressure to allocate larger and larger funds for renovation to physical plants and for purchasing new equipment that was technologically more advanced than what was in use. Budgets were increasingly strained as hospitals attempted to keep current with the state-of-the-art technology. Annual outlays for equipment began running $500,000 per year for every 100 beds.

By 1980, Medicare and Medicaid were accounting for nearly one-half of total patient days in many hospitals and it was no longer feasible to charge other patients enough to make up for losses incurred under allowable costs. Medical staffs, as in the past, continued to press for the latest available equipment and steadfastly refused to settle for anything less. Even in hospitals where depreciation had been conscientiously funded, the price tags on new equipment were considerably beyond replacement funds that had been accrued. The traditional financial equation was no longer viable.

EXTERNAL STRESS

While these changes were happening inside hospitals, external forces were also coming into play and crippling their ability to carry our their mission. Applications for Certificate of Need approvals became a constant source of frustration because of the cost of their preparation, inordinate time delays in processing, and frequent denials on grounds hospital representatives considered superficial or capricious. By the end of the '70s, hospital executives had become thoroughly disenchanted with the governmental process of regulation and were openly discussing these problems. There was a growing feeling that hospitals were being held hostage by the government for problems in the general economy over which they had no control. Inflation was running in double-digit numbers and expenditures under Medicare and Medicaid, brought about by entitlements enacted by Congress, were proving to be more costly than had been anticipated.

Keeping a physical plant and equipment up-to-date, a practice that had been successfully followed for 70 years, had become an unsolvable equation in the face of the governmental pressures that were bearing down. Reluctantly, many hospital executives were reaching a conclusion that previous strategies were not going to be useful in coping with the future. Instinctively, they knew that the road was coming to an end and a new pathway was needed. They realized new strategies would bring profound changes in the organizational structure of the hospital.

The coalescing of these forces had been recognized a few years earlier by a handful of hospitals that were willing to squarely face these issues. These hospitals had already undertaken a serious reassessment of their own organizational structures and developed new strategies. The reluctance of most hospitals to make major changes was understandable when reviewed in a historical perspective. Since 1910, when the Flexner Report was published, hospitals had dedicated themselves to providing the best possible patient care. Over the intervening years, adherence to this concept had led to the development of hospitals that were the finest in any nation. For 70 years, governing boards had guided hospital development by basing their decisions on affirmatively answering one question, "Does the matter under discussion enhance patient care?" If yes, the project was authorized; if no, it was voted down. This single-minded devotion to quality patient care for seven decades had the intended result—a hospital system that was unmatched.

This development occurred during a period of ample resources. Trustees of voluntary nonprofit hospitals believed the public should receive quality patient care at the lowest possible cost. What this really meant was that governing board decisions became a two-step process. The first decision had to do with the quality of care. The second, and always second, was to decide how to finance a project. The two were not considered together, but in sequence. Trustees took pride in believing that if something was needed in a hospital, ways could always be found to pay for it. This philosophy worked, year after year, as long as resources were plentiful.

By the end of the '70s, it became evident that something was amiss. Decisions could no longer be made on a sequential basis. Governing boards and chief executives found themselves devoting more and more time to finance and increasingly unable to fund new technology. Without consciously attempting to do so, they were giving as much weight to financial concerns as to quality of care; both now had to be considered at the same time.

Finances were becoming unstable and unpredictable. Retrospective audits by Medicare, where operating costs of a hospital were being disallowed as reimbursable, often turned modest surpluses into major deficits, sometimes two to three years later, as a result of delayed audits. In states with prospective rate review programs, the margin between income and expense was narrowed to unrealistic amounts. Governing boards trying to exercise prudent trusteeships were finding that hoped-for year-end financial results of approximately a zero balance (or preferably a net positive margin) could lead to unanticipated losses and an inability to fund new and needed services.

As financing and capital formation problems rose to the top of their concerns, more and more attention was paid to the growth of the investor-owned hospital corporations. By the end of the '70s, it appeared that they were becoming a major factor in the hospital industry. These hospitals paid close attention to finance, organizational flexibility, and managerial performance and their results were impressive. Capital formation didn't seem to be a constraint and it became clear that these corporations had an advantage of being publicly traded on the stock market. They had access not only to the bond market but also to equity funds through the sale of additional shares of stock.

ORGANIZATIONAL FLEXIBILITY

In the mid-'70s, arguments frequently arose in some quarters that for-profit chains would never succeed because they "skimmed the cream" and provided inferior care. Leaders associated with community, nonprofit hospitals tended to believe that for-profit hospitals took only paying patients, shunned participation in nurses training and postgraduate medical education, and accepted any physician who applied for medical staff privileges. Because of these practices, it was thought that the public would eventually recognize the advantages of receiving care in nonprofit hospitals and avoid the for-profits.

This did not happen. As the investor-owned hospitals continued to enjoy rapid growth, the voluntary hospitals realized that they were a real competitive threat because their financial strength was a major advantage. Providing health care services at multiple locations and offering a wide diversity of services in a flexible organizational structure were seen as avenues around some of the roadblocks that had been created by government.

The parent subsidiary corporation model appeared to offer several advantages including:

1. A number of nonhospital, but health-related, activities could be undertaken without submitting Certificate of Need applications to a Health Systems Agency if a subsidiary, other than a hospital corporation, was the applicant.
2. Alternative sources of revenue could be tapped without being subject to state rate review if a subsidiary, other than a hospital corporation, was used.
3. Competitive pricing for health services could be employed if a subsidiary, other than a hospital, was used.
4. Greater accountability of management personnel could be achieved by using a parent-subsidiary model.
5. For-profit, as well as nonprofit, subsidiaries could be established.
6. Expanded influence in the marketplace could be obtained if ambulatory services were developed that enhanced the use of a hospital subsidiary.

GROWTH OF CHAINS

The chaining of hospitals and health-related activities was seen to be as useful for nonprofit hospitals as it was for the for-profit field. The strategy for both groups emerged: multiple units of hospitals and other health-related activities operating at multiple locations in multiple corporate structures. Financial strength through size and diversity opened up the road to the future and the race to grow as rapidly as possible became the number one priority for many hospitals.

On April 20, 1981, the voluntary hospital field received a jolt. On that date, the Hospital Corporation of America announced that it had acquired Hospital Affiliates International from the INA Insurance Company for approximately $650 million. This increased the beds and number of hospitals owned or managed by HCA by about two-thirds and resulted in a hospital corporation controlling over 300 hospitals. Governing boards and chief executives of voluntary hospitals who had been thinking about growth through a restructuring of a hospital corporation, but who had not as yet activated any plans, realized that a sense of urgency was required. The move by HCA triggered action by a number of hospitals that had been standing on the sidelines.

By coincidence, at the time of the HCA move, *Modern Healthcare* published a special report in its April, 1981,[1] issue on multihospital systems. It was based on a detailed survey and was significant because it was the first time a trade journal in the health field had taken a long detailed look at an emerging corporate trend. The article identified 176 chains already in existence. In summary form the journal reported as follows:

Type of System	1980 Total Beds Owned/Managed	Less Psychiatry Beds	Percent Change from 1979
Religious	110,740	107,418	+ 4.4%
Investor-Owned	103,280	100,182	+14.0
Secular Nonprofit	56,731	55,029	+ 4.1
Public	21,448	20,805	− 1.2
Total	292,199	283,434	+ 7.1%

Of the 988,000 acute beds (psychiatry not included) in operation in the United States, the 283,434 represents 28.9 percent of the total beds. Should the growth rates experienced between 1979 and 1980 continue throughout the present decade, the results will be startling. If it holds up, 1990 will look like this:

Type of System	1990 Beds	1980 Beds	Change 1980–1990
Religious	165,225	107,418	+ 57,807
Investor-Owned	371,391	100,182	+271,209
Secular Nonprofit	82,243	55,029	+ 27,214
Public	18,441	20,805	− 2,364
Total	637,300	283,434	+353,866

Should this outcome occur, 64.5 percent of the acute beds will have become part of a chain operation, a 125 percent gain over the 1980 level.

This 14 percent growth rate of investor-owned chains may prove to be optimistic in light of the consolidations among chains that are now underway. In all likelihood, some of the existing chains will experience this kind of growth, but a part of this growth will be due to the acquisition of smaller chains. The net result of this kind of activity may be to reduce the overall rate by one-half of the projected rate to 7 percent. This would result in the following configuration:

Type of System	Rate of Growth	Number of Beds 1990
Religious	+4.4%	165,225
Investor-Owned	+7.0	235,787
Secular Nonprofit	+4.1	82,243
Public	−1.2	18,441
Total		501,696

Even at this lower rate, 50.8 percent of all beds would be in hospital corporate chains by 1990.

What is the probability that this growth will take place? Among religious chains, the 4.4 percent current annual increase can be expected to continue. Catholic orders that had been selling off hospitals because of an inadequate number of Sisters to staff them, are no longer thinking of retrenchment. Instead of viewing the operation of multiple hospitals only from a religious standpoint, they are now tying them together financially and managerially to successfully compete with the other chains. The orders are now bullish on growth.

Like the religious chains, secular nonprofit ones can also be expected to continue their growth rate. Executives in these organizations believe that other freestanding voluntary hospitals will prefer to join ranks with them because they are also nonprofit and do not have a religious affiliation. The extent to which this will occur is unknown, but it does provide a freestanding hospital with an alternative it may wish to consider.

To date, the growth of chains has been of a horizontal nature in which one hospital corporation operates a number of additional hospitals in various locations. This pattern varies depending upon the ownership of the chain. In the for-profit sector, the major concerns involve financial and managerial performance. Their hospitals are expected to generate a targeted rate of return and to maintain desired standards of patient care.

The locations of hospitals in a chain are not of primary concern provided that regional supervision can be maintained without undue expense. Locations of additional units are not significant as long as they can be supervised properly and the pro formas are in line with expected results.

The criteria in the other types of chains are somewhat different and more restrictive. They may include concerns about religious aspects or about proximity to the acquiring hospital. In addition, the philosophical basis of serving on the governing board of a nonprofit hospital may, in itself, become an impediment to rapid growth of a system. A look at why this is so may be helpful in understanding why growth rates in the nonprofit chains may occur at a slower rate.

Trustees of nonprofit hospitals serve on governing boards as a community service, without pay and with a desire to see that the community benefits by receiving the highest quality of care obtainable at the lowest possible cost. They tend to see physicians on the medical staff as entrepreneurs engaged in private practice using the hospital, a quasi-public enterprise, to assist in the diagnosis and treatment of patients. Because of its nonprofit status, trustees often believe their institution should not engage in activities that are economically threatening to physicians.

This type of thinking extends to salary levels paid to employees of a hospital. As a community nonprofit service, trustees believe no one should be paid an excessive salary. This is often interpreted to mean that a hospital should pay salaries competitive with other nonprofit hospitals in the area. Fringe benefits follow the same kind of pattern. Outstanding performance may be unrewarded or, at best, not be fully recognized in salary increases.

In the past, this kind of thinking on the part of trustees, particularly with regard to senior management, presented no difficulty in retaining capable executives since no other alternatives existed. Ten years from now, this situation is apt to be changed. When the tables dealing with growth of the investor-owned hospitals are examined, it seems self-evident that the more competent executives in the nonprofit sector are likely to be attracted to similar positions in for-profit chains where managerial performance is recognized by salary as well as year-end bonuses and an opportunity to develop equity positions in the stock of the company. The ability to offer these types of inducements suggests that nonprofit hospitals are going to have increasing difficulty in recruiting and retaining top managerial talent.

This kind of income competition for executives is not unique to the hospital field. In years past, it has been experienced by the life insurance industry, where a number of the large companies were originally formed as mutuals. In order to provide the same kind of incentives and inducements offered to executives in the stock insurance companies, organizations like Prudential and Connecticut General developed subsidiary companies so that top management could be offered equity positions in their for-profit subsidiaries. This is a model that might well be studied by nonprofit hospitals.

DEVELOPING A NEW PHILOSOPHY

Whether or not a freestanding nonprofit hospital elects to join a chain, trustees are now faced with the necessity of developing a new philosophy about their responsibilities. The concept that a trustee represents the community and, therefore, measures performance only against what is done on behalf of the community can no longer be considered to be the total and only responsibility of a board. The nonprofit institution has taken on a role that requires an advocacy of its own. Community service must now be balanced against institutional requirements. At times this will coincide with public interest, while at other times it may not, particularly in the arena of economic factors. In many cities and towns, hospitals now rank as the largest, or one of the largest, employers with a physical plant worth tens of millions of dollars. Thus not only are these hospitals important to medical care but they have become significant economic resources for providing community employment opportunities. Remaining in business to provide modern, up-to-date health care services and to provide employment opportunities are both equally important. Therefore, a hospital cannot remain aloof from happenings in its marketplace.

A hospital needs to keep current information on what is occurring in its service area and, if necessary, take an aggressive posture to protect its market share. When a hospital discovers it is losing market share or is operating at less than capacity, it will have to develop marketing strategies that reverse this trend, possibly at the expense of nearby hospitals. This strategy may take the form of creating a network of primary care centers at some distance from the hospital, erecting professional office buildings, or guaranteeing incomes to new physician practices. In hospitals that have incurred large amounts of long-term debt, aggressiveness in the marketplace may be needed for survival. Marketing is part and parcel of exercising sound financial stewardship.

Another aspect of trusteeship requires abandoning the notion of providing services at the lowest possible cost to patients. In a technological industry that is capital intensive, adhering to this concept will lead away from, and not toward , a successful future. If a hospital is unable to keep up with state-of-the-art technology because it has not accumulated sufficient surpluses or cannot resort to the bond market because of a weak financial history, it is to be expected that physicians will take their hospital practices elsewhere. Admitting a patient to the lowest-cost hospital has no appeal to a competent physician if that low cost is achieved at the expense of up-to-date technology or inadequately trained personnel. To continue to believe in the lowest possible cost may invite a loss of market share, leading to a lowered average occupancy rate, which leads to increased financial difficulties and reductions in the quality of care.

The capital crunch on hospitals is the result of being paid historical costs for plant and equipment depreciation at a time of continued double-digit inflation. New technology necessitates the use of long-term debt, most often through a public sale of bonds. When a bond sale is contemplated, hospital representatives inevitably make a journey to New York City to meet with Moody's Investor Service and Standard & Poor's to obtain a rating for their bond sale. The rating received is a reflection of the degree of risk for the investor. Rating agencies have little interest in the fact that a hospital may have the lowest average cost per patient day in its area if the result is a weak financial picture.

As a freestanding hospital moves toward the health care corporation model of 1990, governing boards are going to have to decide issues on much the same basis as directors of for-profit organizations, even though their basic philosophies are different. Governance behavior will be similar because survival and growth will be dependent upon using the same frame of reference to make financial decisions.

In a large measure all health care corporations will use the same type of management information (for-profit and nonprofit) in measuring financial performance though there are two major differences, neither of which affects the day-to-day operations. When capital financing is needed, the investor-owned must choose either debt or equity or a combination of both. The nonprofit chain can only look toward long-term debt.

The restructuring of a freestanding hospital into a parent-subsidiary health care corporation has a unique advantage from a governance perspective. The parent, or holding company, provides a way of bridging the gap between the past and the future without doing violence to the traditions of hospital trusteeship. In a subsidiary, the hospital trustee can retain concerns about the problems of finance and coordination with other health-related programs. Trustees who have the requisite skills in finance and the ability to weigh competing factors can be encouraged to become directors of the parent corporations.

In creating a parent-subsidiary structure, care should be taken to avoid having a governing board of the hospital also serve as the board of the parent. This dual arrangement leads to patient care considerations dominating all of the board decisions and impedes the process of evolving into a health care corporation. During the formative years, the hospital is the single largest entity in this type of organization, even though it is a subsidiary. Because of the hospital's size and importance, the activities of a parent holding company must be shielded from domination by its major subsidiary and its problems. If the two boards have identical membership, the hospital agenda may well consume the major time and interests of the trustees.

DIFFERENCES IN CHAINS

In the future, secular nonprofit chains can be expected to maintain their service area identification. However, as time passes, governance and management may come to focus on a larger scale, such as a region within the state. Because of the possibility of this identification, it is most apt to move toward a vertically integrated model and ultimately may own and operate two or more hospitals, several nursing homes, and a wide array of ambulatory care programs. Should a chain develop a specific program that is notable, such as a behavioral modification project, it may ultimately franchise this program throughout adjacent states.

Religiously oriented health care corporations are more likely to become horizontally integrated systems not concerned about geographical boundaries, but rather concerned about operating in areas where they have religious activities. This type of system may result in one large corporation or in a parent-subsidiary mode, depending upon the political necessities of bringing together the first few units. A model that may be emulated is one that parallels the structure of the Sisters of Mercy of Farmington, Michigan.

Investor-owned chains are most apt to become a hybrid of the vertical and horizontal systems. Whereas geography may be controlling in shaping the secular nonprofit chain, religious activities will likely dictate where the religious chains locate hospitals. The investor-owned chains will make their determinations on the mix of cost reimbursement versus charges and the potential ability of hospitals to generate bottom lines in keeping with corporate plans. Their future growth will take place primarily in the southeastern, southern, and southwestern portions of the United States. Even though the investor-owned chains began as horizontally integrated systems, they are adding subsidiary activities for real estate management, insurance, and purchasing. More will be added as needs arise.

Overshadowing all of these anticipated developments is the question of whether or not Congress will adopt a procompetition bill for all hospital care, not only Medicare. Should one be enacted, the wisdom of freestanding hospitals moving into vertically or horizontally integrated systems will be more apparent because of an emphasis that will need to be placed on improving productivity. If a bill is enacted, the chains will concentrate their acquisition efforts on hospitals between 100 and 250 beds where they will be able to compete more successfully due to lower operating costs than those of larger institutions.

The leaders of the industry in 1990 will have reached their positions of prominence because they demonstrated their concerns for fiscal viability, and will share a number of common characteristics:

1. Operating expenses will have been maintained at approximately 80 percent of new revenues (gross revenues less bad debts and contractual allowances).
2. For every dollar of assets, there will be a dollar in annual revenue.
3. For every dollar of net revenue, there will be a bottom line of five to seven cents.
4. Long-term debt will have ranged between 40 and 60 percent of total assets with a median of about 50 percent.
5. Depreciation and amortization costs per bed per year will have ranged between $2,000 and $2,500 for the first part of the decade and slightly higher for the latter part.

6. Interest expense per bed per year will have averaged between $2,000 and $2,500, provided interest rates ease off during the latter half of the decade.
7. Operating revenues will have steadily increased by an annual amount of between 15 and 25 percent, fueled by both real growth and inflation.

In the investor-owned health care corporations, two additional characteristics will be found:

1. Net income, as a percentage of shareholders equity, will have ranged between 14 and 17 percent with a median of 15 percent.
2. Corporate taxes will have been between 40 and 43 percent but may decline to lower levels as a result of tax relief.

For hospitals that cling to the status quo, the future will be circumscribed by the limits of tradition. For those that recognize and adapt to a changing environment, chains will be viewed as large, complex sets of organizational relationships that will provide governance and management with the required flexibility to meet a new and different world.

NOTE

1. *Modern Healthcare*, April 1981, 79–102.

Chapter 39

The Theory of Multihospital Systems[*]

The more one reads and sees of the modern multihospital systems, the more one wonders whatever happened to the concepts taught in organizational theory and behavior curricula.

Existing multihospital systems are organizational structures that reflect the past realities of merger negotiations, reimbursement considerations, struggles with the tax codes of the Internal Revenue Service, and an assumption that no matter what external realities must be accommodated, a workable management structure can be evolved.

In other words, theory and reality are poles apart. Any organizational structure can be made to function, but at what cost and at what price to the executives in the system? Long working hours, endless travel, lost market opportunities, and a high level of executive frustration may be the side effects that result.

PURPOSE OF STRUCTURE

The goal of an organizational structure is to achieve managerial effectiveness that smoothly delivers a complex array of health care services with a minimum use of resources at an optimal level of effectiveness. The degree to which existing multihospital systems meet this criterion is unknown because no comparative organizational structure studies have been published that deal with the impact of organizational structure on managerial effectiveness and cost in multihospital systems.

Historically, two types of multihospital systems have been in existence for decades: the Catholic orders and the Veterans Administration of the federal

---

[*]Adapted from *Topics in Health Care Financing*, Vol. 8, No. 1, pp. 75–85, Aspen Publishers, Inc., © 1981.

government. The Catholic orders, until the late 1960s, viewed each hospital as an outreach of their apostolic mission. There was no entrepreneurial motive to organize an integrated system. The Veterans Administration hospitals operated within the bureaucratic structure of the government and, likewise, lacked an entrepreneurial and efficiency motivation.

From the late 1960s on, the development of the multihospital system occurred in two different forms. The large community nonprofit hospital chains typically began their expansion by mergers between hospitals in a horizontal structural arrangement. Investor-owned hospitals also developed laterally, but maintained a corporate governance function that did not change as facilities were acquired.

Since the mid-1970s, multihospital systems have expanded both vertically and horizontally. Their scope of medical care services has ranged from primary care to tertiary care levels, from outpatient clinics and nursing homes to specialized medical care programs with a high level of intensity of services.

In the decade of the '80s, the existing multihospital systems can be characterized as focusing on developing the individual facilities rather than developing interrelationships among the hospitals in the system. The preponderance of central office functions has been centered on acquisition, financial matters of accounting, budgeting, revenue and expense controls, utilization, reimbursement, management control systems, and asset management, with some efforts at training and manpower utilization. By and large, present-day systems have not yet moved from facilities planning and operations to systemwide program planning.

CORPORATE DIVISIONS OR HOLDING COMPANY

In today's environment, the typical organizational concerns are about the use of a corporate model versus a holding company approach. Legal and reimbursement issues dominate discussions even though they are not central to management effectiveness.

Existing theories about organizational structure are sufficiently worked out to be useful as general guides for thinking about the organizational structures of hospital systems.

An organizational structure either facilitates or handicaps management effectiveness. It is never a neutral element in the achievement of an organization's role and mission. A major purpose of an organizational structure is to group workers, functions, and programs into an integrated set of relationships in order to provide a logical, clear, and easily understood system for anticipating future demands for service. In essence, today's decisions about organizational structure of a multihospital system sets the limits as to how the problems and service demands of tomorrow will be handled.

An organizational structure is fundamentally a management structure, whereas the corporation structure is a legal and reimbursement mechanism. Organizational theory deals with the management structure and the interrelationships of functions to carry out a role and mission. It is a rationalization for getting work done within a defined scope of interest.

The history of organizational structure development in acute hospitals has been logical, but incomplete at the governance and chief executive level. The parameters of separate governance and administrative functions have rarely been clearly divided in most hospital organizations, and they are often compounded by ambivalent separation of medical staff affairs with governance and executive accountabilities for medical staff matters. In multihospital systems of more than three facilities such obfuscations have disappeared as medical staff functions have been delegated to the individual institutional level of the organization. The identification of medical staff authority as an individual hospital function separate from governance is one of the essential differences between freestanding hospitals and hospitals operating within a multihospital system.

Containment of medical staff authorities and influences at the individual institutional level has added greatly to corporate stability and strengthened the entrepreneurial functions of multihospital systems to acquire additional facilities.

The hospital organizational structure, beyond the separation of professional and support services, is typically a hit-or-miss proposition. The organizational location of newly created services or programs is often assigned to an assistant administrator with an interest in it or one who has a smaller administrative workload than other assistant administrators. If organizational theory had been followed as a guide for placement in the structure, existing hospital organizational structures would be much more alike than they are now, no matter what the size of the institution.

Most hospital CEOs tend to view organizational structures of different-sized hospitals as being separate and apart from each other. To do so is a misunderstanding, both of organizational theory and the functions of hospitals.

All hospitals have the same primary purpose: the delivery of medical care and hospital services. The particular role and mission of a hospital determines which particular aspects are to be emphasized by accepting responsibility for operating programs to carry out the necessary functions.

FOCUS OF A MULTIHOSPITAL SYSTEM

A multihospital system may have either a broad or narrow focus for its corporate role and mission. If the system is vertically structured this statement would be broad in its definition of medical services: from wellness programs to primary care centers, to acute hospitals, to rehabilitation and skilled nursing facilities. In terms of geography, its scope would probably be restricted to a large metropolitan or regional area within a state.

On the other hand, the role and mission statement of a horizontally structured system would probably be narrow in its scope of medical services, such as acute general hospitals, and broad in its geographical scope, such as the southeastern United States or all states where reimbursement policies are on a charge basis.

Within the boundaries of the corporate role and mission, the multihospital system determines the basic grouping of functions necessary to accomplish its goals. In practice, multihospital systems better understand how to divide functions into activities, tasks, and jobs than how to translate a role and mission statement into objectives and functions that control the total organization.

At the corporate level of the multihospital system, the basic functions should be grouped so as to give emphasis and focus to organizational objectives. A role and mission statement is an expression of the long-term goals of the corporation, while objectives are a subset of this statement that elaborate how the organization plans to accomplish its goals within a three- to five-year perspective.

To do this the organization of a multihospital system must employ a matrix-type structure. That is to say that even though a function must necessarily exist at the individual facility level, such as a division of medical services, radiology, pathology, or pulmonary function, its director must report to both the institutional facility manager and the corporate director of these services.

One of the oldest adages in organizational theory is that each position should have only one superior to whom it reports. Modern theory has replaced this notion because it has been recognized that an educated, intelligent manager can distinguish the differences in his problems and follow more complex routines in order to reach a decision.

If a multihospital system does not have a matrix-type structure, it clearly implies that the organization allows the quality of its services to vary at the institutional level. Without overall corporate control and direction, the level of care is not centrally directed and controlled but is at the discretion of the institutional manager.

If there were an evenness of high-level quality of care in a multihospital system, the corporation should market the corporate name, rather than the name of individual hospitals, because it would uniformly represent high quality to patients and physicians. It would be similar to the old marketing slogan of ''like sterling on silver.''

When hospitals face the issue of expanding their current operations into a larger arena, the paramount concern is whether the structure should be that of a corporate model or a holding company. In both cases, the internal management of individual hospitals and central office functions can operate in similar fashion. This is often overlooked in the political, legal, and reimbursement argument.

In all multihospital systems serving an area larger than the scope of practice of individual physicians, the traditional procedure of individual institutional appointments of members of the medical staff has been followed. This means that the quality of medical care has been retained as an institutional responsibility of the local medical staff. The nature of medical practice and its technology being what it is means that a logical choice for the organizational location of this responsibility has been made.

However, the choice of the overall corporate structure can have a direct impact on how successfully the monitoring and evaluation of medical care is accomplished. In the case of the corporate model, with one corporation operating multiple hospitals, there is no mandated responsibility for this function, other than the typical regulations of the Joint Commission on the Accreditation of Hospitals and Medicare. The function of an individual hospital will be no more, nor less, than in a freestanding hospital.

If the multihospital system has a quality of care committee of physicians at the corporate level, their performance will typically be carried out like other committees, carelessly or meticulously, depending upon its membership and chairman. Committee directives are frequently viewed as less than binding, or are seen as less than serious in intent.

In the holding company, subsidiary units such as individual institutions are incorporated separately with a corporate board of directors who have legally defined authorities and responsibilities. When the subcorporate board has accountability for the quality of medical care and has medical staff members, the probability of serious concern for quality issues is significantly enhanced.

The use of subsidiary corporate boards also provides opportunities for corporate officers not on the corporate board to gain experience through membership on one of the subsidiary boards.

COMPONENTS OF A MATRIX STRUCTURE

A matrix-type structure can be successfully used as the basic organizational scheme of a multihospital system when the underlying factors present are as follows:

1. *Authority and accountability are delegated clearly and accurately defined for each management position.* A clearly defined scope of authority and accountability for each position reduces organizational conflicts and the amount of consultation required before making a decision.

2. *Trained and experienced subordinate executives are managing the multihospital system.* The more training and experience possessed by managers the less time needed to clarify procedures, interpret operating reports, and avoid conflict. Each manager must accept the overall corporate philosophy, its role and mission, and adjust the limits of positional authority and objectives to the greatest extent possible within acceptable boundaries of the position and the traditional mores of its functional field of specialization.

3. *Planning goals, policies, and inputs must be widely distributed within the multihospital system.* Subordinates must know where the corporation is headed and how it proposes to get there if individual institutions are to make a maximum contribution to this effort. Because new information about marketing and regulation is continually developing, upward input of information is required.

4. *Management information and control systems must be adequate to accomplish the role and mission of the multihospital system.* A corporate organization must know to what extent delegated authority and decision making conform to overall standards and to assure that these standards are maintained. The more effective the information and control systems the more corporate affairs become predictable and consistent with its objectives.

5. *High-quality communications for dispersed operating sites are required.* Effective communicating techniques are increasingly necessary for the larger multihospital system in order to maintain predictability and to avoid commitment of large amounts of executive effort at the corporate level.

In all large, complex organizations their typical pyramid organizational structure creates a range of control problems. Either there must be a tall structure with many management levels and short spans of control for top corporate positions or a flat structure with fewer management tiers but wider spans of control for executives. Multihospital systems managements often discuss this issue and typically they desire as few levels of management as possible.

The rationale of deciding what functions are corporate office matters is usually based on the centralization of financing affairs with the use of computers. Other types of decisions that have lead times, such as planning activities, are likewise centralized.

Decisions that require prompt decisions are decentralized to individual hospitals, such as patient care and technology. Multihospital systems have not as yet integrated these decisions into corporate functions, even though economics of scale would be achieved if they did so. A completely developed matrix organization would provide a method of integrating patient care at the corporate level.

Considerations of tall or flat organizational structures are fundamentally based on the degree of direct control desired at the corporate level and the quality of information and communicating procedures. Essentially, multihospital systems have not developed methods for directing and controlling the patient care services. Without centralized control over patient care services multihospital systems are simply systems for maximizing reimbursement and stock market vehicles for its ownership.

Vertical organizational structures do not seem to be appropriate in the health care field because of the nature of the work involved. All health care institutions have a similarity of function, without significant geographical differences. Because of the large number of specialized services, with small numbers of workers in each service, the base of the organization is too broad for a vertical structure. This reality dictates a flat structure.

Even though one-half of all workers in a hospital are assigned to nursing activities, the modern-day development of nursing specialties, such as in operating rooms and critical care units, emergency services, obstetrics, psychiatry, rehabilitation, and pediatrics, have created separate services in which nursing personnel are no longer interchangeable.

To avoid loss of control in operations caused by wide spans of control at the executive level in a flat structure, the chief executive officer needs to delegate his responsibilities on a functionally specialized basis to the executives who report to this position.

There is one function that cannot be delegated from the office of the corporate presidency in a major multihospital system in the existing regulatory environment—that of government relations. The future survival and prosperity of a system is seriously affected by governmental decisions and requires the constant attention and influence of a chief executive officer. To assist in carrying out these duties a small staff may be required under the direction of an executive experienced in interacting with bureaucrats and politicians.

An incidental, but necessary, activity of the president's office in a large system is the handling of corporate affairs, from stock transfers to affairs of the board of directors. This position usually carries the title of secretary of the corporation.

GROUPING SECOND-LEVEL FUNCTIONS

The level immediately below the chief executive officer should show groupings of major functionally specialized areas, with executives in charge of each major functional area having education and experience appropriate to the specific specialty. There are seven areas of specialization: planning, institutional operations, finance, evaluations and training, real estate management, personnel, and marketing.

In small and medium-sized multihospital systems some of these functions may be combined to avoid an excessively large and expensive organizational structure. Whenever functions are combined, there is typically some loss in expertise. In very large systems, where each of the seven areas can be separately staffed, there may be other positions added to further specialize their functions into subspecialty areas when greater depth and control are desired.

The planning function involves the typical activities of developing corporate objectives, estimating demand, program development, demographic characteristics, and design matters.

In small- and medium-size systems the marketing function may become a subsidiary function of planning. The activities of marketing would include determination of acceptability of new programs and services, acquisition of other corporations and hospitals, corporate public relations, and affiliations with other organizations for continuity of patient care.

The finance functions would include accounting, banking relations, capital and equity funding, budgeting, cash flow, reimbursement, insurance, rate setting, and probably data processing. In smaller systems, the management should be operated as a subdivision within the finance division.

The operations function would be focused on the daily operation of the multihospital system's health care services. As the system expanded, it would be appropriate to separate its activities into the major areas of specialization, hospitals providing secondary and tertiary levels of care, and programs at the primary care level such as satellite clinics and health maintenance organizations. As operations are dispersed over larger and larger geographical areas, they should be divided into regional groupings. In very large systems the separation between primary care and secondary and tertiary levels of care should be maintained because of the different technologies, services, and marketing approaches required.

The provision of an evaluation and training function is to lay the foundation for an organized, corporatewide system for integrating patient care services through measurements and judgments about the quality, efficiency, and effectiveness of its operations. One of the major tools used would be a corporate information system. In essence, this function would be an internal evaluation and consulting service for the system. In small corporations, a subdivision could include the personnel functions of industrial relations, recruitment, training activities, and fringe benefits.

Each functional division requires an executive with specialized skills and experience. Generalists in health care administration would be needed at the institutional level and in the operations division. All other dimensions would require knowledge and skills that are acquired through education and experience in generic areas other than health care administration. This kind of structure provides for economics of scale at the institutional level because greater skill is brought to the operating levels than is possible in even the largest freestanding hospitals.

In small multihospital systems, the chief executive officer would have a span of control that is small and manageable, while in larger ones it would not exceed nine positions, seven line and two staff positions.

In Figures 39–1, 39–2, and 39–3 the organizational structures of small-, medium-, and large-size systems are presented, with the guiding organizing principle shown on the left-hand side.

An effective organizational structure for a multihospital system does not just happen; it is the result of adherence to principles of organizational theory that is based on human behavior. However, an effective organization depends both on its structure and the behavior of its executives.

Figure 39–1 Small-Size Multihospital System, Metropolitan Area

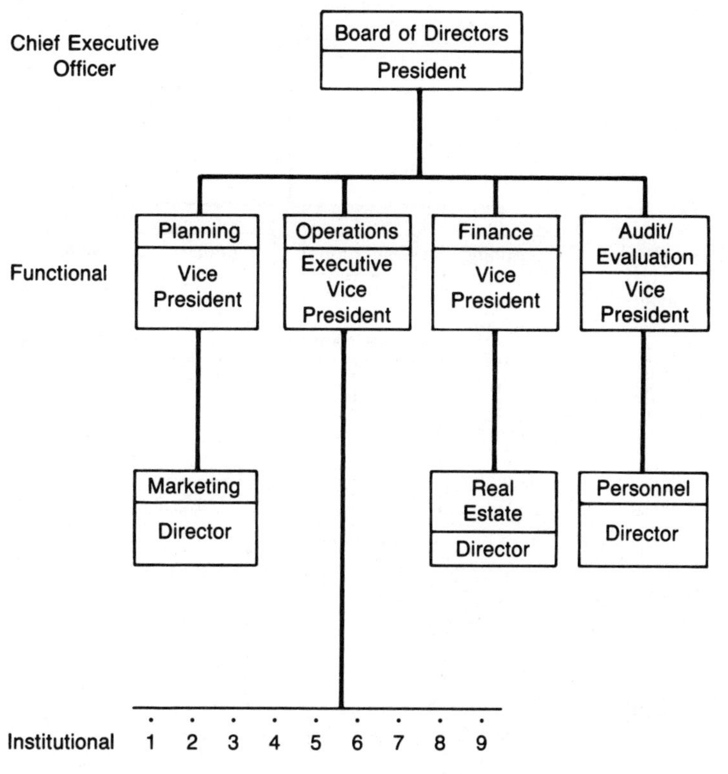

ELEMENTS OF AN EFFECTIVE ORGANIZATION

An effective organization depends upon the following elements:

1. Predictability in behavior of all managers in the multihospital system
2. Consistency in decision making
3. Rational determination of goals and objectives
4. Pinpointing responsibilities at all levels in the organizational structure
5. Providing appropriate authority at each level and control of resources to carry out assigned responsibilities
6. Requiring accountability for performance, including individual and group behavior
7. Recognizing the unique characteristics of the environment in which each institution operates
8. Maximizing the best use of available resources

Figure 39–2 Medium-Size Multihospital System, Regional Area

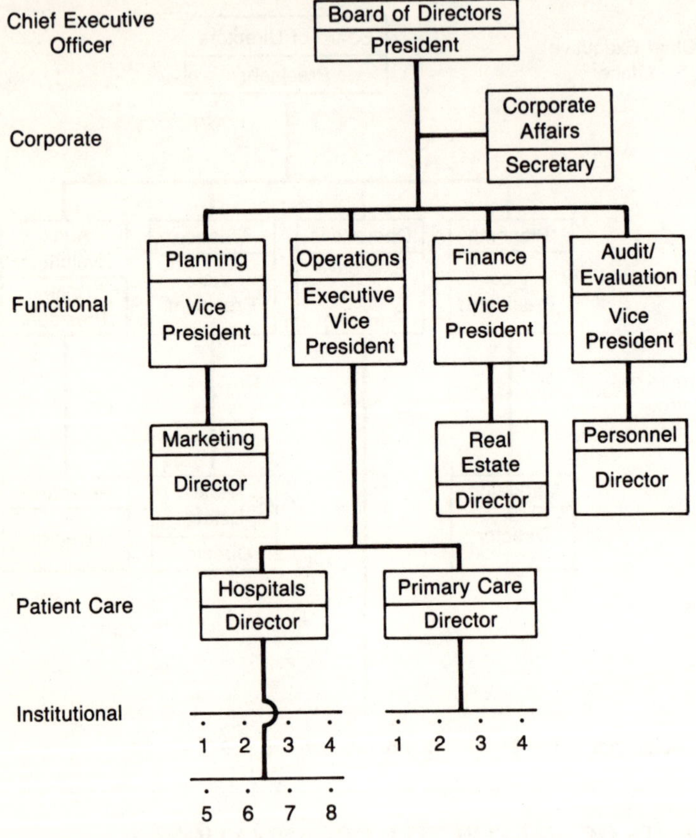

9. Setting priorities for programs that take into account both physical and psychological needs
10. Developing, reporting, and monitoring systems appropriate to the size and needs of the organization
11. Promoting a willingness to monitor the performance of all facets of the organization and its operations
12. Recognizing the need to continuously plan for the future

An organizational audit of a multihospital system against these 12 criteria would identify the areas of organizational structure that are inadequately developed. If corporate control, direction, and maintenance of a high quality of services are to be achieved in an efficient way, these criteria must be developed and initiated at the top of the organization as a framework for systemwide operation.

Figure 39–3 Large-Size Multihospital System, National

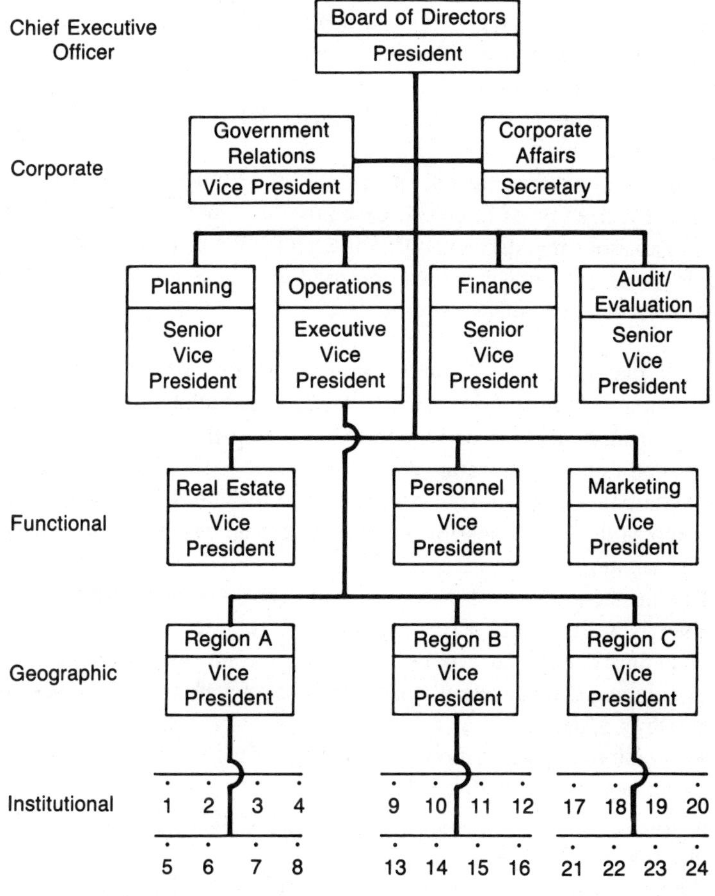

This means that immediately after the acquisition of an operating institution by the multihospital system, an evaluation is required to adjust existing operating systems to match up with the overall corporate systems. This is most easily accomplished by organizationally housing all new acquisition in the evaluation and training division until the new institution has incorporated the corporate systems into its operation through procedure adjustments and additional training. When a newly acquired institution has made the necessary changes, it can be transferred to an operating division already indoctrinated in the ways of its new corporate setting.

The corporate structure diagrammed in the three charts does not imply that individual institutional units would follow the same organizational scheme. Two major functions not included in the corporate organizational structure are operations of a medical staff and community relations. These two functions must remain at the level of delivery of patient care because they are practiced locally. Admission to the medical staff of a health care institution is traditionally an individual hospital function for a variety of sufficient reasons, and control should remain at this level. Likewise, community relations must take place and respond to the local community environment.

The organizational structure of individual units in a multihospital system is determined by size, types of health care programs, and comprehensiveness of services. Variations in individual hospital organizational structure abound. Seven criteria in organizational theory can be used as guides as to how institutional organizational relationships should be developed:

1. When the efficient operation of two or more activities depends on frequent communication between them, or when close timing is required for proper coordination, these functions must be within the span of control of one position in the organizational structure.
2. Operational efficiency is maximized when the authority of decision making is kept at the lowest possible level in the hierarchy consistent with expected performance.
3. To enhance job interest, functions should be so grouped that organizational objectives are clearly perceived in the job routine.
4. Functions should be grouped to maximize the use of employee skills, experience, and education at their highest capacity for the greatest possible length of time.
5. To maximize organizational control, all functions relating to the same objectives should be grouped together when possible to maintain a focus of interest, to maintain flexibility between positions, and to avoid duplication of work.
6. When specific functions require physically related areas, these functions should be grouped near each other in the organizational structure.
7. When common equipment is used by more than one activity or more than one activity is part of a larger service system, they should be grouped together in the organizational structure.

While these criteria apply at the institutional level and will lead to a functional organizational structure, they do not suggest that in all institutions corporate relationships must be completely handled only by the institutional top executive, the hospital administrator. In daily operations, the level of assistant administrator should be assigned some responsibilities for carrying out corporate functions, in addition to a major group of institutional departments such as the physician-directed hospital departments or the service departments.

For example, the assistant administrator assigned the clinical laboratory, radiology, pulmonary function, nuclear medicine, anesthesia, and emergency room service might also be assigned institutional planning and marketing functions and would be controlled by the corporate staff in this work. If problems arose that required intervention by the institution at the corporate level, the assistant administrator would raise the issue with the regional director, this position in turn would take the matter to the director, and this position in turn would take the matter to the director of the operations division. If the issue was not settled between the operations and planning directors, the two would then raise it with the chief executive officer of the corporation.

In practice, this chain of command would seldom be employed, and for less than the most critical issues the hospital administrator, or the regional director, depending on the seriousness of the situation, would negotiate an appropriate decision from the planning director or the staff concerned in the appropriate functional area.

However, the availability of more than one position's involvement at the corporate functional level such as operations and planning will allow differing points of view and information to reach the chief executive officer. Having two avenues of access to the chief executive officer is a strength of matrix-type organizations. If too many unresolved issues are pushed to the top of the corporate organization, the chief executive officer will quickly become aware of inadequate performance by one or more immediate subordinates.

SELECTING THE RIGHT STRUCTURE

The extent to which multihospital systems are more or less costly or efficient is unknown in terms of their organizational structure. The bottom line, net profits, is not a useful criterion. Many investor-owned systems avoid operating in rate-controlled states and high-cost, tertiary level types of hospitals. By careful analysis of reimbursement policies, it is possible to position a hospital and its pricing structure in a reimbursement category where most of the other institutions offer a greater range of services. Typically, the multihospital system is not the least expensive institution, but is in the upper half of the reimbursement range and below the most expensive hospitals.

Expenses can be manipulated in multihospital systems through the allocation methods used for indirect or overhead expenses. Certain types of expenses can be allocated on a rational basis partially to an individual institution and also to the corporation. Different justifiable methods result in differing results.

To determine the efficiency of multihospital systems, financial data would need to be analyzed as follows:

Each Hospital

$$\frac{\text{Direct Institutional Operating Expenses}}{\text{Total Expenses (or per Occupied Beds)}} \times 100 = \text{Percent of Total Expenses}$$

$$\frac{\text{Indirect Institutional Nonoperating Expenses}}{\text{Total Expenses (or per Occupied Beds)}} \times 100 = \text{Percent of Total Expenses}$$

Multihospital System

$$\frac{\text{Total All Institutional Operating Expenses}}{\text{Total System's Expenses (or per Total Occupied Beds)}} \times 100 = \text{Percent of Total Expenses}$$

$$\frac{\text{Total All Institutional Nonoperating Expenses}}{\text{Total System's Expenses (or per Total Occupied Beds)}} \times 100 = \text{Percent of Total Expenses}$$

The greatest claimed efficiency in a multihospital system is assumed to be based on economies of scale achieved through larger size. Typically, purchasing, insurance, and equity costs are given as examples. However, multihospital systems also aim at employing institutional managers who are more financially concerned than the typical hospital administrator and have greater authority to make operating decisions. In other words, the climate of institutional management is significantly different in a multihospital system from that of a freestanding institution with a governing board's restraint, particularly in medical staff affairs.

In a multihospital system, a matrix-type organization with functional specialists at the top level handles the most complex of institutional management tasks, other than daily operations, medical staff matters, and community relations, which are removed from the operating level. Locating these functions at the corporate level should reduce the total institutional management effort required and allow for greater spans of control, or fewer assistant administrators at the institutional level. In addition, it should also provide for a more skillful handling of the functions removed to the corporate level. In essence, each institution's management does not have to duplicate efforts or all other institutions to solve the same problems, but it can be guided by the corporate system for necessary inputs.

Since conceptual skills and in-depth knowledge are the highest-order characteristics sought in hospital executives, their concentration at the corporate level should allow a system to have institutional management costs at a lower level of expense than is possible for a freestanding institution. The larger the multihospital system the more likely that this economy of scale should be reflected at the department director level as corporate systems are gradually expanded to standardize departmental operations.

To determine the most efficient organizational structure of a multihospital system the cost and efficiency of corporate structures can compare in the following ways:

Multihospital Systems

$$\frac{\text{Total Number of Supervisory Positions}}{\text{Total Number of Nonsupervisory Positions}} = \text{Number of Employees per Supervisors}$$

$$\frac{\text{Total Number of Management Positions}}{\text{Total Number of Nonmanagement Positions}} = \text{Number of Employees per Manager}$$

$$\frac{\text{Total Corporate Supervisory Expenses}}{\text{Total Corporate Nonsupervisory Expenses}} = \text{Supervisory Expense per Employee}$$

$$\frac{\text{Total Corporate Management Expenses}}{\text{Total Corporate Nonmanagement Expenses}} = \text{Management Expense per Employee}$$

No data are currently available in the health care industry regarding an optimum ratio and cost for these calculations. Data available in organization literature indicate a generally acceptable standard of between 12 and 16 employees per supervisor and between 35 and 40 employees per manager. Whether or not these ranges would apply to the health care field is unknown.

The organizational challenge ahead for multihospital systems is to move beyond the present state of integrated financial functions into a system of integrated patient care systems that will assure uniformly high-quality service in all of its institutions. Until a matrix-type organization is implemented, quality of care issues will remain the domain of the institutional administrator, almost untouched by the corporate office.

Modern medical knowledge, organizational theory, sufficient numbers of well-trained and experienced health care administrators, and high-speed communicating and information systems are all available to be brought together to take advantage of the clinical, managerial, and capital resources of multihospital systems. If success is achieved in integrating patient care systems at the corporate level, the growth of multihospital systems will be explosive in the decade ahead.

Chapter 40

Alternative Delivery Systems to Diversify Hospital Revenues[*]

During the 1970s two major trends dominated the health field. The first, increasing regulation, was widely recognized and often debated. The other, deregulation leading to increased economic competition, went largely unnoticed, though much of it took place, as will become increasingly evident during the next few years.

REGULATION EFFORTS

As regulations steadily increased during the past ten years, the fiscal noose gradually tightened on hospital revenues. The more it restricted, the greater the interest in finding ways to alleviate fiscal restraints. Two possibilities emerged: health maintenance organization (HMO) and multiple corporate structures held together in a variety of ways. The first, the HMO, has been more easily identifiable because it has characteristics that stand out in bold contrast to the rest of the health care field. The other is much less sharply defined because it has evolved within the structure of the hospital organization. Both have arisen from the same base, a real concern with the fiscal imperatives of health care.

The development of multiple corporate structures was the direct response of hospitals to increasing regulation. When the federal government announced that it looked more favorably on hospitals that undertook cooperative activities with other institutions in the same service area, the result was joint laundries, joint purchasing agreements, shared ambulances, and other administrative arrangements. To a limited degree, hospitals traded off clinical services.

After a few years, it became apparent to hospital executives that these steps had neither stemmed the flow of regulations nor effectively contained costs. Hospitals

---

*Adapted from *Topics in Health Care Financing*, Vol. 8, No. 1, pp. 49–56, Aspen Publishers, Inc., © 1981.

also came to appreciate that trading off of clinical services usually led to a dissatisfied medical staff that could only be placated by having as many clinical services as possible under one roof. New approaches were needed and this led to the next stage of development.

The government's efforts at regulation have been directed toward inpatient activities in the hospital and nursing home. These controls have not been meaningfully applied to physicians services, drugs, dentists, eyeglasses, and other professional services. The result is a health care industry with lopsided controls, 48 percent of government expenditures represented by hospitals and nursing homes coming under strict regulation and 52 percent largely uncontrolled. The recognition that ambulatory services had the fastest growth rate and could take place in the uncontrolled sector of the industry, if the organizational arrangements were properly positioned in the legal structure, led to a dispersal of numerous hospital activities away from the hospital site that previously had been under the hospital's umbrella. Institutions that had built professional office buildings in order to attract physicians to their facilities began to see great logic in spinning them off as separate corporations. By doing so, they had the best of two worlds. Not only did hospitals discover that their original rationale could be maintained, but they avoided arguments with Medicare and Medicaid as to the allocation of overhead expenses. They also realized that if they established their organizational structure properly, they could avoid filing for a Certificate of Need approval.

Once hospitals began to appreciate the fact that multiple corporations open up avenues that could be financially exploited, but remain in conformity with the laws of the land, they began to search for other possibilities for diversifying revenues. Primary care centers, ambulatory surgery, home health care, and contract management of hospitals became candidates.

SERIOUS QUESTIONS

As hospitals have become technology-oriented enterprises, they have required larger and larger amounts of capital funds. At the same time, the government has been working in the reverse direction, trying to limit their flow of capital expenditures. The resultant pressures have forced hospitals to seek alternatives.

Some hospitals have created real estate corporations solely for the purpose of creating surpluses that can be used to fund hospital activities. Not only do these subsidiaries buy and sell investment property, they may also hold title to the physical plant of the hospital.

In their attempts to secure sufficient funds to keep abreast with new and improved equipment, the obvious choice has been the creation of new corporations that are related to the hospital. This approach is not new to hospitals that have had separate foundations even though the hospital itself might be a 501(C)3 tax-exempt organization and could accept gifts directly from a donor. The difference lies in the number of corporations now being created and in the mixing of for-profit and nonprofit corporate organizations under an overall plan. Hospitals are creating health delivery systems that reach far beyond inpatient type of activities that have historically characterized their operations. The need for a broader financial base to support technological advances has pushed hospitals into becoming systems of health care extending their range of interest to include many activities that traditionally were not considered areas of legitimate consideration.

As hospitals have opted for multiple corporations, they have had to face two problems:

1. Who would be the directors and officers of these organizations being created?
2. How should these new organizations be related to the hospital?

If a hospital had a large governing board, the usual approach was to spread trustees across the other corporations and forego trying to create a parent organization with several subsidiaries. Reliance was on trustee involvement in all corporations they established in the hospital to provide informal control of the whole structure. As the number of additional corporations grew, the pool of available trustees dried up since it was unrealistic to expect trustees to serve as directors of three or more corporations. It became necessary to find another approach.

This led to the establishment of a for-profit holding company as the model for reducing trustee time and involvement. In moving to this prototype, hospitals entered this arena with mixed feelings. By creating a for-profit parent holding company, the hospital governing board composition could be left undisturbed as a subsidiary and the new holding company was free to make decisions on the size and composition of the boards of the subsidiaries without undue concern over representation of all concerned parties.

Hospitals are rapidly moving to the parent-multiple subsidiaries model as the best way to create additional sources of revenue and at the same time minimize adverse reimbursement restrictions. In looking at the need for increasing hospital revenues, they are changing the fundamental focus from inpatient care to one that is concerned with a total health delivery system in one organizational scheme with centralized management over all subsidiary corporations in the system.

The transformation of hospitals into health delivery corporations has occurred in the private sector, as yet unrestricted by governmental intervention. The government has not only passed laws and developed rules and regulations for controlling hospitals, it has been moving legislatively since 1973 to free hospitals from some restraints, under selected conditions.

In 1973, Public Law 93-222, the Health Maintenance Organization Act, was enacted. As experience developed, some of the requirements in the original law were modified and eased, first, in 1976 with amendments contained in Public Law 94-460 and in 1978 with the modification of Public Law 95-539. Additional amendments were made in 1979 with the passage of the amendments to the Health Planning Act, Public Law 96-79, which provided specific exemptions to the Certificate of Need approval process for hospitals that had 75 percent or more of their admissions from health maintenance organizations.

Because of the legislation that has been passed which exempts HMOs from much of the existing regulation, hospitals are studying the establishment of HMOs for the same reasons hospitals are creating multiple corporations, as well as from an awareness that industry and labor have joined government concerns about health care costs. All three are actively seeking an alternative health delivery system that makes economic competition an important element in the decision making of those who use the system.

By 1980, nearly 220 HMOs had been created. In some sections of the country, HMOs are still relatively unknown, but this will change dramatically as marketing programs are developed and advertising campaigns using radio, television, direct mailing, and newspapers to promote enrollments. As public awareness increases, so will the number of subscribers, and the interest of hospitals will become more serious and widespread. There are several reasons for hospitals to become active participants. HMOs are a marketing tool to fill empty beds, they protect the inpatient share of a hospital's market, help diversify revenue sources, and represent a new challenge to management.

It is expected that HMOs will grow at a substantial rate during the '80s. In 1976, there were 6 million HMO members; this figure grew to over 8 million by 1979 and 13 million in 1984. The growth rate has been running at 20 percent. If this rate is sustained throughout the '80s, there will be 42 million subscribers by 1989, which will represent 17 percent of a population of 242 million people.

This potential has already attracted considerable interest among a variety of groups. Each has its own set of reasons for their interest. Thoughtful hospital executives need to appreciate that the competition for becoming leaders in this field is going to be fierce and will not automatically belong to the general hospital but may ultimately be vested in others.

FOUNDERS

Consumer groups and unions have the longest history of involvement in capitation plans. In 1913, the International Ladies Garment Workers Union established a health facility in New York City. This was followed by the Group Health Association in Washington, D.C., and by the Group Health Cooperative of Puget Sound, Washington, in 1947. Then the United Automobile Workers created the Community Health Association in Detroit. The common thread among these groups was the provision of prepayment coverage for a defined clientele.

Corporations first became interested when Edgar F. Kaiser asked R. Sidney Garfield to organize a hospital-based group practice prepayment plan in 1937 in order to care for union construction workers on the Grand Coulee Dam. As the Kaiser-Permanente Foundation grew and attained national visibility, several industries in the Twin Cities of Minnesota (in the early '70s) embarked on HMO development. By 1976, the R.J. Reynolds Industries in Winston-Salem, North Carolina, established a private company plan and in 1978 the Ford Motor Company organized the Metro Health Plan in Detroit. Here again, the common theme was identifiable: major corporate employers seeking ways to trim the annual increases in premium rates they were paying for employee health benefits. For 1978, the Ford Motor Company indicated it had saved $3 million on only 5 percent of its work force who belonged to the HMO. For the same year, General Motors claimed a $5 million savings on 5 percent of its employees.

Not to be left out, the health insurance carriers recognized the developing trend and began to examine the degree to which they should become involved. In 1956, Group Health Mutual Insurance Company of St. Paul, Minnesota, offered a capitation plan. Connecticut General Life Insurance Company, working with the Johns Hopkins University, put together a plan in 1969 for the residents of the newly created Columbia, Maryland, development city being built by the Rouse Company. CNA Financial Corporation sponsored Inter Group in Chicago, which commenced operations in 1972. Likewise, the Prudential Insurance Company established Prucare in Houston, Texas. Seeing the need to move rapidly, INA, which had had several years of experience behind it, purchased HMO International of Los Angeles in 1978 and in the following year bought ABC-HMO in Phoenix, Arizona. Early in 1980, the John Hancock Life Insurance Company announced its entry in the race with the formation of an HMO service subsidiary, Hancock/Dikewood Services, Inc.

While unions, large corporations, and insurance companies were gaining needed experience, the Blue Cross/Blue Shield plans were also moving in this direction. By January 1980, Blue Cross was operating 39 HMOs with a combined enrollment of 693,000 members. These efforts were further enhanced by providing a variety of selected services to HMOs, including billing and collecting premiums, processing claims, marketing, out-of-area emergency coverage, and actuarial assistance. While having a market share of less than 10 percent of the HMO market, Blue Cross had put in place organizational machinery for accommodating the growth of subscribers as it occurs.

FRONT-RUNNERS

Given what has taken place to date, what will happen to hospitals? If current rates of HMO increase are sustained for the next several years, what is apt to occur in hospital revenues? The scenario seems to indicate that the fulcrum of leadership in the health delivery system will shift away from the general hospital to the operators of HMOs who are exempt from regulations affecting hospitals. In some cases, these will be the multiple corporations formed by hospitals; in others they may be business corporations, medical societies, or multispecialty group practices, or prepayment carriers with long experience in health insurance.

When these possibilities are weighed, the front runners appear to be the prepayment carriers and, within that category, the commercial companies seem to have an edge over Blue Cross. In both cases, the carriers collectively have some distinct advantages over the other sponsors. Because they are in the business of providing coverage against illness, they are more experienced and apt to make fewer mistakes. Already in place and used daily is a marketing organization and an information processing system that can be readily adapted to the needs of an HMO. Having extensive experience with reimbursement and a database of actuarial information of claims experience on which to develop a benefit package and premium level, they are in a position to offer realistic and financially sound programs.

The organizational structure of a prepayment carrier is such that it would require little or no modification for an HMO. The major problem to be dealt with is an understanding of the controls that are essential to the successful operation of an HMO. This problem would not be totally unfamiliar to carriers because of the claims review process they now employ.

Insurance carriers have an additional unique advantage. As financial institutions that control large sums of money, they not only have available resources for financing the start-up costs of an HMO, but an inherent ability to stay with it in the event of mistiming or misjudgments in premium and claims management that might otherwise lead to a cash shortfall.

By contrast, hospitals lack marketing experience and actuarial know-how and have an organizational structure designed for patient care. To some extent, hospitals have applicable information processing experience. Their greatest asset is an understanding of physician behavior and of cost controls. Hospitals are not totally disadvantaged when it comes to capitalizing the front-end costs of an HMO, particularly if the hospital is large and has been operating in a favorable reimbursement climate.

Medical groups are likely to be severely limited in their ability to sponsor an HMO if they attempt to go it alone. The main advantage they have is the enrollment of physician providers because, more than any other group, they have the greatest credibility with their peers. However, physician providers would have to develop the knowledge and organizational structures to provide HMO sponsorship.

Business corporations have substantial limitations that are likely to prevent them from becoming major sponsors of HMOs. Not only will corporate executives recognize that their knowledge about the health care industry is limited, but HMOs are far afield from their own areas of expertise. Large corporations would not encounter capitalization problems since they annually pay large premiums for health care. However, there might be a reluctance to take the heat from employees who express dissatisfaction with the company HMO. It is unlikely that many corporations will follow the path of R.J. Reynolds Industries.

These four groups, carriers, hospital, medical groups, and commercial corporations, can be visualized in terms of relative strengths and weaknesses by attaching subjective weights to major elements that are important in the successful operation of an HMO (see Table 40–1).

When viewed from this perspective, the point spread between the carriers and the three other groups indicates that the carriers will ultimately dominate the HMO marketplace if they move aggressively in the next few years.

It will be difficult for hospitals to surpass carriers, who have six incentives for sponsoring an HMO:

1. Opportunity for generating net revenue from a capitation plan.
2. Protection of existing enrollments in health insurance plans by providing subscribers with a dual choice
3. Potential for creating an increase in their life insurance program
4. Potential for a high rate of return on invested assets

Table 40–1 Potential Capability for Entering the HMO Scene

Factors	Prepayment Carriers	Hospitals	Medical Groups	Commercial Corporations
Organizational Structure	3	1	0	0
Experience with Reimbursement	3	2	1	1
Actuarial Know-How	3	0	0	0
Marketing Know-How	3	1	0	0
Information Processing Experience	3	2	1	2
Utilization Control Experience	2	2	2	0
Understanding of Physicians	2	2	3	0
Capitalization Strength	3	1	0	2
Total	22	11	7	5

Key: 3 = Of great importance or well experienced.
    2 = Of some importance or some related experience.
    1 = Of limited importance or limited related experience.
    0 = Of no importance or no experience.

5. Product differentiation and market stratification
6. An increased base for spreading indirect costs of operation

To gauge the importance of the health field to a carrier that has been vigorously pursuing this interest, the 10K report of the INA Corporation was examined for 1979 (see Table 40–2).

The 8.9 percent return on investment from health care is more than double the next best producer, property and casualty insurance. In 1979, health care contributed revenues of $553.3 million to INA, with an operating income before taxes of $41.4 million, a 7.5 percent return on sales. INA's investment in its health care activities was $467.5 million, which resulted in an operating income before taxes of the $41.4 million, an 8.9 percent return. The reasons are self-evident from this example for a carrier's interest in HMOs.

Hospitals have an entirely different set of reasons for being interested in sponsoring HMOs. These are:

1. A marketing tool for filling empty beds
2. A means of applying a marginal cost concept in determining prices offered to a capitation plan
3. An escape from the Certificate of Need approval processes
4. A need to diversify revenue sources and avoid reimbursement formulas that pay less than full cost
5. A desire to maintain leadership in the health field
6. A strategy to acquire an early franchise in a given service area
7. A broadened challenge to management
8. An opportunity to gain experience in a significant development in the health care field

These are compelling reasons for hospitals to seriously explore HMOs. Because the hospital organizational structure is not suitable for the operation of a capitation

---

Table 40–2 INA Report

	Revenues	Operating Income Before Taxes	Return on Investment
Property and Casualty Insurance	68.8%	66.3%	3.6%
Life and Group Insurance	18.6	20.8	2.8
Health Care	12.6	12.9	8.9
Total	100.0%	100.0%	

Source: 10K Report, INA Corporation, 1979

Table 40–3 Changes in the Use of Selected Hospital Outpatient Services, 1972–1978 (Numbers in Thousands)

	Emergency Visits			Outpatient Clinics			Referred			
	Number of Visits	Per 1,000 Population	Percent Change per Year	Number of Visits	Per 1,000 Population	Percent Change per Year	Number of Visits	Per 1,000 Population	Percent Change per Year	Civilian Population July 17
1972	55,660	269.5	—	53,244	258.0	—	53,764	260.4	—	206,500
1973	61,306	294.6	10.1	54,306	261.0	2.0	57,456	276.1	6.9	208,100
1974	66,785	318.5	8.9	54,917	261.9	1.1	67,238	360.6	17.0	209,700
1975	68,937	326.1	3.2	50,729	240.0	7.6	71,007	335.9	5.6	211,400
1976	71,864	351.5	4.2	54,949	258.0	8.3	74,434	349.5	4.8	213,000
1977	72,609	338.2	1.0	51,351	239.2	6.5	74,849	348.2	0.4	214,700
1978	76,123	351.8	4.8	N/A[1]	—	—	N/A	—	—	216,400

[1]Breakdown discontinued; total is 125,807,811.

Source: American Hospital Association, *Hospital Statistics*, annual edition, 1973–1979; U.S. Department of Commerce, Bureau of the Census, *Statistical Abstract of the United States,* 1979 edition; TriBrook Group, Inc.

plan, those who proceed are most likely to think in terms of creating a parent-subsidiary model that parallels the holding company used by conglomerates and in which a hospital and an HMO are subsidiaries.

PROGNOSIS

Hospitals that are only concerned with finding alternative sources of revenue will come to recognize that they have not been planning on a bold enough scale. The hospital industry has become a mature industry plagued with overcapacity that will gradually become more severe and faced with a heightened need for larger and larger amounts of capital funds to support technological changes. An answer for continued success lies in becoming health care corporations concerned with all aspects of health care, not just inpatient services (see Table 40–3).

In summary, most hospitals have been job shops dealing with only two products: inpatient care and outpatient services provided on site. The future belongs to hospitals that are knowledgeable in health care and can combine traditional activities with an aggressive marketing organization. This must be supported by a financing arm that can compete head-to-head with sophisticated insurance carriers, while adding new and imaginative programs. Hospitals that restrict their efforts to finding alternative revenues will not remain among the leaders. Leadership will belong to those hospitals with the courage to take risks and become health care corporations.

If a sponsoring organization is a hospital, the risks are greater than for other organizations. Because an HMO is based on a capitation method of payment, a medical staff is most likely to be against hospital involvement. Physician payment in an HMO is capitated and is not traditional fee for service, which may make it difficult for a hospital during the initial stages of development.

If an HMO successfully enrolls a substantial number of insureds, a hospital may see a decline in the annual number of admissions, since HMOs usually decrease utilization by one-half or more. In a static market, this decrease may spell financial difficulties for a hospital. Therefore, it is important for a hospital to review carefully its market share of the service area. The only avenue open to a hospital is to increase its share by soliciting HMO business to offset any potential losses that may result from an independent HMO.

In spite of these risks, a hospital that remains in the forefront of health care is going to have to face the competition and adapt to rapidly changing conditions.

REFERENCES

Falkson, Joseph L. *HMO's and the Politics of Health System Reform*. Chicago: American Hospital Association, 1980.

Lindsay, Cotton M., ed. *New Directions in Public Health Care: A Prescription for the 1980's*. San Francisco: Institute for Contemporary Studies, 1980.

MacLead, Gordon K., and Mark Perlman. *Health Care Capital: Competition and Control*. Cambridge, Mass.: Ballinger, 1978.

Part VIII

Looking around the Hospital Field

Chapter 41

Educating Health Care Executives

There is a popular song from a Broadway show that says, ''on a clear day you can see forever.'' The health executive version is, ''On a clear day, if you are lucky, you might see tomorrow.''

In an era of tumultuous change the question is, ''What skills and knowledge are needed to be a health care executive in the future?'' An accurate answer to the question is necessary if graduate university programs are to prepare today's students for tomorrow's experiences.

It is fruitless to try to equip students for the twenty-first century with present-day changes occurring at a rapid rate. A few years ago the only people who knew what the initials DRG stood for were a handful of researchers at Yale. MRI, or Magnetic Resource Imaging, appeared only a short while ago, and until just recently lithotropers would have been thought to be some kind of break dancing.

ROLE OF THE FACULTY

Despite the speed of change, a university faculty needs to provide a curriculum that will give graduates a set of skills that make them employable with a chance to rise to the top of their field. In fact, the survival of the faculty requires that a reasonable number of graduates reach visible levels of leadership. If, 20 years later, these graduates are still in charge of hospital security and the laundry, the professors had better see if they can become laundry managers because they won't have any security.

The curriculum need for health administration is to determine the skills needed for the next decade and to build courses around these needs. A safe bet for the faculty is to tell all students they must become life-long learners so that if they fail at mid-career the faculty is protected—the failures were not life-long learners.

With the ungluing of the health care market, the field is moving from a social service orientation to a corporate business, providing social services within affordable financial limits.

At the present time the best guess about the future is that in the next decade the majority of hospitals and long-stay institutions will be consolidated into a limited number of national chains of both investor-owned and nonprofit hospitals. The future practice of health administration will therefore be in large organizational structures requiring high levels of functional skills. There will still be a significant number of freestanding hospitals integrated both vertically and horizontally within a local market area.

PLACEMENT PATTERNS

As a response to the changing roles for health executives the placement pattern for new graduates has shifted. The historical pattern was for the majority of program graduates to move into hospital administration, with an assist from the "old boy" network, on completion of the administrative residency. Currently, about one-half of the graduating students accept positions in general hospitals or related institutions, while 40 percent begin their careers in clinics, health maintenance organizations, community health centers, or businesses serving the health field, and 10 percent join consulting firms in health care. The pattern varies to some degree by individual university programs.

The basic curriculum issue is to identify the knowledge and skills needed to function in a variety of settings. Historically, the curriculum had as its goal the preparation of students to become assistant administrators, or a hospital administrator in a small hospital, after the administrative residency.

The origin of this model was the hospital administration program in the Graduate School of Business at the University of Chicago in 1933. Later, other universities sponsored graduate programs in colleges of business administration, public health, and allied health, and medical and graduate schools. Since the early '50s, the academic world has had a prolonged discussion on the proper university setting for hospital administration programs. This issue is unresolved but the compromise has been to adjust curriculums, whatever their setting, so that about 60 percent of the content is identical, irrespective of the college or school within the university.

The remaining 40 percent reflects the basic interests of the school in which a program is located. The business administration setting for health administration students puts an emphasis on attitudes and skills useful in the business world. With hospitals becoming economically competitive, as well as subsidiaries of larger organizations, the values of marketing, finance, and organizational behavior, which are core subjects in business administration, provide a solid basis for students planning careers in hospitals.

Career success in the new era requires competence in two knowledge and skill areas. The business administration curriculum provides the general characteristics while industry-specific knowledge is provided in the health care curriculum. Career success requires a basic theoretical understanding of both.

There are 62 graduate health administration programs in North America with more than 5,000 students. Approximately 1,500 students are graduated annually. Of the 62 programs, 29 percent are based in schools of business administration, 44 percent in medicine, allied health, or public health, and 27 percent in graduate schools. The most common degree awarded is a master of health administration (MHA), while 18 percent of the graduates receive a master of business administration (MBA). In addition, there are over one hundred undergraduate programs serving local or regional markets. Typically, they develop middle management for a variety of health care activities.

As might be expected, there is an accrediting organization for health administration programs. The Accrediting Commission on Education for Health Administration was established in 1968 on the initiative of the Association of University Programs in Health Administration. For graduate programs two academic years are required for accreditation. In addition some programs require a residency period, but it is not needed for accreditation.

BACKGROUND

Students in graduate programs typically come from two different backgrounds. One group are recent college graduates in their early twenties. The other group are in their late twenties and early thirties and have five to ten years experience in a clinical profession in health care. The older students enter health administration programs because they realize that they have been dead-ended in their careers and need a master's degree if they are to move into an executive position in health care. Recently, physicians, some with American Boards, are entering health administration programs because they recognize the changes that are taking place require a different set of skills than the ones learned in medical school for physicians seeking to practice administrative medicine.

Another shift has been an increase in the number of registered nurses applying to graduate health administration programs. They have one of two different motivations: some are escaping from nursing while others are seeking to be better prepared in order to become directors of nursing. They believe this degree to be preferable to a graduate degree in nursing administration. In the last decade there has been an increasing number of women in programs in health administration. Currently, a little more than one half of the students are women. Many of them see health administration as a superior opportunity for a woman executive without being aware that 30 years ago hospital administrators were predominately women.

ACADEMIC PROGRAM

A key part of a program's success is the selection of its students. Because career success depends upon being motivated to be a manager and to think conceptually, graduate programs seek students who are more broadly based. High grades in undergraduate work and high scores on aptitude tests are not the only criteria for admission. A recent course graduate does not possess executive skills in a polished form, but must possess sufficient skills to work effectively. Greater skills are acquired through experience. In the competitive health care environment new graduates must be able to justify their salaries through competent performance. The days of gradually working into a position are gone.

Moving directly into a general management position after an administrative residency, or upon completion of a campus program, when a residency is not required, is disappearing. Functional specialists are now needed for finance, marketing, organizational development, strategic planning, and computer technology. Even the chief executive of a hospital in a chain of hospitals has different performance requirements from one in a freestanding hospital. In a multicorporate system the hospital executive must be an organization person; one that can work in a matrix structure with rational accountabilities and a strong support system.

In planning a health administration curriculum the dilemma is that future health care executives have two fundamentally different career choices. One is as a generalist in a line position in a hospital; the other is as a functional specialist in a complex corporate structure. The curriculum must respond to the needs of both. This is responsibility further complicated because students can now opt for careers in HMOs, specialized single-purpose national firms operating ambulatory surgery centers, or a network of primary care programs, or in investment firms that provide capital to the health field, or government, or health consulting firms. Graduating students have a wide range to choose from in the health care field. Slightly less than one-half of the students now have their first professional position in a hospital. The problem of the graduate health administration program is the same as the historical problem of a graduate school of business where the faculty is faced with the same issue. MBA graduates go into a wide variety of businesses, from retailing, plant operations, finance, marketing, information processing, banking, to whatever else the business world is doing.

The difference between the MBA and the MHA curriculum is related to the fact that a business firm initially employs graduates at a lower organizational level and then provides a gradual progression to higher corporate levels. In the health world the generalist, and up to this point, the functional specialist, usually begins at a higher corporate, or responsibility level, and must quickly learn to meet higher performance standards. This difference is due to the uniqueness of health care organizations, which have large numbers of professionally skilled personnel including physicians, nurses, technologists, and technicians. There is little room at the starting gate for the generalist. The generalist's role in health care is to hold together a large number of specialists.

RELATING TO THE MBA CURRICULUM

The school of business curriculum meets the diverse interests of students by providing fields of concentration. A core curriculum is required of all MBA students to equip them with the knowledge common to all business activity: accounting, decision sciences, marketing, finance, macro and micro economics. Once this part of the program is completed, the student elects a field of concentration to develop additional knowledge for a particular area of business, whether finance, accounting, real estate, insurance, computers, industrial relations, production, or marketing. The goal is to provide a student with sufficient skills in a functional area of business as well as the general knowledge needed for any field of business.

Because the health administration executive usually begins a career at a higher organizational level, greater depth and breadth are required. The health administration curriculum must be more extensive than the field of concentration selected by an MBA student.

Because the core curriculum of the MBA is necessary in health administration and the industry-specific requirements are more comprehensive, the curriculum for graduate health administration includes both the MBA and MHA areas of knowledge and thus a longer period of time is needed in the academic program. To get students to accept longer training there must be a recognizable payoff for an individual selecting this field in the number and value recognition of the degrees awarded and first-job opportunities.

In the last few years the MHA degree has been diminished in the minds of employers because the graduates they hired lacked sufficient skills and understandings of performance requirements in the new marketplace economy of health care. The present demand is for new graduates to have greater skills in financial management, strategic planning, accounting, marketing, business economics, and management information systems—the knowledge areas developed in the MBA curriculum.

Recently, the Institute of Health Administration of Georgia State University recognized a need to reorganize its curriculum to prepare students for the emerging era. It was obvious that an MHA degree was not able to adequately prepare graduates for a variety of different health administration positions. The result was the development of a two-academic-year program that awarded two degrees, both an MHA and an MBA, while maintaining, in addition, a third-year administrative residency and also providing students with an opportunity to have a field of concentration for the MBA degree. As a result of this new curriculum, students have selected finance or accounting as a field of concentration when they were interested in being a chief financial officer, marketing when they perceived the demand for marketing positions in health care, and insurance if they believed HMOs to be the wave of tomorrow.

Administrative residencies are selected to support one's choice of a career objective in a particular area of health care. If a student is interested in mental health, association work, HMOs or insurance, ambulatory care, or investor-owned hospitals, the residency is in that type of organization. However, part of the residency period is spent in an acute care hospital setting to provide this experience, because it is the most complex health care organization and is the foundation of the health care delivery system.

In recent years graduates have been placed in both generalist and functional specialist positions of their choice and have demonstrated that they are better prepared than graduates of the stand-alone MHA curriculum. Depending on the choices students make while on campus, they graduate with a deeper grasp of the functional skills required and with a more comprehensive set of business organizational skills.

No prediction can be made as to which graduates will eventually become chief executives of large health care organizations in 20 years. If the pattern is the same as in business and industrial firms, success will depend on individual motivation and the particular circumstances in the firm. The goal of the university curriculum is to prepare graduates for the foreseeable future with adequate knowledge and skills to become competent executives.

It has been observed that physicians are apt to again be the predominate choice of health care organizations for chief executive positions. This is more wishful than factual because the skills needed for the future executive are not those developed in a medical school or in clinical practice. The emerging need is for conceptual skills rather than technical skills in the health field.

The difference between yesterday and today is that there is less tolerance for inept behavior or poor judgment. The residency period provides a transition from the theoretical to the practical, where the lesson is learned as to the level of performance that is expected in the organization.

Chapter 42

The Rules of the New Game

OUTRUNNING THE PAST

Since 1966 hospitals have moved from one crisis to another. We have learned along the way that our resources are not infinite, but finite, and we must begin to make choices. No longer are all things immediately possible.

The 1960s belief that one-class medical care for all was possible resulted in the Medicare and Medicaid programs becoming law. Since then we have gradually learned that the political promise was larger than the public purse. First came Medicaid cuts as state funding faced the reality that state and local taxes have ceilings. The national reality did not emerge until the late 1970s when the costs of living spiraled upward, fueled by an inflation rate that began to make a shambles of conservative financial perspectives.

Now we are worrying about 200-plus billions in annual deficits, antiquated B-52 bombers, and a host of social problems. Along the way, federal bureaucrats have learned that modern medicine is an intensive user of both capital and labor, unlike the economic textbook belief that capital was a substitute for labor. The Canadian, Australian, British, Japanese, and Scandinavian economies have learned the same lesson about medical care costs.

The truth of the matter is that all modern developed nations have outrun economic theory. All of their medical care systems are being attacked by their political leadership because of an inability to mitigate cost increases. These governments are reacting in similar fashion—cutting back on payments to their medical care systems in order to leave political promises intact.

In 1981 the Medicare program covered 40 percent of all patients hospitalized in the United States. Since the population now lives longer, people between 65 and 74 years of age use three times the amount of hospital care than the population 64 years of age and younger; and for those age 75 and older, patient usage is eight times this rate.

To cope with this phenomenon, the federal response has been to reduce payment to hospitals so that a dollar of payment has shrunk to 68 cents. With the passage of the Tax Equity and Fiscal Responsibility Act, the net effect was a further reduction to approximately 60 cents on the dollar in 1985.

In the 1980s the name of the game for hospitals is survival. There is both good news and bad news. The bad news is that many hospitals will become insolvent and disappear, while others will experience new levels of reduced ambience, lower quality of care, and a freezing of new medical technology. The good news is that hospital care will still be around, but many hospitals will have new ownership and management.

TRUSTEES FACE A NEW REALITY

Hospital trustees are now facing a new reality. In the past when there were differences in viewpoints about what the hospital should do next in new programs and major capital expenditures, trustees could accommodate them all with a little extra time and more money. The days ahead have difficult choices in store. A new ballgame is emerging in most hospital board rooms.

Several major forces can be identified that are pushing and pulling on the health field. Some of these forces have major implications for nearly all hospitals, while others that are currently viewed as significant are, in fact, merely popular topics and are not sufficiently viable to make a dent in the foreseeable future.

An unrealistic idea is the development of a rational model of a national health care system neatly articulated between levels of care; the delegation of health care financing to the states from the federal government; and the deregulation of the health care field similar to the airlines and trucking industries.

Since 1948, when the Hill-Burton Law was passed, Congress has repeatedly put one planning law after another on the books trying to move the country into a territorial franchised system. Each succeeding act recognized the failure of an earlier act, proposed new approaches, provided greater and greater amounts of funding and restrictions, only to lead to another failure.

The impact of federal involvement in financing health care has thrust trustees and hospital executives into an intensive search for new programs searching for ways to balance the altruistic mission of the institution with prevailing economic factors.

Over the past several years, there has been a growing recognition in political circles that a grand design in health care was an impossible dream and that market forces should be allowed to rationalize the system. In spite of this fact, there is a reluctance within Congress to abolish all controls because of a fear that removal of controls would lead to unacceptable high costs. However, the evidence continues to mount that government mandates and incentives are not sufficiently focused to eliminate wasteful duplications in service. Congress is on the edge of a blade, undecided between a new round of legislation or of adopting a hands-off policy except for Medicare.

Market forces are messy and seemingly disorganized to those who favor precision-type models. From a governmental perspective the way to control costs and services most effectively is through a highly structured model. The idea that looseness is desirable is seldom considered when model builders are at work. Their goal is to maximize operating efficiencies through federal statutes that assure adherence to the adopted model. This goal ignores reality where change is always in process. Laws of this type freeze the possibility of future modifications to meet future changes.

An example is P.L. 93-641, which created the Certificate of Need process. Hospitals developed multicorporate structures to avoid Certificate of Need and restrictive reimbursement regulations. On a macro basis, a comparison of a centralized bureaucratic society, such as the U.S.S.R., with the greater effectiveness and efficiency of the United States market forces system reveals the advantages of a loose system. Grand designs do not work in the health field or elsewhere.

As long as the master designers have a following and Congress does not legislate deregulation, the hospital field will remain in a state of unrest. Pressures for increased access to health care while maintaining comprehensiveness of benefits, and at the same time keeping up pressures for cost containment, lead to problems rather than progress.

As the administration encourages deregulation, everyone from cabinet officers to mayors and governors supports running health programs at the city and state levels so long as the federal government puts up the money, not a likely prospect in an era of $200 billion annual deficits. Washington does not trust lower levels of government to spend federal grant monies wisely so Congress continues to tie strings on federal money sent to the states. States do not have, nor are they likely to have, enough money to support large health care programs. Decentralization of health care programs is an attractive concept but there is no reason for thinking that Big Brother is going to climb off the shoulders of the health care industry. In regulation of health care the best bet is that the future will look like the past.

MAJOR FORCES NOW OPERATING

There are several major forces now operating that are not myths. The most obvious is the increasing pressure on hospital revenues through the Tax Equity and Fiscal Responsibility Act (TEFRA) of 1982. When coupled with state rate control commissions and reimbursement restrictions by Blue Cross and Medicaid programs, even investor-owned hospital chain stocks are likely to be in for serious declines on the stock exchanges. When business coalitions and HMOs, plus emergicenters are added to the equation, certainly the percentage of health dollars going to hospitals will sharply decline. The next round of pressure will see a decrease in first-dollar insurance coverage, a reduction in health benefit packages, and perhaps the total adoption of a pro-competition strategy.

The hospital field has discussed declining revenues from Medicare and Medicaid since the beginning of these programs but cost shifting to nongovernment sources of patient revenue hospitals minimized the losses incurred from government programs. All health insurance purchasers are now getting as miserly as the government. Reality has arrived and hospitals are in for a hard time financially.

A second major force is the growth of multihospital systems. During the decade of the 1970s, the investor-owned chains came first, followed by community and religious nonprofit chains. Chains have grown primarily through the acquisition of existing hospitals by purchase, lease, or management contracts. What is evolving is the demise of locally controlled hospitals and their replacement by health care corporations. Medical staff matters and community relations remain at the local level while management planning and financial matters are directed at the corporate level. The growth of multihospital chains has largely occurred because the local boards of trustees have failed to appreciate the new forces impacting on a hospital.

The growth of hospital chains is the redevelopment of for-profit corporations. Fifty to sixty years ago, there were a substantial number of for-profit hospitals. Their number declined in the 1930s, 1940s, and 1950s because of the Great Depression, World War II, and the establishment of Hill-Burton hospitals. With the rapid growth of health insurance and the stabilization of hospital revenues, accompanied by the speed-up in newer medical knowledge and technology, the for-profit hospitals reemerged in the 1970s. The 1980s have seen the spread of the for-profit concept to the related health care services, surgicenters, emergicenters, dialysis centers, home health care, reference laboratories, and drug programs.

In 1981, the number of hospitals operated by multihospital systems was 1,877 out of a total of 5,842 community hospitals, or 32 percent. The number of beds in multihospital systems was 351,408 out of a total of 983,694 community hospital beds, or 36 percent.

The distribution of multihospital systems by type of ownership was 28 percent investor-owned, 39 percent Catholic, 6 percent other religion, and 27 percent voluntary. The regions of the country with the highest proportions of multihospital system beds were South Atlantic, Pacific Coast, and West-South Central locations. The regions with the lowest proportion of system hospitals were New England, Middle Atlantic, and East North Central areas.

This expansion of multihospital systems, coupled with restrictive Medicare reimbursement regulations, Certificate of Need legislation, and competition from entrepreneurial physicians, has led to the vertical integration of health care services into multicorporate health structures that previously did business as a one-hospital corporation. In many hospitals it is no longer unusual to have from two to six corporations integrated into a parent-subsidiary arrangement, with a central management structure. These multicorporate structures have focused primarily on becoming competitive with local physician enterprises in the services listed, as well as such areas as medical office buildings, retail pharmacies, occupational medicine, wellness centers, and retail health product stores. Two other areas have been tried, nursing home facilities and housing for the elderly, with mixed results.

The third major force is an increasing supply of physicians. In some cities and regions there is already an oversupply of physicians. Since about 1960 the number of physicians graduating annually has increased from 7,500 to the recent level of 17,500. In addition there has been a large increase in foreign medical graduates who now total about 20 percent of all active physicians in the United States.

This increasing supply has created an opportunity for hospitals to move away from being controlled by medical staffs. An improved bargaining position with private practicing physicians has led to new staff appointments only when an applying physician has committed to exclusive use of the hospital's laboratory, X-ray, and pharmacy. In other instances hospital-based physicians have been converted from fee-for-service to a salary. A federally sponsored committee has estimated that by 1990 there will be 70,000 surplus physicians.

What the ultimate effects of a surplus of physicians will be is unknown, but it is clear that their leverage on hospitals is rapidly disappearing. The increasing competition is creating sharp distinctions between physicians with medical staff appointments and those who lack them.

The last major change is in the role of the hospital trustee. Over the past decade there has been an increase in the number of chief executives and physicians serving as hospital trustees. Boards are struggling to integrate the organizational structure by bringing the internal leadership and management into the policy-making roles. Most governing boards of independent hospitals have failed to observe that investor-owned and voluntary multihospital corporations have the majority of their board memberships filled from among key management and medical positions. In fifteen years the chains have acquired one-third of the beds and facilities in the industry. Obviously, the difference in their mode of governance makes a difference.

The sum of these forces at work is that a successful hospital will move into related health care markets and into the turf traditionally claimed by physicians.

EXECUTIVE TALENT

In looking across the whole spectrum of health care services, it is evident that the main source of all health care executive talent is located in hospitals. There is little truth in the observation that a skilled executive can switch industries and operate with the knowledge needed for each kind of industry. This is particularly true for the health care industry where medical care imperatives often override business decisions.

Health care managers, other than those in hospitals, can be typified as skilled professionals in a clinical or therapeutic field but lacking in management knowledge. Hospitals are the major management pool for developing all of the health care related businesses. Hospital executives have the experience to negotiate and compromise differing viewpoints, as well as knowing whom to involve, when to involve them, and how much to expect of them. The future places a premium on seasoned, mature judgment based on solid experience. A tough-minded health care executive with real leadership skills will produce an organization capable of high performance.

Administrative skills will be severely tested in the years ahead. The development of primary care and emergicenters on a freestanding basis will cause a major struggle in medicine that has been avoided for the last two decades. Sooner or later there is going to be a ''shootout'' between primary care physicians and specialists.

ECONOMIC PRESSURES ON PHYSICIANS

With the rapidly increasing number of physicians, many are going to staff freestanding medical ventures. These physicians will ignore the tradition of offering their patients free choice in consulting a specialist and instead will steer patients needing other services to the practices of cooperating specialists and hospitals. Many senior specialists will experience a steady erosion in their practices because patients have been pressured into accepting another specialist tied to a freestanding group.

As a new reality is created, local hospitals are going to become battlegrounds between blocs of specialists and primary care physicians. At the national level, the AMA and AHA are sure to have some interesting days ahead.

As economic competition develops, trustees will find many of their judgments on the line. They will no longer be able to hide behind the screen of community service to rationalize the status quo. Their accountability and good judgment will be tested more severely than at any time in the past.

In dealing with hospitals, physicians will be hard put to think that economics has equal priority with their own professional interests. They have been accustomed to viewing their role as the initiator of important hospital changes. From their point of view, the role of the hospital chief executive and the trustees has been to provide the support systems for the diagnostic and therapeutic orders of physicians. They see the hospital as a patient care institution where all other concerns are of secondary importance.

It is important to make the medical staff knowledgeable about the financial affairs of a hospital because some still believe that a hospital is a bottomless barrel of resources and can finance all of its activities unencumbered by restrictive reimbursement. They may know about DRGs and their impact on how they practice and what they write into medical records, but they are probably unaware of the impact of DRGs on the hospital's total financial situation.

In hospital-sponsored or cooperative ventures outside the hospital, physicians expect the hospital to manifest loyalty to them by not providing unnecessary competition. The reverse is also true. A physician needs to ask himself a question each time an opportunity is presented to use a nonhospital medical service by referring a patient elsewhere. If the hospital is able to provide the same service, at the same level of quality, and at a comparable cost, then the physician ought to say, ''Why am I supporting a nonhospital business or sending a patient away from the hospital? I expect the hospital to provide me with a place to work when I have patients who are in need of inpatient and outpatient care; why should I refer patients somewhere else?'' Sooner or later it will be realized that a two-way street exists.

When a hospital contemplates going into those health care businesses that are a direct competitive threat to physicians, consideration should be given to converting from a nonprofit to a for-profit corporation. The 1981 tax code amendments were aimed at lowering tax penalties for the accumulation of capital funds. These changes significantly eroded the benefit of tax-exempt status. The reduction in the highest marginal tax rate from 70 percent to 50 percent diminished the taxes that can be saved by charitable giving and, likewise, increased the cost of a contribution.

At the same time, the tax burden on for-profit hospitals was reduced. Corporations can depreciate the cost of a new building over 15 years, new equipment over three to five years, and earn significant investment tax credits on equipment. In addition, taxable corporations may ''rent'' tax credits and deductions that they cannot use to other taxpayers. These unused deductions and credits are not available to nonprofit hospitals and are thereby lost. A corporation that will pay no tax because it already has sufficient deductions to offset income may rent its unused tax benefits and earn additional tax-free revenue.

In sum, as a result of the tax laws, investor-owned hospitals can be expected to pay substantially lower taxes than before, while charitable contributions to exempt hospitals become more costly to the donor.

Hospitals, like other institutions in our society, must adapt to the rapidly rising cost of new medical technology, the impact of inflation, and increasingly restrictive reimbursement. These are forcing hospitals to look elsewhere for additional sources of revenue.

Many hospital boards struggle over the particular corporate structure to be put in place. Questions about who controls what are at the center of debate. These questions may be discussed for one or two years before making a decision, thereby losing opportunities.

About two-thirds of the hospitals over 250 beds have put in place either a multicorporate structure or have completed the legal, tax, and mortgage planning needed to finalize new corporate structures. The generally-agreed upon best structure is the parent/subsidiary arrangement. How it is developed for an individual hospital depends upon endowment restrictions, mortgage indenture clauses, state laws, and the freedom to reshuffle assets. Where restrictive clauses interfere with a direct corporate reorganization, use is made of operating leases and management contracts.

EMERGING SYSTEMS OF HOSPITALS

A new level of multihospital systems for voluntary hospitals has emerged through mergers of existing systems. In the West, Lutheran Hospitals of Southern California and the Phoenix-based Good Samaritan System have merged their holding companies with a principal goal of capital aggregation and formation of a larger system.

In Kansas, Health Frontiers (originally Wesley Medical Center) in Wichita brought 33 hospitals and about 3,100 beds into a common regional alliance and the Seventh Day Adventists have formed a national organization of their own hospitals.

The hospital field is changing in historic ways with the emergence of billion-dollar systems. On the health insurance front, both Blue Cross and commercial carriers are putting preferred provider organizations into place. If the hospital meets contract conditions, the patients' bills are paid in full; if not, the patient makes up the difference.

As PPOs grow and there are further reductions in Medicare and Medicaid reimbursement, a two-tier hospital care system will reemerge. When these two programs were developed, Congress believed it would close the gap between the outdated 20-bed wards painted battleship gray and the color-coordinated, carpeted private-room hospitals. For awhile this expectation looked like a reality.

With the enactment of TEFRA the message from Congress became much clearer. The hospital response will be the same as it was 20 years ago, a two-tier hospital system. One tier will limit its quality and service to the level of the dollars available, the other will serve the private market in the style to which patients have become accustomed. Separate hospitals are required since an individual hospital cannot accommodate both levels of care. Survival may mean canceling the participating contract with Medicare and Medicaid. If a hospital is the first in its local area to do so, it will survive; if it is the last, it will gradually sink into obsolescence and unattractiveness to both patients and physicians.

The federal bureaucrats who design reimbursement regulations don't believe that hospitals will terminate their program agreements. In the early 1970s, they didn't believe nursing homes would do so either. Today try and find a nursing home still in the Medicare program.

The days of friendly competition between neighboring hospitals is headed into the sunset. The only reason remaining for cooperation is if it assists the bottom line. It is too bad that the niceties of cooperation with our professional neighbors is lost, but survival depends on an ability to be around after the smoke clears.

As institutions move into the era of economic competition, the risks of failure increase. Administrative staffs of hospitals should remember that when risk taking fails, trustees will put some distance between themselves and the staff. On the other hand, if successful the administrative staff will be regarded by the trustees as simply doing the job for which they were employed. Those who philosophically see themselves as conservators of community funds are apt to look for a scapegoat if a risk turns out badly. Success will probably be buried since the rewards for risk taking become part of the stream of revenues required to keep the hospital up-to-date in new technology and plant.

The successes of yesterday are not an argument for continuing to do business as usual. The rules of the game have been significantly changed and need to be understood in order to play in the new ball game. Survival depends on playing by the new rules.

Chapter 43

Looking around the Corner of 2000 A.D.*

The game of speculating about what is going to occur in any industry is fraught with future possible danger, or embarrassment when one's predictions prove to be wide of the mark. In spite of these risks, it might be interesting to look ahead to the time when we enter a new century and see if it is possible to predict some of the major thrusts and shifts that seem most likely to occur in hospitals.

MAJOR TRENDS

An uncontrollable federal deficit appears to be a chronic problem. Transfer payments, balance of trade deficits, and defense expenditures will probably be reflected in continuing unbalanced budgets.

If the share of the gross national product devoted to personal health care expenditures increases from the 9.0 percent in March 1980 to 12 percent by 1990, total expenditures for health care will be $753.6 billion, a three-fold increase (see Table 43–1).

This increase will take place at opposite ends of the spectrum. At the lower end, where provider units are the smallest, growth will be of a cottage industry type and will occur among those who offer professional services on a fee-for-service basis. These services will include physicians, dentists, clinical psychologists, podiatrists, optometrists, and other health-related professionals.

The largest single increase among professionals will be for physicians, since there will be 596,800 practicing physicians in 1990 and the ratio will stand at 2.45 physicians per 1,000 population. These new physicians will not be locating in rural areas, but will establish practices in medium- and large-size commu-

---

*Adapted from *Health Progress*, Vol. 62, No. 4, pp. 48–53, with permission of The Catholic Health Association of the United States, © April 1981.

Table 43–1 Personal Health Care Expenditures (in Billions)

	Dollars 1980[1]	Dollars 1990[2]	Percent 1980	Percent 1990
Professional Services	$ 88.2	$317.4	40.2%	42.1%
Public Health, Research				
Construction of Medical Facilities	16.3	42.0	7.4	5.6
Hospitals and Nursing Homes	106.9	367.8	48.8	48.8
Prepayment and Administration	7.7	26.4	3.5	3.5
Total	$219.1	$753.6	100.0%	100.0%

Source: Office of Research, Demonstrations and Statistics, Health Care Financing Administration; Estimate by author.

nities. The $88.2 billion spent for professional services in March 1980 will grow to $302.9 billion by 1990, including drugs and drug sundries.

Many of the new physicians will join existing practices, either in single specialty or multispecialty groups. If they don't, they will enter solo practice, either in understaffed specialties or into emerging specialty services that are unique in the community, some of which may be in direct competition with institutional-based services. Because they prefer a fee-for-service mode, they will be favored for referrals by their colleagues in other specialties who will prefer to refer to a physician rather than to an institution or agency for a particular service. Many patients will also favor this arrangement because it is highly personalized. A parallel can be drawn between this development and what has occurred in retailing when broad-line, large department stores experienced stiff competition from specialty shops that carried an extensive but limited number of items.

Since 200,000 additional physicians will be coming into practice by 1990 (see Table 43–2) the share of the total personal health care expenditures may rise slightly above a constant market share to $317.4 billion, a 5 percent increase. It is unlikely that very many of the professional corporations at this end of the scale will be larger than $5 million, and most will have billings of less than $1 million.

THE DEVELOPING SPECTRUM

At the upper end of the scale will be health care conglomerates with annual gross billings in excess of $1 billion. As a conservative estimate, by 1990 there probably will be 25 to 35 organizations that will grow out of existing hospitals and 10 to 15 that will develop out of nursing homes. Of the $367.8 billion spent on hospital and nursing home care in 1990, the hospital-based conglomerates may represent 11.5 percent of total revenues, approximately $35 billion. Among the $63.3 bil-

Table 43–2 Supply of Active Physicians (M.D. and D.O.) by Country of Medical Education Using Basic Methodology: 1974 and Projected 1975–1990

Category	1974	1975[2]	1980	1985	1990
		Number of Active Physicians			
All Active Physicians [1]	362,500	377,500	477,800	523,600	596,800
U.S.-trained	286,000	295,800	352,800	419,300	486,900
M.D.	272,400	281,700	335,100	396,100	457,000
D.O.	13,600	14,100	17,700	23,200	29,900
Canadian-trained M.D.s	5,600	5,600	5,500	5,600	5,600
Foreign-trained M.D.s	70,900	76,100	89,400	98,700	104,500
		Rate per 100,000 Population			
All Active Physicians	171.1	176.8	201.5	224.8	245.1
U.S.-trained	135.0	138.5	158.8	180.0	200.0
M.D.	128.6	131.9	150.8	170.1	187.7
D.O.	6.4	6.6	8.0	10.0	12.3
Canadian-trained M.D.s	2.6	2.6	2.5	2.4	2.3
Foreign-trained M.D.s	33.5	35.6	40.2	42.4	42.9
		Percent Distribution			
All Active Physicians	100.0%	100.0%	100.0%	100.0%	100.0%
U.S.-trained	78.9	78.4	78.8	80.1	81.6
M.D.	75.1	74.6	74.8	75.6	76.6
D.O.	3.8	3.7	4.0	4.4	5.0
Canadian-trained M.D.s	1.5	1.5	1.3	1.2	0.9
Foreign-trained M.D.s	19.6	20.2	20.0	18.9	17.5

[1]Assumes that the percent active of the AMA "not classified" M.D.s is the same as the percent "professionally active" of the classified M.D.s including those with address unknown.

[2]Available estimates for 1975 and 1976 for active U.S.-trained M.D.s are 282,800 and 290,900 respectively; active FMGs are estimated at 76,200 and 79,700 respectively. Active Canadian-trained M.D.s are estimated at 5,500 for both years.

Population figures used (in millions): 1960: 185.4, 1970: 206.1, 1974: 211.9, 1975: 213.5, 1980: 222.2, 1985: 232.9, 1990: 243.5.

Source: 1974-M.D.s; Roback, C.A., Physician Distribution and Medical Licensure in the U.S., 1974-75 editions, Center for Health Services Research and Development, AMA, Chicago, for each year; Foreign and Canadian-trained M.D.s: *Profiles of Medical Practice,* AMA, 1971-75 editions; D.O.s: Survey of Osteopathic Physicians 1974, AOA, 1975; Population: U.S. Bureau of the Census, Current Population Reports, Series P-25, No. 635.

lion that will be spent on nursing home care, it is likely that $15 billion will go to organizations that have billings in excess of $1 billion. Together the $1 billion plus health care corporations should account for approximately $50 billion of the $367.8 billion, or 14 percent.

Ranking just below them will be a number of health care corporations with revenues between $500 million and $1 billion dollars. Assuming there may be 250 hospitals at this level and 50 nursing homes, this group will probably account for another $12.5 billion for hospitals and $5 billion for nursing homes, a total of $17.5 billion, or another 4 percent. Thus, by 1990, nearly one-fifth of all revenues to hospitals and nursing homes will be paid to large health care conglomerates.

What will these organizations look like? What will be their impact on the health care field in general? Will those of large size bring about changes simply because of their scale? Will the proliferation of small, multiple units in professional and ancillary services be a factor for change?

The answers to these questions are already evolving. At the high end of the scale the formation of the health care conglomerates commenced in 1969 and is sweeping the country. Existing hospital corporations are being converted into parent-subsidiary models concerned with personal health care extending from wellness and fitness programs at one extreme to highly skilled intensive care programs at the other extreme. Because of the need to more effectively respond to a rapidly changing external environment the freestanding general hospital is undertaking the task of channeling various activities into separate, but related, corporations set up operationally as independent profit centers.

This organizational change is, at present, a response to government regulation and inadequate reimbursement from government sources. In order to avoid onerous restrictions, hospitals are creating subsidiaries. Largely unrecognized in this shift is a new organizational vehicle that has been created that has considerably more flexibility than previously existed. This vehicle, the conglomerate, will be used to advantage as hospital executives realize the potential that has been created for moving into new areas of activity. Rapid growth will follow. The major components of a conglomerate will be one or more general hospitals, a philanthropic foundation, one or more nursing homes, a contract management company, a real estate corporation, professional office buildings, and a system of primary care centers. As the parent-subsidiary model takes hold, it will have many diverse and unexpected roles in the coming years. By 2000 A.D., it may well be the dominant organizational structure in the health care field.

Taken together, both ends of the spectrum suggest that the health field will become both more professional and more personal in dealing with patients. It will be more professional at the $500 million-plus size. It is already evident in those organizations that have achieved this size level and will become increasingly apparent as they continue to grow and others join them. The level of professionalism expected of physicians will be much higher in such organizations because individual incompetence and sloppy clinical performance will be less tolerated. This will be true for two reasons:

1. The large conglomerate, because of its size, can purchase and/or develop sophisticated quality of care control programs and have them managed by statisticians. The quality control staff will not be concerned with the reactions of individual physicians because it will be working at corporate headquarters. Staff reports will supply individual hospitals with results on physicians who are not measuring up to the established standard.
2. Risk management programs will be linked with a quality of care effort in order to minimize the reserves that will have to be established for pending claims.

IMPROVING QUALITY OF CARE

Both types of programs will routinely and regularly be used to assess the quality of care in each institution and to note individual physician performance that falls below established standards of performance. At the corporate level the senior management will be mindful that the reputation of the corporation comes first. The size of corporate long-term debt will make corporate executives acutely aware that a reputation for clinical excellence is to be prized when dealing with investment bankers. It is that reputation that attracts competent physicians, who are needed to maintain market positions in a competitive climate. There will be a corporate concern to see that a system for monitoring individual clinical performance is in place and working well. The overall result will be an ever-increasing standard of professionalism. Individual physicians who chose to ignore a push for excellence will find senior executives far more concerned about the corporate image and fiscal health than they are about the feelings of any dissident physician who might tarnish the organization.

By the turn of the next century, improved measures of clinical performance will probably have been developed and implemented. Software packages will be numerous for measuring clinical performance tasks and continued progress on data-processing equipment will take much of the drudgery out of extracting the necessary input information from patient charts. Large hospital corporations will have the resources to undertake the tasks involved. At the top of the organization, it will be viewed as an important program in providing assurance that the ability to meet long-term financial commitments has been protected as much as possible. In general, the largest health care corporations will be recognized within the industry as providing the best patient care that is available by 2000 A.D.

OVERSEAS OPERATIONS

A second characteristic of large conglomerates is that many will become multinational organizations managing, and in some cases, owning hospitals and other health-related facilities in foreign countries. Often recognized, but not thought of as a salable service overseas, is the fact that the United States has the finest health care system in the world. Unlike the rest of the world, the need for talented management as well as clinicians was recognized in this country in the early 1930s. Since then, the specific skills required for health care management have been honed in graduate programs in universities and career paths have been developed. The wisdom of this is now apparent to the rest of the world.

In the next 20 years, health care management will be exported overseas by the large $500 million-plus organizations that decide to sell their services to foreign health care organizations. The long lead developed in hospital management skills is an exportable commodity that as yet is almost totally unrecognized. Many foreign countries are aware of the U.S. talent and will be signing contracts in increasing numbers to purchase sophisticated management skills, software packages, and management information systems, as well as training programs for a number of health-related professionals and technicians.

The demand for these services will be generated by foreign nationals who received all or partial medical training in this country and have come to appreciate that the only way their own systems can be substantially improved is by inviting an American health care organization to operate in their country. Because of the kind of commitment required to respond to these invitations, only corporations that have revenues in excess of half a billion dollars will be in a position to easily do so without undue risk. Since competition will be growing stiffer in this country, health care conglomerates desiring to continue to grow rapidly will see overseas development as one of their more favorable opportunities.

The possibilities for overseas development are highlighted when a list of items exported by the United States is reviewed. Today one item that stands out is farm products. Health care services are not on the list; yet, like farm products, our health care services are the best in the world and will remain so for the foreseeable future. This is already understood by American health care organizations now operating overseas. In spite of enormous difficulties, hampered by U.S. governmental regulations, these corporations are daily demonstrating that Americans are unsurpassed in their abilities to manage health care enterprises. Over the remaining years of this century the pioneers in this movement will be joined by others who see these opportunities to export American know-how. By 2000 A.D., American health care management will be dominant in the free world because large conglomerates had the flexibility and the fiscal muscle to be able to take risks in overseas developments without placing an undue strain on domestic corporate resources.

Large corporations that develop overseas operations will tend to favor one or two countries over other countries. Since most developed countries have centralized hospital systems operated by a federal ministry of health, a conglomerate that first gets established in a country is likely to enjoy a favored status and be first in line for providing additional services in that country, particularly if it enjoys a good working relationship with ministry officials. Thus, by 2000 A.D., if a map of health care systems is examined it will tend to reflect this kind of development. Overseas growth will also be stimulated by the training capabilities of a health care corporation.

NEW TRAINING CONCEPTS

At the $500 million-plus level, there will be a trend for corporations to develop their own training programs, of an in-service type for professionals in hospital departments and of a work training nature for nonprofessionals. When training programs are used only a few times before going on the shelf, the cost per participant is astronomically high and becomes a real barrier to high-quality training. If developmental costs can be spread across a useful life of 25 to 50 users, economics are no longer insurmountable. With large numbers of employees in a corporation, training centers will develop where editorial and graphics personnel can be employed to supplement activities of specialists developing training programs for a wide variety of nonphysician hospital personnel.

As these training programs mature and the results are apparent to all, the senior management of a conglomerate will realize that they add a unique dimension to the organization's overseas operation. At minimal cost, translations and adaptation of material can be made for use in host countries within a training center. Teams will then be sent overseas for a few weeks at a time to teach foreign nationals the latest techniques and procedures. Over the next 20 years, training centers will be developed in most of the large conglomerates and it will become commonplace to conduct in-service programs in foreign countries as a routine part of their regular operations.

LOBBYING ACTIVITIES

While this is going on, other changes will be taking place. Domestically, the handling of federal legislative matters will be undergoing a transition. Multiple lobbying offices will be established in the District of Columbia. There will be a desire among the very large hospital and nursing home conglomerates to have a direct influence on legislation affecting their operations. They will be unwilling to permit national associations to have an exclusive on this activity. The results will not be devisive in terms of the interests of the health field, but rather in 20 years will be recognized to have had just the opposite effect, a reinforcing of common viewpoints repeatedly being made known to the Congress.

This outcome will be an enhanced influence on legislation because of the diversity of health groups making their thoughts known on The Hill. Much of what these groups want will be the same because the matters for which they seek relief will be common to all health care institutions. Solutions proposed by them will at least be similar, if not identical, in most cases. Rather than discourage this movement, national associations should welcome additional support. Even though the efforts will lack coordination, which will be a concern of some, joint efforts will turn out to be a real strength. Many people taking the same position will carry more weight in the minds of legislators than one or two groups representing the entire medical and hospital field.

This change in role will affect the American Hospital Association. Large conglomerates will not be willing to pay dues at the level now called for under the AHA rate structure, particularly when they provide their own educational programs and lobbying efforts. Ultimately, this point of view will be recognized and the AHA will have to modify its programs and shift emphasis. Within the decade of the 1980s, it will be necessary to rethink allocations of expense, trimming some programs, eliminating others, in order to survive under reduced income. It is likely that the AHA will shape its role to become the representative in government circles of the freestanding independent hospitals. On selective issues, the AHA may still be the spokesman for the field as a whole, but it will have a more restricted role than the one now played. The AHA's positions on legislation will continue to be important, but it will not be the single authoritative voice that it is today.

THE MIDDLE OF THE SPECTRUM

In the middle of the hospital spectrum, between the over $5 million but less than $500 million range, will be freestanding hospitals and nursing homes. The bulk of these institutions will be in rural and suburban areas. Rural institutions will survive, often not in compliance with federal and state regulations, but not particularly concerned about it because they may be the only health care provider in the area. As stand-alone institutions rural hospitals can clearly demonstrate that without the services they provide, the residents in their area would have no service at all. Community pride will enable them to survive even though they may encounter financial difficulties.

Sharing the middle of the spectrum with rural hospitals, but at the upper end, will be suburban hospitals that have a satisfactory mix of sources of revenue and a solid occupancy level. With a strong financial picture and a competent medical staff, and not threatened by competition, they are apt to remain freestanding, so long as these factors remain favorable. By 1990, over half of all hospitals will still be in this middle range, but the figure will slowly decline over the following ten years so that by 2000 A.D., this middle group will likely constitute less than one-half of all existing hospitals and may account for perhaps one-third of all hospital revenues.

During the twentieth century the sole criterion for determining the effectiveness of a hospital has been its standard of patient care. Nothing else was regarded as being important when compared with this measure. How to determine quality was never solved. No objective measures were developed that could be added together to reach a conclusion about the quality of care and the opinions of leading physicians associated with a hospital usually served as a substitute for a numerical determination. Surveys of the Joint Commission on Accreditation of Hospitals (JCAH) with resulting accreditation, coupled with the opinions of leading physicians expressing themselves satisfied with quality, were considered by most governing boards as all that was required, so long as a stable financial condition was maintained. This constant and sustained focus on quality of care over decades brought about the intended results—a hospital system dedicated to quality. But, in doing so it also laid the groundwork for the changes now impacting hospitals. The single-minded devotion to quality of care has meant a modern up-to-date hospital with a wide array of expensive, complicated equipment, manned by well-educated personnel who are experienced and specialized. The costs for maintaining this posture in the future can no longer be subordinated to the primacy of patient care but must be given equal consideration. Patient care still remains important, but it has now been joined by economics and organizational flexibility.

The joining together of patient care, economics, and organizational flexibility has led to the development of health care corporations. The hospital is a subsidiary, albeit the major one, of the conglomerate, a vertically integrated system dominated by these three major factors.

Traditionalists will rightly question what will happen to patient care if it becomes a subsidiary in an organizational model where two other factors must be considered. With the individual physicians' voice muted at the corporate level, traditionalists fear that the diagnostic and treatment aspects will be downplayed.

However, as students of organizational structure see it, such an outcome need not occur. If the organizational structure is properly developed, the role of a physician as the advocate of patients can be enhanced. To a physician practicing in a health care corporation setting versus a freestanding hospital the difference will not be noticeable on a day-to-day basis, even 20 years from now. Yet differences will be there and will be observable in subtle ways. Since a corporation is designed with finance as a major consideration, a hospital will continue to have the latest in available equipment and a wider range of services than the freestanding hospital, which will have to increasingly defer capital expenditures as it uses its depreciation funds for operational purposes because of the growing limitations of cost reimbursement.

In addition, a physician in a health care system will find it is easier to transfer a patient out of the hospital to a nursing home or other health care facility because of the interlocking of activities in a conglomerate. The attending physician, by writing in a patient's medical chart, can trigger a series of procedures for arranging whatever is needed, requiring no further effort on his part. By 2000 A.D., physicians operating in this environment will look back on the lack of coordinated vertical services for this type of problem with no regrets and a considerable feeling of relief.

While a physician's role will remain largely unchanged, the same will not be true of management personnel. There will be a heightened sophistication in management. Decisions at the top will require a balancing of all the factors inherent in a situation being analyzed. Patient care will be of importance, along with financial, political, legal, and social considerations. Short-term needs will be weighed against long-term goals. All in all, decision making will tend to become more objective and less subjective. Career paths to the top will not be clearly marked, the top post in some instances going to those trained in hospital administration, in other situations going to those trained in finance, law, or marketing.

INNER-CITY HOSPITALS

The need for a balanced corporate interest will result in less identification with inner-city health problems. Hospitals that are freestanding always maintain a close identification with the community in which they are located. Over the years if a hospital has survived a changing neighborhood and service area, it is likely to remain freestanding. Large health care corporations are not apt to want these institutions as part of their system. When analyzed for possible acquisition, inner-city hospitals will not pass corporate muster. Today this may not seem true since city and county governments are now turning to large health care corporations and signing management contracts for operating hospitals in the inner cities. For several reasons, this trend is not likely to be long-lived.

Many city and county governments are anxious to get out of the hospital business. They believe that tax dollars will go further if a hospital is managed by a large health care corporation. The health care corporation is interested in obtaining inner-city management contracts because these corporations are still in a developmental stage where a desire for an expansion of revenues, additional units to manage, and testing of information systems dominate their decisions. The risk is minimal to these corporations since capital outlays are not required, only additional working capital and on-site managerial personnel.

This does not change the basic problems of inner-city hospitals. As inner-city hospital costs continue to rise and the tax base continues to decline, local governments will realize that their hoped-for results are not achieved. On the other hand, management corporations will discover that local governments are increasingly difficult to deal with because the management fees a government is willing to pay are no longer adequate to do the job at hand. An inability to pay for the care required with ceilings placed on fees will be insurmountable handicaps to proper management. Once recognized, these contracts will be terminated, probably to the relief of both parties, who will be blaming each other for the situation that has developed.

This series of events can be expected to occur over and over again. By the time the health field enters the last decade of this century, public hospitals may be again directly operated by governmental agencies. Unless existing methods of paying for hospital and medical care are drastically changed, the result will be a two-tier system of care by 2000 A.D. Public hospitals will still have their traditional problems: inadequate funding, insufficient equipment, obsolete facilities, not enough trained personnel, and a lack of physicians to provide care: all arising out of an eroded tax base, a problem beyond the scope of a health care corporation's contract with a governmental unit. Eventually, these corporations will move on to greener pastures where high standards of management and quality of care can be maintained.

THE WIDENING GAP

If financing mechanisms do not change, the gap between public hospitals and the rest of the hospital field will continue to widen well into the twenty-first century. Even though a surplus of physicians will be real by 1990, they will still shun inner cities despite the fact that funding may be available for paying physicians at levels commensurate with what they will be able to earn in other settings. Many physicians will settle for working on a salary rather than establishing a fee-for-service practice in an inner city. Even if public agencies offer financial inducements equal to suburban offerings, the vast majority of new physicians coming into practice will not practice in the inner city. Like other professionals, they will opt for suburbia.

By 2000 A.D., the only hope for a single standard of care in metropolitan areas will likely rest with the enactment of a major bill by Congress to change reimbursement systems. If present trends prevail, it is inevitable that a two-tier system will again evolve. If at the state level regulation of hospital revenues occurs through rate review mechanisms or diagnostic related group approaches, the answers are going to come out the same.

In a generalized sense, it appears that the only way this outcome can be avoided is to seriously and meaningfully introduce competition into the health care arena. Fewer regulations and reimbursement on a pricing basis, rather than on a cost basis, may benefit inner-city hospitals. On the other hand, it may turn out that these measures will also be inadequate and will have made no difference anyway.

By 2000 A.D. health services will still be maldistributed, physicians will still avoid rural areas and inner cities. The poor and the needy will still be receiving episodic care and the local emergency room on a Saturday night will continue to resemble a M.A.S.H. unit. However, on balance, the health delivery system will be considerably improved, providing greater depth and breadth from wellness to intensive care.

The present adversary relationship with government will have given way to one of neutrality. HSAs and PROs will disappear from the scene and will be remembered as fumbling attempts to deal with a problem that only resulted in showing government in a bad light because they operated on the premise that centralization of decision making was the best solution to health cost increases.

Looking back over the last half century from the vantage point of 2000 A.D., it will be well to remember that in 1950 personal health care expenditures stood at 4.5 percent of the gross national product, at 9.1 percent in 1980, and at 12 percent in 1990 before leveling off at about 12 percent. Yet, the conclusion in 2000 A.D. about the health care system in this country will be the same as it was in 1950 A.D.

The American health care delivery system has continued for over 50 years to be the finest in the world, still plagued with problems and dilemmas but unmatched by any other country. When the health field landscape is surveyed, those who have participated in its trials and tribulations and in its accomplishments and triumphs should be pleased by what they will see.

Chapter 44

Ten Years Hence

SOCIETAL FORCES AT WORK

The fact that a large-scale health care organization can focus its services effectively at a local level in a sensitive way is an accomplishment that negates the traditional opinion that essential community medical care needs are best met only through totally independent community hospitals.

Why is this significant? Because it is essential to understand the broad sweep of forces impacting hospitals by focusing on the macro level of health care. People seldom do this because they have their minds on day-to-day affairs.

Since the Vietnam War period, changes in society have moved from small to large events, from urban to rural and rural to urban, from abundance to scarcity and from less to greater knowledge. The past decade is characterized by rapidity of change. We have learned that what one generation believes is not what the next generation may value.

Health and medical care are part of this trend. Adherence to hospital traditions of 50 or more years is not necessarily an assurance of future successes in a changed society. The problem is to sort out the essential values from among the traditional practices.

In spite of the fact that all kinds of hospitals are rapidly joining existing investor-owned and nonprofit corporate systems, creating new ones, and merging existing systems into super systems, there is a widely held opinion that an individual hospital management has the total competence to readily manage all aspects of the operation. The reality is that the complexity and speed of ongoing change usually exceeds the capacity of an administrative staff to cope with these changes and to properly present them in perspective to the trustees.

The last two decades saw a tremendous increase in medical knowledge and in the complexity of instrumentation, new drugs, fiber optics, nuclear medicine, computerized imaging, transplantation, hospice, urodynamics, and noninvasive techniques of diagnosis on the hospital scene. At the same time, the organization and delivery of medical services largely remained stationary. Change didn't begin until financing was impacted too heavily by restricted spending on discretionary health care by government, industry, and individuals. Medical care organizations and associations were slow to respond and the initiative for change came from outside the field.

The cumulative effects of these external activities have stimulated initiatives in the medical care field. Throughout the next decade, changes will continue to occur but at a higher rate with new medical knowledge, revised government entitlements, amended funding mechanisms, and new ways to provide care to patients.

In what ways will these changes alter the financing and delivery of medical care in the next ten years? What will the organization and delivery of care be like? Looking only at the financing and delivery issues and not at the development of medical knowledge and technology, these changes can be identified.

The driving force for modification of the existing system is taking place in the financing mechanisms because they impact the factors of supply and demand, particularly in the Medicare and Medicaid programs. These changes will not affect all hospitals to the same degree, nor at the same time. However, the economics of the field will create a radically different health care system in ten years.

DEMAND-SIDE ECONOMICS

Controls on the demand side of health care have been explored, tried, and evaluated since the early 1970s through federal funding of health maintenance organizations (HMOs), increasing use of higher levels of co-insurance and deductibles, and the development of tight utilization review systems. The results are mixed.

For the last ten years, HMOs have struggled to gain a foothold in parts of the country where they had not previously existed. Many failed and a few marginally survived. In the process, the lesson learned was that capitation plans can significantly lower hospital utilization rates from preexisting levels. To successfully operate an HMO, it was discovered that greater capitalization was a requisite and that support of corporate management was essential to achieve adequate enrollment levels in a reasonable time period. Lately, the popularity of HMOs has been gaining greater public participation and its growth curve has turned sharply upward. It now appears reasonable to believe that by the mid-'90s at least 20 percent of the population will be enrolled in an HMO.

A second demand factor that has been ignored since the inception of Medicare is the growing number of beneficiaries. Between 1970 and 1990, the Medicare population is projected to increase 21 percent to 31 million, while the total population is estimated to increase by 8 percent. When it is realized that the 65- to

74-year-old population uses three times the hospital care of the under-65 population, and the 75-plus population uses eight times as much hospital care, it is clear that the major cause of inadequacy in Medicare funding is extremely high utilization. In HMOs, the 65-year-plus population uses only one-third the number of patient days used in the traditional fee-for-service arrangement.

In controlling utilization, patients are the key. Physicians have been unable to substantially reduce hospital usage through prospective or concurrent utilization review. Lower hospital usage can be accomplished in one of two ways: mandated Medicare coverage in HMOs or the establishment of a Medicare voucher system. Because physicians are most likely to politically oppose a mandated HMO solution, the probable solution is the enactment of a Medicare voucher system.

There are two strategies for relieving the pressure on Medicare funding and the federal budget. One is to establish a means test for Medicare beneficiaries and the other is to make health insurance benefits taxable above a set amount. Both choices are aimed at stabilizing governmental finances.

Another concept has gained widespread popularity—the establishment of preferred provider organizations (PPOs). Under their programs utilization is reduced through tight controls and physician and hospital services are discounted. Another proposal under consideration by Congress has been the creation of an all-payer system to prevent cost shifting by hospitals and physicians from government program shortfalls to nongovernmental patients. A short life can be predicted for such strategies. Until patients are held to some degree of financial risk for their medical care decisions, the existing and proposed programs will have minimal impact on the costs of medical care.

In essence, the costs of medical care are where they are today because control of the demand for medical care has not been faced in a realistic way. The governmental activity has been aimed at controlling increasing medical care costs, the supply side not the demand side, because of political considerations.

GOVERNMENTAL ACTIVITIES

Shortly after the enactment of Medicare in 1965, the first planning laws were put in place, followed by Certificate of Need state legislation and progressive restrictions in the definition of reimbursable Medicare costs. This was later followed by mandated utilization review through PSROs and state rate review commissions. In industry circles, business coalitions and preferred provider organizations were established. Government then came along with the tax equity and fiscal responsibility law and the prospective payment system for Medicare. This authorized the diagnostic related group method of paying for hospital care on a fixed amount basis.

While this was taking place on the hospital scene, the growing supply of physicians was expected to control the rise in the professional components. In two decades, the number of medical school graduates increased from 7,000 annually to 17,500 with an additional 20 percent of physicians being added from among foreign medical graduates.

It has become increasingly clear that an overabundance of physicians will not cause a reduction in their fees. Congress is now considering legislation to establish a fixed-payment system for physician fees to Medicare patients and later to all patients. At present, there are about 400,000 practicing physicians and an expectation that in the next 20 years, the supply will increase to more than 600,000.

The result of an increased physician supply is being felt in several regions of the country, as well as in specialty fields. In large cities, it is a rarity for physicians to enter solo practices, while in the semirural areas practice specialties not previously present are becoming available.

In addition, HMOs, minor emergicenters, and walk-in primary care facilities are finding well-qualified physicians to staff these programs on a salary basis. These new programs are financially successful because they provide quick responses, qualified personnel, attractive environments, and courteous service. The basis of their marketing plan is to attract patients away from existing physician practices. In some cities and towns, 70 percent of the patients come from this source.

Behind all of these efforts is the desire to slow the rate of increasing medical care costs and to eventually cause a reduction. Supply side externally generated economic controls cannot accomplish this goal, while the use of a fixed price system of paying for Medicare patients is likely to cause financial chaos in hospitals.

Supply side economics can be used to internally develop new responses by physicians and hospitals. Incentives to do so are present. Some physicians and organizations will respond, others will choose to think and behave as if the traditional ways of deliverying medical care will prevail. It is predictable that many of the traditionalists will not be on the medical scene by the mid-1990s.

THE NEXT DECADE

In the next decade, the supply side of medical care economics will find new avenues for delivering care. However, it is unrealistic to believe that internally developed supply side changes alone will reduce the total cost of medical care or that externally imposed supply side controls will do so. Any additional external controls are likely to create serious disruptions in the delivery of medical care.

If a reduction in medical care costs is to occur, demand side factors need to be manipulated by requiring patients to personally be responsible for medical care in excess of either a limited number of dollars or beyond a specified level and type of care.

Obviously, there needs to be a limitation on the financial liability of patients with catastrophic illnesses. The logical choice is a dollar limit for medical care, an uninsurable corridor on top of the basic amount, and above that level, catastrophic coverage, probably limited to certain broad types of care. An example of such a program would be a fixed number of dollars, adjusted by age and sex, such as $1,200 for a male patient 30 years of age, and $2,700 for a male patient aged 66. The corridor amount would also vary by age, say $3,500 for a 30-year-old and $2,800 for a 66-year-old patient. Once through the uninsured corridor, catastrophic coverage would make payments, but might not include such things as heart transplants in patients over 65.

Many variations in such a program are possible. However, this concept provides a new way to involve patients in the economics of medical care. Morbidity and mortality tables, insurance carrier experience, and medical inputs would be necessary to arrive at realistic financial levels for implementation.

If the trends and changes just described determine the characteristics of medical care delivery by the mid-'90s, what will the system look like? At a minimum, it will have the following characteristics:

- There will be no regulation through planning and Certificate of Need laws.
- Preferred provider organizations and diagnostic related group payment methods will have been phased out.
- Marketing strategies and techniques will be extensively used by medical care organizations.
- An all-payer system based on the use of vouchers will be widespread.
- HMOs will be the source of about 20 percent of all medical care by 1990.
- Medical and allied health care educational programs will not be funded by hospitals.
- There will be significantly fewer acute hospitals, particularly in rural and semirural areas.
- A high proportion of hospitals will be consolidated into large multihospital systems.
- The number of hospital admissions will substantially decrease and ambulatory care greatly increase.
- Acute hospital services will be highly intensive and patients will be transferred to semi-ambulatory and self-care facilities on the hospital campus for recuperation.
- Most of the ancillary and support services of hospitals will be leased from large corporations specialized to provide a single service.
- Hospitals will have developed health care service malls similar to shopping malls with the hospital as the anchor firm.

- There will be a substantial increase in all types of long-term care facilities on the health care campus.
- Most hospital systems will be of the investor-owned type.
- The number of small multihospital systems will be substantially reduced.
- There will be a large increase in the number of employed physicians, particularly for the delivery of primary care services.
- Physician services will be marketed directly to the public by large health care corporations.

This listing of likely medical care delivery attributes in the next decade is at best sketchy, but it suggests the radical changes that will occur. Such changes will not be popular because they are at variance with existing traditions. However, economic reality will prevail.

Chapter 45

Imperatives in Health Administration Education

When the education for a health administration career is contemplated, it quickly becomes apparent that there are three major elements for achieving career success; administrative knowledge, administrative judgment, and administrative behavior. The question is not only what is currently needed, but what will the needs be in 1990 and 2000 A.D. and beyond.

About the only thing really known is that a prediction of future characteristics of the health administration field is in itself a risky business, even for a few years. Separating these characteristics into three major elements and predicting what will be needed in each element is even more difficult.

The usual academic ''cop-out'' is to set a goal of preparing and motivating the student to engage in life-long education, then any curriculum omissions, or lack of foresight, can later be laid on the doorstep of lack of motivation of the career executive to pursue life-long learning.

ADMINISTRATIVE BEHAVIOR

In terms of the three basic elements, the one factor that most determines career success is administrative behavior. Too frequently one encounters a health care executive who knows how to deal with his board, medical staff, and community but who leaves a trail of unfilled hospital goals and objectives behind him. He is a nice chap that fitted into the milieu of governance and community, but left a hospital that has not improved in any substantial way through his leadership.

Unfortunately, administrative style is too frequently a criterion used by boards or trustees for gauging administrative accomplishment rather than what has actually improved in the hospital.

Different personalities and the value systems of trustees establish the unwritten criteria used for judging desirable administrative behavior. If an executive is working for a board of trustees in Boston composed of socially elite persons with inherited wealth, he needs to have social graces and a taste for conservative business suits. If it is a consumer board in the inner city, a beard and open-necked shirt is the standard of dress. Administrative sensitivity to trustee characteristics is essential for making trustees feel secure and confident about their management personnel.

Along with the outward, observable characteristics an executive needs to acknowledge the limit of what trustees are willing to think about and debate. In a hospital where physicians are perceived as the bastion of free enterprise, an agenda item to discuss the hospital's initiation of an HMO is clearly an off-limits subject. In a situation where physicians are seen as a necessary but selfish profession, the inclusion of an HMO on the board agenda will be welcomed.

Administrative behavior is what it is because trustees establish the ground rules by which executives are employed and terminated. The teaching of appropriate management behavior is an untouched aspect of administrative skills in the academic setting because classroom pedagogy has not developed adequate techniques for doing so. The limitations of the classroom for teaching appropriate administrative behavior are recognized and can only be realized by including in the curriculum a hospital residency. Its purpose would be to expose the student to a hospital president, as a preceptor, who has developed behavior skills and can serve as a role model for the student.

A faculty recognizes that students subconsciously accept faculty behavior as a role model that reinforces the students' understanding of desirable behavior. Each member is aware that he is a role model and must practice appropriate behavior in all student contacts. When students do not get this message, they should be separately counseled by a faculty member. Considerable time, effort, and discussion of the faculty should be spent in this activity. If a university is to gain a reputation and have the respect of the field of practicing hospital executives, a major component is to have graduates who understand and practice appropriate administrative behavior. By itself, administrative behavior does not lead to becoming an effective executive.

In the future, it would be desirable to find a way to develop student sensitivity within the curriculum about this major component of success for an executive. However, the methodology to do so is not clear, nor probably cost-effective in the university setting.

The American College of Healthcare Executives has a Kellogg grant to develop a self-assessment program because inappropriate administrative behavior is probably the primary cause of executives getting into difficulties. There is a need for assessment of this factor. However, the more one looks at behavior assessment, the more one finds difficulties. The assessment of administrative behavior requires the development of a methodology that is both rigorous and valid. It is a tough problem because it involves one rater to one student. The greatest difficulty is that there is no one identifiable appropriate behavior. Circumstances and environment determine what is appropriate in any given situation.

ADMINISTRATIVE JUDGMENT

The next most important element in career success for hospital executives is administrative judgment. Hopefully, graduate programs in health administration are turning out graduates with sufficient abilities to perform satisfactorily in their first career position. A curriculum usually includes courses that the faculty believes will aid students in developing judgment. These cover administrative practices, health care planning, and organizational policy. More important, a faculty should see the administrative residency of nine months as the best way to develop this area of administrative skills. While most university programs have entirely eliminated the residency, or fit it into the summer period between academic years, the belief that it is important has steadfastly been held to in a small number of graduate programs.

The latest revision of the accreditation standards for health administration requires two academic years on campus and provides no credit for the residency period. At Georgia State, the response was to move from five quarters on campus to six quarters, or two academic years, and to maintain a three-quarter residency. The residency was strengthened by improved quarterly evaluations and the use of a hospital administrative survey report. The goal is to have residents synthesize what they are learning into a coherent viewpoint of what administration is all about, to see the forest as well as the trees.

Faculties know that one of the major problems regularly faced by health care executives is adequately defining an issue, recognizing its essential core elements, and being able to state them in measurable terms. In the classroom, the problem is to provide the general principles for developing this skill. These are taught in an MBA curriculum, which applies to different industries. The classroom instructor can never take sufficient time, or lacks industry-specific knowledge, to demonstrate the applicability of a principle in several industries, so specific problems in a particular industry remain undefined. If case studies are used to bridge this gap, the problem as presented to students is already defined and no practice in problem definition occurs. The administrative residency gives the student experience in problem definition. For persons in general management, the real-world, useful skill is problem definition, not problem solving. Problem solvers are department directors in hospitals and problem definers are the administrative staffs in hospitals.

Excellency in administrative judgment is also based on an ability to arrive at workable, acceptable decisions when available data are less than complete. Sound administrative judgment is based on an ability to cope with uncertainty. With greater experience, a capable executive is able to cope with uncertainty by closing information gaps through reasoning from previous experiences that are related to the problem at hand.

SELECTING A DECISION PATH

A related skill that is not well understood pedagogically is the ability to finally select a decision path from a series of alternative possibilities. A skilled executive typically selects an option that maximizes the possibility of either accomplishing more distant goals or of providing flexibility for shifting to a different course of action if unforeseen obstacles appear. How one teaches this skill is not well worked out in the classroom. Again, the residency probably provides a much better educational experience for acquiring this skill than the campus classroom. The one difficulty is that a resident must remain objective and aloof intellectually, to a degree, to maintain this perspective. This is probably the proof for the frequently stated belief that a poor preceptor, one who lacks sufficient administrative judgment, may be a good teacher because the student learns what not to do and how not to think. Certainly, this is not the preferred way to teach administrative judgment. These lessons are better learned and reinforced if a resident observes an executive who has excellent administrative judgment.

The term "administrative judgment" covers a large, complex array of activities for the hospital executive. These activities include planning and organizing, achieving organizational goals, quality of medical services, allocation of resources, crisis resolution, compliance with regulation, marketing, and sensitivity to behavior. A nagging question remains, if an executive has above-average judgment in some areas, is he competent in other areas? There are no published studies that have analyzed this component of judgment. If success in one area is achieved, does this imply the use of good judgment in all other areas, or is there an unrecognized halo effect that convinces people that there is uniformly good judgment on all dimensions?

In practice, there is a tendency to subconsciously identify strong and weak areas of administrative judgment when evaluating a person's performance. However, we need to know much more about why there is a difference in judgment on different issues. Is there a quality of mind or a way of thinking about problems that is so basic that the same skills apply? If so, what does a mind gain from having an in-depth knowledge of the issues involved? Administrative judgment is a blend of in-depth knowledge of an area and ability to think both intellectually and emotionally. Even though hard facts and uncontrovertible data point in a specific direction, implementation must be tempered by how the various players will behave in the process.

For example, an executive may decide that there is sufficient demand to establish three primary care centers on the perimeter of the hospital's market area.

Failure to do so is seen as eventually leading to a decline in the hospital's market share. Since physicians are needed to staff these centers, approval by the medical executive committee may be sought. An understanding of physician behavior is needed.

Excellent administrative judgment is obviously a composite of many variables to which weights are subconsciously assigned. The mind probably does not measure fine graduations in weighting, but operates at a more macro level, such as deciding that a specific factor can be overcome with a little foresight and political action. Another factor may be viewed as a real stumbling block requiring persistent and sensitive presentations over time in order to overcome resistance and gain support. Other times, an alternative may be seen as not being worth the effort because the cost of overcoming the difficulty outweighs the gain. Under such circumstances, the matter should be shelved. The unknown element in the process is why some executives can weigh these variables more accurately than others, even when all of the influencing variables are well defined.

One way to teach residents the skills needed for excellence in administrative judgments is to ask them to put in writing the major alternative decisions that are possible and then have discussions with preceptors regarding the completeness of their lists. By defining the positions that participants in the final decision are likely to take, and the reasons for doing so, residents gain insights. This should be followed by asking the residents to outline a process and counterstrategies of management that can be used to overcome the positions taken by others. Following the completion of the decision process, a "postmortem" between preceptor and resident, reviewing what didn't happen, as well as what did happen, analyzing how each decision maker played his role, is a valuable lesson.

This kind of teaching cannot be accomplished in the classroom. The closest approach is role playing, but this activity lacks vitality and the depth of feeling that one experiences in a real-life situation.

Tactical and strategic skills can be sharpened by practice and tutoring. However, if the tutor doesn't have a high level of such skills, the resident will not develop them. They may be developed later in his career, but he will have been short-changed in the residency period by a preceptor who does not analytically understand their use and application.

The development of administrative judgments is expected to come with experience. However, the on-campus period can be used to give the student insights into the way various groups in a hospital are likely to approach issues and the reasons that these perspectives are held. For example, there are faculties and preceptors who tell students that the physician is the antagonist of the hospital administration. This kind of teaching is not useful, but it is a viewpoint that sooner or later may cause obstacles to the student becoming a successful hospital executive. It would be constructive, however, to explain to students the reason why physicians feel and behave as they do and to get students to understand why such behavior is rational from the physician's perspective, type of training, and status in the community and hospital.

Administrative judgment is based on a knowledge of hospital management and a blending of this knowledge with an understanding of individual, group, and community behavior. Too frequently an unsuccessful hospital executive places blame and points a finger at physicians, trustees, or employees without realizing that it is his responsibility to gain acceptance of his ideas. These executives unknowingly generate barriers to acceptance rather than reducing or eliminating them through more controlled behavior.

ADMINISTRATIVE KNOWLEDGE

When the value of administrative knowledge is considered, a university often assumes that this is the only subject area to be included in the curriculum. Yet how does one decide what to teach and where does this knowledge come from?

In the hospital administrative curriculum, the test of usefulness to practitioners in the field is more important than esthetics or the traditional university criteria, such as in creative writing, theoretical physics, or mathematics. The criteria of usefulness is daily tested by the performance of the graduate as a practitioner of hospital administration. How well do a program's graduates perform; do they perform better than nonspecialty trained managers and does their performance exceed that of other approaches and hospital administration programs? To look carefully at this aspect does not imply that university programs in health care administration are trade schools turning out artisans. Rather, a utilitarian criterion is primary. The scope of administrative knowledge needed by a modern-day health care executive is complex, diverse, and draws on basic knowledge from several academic disciplines.

The role of a health administration faculty in acquiring knowledge is to take the empirical findings of many fields and evaluate their applications in the health field. There is more art than science in developing such applications. The test can only be found in their usage, which is why faculty members need a close and continuing association with practitioners.

Basic to the development of successful health care executives is the appropriate selection of students. As gatekeepers for the profession, the faculty is faced with a serious responsibility. Students should be selected on the basis of their potential as realists who can translate academic knowledge into practical decisions when embarked on their careers.

WOMEN IN GRADUATE HEALTH PROGRAMS

The rising number of women students in graduate programs in health care administration should be of concern. About one-half of the students are women.

Many are geographically limited because they subconsciously place greater importance on their husband's career than they do on their own. Despite long and loud protestations of single women, once engaged or married, most want to be with their husbands, rather than believing the husband should move to where the wife's career takes her. This is not to say that all women act this way, only that the predominance of women graduates exhibit this kind of behavior. This may change in the years ahead as there is greater acceptance of equality between husband and wife but, for the present, it is not the case.

Beyond the residency period, this matter becomes more serious since the young female career health care executive is faced with the same decision over and over again. Chief executive officers are aware that a potential female executive has a position tenure that is only as long as the time her husband is employed locally. Because of existing laws, the chief executive may not ask questions on this topic, but will find a subterfuge reason for selecting a man rather than a woman, rather than reveal his true concern.

Forty years ago, hospital administration was dominated by women from religious hospitals. It was a different era. Looking ahead, it seems probable that most women entering health career administration will have careers at the assistant administrator level with few holding chief executive officer positions. Trustees will hold the same unexpressed reservations as chief executives of hospitals.

Women do have a place in health care administration. In the early stages of their careers, they are likely to be slotted into staff positions where high analytical skills, mutual trust of the chief executive officer, and objective thinking are primary. A woman in her late thirties or early forties who continues her career will find she is an equal of her male counterparts and there will be little concern about limited tenure and prolonged leaves of absence to have a child. Some of these women will become chief executives.

DEVELOPING NEW KNOWLEDGE

The acquisition of new health administrative knowledge once the student begins a full-time career is another facet that needs consideration. The health field has a plethora of short educational courses on more subjects than one can possibly attend. The problem with the variety of postgraduate courses now offered is that they are basically a reiteration of existing knowledge. Where does a senior administrator go for new knowledge? The education programs of the American College of Healthcare Executives are now the best available, but these are limited by what the college staff believes will lead to sufficient registrations to justify the costs of the seminar.

The career administrator must become a life-long student who persistently reads professional journals and new books, as well as periodically attends appropriate short courses. Often overlooked are the daily work experiences. In a learning environment there are many teachers at hand, department directors and physicians, who all have a real interest in having the chief executive understand their problems.

At the university level, the development of new knowledge can be measured by observing how much a course syllabus is changed from year to year. Experience indicates that about 20 percent of the material in a course syllabus should be deleted and about that same amount of new material added each year. In a five-year period, the course material should be completely revised. In other words, a career administrator faces learning a totally new scope of knowledge over six times during his active career. Dr. Malcolm MacEachern's classic book *Hospital Organization and Management* describes the world of hospital administration of 1930. That was a much simpler time with not much expectation for change. To duplicate this 1,000-page book today would require writing about a 10,000-page book, with the knowledge that within five years such a massive effort would result in merely recording one phase of development and would be seen ultimately only as a historical document. When first published, MacEachern's book was a standard text for over 25 years.

The ultimate goal for preparing students for careers in health care management is to equip them with a philosophy and an understanding of the environment. Important organizational relationships also need to be understood. The component parts of administrative knowledge, administrative judgment, and administrative behavior need blending if a skilled manager is to be developed. With solid experience and a life-long learning curve, the limits of an administrative position are transcended as the capable chief executive becomes a health care statesman. The world is short of people who understand the externalities of our society and relate them to their daily operations. To articulate these relationships in a meaningful way is a skill learned in the crucible of experience.

The imperatives for health administration education call for a deeper understanding of the demands of society than has been needed in the past. Enlightened faculties are critical to the well-being of the future in health care.

Chapter 46

The Future of Health Field Consulting

PAST GROWTH

A quarter of a century ago consulting services were offered by successful administrators who had retired or by a person who had held a chief executive's position in a hospital, often under strained circumstances. It was not a career that was deliberately chosen or a career path that had been worked out, since none existed. Those who entered saw an unmet need and had a belief that there would be sufficient demand for their services to enable them to engage full-time in this activity. As their practices grew they added staff members, initially drawn from the ranks of hospital executives. Gradually, there was a recognition that the skills of management were different from those required of consultants.

Where early assignments drew from knowledge of hospital operations, the types of projects began to broaden and diversify requiring more and more analytical skills. The base of knowledge began to draw from other areas: accounting, finance, corporate structures, nursing, personnel, marketing, and statistics, if desirable results were to be obtained. As these additional talents were required by clients, new and additional types of assignments were available. Throughout this developmental stage, consultants were aware that the value of their services was dependent upon staying on the cutting edge of the hospital field.

The need to respond to client requests led to an increasing number of projects, which led to larger staffs, coupling generalists with specialists and this in turn led to increased competence in more and more potential areas of practice. The transferability of administrative skills to consulting skills diminished as the importance of technical talents became more important.

The stage has now been reached where familiarity with the health field and, in particular the hospital, is necessary but no longer of overriding importance. It is now only one of the many skills of a competent consultant, one that requires several years of hands-on consulting experience to learn. The well-worn expression "If you can't manage, you can always go into consulting" is now reversed—"If you can't do consulting, you can always go into management." Consulting is no longer the haven for those with limited abilities, but attracts the best and the brightest of the students who have completed their graduate studies.

FUTURE DIRECTION

Consulting in the health field will continue to grow and expand in the years ahead because of the talent now in consulting firms. Many have become committed to life-long careers in consulting. They enjoy the challenges and are adept at handling the increasing complexities of the field. The sophistication of consulting staffs today and their strong commitment to their work is joined by an entrepreneurial spirit that develops early in a consulting career. This combination strongly suggests that the competitive nature of consulting will enable its practitioners to continue to develop services that are unique and in demand. The fluid and changing conditions prevalent in the health care field provide more opportunities than ever before for health field consultants. It is a time for imagination based on solid conceptual skills and experience. These skills will continue to be recognized by health field clients.

At some point in time, should the hospital field be nationalized the result would be disastrous for consulting. Overnight, the number of consultants would shrink precipitously. Short of this occurrence, the future should see an increasing use of consulting services, though the road ahead will not be smooth. Periodic ups and downs will be due to events that are happening at the time, but the overall trend over the next decade should continue upwards, perhaps, as much as 50 percent higher than at present.

FIELDS OF COMPETENCE

Within the fields of competence there is apt to be considerable shifting in volumes of work over the next decade. A review of these may be helpful.

The demand for strategic marketing plans, which has been a mainstay of existing firms, should continue to be strong in the years ahead. However, the results of these studies are going to contain much more proprietary information than in the past because of the growth of economic competition between hospitals. This shift will limit the abilities of individual firms to serve more than one client in any given service area because of conflicts of interest. Firms will need to seek a wider dispersion of clients in this field of competence.

Increasingly, hospitals are seeking reliable studies on consumer attitudes about the services they provide and are no longer content to depend on the opinions obtained in patient polls. As competition stiffens, hospitals will use this technique more and more in shaping their business plans. Though consumer surveys are inexpensive when compared with other consulting services, they will incur substantial growth in volume, but remain a secondary source of revenue to a hospital consulting firm.

Market research projects will become more important in consulting firms as they provide services to a broad spectrum of health care programs. As hospitals undertake joint ventures with groups of physicians and others in the community, knowledgeable outside consultants will be used to undertake the preliminary planning. While the methodologies used to conduct these studies will be well known to consultants, they will be applied to a wide variety of health activities and will become a substantial market in the future.

The use of executive recruiters should see a substantial increase in demand. As a result of the changes in the financing mechanism, there is going to be increased tension between medical staffs and chief executives of hospitals as the availability of resources decreases. This will lead to greater administrative turnover and provide increased opportunities for executive recruiting. There are also new positions being created as a result of hospitals moving into parent-subsidiary corporate structures as well as new staff positions being developed within hospital chains. The result will be increased recruiting, which will be attractive to executive recruiters who have not previously served health field clients. All in all, competition may be keener.

The same degree of growth will occur in the seminar field. Consulting firms are being asked increasingly to conduct retreats for individual hospital clients. These will grow in numbers and result in repeat assignments, but will remain a secondary source of revenue. On the other hand, it is unlikely that publicly offered seminars by hospital consulting firms will ever be a significant source of revenue. The costs of preparing, advertising, and conducting public seminars can, at best, be a loss leader. The seminar field is highly competitive and dominated by nonprofit organizations that do not recapture all of their expenses or have a built-in audience from a particular professional field. This restriction works to the disadvantage of consulting firms that will have to find a market in an overcrowded field.

Management training and development programs are not apt to be attractive to consulting firms. This is a specialized activity requiring different sets of skills from those possessed by consulting staffs and is marketed through different channels of communication at organizational levels not typically reached by consultants.

As hospitals restructure into health care corporations, the volume of organizational studies will increase. Since managing multiple operations on multiple sites is more complex than operations on a single site, assistance will be sought. Inevitably, organizational studies involve governance and senior management, along with defining interrelationships of positions and personalities. In order to maintain objectivity, outside firms will be used for these studies. Even systems that have their own consulting staffs will turn to outsiders because internal staffs would be suspect in this area. Some consulting firms will gain a reputation for this service, which will comprise a substantial part of their practices.

For the foreseeable future consulting services for management information systems, the articulation of clinical and financial data for DRGs, and financial feasibility studies will remain in the domain of the major accounting firms that have developed consulting practices in hospitals. Given the size of these firms and their audit practices, they have a lock on this market that will not be dislodged by hospital consulting firms.

The preparation of Certificates of Need, which has yielded substantial revenues for the past few years, will remain at existing levels but as economic competition matures, the need for health system agencies will disappear and they will be phased out. Along with their demise the consulting work associated with the preparation of CONs will gradually fade.

Departmental specialists that limit their practices to one field, such as the laboratory, dietary, or X-ray, will continue to survive, but the volumes of these activities are unlikely to grow. In the main they will be one- to two-person operations that will subcontract with a larger, more diversified hospital consulting firms as well as continuing to operate independently.

Productivity studies aimed at increasing institutional efficiency are likely to have the greatest increase due to a movement away from cost reimbursement and toward a pricing structure. To date, this area has never been in demand because of the widespread use of cost reimbursement as the dominant method of paying for hospital services. As pricing moves to the forefront, concern with productivity will rise and assistance will be sought from outside consultants.

The nationwide decline in hospital admissions will also add impetus to studies in that area. Within the consulting field the response to this growing demand will be from two directions. Hospital consulting firms are most apt to propose providing assistance that relies on judgment and experience in hospital operations, rather than on industrial engineering techniques. However, short-interval schedulers, using industrial engineering skills and relying on experiences gained in industry, can be expected to see the hospital field as an attractive opportunity. They will be the chief competition to existing hospital consulting firms. In addition, competition will come from corporate staffs of multihospital systems who will offer this service to hospitals in their systems.

The facilities planning services, which have been of major importance to the larger health field consulting firms, appear to be in a retrenchment phase. This will continue until such time as the federal government develops a firm position on paying for capital expenditures. The longer the government delays, the greater will be the pent-up demand for facilities studies. When the government publishes a capital payment formula there will probably be a surge of activity in this field.

Hospitals are dynamic, changing organizations, where departmental volumes of activities are constantly shifting at disproportionate rates, resulting in a need to modify physical plants. This arena will continue to be of prime importance indefinitely, though individual projects may be smaller or scheduled over a longer period of time than in the past. Since consultants are typically retained prior to architects, it can be anticipated that facility planning may include the schematic design stage and contract development in an effort to protect or expand revenues. When this occurs, consulting fees will be proportionately higher and architects' revenues decreased. In investor-owned chains, this service may be provided by the corporate staff and outside consultants may be excluded. In nonprofit chains that have autonomous, affiliated hospitals, outside consultants will continue to be called upon. Firms with existing substantial practices in facility planning will remain in the forefront. Newcomers will discover that facilities planning is a difficult field in which to become established.

Equipment planning will continue hand in hand with the volumes achieved in facilities planning. Over the next few years, independent equipment planners are likely to fade from the consulting scene as these specialists are added to the facility planning staffs of the more diversified hospital consulting firms. Since equipment planning is one of the later steps in facilities development, the independent equipment planners will find fewer and fewer opportunities to bid on projects because the facilities project has included it as part of the services being offered.

Consulting services to group practices of physicians will appear to be a market opportunity as group practices grow in number the next several years. Some firms will attempt to build part of their practice in this area but will discover the market place to be too thin to be a worthwhile activity. The need for consulting services will be present, but the demand will be insignificant because of the unwillingness of group practices to pay the level of fees quoted to them.

COMPETITIVE FORCES

Over the next decade competition will increase among consultants. It will not only be from firms already in the field, but from those that had not previously entered the consulting arena. There will be considerable movement in and out of the field. Most of those who enter will not remain, even if they have substantial capitalization. Companies that are major suppliers of products to the health field will be among the casualties that try and fail. Even though supplier firms have financial staying power, corporate management will view their consulting division as another product division in the company. The results will not be in keeping with initial expectations and after a few years this effort will be phased out.

Chains of hospitals will also establish internal consulting groups to be used by hospitals in the chain as well as selling services in direct competition to unaffiliated hospitals. In time, the consulting practices of such groups will largely be limited to affiliated hospitals. The services are likely to be limited to improving internal operations and space planning.

In both approaches, by hospital supply companies and chain operators of hospitals, long-term survivability in consulting is questionable because corporation executives who create them lack the necessary understandings of what is required in terms of talent, salary levels, and fringe benefits, and, moreover, have false expectations about results. These sources do not pose a serious competitive threat to independent health field consulting firms.

Concern may be felt about the trend in larger hospitals to employ a director of planning in the belief that this person will provide the same services previously purchased on the outside. It is probable that the collection of basic data will be accomplished by the in-house staff, but because of a familiarity with the consulting field, the director of planning is apt to be the internal person who will in fact trigger the use of outside consultants. This is so because he will recognize a project's requirements as being beyond the skills of the in-house staff. Overall, it can be anticipated that the growth of in-house planners will contribute to growth in consulting.

Since the capitalization needed to enter consulting is modest, the future may well see experienced consultants in existing firms break away and start up new firms. This is likely to occur more frequently in the future as individuals decide early in their careers to make hospital consulting a life-long activity. If they find their own progress blocked, they are not as apt to seek employment in a hospital as they are to start their own firm or seek a position in another consulting firm.

CONSULTING AS A PROFESSION

Today, hospital consulting is a profession. It has a professional society that provides a credentialing process certifying competency levels of members. Growing numbers of persons who provide consulting services in the health field are joining its ranks. In a real sense the professional association has brought stability to the field. It has also been helpful to graduate students by drawing attention to this field of endeavor as one having potential for life-long careers. Today, many students deliberately plan careers in consulting. This level of commitment for the long term provides the best assurance that the future of health field consulting will be brighter than ever before. The quality of the persons entering the field and the quality of the work performed continues to improve every year. Under such circumstances it can only be concluded that bright, dedicated, and self-disciplined consultants are going to find increasingly better ways to serve the clients in their chosen fields of endeavor.

Chapter 47

Reflections on Ray E. Brown: Model Hospital Executive

Occasionally in life one meets a totally unique person who leaves a deep imprint on one's professional life. Ray E. Brown was such a person. Among hospital executives, Ray was a giant who stood head and shoulders above his colleagues. It seems appropriate for the authors to share their thoughts about a person who was regarded by his colleagues as a national resource, who led the field, by example, during the decades of the '50s and '60s. For those of you who knew Ray, we hope this stirs fond memories. For those who never had that opportunity, we think you may simply enjoy these personal comments about a man who contributed much to the advancement of our profession. In his career, Ray was a full professor at the University of Chicago, Duke University, Harvard University, and Northwestern University, in addition to his other activities.

One of the delightful experiences in life is to be asked to honor a friend, one's teacher, a person who was unselfish, totally absorbed in his chosen field, and a pragmatist. He saw both good and bad in people, but recognized that we are all human and in need of strength of will and perseverance if we are to reach a personal goal.

Despite Ray's reputation as the totally rational man, we clearly remember his weakness at the poker table where he was sure that a one-card draw would complete an inside straight. He saw life as a large poker game in which both luck and good sense played a role. In one's career and in the accomplishments attained, he held the same viewpoint. He thought of hospitals in the same way.

Throughout his career, Ray progressively became more interested in the concept of organizational effectiveness, never questioning the need for it, but rather examining the why and how of the organizational environment. He believed in the administrative process as the primary vehicle for achieving organizational effectiveness. His entire professional career was based on an insatiable curiosity about this idea and how it worked in the real world. In effect, he was a real-world researcher who carried a title of superintendent or vice president of the University of Chicago.

He was regarded as an administrator and executive of great competence but who, in fact, was a persistent researcher gathering insights in a variety of environments. Had he been willing to accept the limitations of existing social science methodologies, he would have become a pure scientist. He didn't because he saw the intricacies involved in understanding organizational effectiveness as being beyond the techniques of social science. Had he accepted these limits he would have been a full-time professor rather than an administrative officer in a university who, incidentally, was a full professor.

Ray's mind set explains to a substantial degree why he was, throughout his professional career in hospital administration, always associated in one way or another with universities. He needed to be continually aware of happenings in the analytical world so that he could include these developments in his own reasoning.

The real world and its potential for goodness was the key to his interest in hospital administration. In his chosen field he saw a real chance to contribute to humanity because he strongly felt a need to be his brother's keeper. Ray did not have the time, even though he possessed the intellect, to work out new methodologies in the social sciences. He wanted a more direct way to contribute his talents and energies to his fellow man.

These essential characteristics, then, are the essence of the Ray Brown we knew. He was a man for whom no challenge was too great in hospital administration, who delighted in using his very bright mind continually on the critical health care issues of his times, and who willingly responded to every request for leadership if it was remotely possible to squeeze it into an always overloaded time schedule. Ray's definition of a vacation was an escape from the daily rigors of an administrative position in order to have time to think, uninterrupted, about the administrative process in health care in order to improve organizational effectiveness.

Our society today is much in need of Ray's touch. The 30-plus years of his professional life occurred mostly during a period of unparalleled expansion of resources committed to health care. He welcomed the arrival of additional resources because they provided increased access to good medical care. At the same time these new resources were channeled into an existing institutional structure that maintained the status quo. It was not a time for serious innovation.

For example, the idea of a health maintenance organization, by whatever its name, would have, and did for Kaiser-Permanente, lead to intransigent opposition from national organizations. Yet, Ray, who was politically sensible, did not publish crusading articles in support of Kaiser, but privately saw the worthwhileness of this form of medical care delivery, with the caveat that there was a limit to paying physicians a bonus for not doing what might need doing when it came to hospitalizing patients. He would have supported the health maintenance organization concept as we now know it, but he would have been leading the charge on the measurement of quality medicine in these types of organizations.

During his time in health care, the major drive in our society was toward bigger being better. We went from jeeps to oversized "gas guzzlers" dripping with chrome, and everybody had a better ride. Now there are some serious thoughts that the wheels are about ready to roll off.

The same phenomenon has happened in health care that occurred in the automotive industry. What was previously successful will not work tomorrow. It is a day for considering as acceptable what was unacceptable yesterday. Ray Brown would have been exhilarated by this opportunity. His legacy of pragmatism and courage, which he instilled in those whom he touched, is the foundation on which we build new approaches to organizing medical care.

One of his basic principles was the desirability, and necessity, for all Americans to equally share the benefits of modern medical care. He was a supporter of social insurance as the vehicle for providing equal access to medical care. The shortfall that happened in Social Security funding and the possible deficits in Medicare in the years ahead would have troubled his sense of responsibility, but he would also have viewed the situation as an opportunity to create a more permanent solution.

He would have disputed the need to fix hospital prices through a diagnostic related group mechanism and would have disputed the unilateral prerogative of the Secretary of Health and Human Services to set prices. As a believer in free-market mechanisms, he would have sought a way to ensure the wide availability of medical care services, but would not have insisted on a right for all hospitals to survive.

In writing about organizational effectiveness, he once said:

> How hospitals develop and how they are run will depend upon how hospitals are evaluated. Effective administration of any sort always accommodates in the long run to the evaluations of those it attempts to serve. The evaluations of the hospital reflect to administration the thinking of those affected by the hospital and fix the image that hospital administration seeks to follow. This means that the evaluation of hospital administration is not so much concerned with the process by which hospitals are administered as it is with the purpose for which they are administered.[1]

He recognized the power of the purse as a meaningful evaluation system. Consequently, he would have argued for a Medicare voucher system in which the patient had a choice of hospital and physician, as well as in selecting a health maintenance organization, an independent practice association, or fee-for-service medicine. For routine medical care he would have supported a voucher system authorizing a fixed annual dollar amount for each Medicare participant, perhaps adjusted by age with increasing dollars for each decade over 65 years of age.

As a realist, he would have recognized the need for catastrophic coverage. However, he would have provided against overutilization by insisting on an uninsurable corridor of a meaningful amount that would be paid by the patient before triggering catastrophic payments. Pragmatically, he knew that unlimited protection for medical expenses would only lead to excessive utilization. He viewed deductibles and co-insurance schemes as being of limited usefulness. Once the threshold is passed, or a low co-insurance feature is used, there is no meaningful control on utilization. Likewise, he was aware that for the vast majority of retired people, an out-of-pocket expenditure of $2,000 was taken more seriously than a $200,000 bill since there was no possibility of ever repaying an indebtedness of that magnitude, while a reasonable debt would stimulate repayment.

Ray would have superficially accepted the use of a diagnostic related group payment mechanism because of the circumstances surrounding its enactment by Congress. Fundamentally, though, he would have had reservations about its long-term successful implementation. He would have recognized that a DRG system based on a mean of Medicare hospital charges essentially means that roughly one-half of all hospital payments on each DRG are less than adequate from an administrative perspective. Therefore, financial difficulties at some point in the future would occur.

One of Ray's observations about people was that everyone had at least 10 percent larceny in their hearts. He recognized that perfect market forces do not exist, except in an economist's hypothesis. He was aware that, sooner or later, both hospitals and bureaucrats would protect their particular interests. He would have reasoned that the initiative for a DRG system was the result of hospital, physician, and patient financial abuse of a cost-based system, which would lead, in turn, to an abuse by government of the DRG system.

Because of foresight his reaction would have been to begin thinking about ways for hospitals to react when they went bankrupt. He knew that Blue Cross and the commercial health insurance carriers would adopt a DRG payment system to escape large-scale cost shifting in hospital rate structures. His mind would have focused on how to use free-market forces to promote efficiency in the use of hospital resources and judicious use by consumers.

Ray was basically a free enterpriser, but within limits. He believed in the worthwhileness of people and their right to personal dignity and accepted the constitutional right of Congress to legislate limits on personal and institutional freedoms. At the same time he recognized the weakness of Congress in reining in the role of government. These two conflicting rights, personal freedom and congressional authority, would have made him consider whether or not a ceiling should be placed on nontaxable health care expenditures. Because he was an astute compromiser of conflicting goals, it is probable that he would have suggested a program that focused both rights on the same goal. He probably would have said that it was acceptable to tax excessive health care expenditures if these taxes were segregated and used to provide catastrophic medical coverage.

On the issues of business coalitions and preferred provider organizations, he would have followed his free-market beliefs, which is to say that they are manifestations of a market philosophy and are appropriate mechanisms for these times.

To people familiar with his many writings and speeches, he was seen as a man of enormous abilities and complex thoughts. To those who knew him well, Ray Brown's complexity was his ability to apply a handful of fundamental beliefs about the nature of mankind. These were reflected in countless ways. Experience had taught him that people are capable of expressing numberless nuances of a central concept. In that process people twist, willingly and unwittingly, a major idea into a personal or institutional purpose, to give themselves an additional advantage. In typical nonargumentative style, he expressed this notion as follows:

> Evaluation is always a complex form of measurement because it attempts to measure the value or worth of a thing. Value is a subjective concept in that it depends more upon the notions of those affected by a thing than the qualities of the thing itself. The more purposes a thing is supposed to serve the more difficult it is to evaluate it properly. The greater the number of individuals or groups it affects, the greater the variations in evaluations that are likely to occur. This problem of diversity of purpose and of groups affected is enormously complicated if some purposes are in part in competition with one another. This is the quandary of trustees and administrators. It is also the problem of those who attempt to evaluate hospital administration.[2]

If he had been asked his opinion about the development of both investor-owned and nonprofit multihospital systems in the last decade, he would have encouraged their growth, not as a way of satisfying personal goals, but as a device to gain economies of scale. He was aware that limits exist on a freestanding hospital since it cannot maximize efficient use of resources. At the same time he placed a higher value on serving the physical, spiritual, and psychological needs of each patient rather than maximizing profits. He recognized that a hospital could reach a bureaucratic size that would prevent meeting all of the needs of individual patients. He would not have sacrificed the one for the other.

What he would have done is keep those functions necessary for quality patient care at the local level and centralize other functions at higher organizational levels to improve economies of scale without adversely impacting direct patient care.

Ray recognized that the hospital marketplace is a local one, except for the tertiary medical center that serves a regional market. He would have supported the idea that local hospital monopolies should be prevented and would have favored applying antitrust laws locally to prevent a multihospital system from unfair manipulation of a local market.

If questioned about the greater desirability of nonprofit hospital systems or investor-owned systems, he would have surprised some people. He believed in health care for all as a worthwhile ideal. He would not have been against profits for investor-owned systems. He would have taken the position that as long as society allowed profits to be earned by providing health care services he could understand why investor-owned chains existed. In fact, he would have thought it desirable to have hospital services available in markets that would not otherwise have hospitals. To him it was more important to have reasonable availability of hospital care, no matter its corporate form. If price determines the availability of hospitals, as it does in today's market, the fundamental issue is not price, but equality of competition in seeking to provide patient services.

In terms of current happenings, he would have favored the elimination of return on equity for investor-owned hospitals, provided a cost-based system of reimbursement was eliminated and replaced with a price-based system. What he would have said to the investor-owned systems is, now prove by a fair test in the marketplace that you are more efficient. Given the recent tax code changes, which favor the higher retention of earnings by for-profit hospitals to stimulate capital formation, he would have advised the nonprofit hospitals to convert to a for-profit corporate form to gain the same advantage. Because of his free-enterprise orientation he would have watched the results with sophisticated interest.

In his heart Ray was a Jeffersonian Democrat. He believed that somehow, some way, the public is the best judge of what is best for them. If the public is provided with a score sheet that equitably measures performance, citizens will vote with their feet. That is, given equal compensation for equal performance, the public will choose to buy their medical care services from hospitals they believe best serve their needs. While different qualities of medical care may be difficult for the nonprofessional to distinguish in detail, the public will recognize the differences in hospital and physician performance that lead to rapid recovery or slow, painful recovery for the same price. How it is accomplished is not of concern, only that they know the difference, and therefore use those institutions and medical practitioners that best meet their medical and economic imperatives.

One of Ray's favorite observations about hospital administration was that, at best (given the existing three-cornered hospital structure of governance, medical staff, and administration), it is probable that an effective administrative process can influence 10 to 15 percent of the efficiencies and outcomes of the operations of the hospital. He did not bemoan this state of affairs but accepted it as a reality of the times and the result of earlier battles won and lost.

He also frequently commented that the effective hospital executive was the only patient advocate available in most hospital settings. In his mind the typical trustee was fulfilling a personal psychological need that was unmet in his own business affairs. He saw physicians as perceiving patients as a way to repeatedly examine their insights into scientific medicine. Though he knew these were not universal truths, he saw sufficient evidence to be aware that this was the basis for much of what he observed.

Both of these observations would have been on his mind as he thought about the course of events that lies ahead of us. It is quite clear that we are beginning a reorganizing process in medical care that will increase the influence of the hospital executive. The public's message to the health care establishment is that the total separativeness of medical care and its cost is no longer tolerable. As quality medical care and medical economics are blended into a new unity, the value of balanced, disciplined judgments in mixing medical and business decisions will substantially increase.

An increased opportunity for administrative effectiveness would have pleased Ray. He would have exhorted hospital executives to make the most of the new opportunity and he would have sought a position that would allow him to show the field how to do it. In a situation of equal competition he would have been a fierce competitor. Patients, hospital personnel, and physicians would be the beneficiaries, and those associated with his hospital would experience a real-world definition of meaningful personal effort.

Throughout his active management career Ray's interest in university-based education for hospital executives never flagged. He encouraged curriculums that integrated operating knowledge, skills, and understanding of human behavior with insights about the thinking processes and imperatives inherent in medicine. He regarded development of large-scale multihospital systems as requiring a combination of traditional training in hospital administration for the successful management of a medical care enterprise along with the business skills honored in the graduate schools of business, as basic to a billion-dollar health care corporation.

Throughout Ray's career he was often asked if he thought the qualifications for appointment as chief executive officer of a hospital should be limited to physicians. His invariable response was vintage Ray Brown: whoever had the best skills for the responsibilities of the position was the person to select. If a physician had medical skills without the necessary administrative skills he would be a poor choice, while a nonphysician with administrative skills but no understandings about the dimensions of medical care would likewise be a poor choice. He believed that motivated, intelligent people could acquire any knowledge they wished to have without following a formal university curriculum. On the other hand, a university curriculum, prepared by knowledgeable teachers, in his opinion, provided a faster and more sure-footed way to reach a selected goal. This is why he remained interested and associated with universities. He believed the profession of hospital administration was a worthwhile way to spend one's life because it served humanity in a significant way.

While Ray was a disciplined person, he was also a pioneer. He wanted to be a part of the cutting edge of a developing profession. At a different time and place he would have been attracted to exploring space as an astronaut. He was always more demanding of himself than of an associate. He had an intensity of purpose without any arrogance in performance. He was a man of his times, understanding how we arrived at where we were in health care and enthusiastic about moving ahead to higher levels of organizational effectiveness. In many ways he created the conditions that are now moving health care into a more rational delivery system. He would have been optimistic about its future, while cautioning hospital administration to remain oriented to the goals of delivering quality hospital care and avoiding the temptation to use an enlarged administrative process for personal advantage.

During his career Ray published over 180 articles in the leading journals. In addition he co-authored one book and authored another, *Judgment in Administration*. The latter never received the acclaim it deserved from the business community, probably because of his hospital background. Nevertheless, it stands as one of the most thoughtful books ever written about management.

In recalling events about Ray, the classic one that took place in the spring of 1964 succinctly tells it all. President Lyndon Johnson asked his advisers who was the most knowledgeable man in the United States on health care.   Told that it was Ray Brown, he instructed the White House operator to track him down and get him on the phone. Ray was located in a large city several hundred miles from home, just completing a speech. Called to the phone he picked it up and said, "Hello, this is Ray Brown." The voice on the other end said, "This is the President." Ray said, "The president of what?" The voice said, "The President of the United States."

NOTES

1. Ray E. Brown, *Judgment in Administration* (Chicago: Pluribus Press, Div. of Teach 'em, Inc. and American College of Hospital Administrators, 1982), 135.

2. Ibid., 180.

Epilogue

Chapter 48

Doing Good—At What Price?

The dawn of a new era arrived on the hospital scene a few years ago. Hospitals are now under fire from the public as they adjust and readjust to the new environment in which they must now operate. The good old days of friendly and gentlemanly rivalry have disappeared along with cost reimbursement. The reshaping of the hospital industry is underway but no one seems to know the configuration that will emerge as the dominant pattern.

For the past 50 years hospitals and physicians grew and prospered by "doing good." As medicine and hospital care became more costly, those representing the public interest increasingly insisted on economic competition as a means of curbing rising costs. "Doing good" is still important but it is no longer the sole criterion used to judge the worthwhileness of the care being rendered. A second dimension, at what price, has joined doing good as being primary in importance.

Historically, the building blocks for the health field were community general hospitals, fee-for-service physicians, and nonprofit prepayment plans (Blue Cross). Around this core were nursing homes, retirement homes, visiting nurse associations, and large state-operated psychiatric institutions. Each had a clearly defined role and the health system operated in an orderly fashion. The goal of a hospital in this system was to increase its comprehensiveness in providing acute care services and to have specialists and subspecialists in substantial majority on the medical staff. Pride was taken in being the most expensive hospital in an area if it was attained by offering more services than any other hospital in the community. Success meant becoming a tertiary care hospital, a referral center, or a medical center. "Doing good" for every patient for everything that might be physiologically wrong was what an acute hospital was all about.

This goal began to be challenged in the decade of the 1970s when there was a widespread recognition that the resources of the country were finite and the availability of funds for health care were no longer unlimited. In order to restrain hospital expenditures, which annually rose much faster than the consumer price index, the federal government undertook a variety of programs. None of these could be counted as successful. During this period, business and industry were passive but unhappy with annual increases they incurred in premiums for employee health insurance. With the economic recession of the early years of the 1980s passiveness was replaced with an aggressive posture towards containing hospital costs and thereby premium increases. In looking around for a point of attack on the problem, business and industry discovered that hospitals were paid for all of the operating costs they incurred, justified or not. This shocked businessmen accustomed to a price system, who quickly appreciated that hospitals could not economically fail since they operated on a cost reimbursement system.

In the mind's eye of trustees, physicians, and management, "doing good" was an adequate justification for a built-in revenue system that protected hospitals from economic failure. But once the business community came to understand that hospital payments were quite different from anything else they were familiar with, they began to look for ways that would bring economics into play. The result was a two-pronged strategy.

Large corporations came to understand that over the course of years in labor management contract negotiations they had bargained away the relationship between an incident of illness and any economic consequence for a patient. By paying first-dollar coverage with no deductible, corporations had unknowingly unhooked them, thereby encouraging uncontrolled usage of health services. The recession of 1981 to 1983 provided an opportunity to redress this oversight.

Taking this step corrected only one-half of the problem. Companies still felt a need to introduce economic competition into the health field marketplace. In casting about for an appropriate mechanism there was a rediscovery of capitation plans and national interest was quickly focused on them. Capitation plans had been on the health scene for nearly 50 years and had received a boost in 1973 when Congress passed the Health Maintenance Act in order to encourage the development of HMOs. By the time the decade of the 1980s began, new HMOs were springing up across the country and focusing their marketing efforts on large employee groups. Feeling threatened by this surge of interest in capitation plans, many hospitals and physician groups banded together to offer large employers discounts through preferred provider organizations.

What had been a neat, orderly, and disciplined prepayment industry has become a jungle of competitive interests in the short span of a few years. All of the participants, old and new, are avidly chasing the insurance dollar. Both the business community and the federal government are delighted. They had changed an uncontrollable expense into a controlled expense. For hospitals and physicians, their gravest fears have been realized. "Doing good" has been joined by at-what-price service. Economic competition has arrived. Occupancy rates in hospitals, which had dropped 10 to 15 percent accompanied by layoffs of personnel, occurred for the first time since the depression of the 1930s. Hospitals have become a mature industry with an overabundance of beds that will continue to increase in the years ahead.

The second major component, physicians, also faced significant changes in their marketplace. Office visits per capita have steadily decreased as a result of the reintroduction of copayments and deductibles in prepayment plans. At the same time, the number of physicians in active practice increased by 50 percent in a period of ten years. Physicians realize that as capitation plans grow, patients no longer have free choice of physicians but must seek care from physicians who have contracts with a capitation plan. This contract between the plan and the physician calls for a negotiated price, eliminating the "usual, reasonable, and customary" (URC) fee that traditionally governed payment for physician's services.

The third major building block, prepayment plans that paid hospitals on a cost reimbursement basis and the commercial carriers that paid on a billed charges basis, came under intense pressure from the newly formed capitation plans. In order to protect its share of the market, the prepayment plans developed their own capitation plans thereby giving the insured groups a choice.

While these changes were taking place, the federal government shifted its method of Medicare payment to hospitals. By the mid-1980s, this accounted for 42 percent of all patient days of care in acute, general hospitals. Over a four-year phase-in period, cost reimbursement would be abandoned and a fixed-price payment schedule adopted for 467 different diagnoses. This move further threatened the revenue base of hospitals.

The freestanding voluntary, nonprofit community hospital that had been the cornerstone of the health field in the twentieth century now finds itself under fire from every direction. Physicians and medical staff are now developing competing outpatient services in their offices, PPOs are insisting on larger and larger discounts, HMOs are putting the hospitals at risk, while the federal government through its Medicare and Medicaid programs is increasing constraints on payments to hospitals, and within the hospital field hospitals are selling out to large investor-owned chains or joining chains if they are nonprofit. In the course of a few years, one-third of all of the acute hospitals have left the ranks of the freestanding and are in chains. By the mid-1980s the rush was on to join a hospital system. Institutions that have not already done so are now looking around for partners and feeling threatened that they have not moved more quickly.

Looking to the future, it is evident that it will be quite different from the past and for the next few years economics of care are going to have a leading role, forcing quality of care issues into the background. Hospitals that join nonprofit chains will, in time, become skeptical of the ability of chains to compete successfully with the for-profit chains. Because nonprofit chains do not have a common decision-making structure and lack a combined balance sheet their efforts are restricted to activities that are commonly agreed to by a majority of the participants, such as a joint purchasing program. The emphasis is on programs and services that have only a limited financial impact on the operations of hospitals.

The greatest weakness of nonprofit chains has not yet been recognized. Since hospitals in this kind of system are financially independent, they are not responsible for the fiscal condition of any other hospital in the system. As competitive bidding develops among hospitals for HMO contracts, this lack of common ownership will work to the disadvantage of nonprofit chains. For-profit chains will be better positioned because the loss of an HMO contract in any particular area of the country can be offset by gaining one in another region. As long as the net result of contracts lost and contracts won is stable, for-profit chains will remain viable. This is not the case for nonprofit chains where the loss of a single contract may be of such impact that a hospital cannot financially survive. Since HMOs now involve 10 percent or less of the population, the likelihood of this happening in the near future is remote, but in ten years when a majority of the public may have such coverage this will become a serious matter. Nonprofit chains will lack the financial strength that comes with common ownership.

Among the large for-profit chains, corporate interests have shifted and they are no longer aggressively seeking to expand the number of hospitals they own. Rather, they have now focused their attention on establishing, and/or purchasing capitation plans. This strategy in an economically driven marketplace is highly responsive to the interests of corporations with large numbers of employees. By offering a benefit package that is competitive and in addition guarantees to hold premium levels constant for three years they are now quickly moving into the forefront for the purchasers of health insurance. Their ability to offer a cost-controlled package is due to one organization running and controlling both the prepayment arm and hospitals in the program. In order to successfully compete against this competition hospital chains and commercial insurance carriers are going to have to offer a similar type of program.

In the next decade, free choice of physician by patients will decline at the rate that enrollment in capitation plans grows, since physicians will have to contract with plans to provide services. Because of this financial arrangement, the basis of payment, which has been reasonable, customary, and usual, will be replaced by a negotiated rate between a plan and a physician. The shift in the basis of payment will lead to lower fees for individual units of service. The impact on physician incomes is likely to be dramatic because of a decline in the average number of visits per person as a result of coinsurance requirements in health insurance as well as a rapid increase in the number of physicians in practice. In all probability, physician incomes are apt to decline by one-third in the next several years because of these two factors. In addition, the cost of malpractice insurance has risen rapidly and sharply, with the annual premium ranging between 10 and 40 percent of gross income.

In the face of these trends, the influence of a physician in the health care picture is going to diminish. Because the supply of available physicians is becoming greater than the demand for their services, greater flexibility in making financial arrangements with individual physicians will result in a move away from fee-for-service practice. Pricing will become more dominant than the quality of physician services in spite of any actions physician groups might take to thwart this outcome.

Among prepayment plans, economic competition will also lead to major changes in the way they do business. For the next several years, the prepayment arena will be a jumble of new entrants and existing carriers all attempting to create a market niche for themselves. Inevitably, a shake-out will occur. Some will fail, some will grow, some will be absorbed, and ultimately only a handful will dominate the national scene, but with strong, local HMOs in some market areas.

At the present stage of development, the winners and the losers cannot be predicted. Some of the winners will come from the ranks of the investor-owned hospital chains, others from traditional insurance carriers, and others from aggressive entrepreneurial groups that enter the marketplace early and make the right decisions. Local HMOs that survive will likely be the ones sponsored by one or more local hospitals to capture their community marketplaces early on and prevent other groups from entering.

Hospitals as an industry are in an overbuilt condition as a result of shorter lengths of stay. Occupancy rates have fallen, even though the number of admissions has not declined but remained at about the same level. With capitation plans now enrolling approximately 10 percent of the population and the likelihood of a rise to 50 percent by 1995, excess capacity will grow since capitation plans typically use only one-third the number of patient days usually consumed under cost-reimbursement and indemnity forms of coverage. Of the 5,220 community hospitals, many will disappear in the years ahead because of a lack of patients.

With all of the cross-currents of events at work in the health field it is difficult to forecast the size and configuration of the field by the time the next century rolls around. Trends are easily identifiable, but how far each goes, how one trend interacts with another, these are the imponderables that will determine whether the health field becomes larger or smaller, or continues to be dominated by general hospitals as the centerpiece of the health field, or whether quality of patient care improves or deteriorates. These factors are unknowns.

By the time the twenty-first century is entered, the balance between "doing good" and "at what price" will have stabilized. The time when this takes place can be visualized as a balance with patient care on one side of the scale and price on the other side. Where the scale comes to rest depends less on health care issues and more on economic outcomes in the general economics of the country. Three basic scenarios can be forecast:

1. "Doing good" and "at what price" are equal.
2. "Doing good" dominates and "at what price" becomes secondary.
3. "Doing good" becomes secondary and "at what price" dominates.

Under each scenario outcomes will be quite different. Over the course of the next decade and a half, as reversals occur, the element that will dominate will be an equilibrium between the two by the end of the century. In all probability a balance between quality and price is the most likely outcome.

"Doing good" has dominated the health scene for over 50 years and has only recently been challenged by "at what price." Because of its newness, "at what price" has received much attention and "doing good" has been neglected. Should this trend continue unabated until the next century, the result will be a two-tier medical care system, one for the haves, the other for the have-nots, and will include those patients enrolled in the Medicare program if it continues to reimburse hospitals under a DRG system.

Given the rise of economic competition in the health field, it is difficult to imagine that doing good will continue to dominate. Physicians would prefer not to consider cost as an inhibiting constraint on their ordering of tests. Though physicians will be pressured to do so by the payers of the health bill, physicians may elect to ignore pressure in order to protect themselves from a malpractice standpoint. With annual premiums reaching astronomical proportions for malpractice insurance, physicians may routinely take the viewpoint that they order tests and prescribe treatments from a legal standpoint, rather than from a standpoint of what is needed for patient care. Under such circumstances, "doing good" will become a rubric for quality patient care. In the event that legislation is not enacted at both the federal and state levels to moderate malpractice suits, physicians will be forced to practice medicine from the standpoint of "If I'm called into the courtroom to defend myself, I can demonstrate that I have ordered every conceivable test and procedure that demonstrates competence on my part."

Without some form of protective legislation for physicians, the outcome by the end of the twentieth century will be a health system that ignores the economics because it is physician driven by a concern for malpractice judgments that could ruin them economically. This pattern of behavior will be recognized as a public issue in the next few years and legislation will be enacted by the end of the decade to prevent continuation of large malpractice judgments. It is unlikely that "doing good" will enjoy more support than pricing considerations because of the current malpractice crisis.

In the mid-1980s, with all of its furor and interest in economic competition, the future of the health field may seem to be greater and stiffer economic competition, as far ahead as one can see. Such, however, will not be the case. As economic screws are tightened, those doing the tightening will not know when a point is reached that jeopardizes patient care and will continue to force concessions from hospitals. Some hospitals will resist, in order to protect patient care, but a large majority may well ignore internal warnings and continue to meet the demands of the bill payers, either capitation plans or the federal government. Eventually, a number of horror stories will surface, and as they increase there will be a belated public outcry about the deterioration of the quality of care that has taken place in American hospitals. When this happens there will be a loosening of purse strings. Hospitals will then move back to a balance between "doing good" and "at what price." By the turn of the next century, equilibrium should be achieved. How long a new equilibrium lasts, what directions and trends then ensue, is for the next generation to determine. In the meantime, the health field will be characterized by volatility and uncertainty. To those who enjoy challenges the opportunities will be unsurpassed.

Index

A

Accreditation Commission on Education
for Health Administration, 381
Administrative educational programs.
See Education
Administrative judgment, 415-16, 417,
418
Administrators, 55. *See also* Chief
executive officers (CEOs)
economic competition and, 11
investor-owned hospital, 322
multihospital second-level, 355-56
Admissions, consulting services and,
424
Admitting privileges, 276
Advertising, 254
Ambulatory care, 87
American College of Healthcare
Executives, 414, 419
American College of Surgeons, 275
American Hospital Association, 402
Anderson, Odin, 21
Anesthetists, 280, 312, 313
Arbitration (management contract),
95

Architect (choice of), 73
Autonomy, management contracts and,
93

B

Barnard, Chester I., 110
Bid contracts, 26, 177-78
Billing
hospital overbilling and, 162
Medicare and, 314
Blue Cross, 73, 112, 134, 320, 387, 392
capitation plans and, 28, 29
competition and, 5
forming of, 3-4
industry restructuring and, 24
Board of trustees, 251
CEOs and, 14, 15, 60, 61, 62-63,
178-79, 183-84, 187, 189, 191,
194, 195, 334
termination and, 197, 198, 199
characteristics and composition of,
67-68
cost control and, 109-114
developing responsive, 333-36

economic issues and, 386-87, 390
external health care industry stresses
    and, 339
finance and change and, 56
freestanding hospital, 345
health care industry trends and,
    318-19, 321
hospital construction and, 47-48
judgment of CEOs and, 332-33,
    413-14
management contracts and, 91-92, 96
    control and, 93
    reports and, 94
medical staff self governance and,
    258-59, 260-62, 264
multihospital systems and, 339, 341,
    343, 345
nonprofit hospital, 343
organizational structure and, 59-61
    centralization and, 63-64
        giving more authority to CEO and,
            62-63
        physicians on board and, 61-62
physician contracts and, 292-93
physician dominated, 328
physicians and, 390
planning strategies and, 39, 42, 43
revenue and, 367
selecting, 66-67
voluntary hospital, 341
Brown, Ray E., as model executive,
    427-34
Budgeting, 18-19, 23
    CEO and, 182
Building projects. *See* Construction
    (hospital); Construction projects
Business coalitions, 431

C

Capital, hospital planning deregulation
    and, 100. *See also* Finance
Capital construction projects. *See*
    Construction (hospital); Construction
    projects

Capitation plans, 438, 439, 441. *See
    also* Reimbursement
    concern over plans of, 29
    control of plans of, 30, 31
    health care industry and, 5-6, 324-26
        oligopsony and, 6-7
    HMOs and, 27-29
    hospital revenues and, 368-69
    shared ownership and, 8-9
Catholic hospitals, 349-50
Centralization, 63-64
Certificate of need (CON), 25, 387
    construction project case example
        and, 76-78
    consulting services and, 424
    planning regulation and, 99, 105
Chief executive officers (CEOs). *See
    also* Administrators
    abilities of, 188
    alternative career routes of, 190
    board of trustees and, 14, 15, 60, 61,
        178-79, 187, 189, 191, 194, 195,
        334
        broader power to CEO and, 62-63,
            183-84
    Brown as model of, 427-34
    business activities and, 187, 239
    capitation and, 6-7
    changing organizational relationships
        and, 14
    changing role of, 193-96
    character of, 207-208
    construction project case example
        and, 72-79
    corporate restructuring and, 17-18
    cost control and, 109-114
    decision making and, 177-78, 183-84
    economic competition and, 177,
        180-81
    education of
        academic program and, 382-83
        health administration and, 413-20
        MBA curriculum and, 383-84, 415
        new graduate placement and,
            380-81
        student background and, 381

student years of, 207-211
university faculty and, 379-80,
    414, 415
emotional and behavioral traits
    of, 209
entrepreneurial instinct and, 181-82
expanding role of, 68-69
finance and, change and, 56
future trends and, 20
governance and organizational
    structure and, 65-66, 190-91
hospital construction and, 47-48
hospital productivity and, 215-16
investor-owned hospitals and, 189
judgment of, 332-33
leadership and, 18-19
management changes and, 11-12, 20
management contracts and, 91-92
management evaluation and, 12-13
medical knowledge and, 252
medical staff and, 16-17, 179-81, 195
    organization and, 261-63, 267,
    271, 273
multihospital systems and, 331, 351,
    362
in nonprofit hospitals, 179, 187-91,
    194, 239
performance of, 188-89
personality of, 207, 208-210
physicians and, 68, 69, 177, 179-80
    conflict with, 57-58
        development of, 58-59
        medical practice and, 252
    contracts and, 297, 305
    hospital-based, 289, 291, 292
political skills and, 12
professional background of
    (education), 207-211
recruiting of, 423
regulation and, 178-79
retaining of talented, 326
risk taking and, 15-16, 177, 179,
    181, 195
salary of, 189
source of talented, 389-90
style and, 208, 209, 210

teaching hospitals and, 19-20, 182-83
termination (case example) and,
    197-206
transitional aspects of position of
    coping with organizational factors
        and, 241-44
    keeping organizational and personal
        worlds separate and, 235
    organizational ambiguity and,
        240-41
    scheduling frustrations and, 237-40
    stress and, 236-37
    voluntary hospitals and, 341
Clinical chief, election of, 261
Clinical services, 40-41, 223, 229,
    230-34, 366
Clinical skills, 269
Chrysler Corporation, 216
Collective bargaining, 22
Communication, multihospital system
    and, 354
Community interests
    board and, 66-67
    hospital and, 38
    hospital type and, 319
    multihospital systems and, 360
Community needs, hospital planning
    and, 100
Competition, 326, 328, 438
    construction programs and, 47-48, 50
    consulting services and, 425-26
    cooperation and, 15
    deregulation of hospital planning and,
        99-107
    economic (between providers)
        change in organizational
            relationships and, 14
        corporate restructuring and, 17-18
        future trends and, 20
        leadership and, 18-19
        management change and,
            11-12, 20
        management evaluation and, 12-13
        medical staff and, 16-17
        political skills of CEO and, 12
        risk taking and, 15-16

teaching hospitals and, 19-20
trustees and, 14, 15
health care industry and, 4-5, 24, 25,
    26, 30
oligopsony and, 6-7
medical practice and, 248, 250-51,
    253, 255
medical staff and, 263-64
planning and marketing strategies for
    clinical services and, 40-41
    organizational structure and, 42-44
    skills and techniques used in,
        39-40
    use of, 37-39
shared ownership and, 8, 9
unknowns of
    American concept of
        competition and, 33-34
    patient and physician and, 34
    two-tier care system and, 35-36
Confidentiality
    management contract and, 95
    physician contract and, 302
Conflict of interest, management
    contracts and, 95
Congressional Budget Office,
    Medicare's Hospital Insurance Trust
    Fund and, 135-37, 142, 144, 146, 151
Construction (hospital). *See also*
    Construction projects
    assumptions governing, 46-47
    case example
        choice of architect, 73
        costs and, 73-74, 75, 78
        financing and, 75-76
        fund-raising drive and, 74
        health planning agency approach
            and, 76-78
        prior building programs and, 74-75
        project review committee and,
            76-77
        steps in, 79
        strategic plan and, 72-73
    forecasting trends in, 45-46
        phases based on, 47-51
    planning and, 71-72

Construction projects. *See also*
    Construction (hospital)
    consulting services and facilities
        planning and, 424-25
    hospital building
        assumptions governing, 46-47
        forecasting trends in, 45-51
        nonprofit system, 83
    Medicare and, 163-64
Consultants
    management, 14, 92
    physician contracts and, 294, 303
Consulting services
    competition and, 425-26
    consulting as a profession and, 426
    fields of competence of, 422-25
    growth forecast for, 422
    past growth of, 421-22
Consumer
    industry change and behavioral
        alterations and, 25-26
    hospital revenues and, 368-69
    consulting services and attitudes of,
        422-23
Contracts. *See also* Bid contracts;
    Management contracts
    physician
        basic elements of, 299-303
        negotiation of, 293-97, 305-310
Corporate structure. *See* Organizational
    structure
Cost containment, 22-23, 27, 387, 410
    appropriate strategies for, 112-14
    CEO, physician, and trustees and,
        109-112
    during the 1970s, 437-38
    economics and, 114-17
    efficiency and, 224-25
    government and public attitudes
        toward, 109
    Medicaid and Medicare and, 120-22,
        134
Costs. *See also* Cost containment;
    Operating costs
    analysis of, 35, 406
    CEO and patient care, 182

competition and, 4, 33, 36
construction project and, 73-74, 75, 78
efficiency and, 224-25, 227
equipment, 286
hospital-based physician and, 291
industry restructuring and, 22-23
organizational change and, 57, 58-59
planning and marketing and, 43
productivity and, 214
quality of care and, 26
trustees and patient, 344
Cost shifting, Medicare and, 132-33

D

Dallas, 3, 28
Data
collection of, 41
decision making and, 252
efficiency and, 227
multihospital financial, 361-62
Debt versus equity finance, 81-82, 88.
See also Finance
Decision making, 177-78, 183-84, 252,
332, 439
Decision path, administrative education
and, 416-18
Demand-side economies, 408-409
Department of Health and Human
Services (HHS), 25, 314
Department of Justice, 24
Depreciation, 338, 346
Deregulation, 365
of hospital planning, 99-107
withdrawing from Medicaid and
Medicare and, 122-24
Diagnostic procedures
medical staff organization and, 269
new construction and, 45
Diagnostic related groups (DRGs), 4, 5,
277, 424, 442
Brown and, 430
CEOs and, 68
health care industry and, 321,
322, 328

hospital-based physicians and,
285, 286, 287, 313
medical staff analysis and, 259, 260
Medicare analysis and, 142, 145,
166, 168, 170, 172
physicians and, 391
productivity analysis and, 213, 217
Diagnostic and treatment services
building, 85, 87
Dole, Robert, 153

E

Economic Stabilization Program, 23
Education
Brown on administrative, 433
CEO
academic programs for, 382-83
degree programs for, 69
MBA curriculum and, 383-84, 415
new graduate placement and,
380-81
student background and, 381
student years and, 207-211
university faculty and, 379-80,
414, 415
CEOs and costs of programs for,
182-83
in health administration
administrative behavior and,
413-15
administrative judgment and,
415-16, 417, 418
administrative knowledge and,
418, 419-20
decision path selection and, 416-18
women in, 418-19
physician contract and, 300
Efficiency
comparing, 225-26
defining, 223
limitations of concept of, 226-27
measuring, 224-25, 227-34
multihospital system, 363
productivity and, 214-15, 220, 224
professional judgment and, 229

Elderly. *See also* Medicaid; Medicare
  entitlement programs for, 119-20
  hospital costs and, 153-54
Emergency Maternal and Infant Care
  (EMIC) Program, 3
Employers, health insurance and, 35
Equipment, 338
  consulting services and planning for,
    425
  cost of, 286
Ethics, 278-79
Expansion program, 39
  case example of, 72-79
  Medicare and, 163-64
Expenditures on health care, 33

F

Families, health care system structure
  and, 35
Fee-for-service concept, 396
  cost control and, 113-14
  fixed fees and, 249
  Medicare and, 314
  physician contract and, 300, 301,
    306, 307
  URC fee and, 439
Finance
  confrontation between management
    and physicians and, 57, 58-59
  construction project and, 75-76
  cost control and, 112
  debt vs. equity, 81-82, 88
  forecasting and, 405-406
  government and, 386
  hospital chain success and, 346-47
  hospital productivity and, 216,
    219-21
  hospital revenue and, 365-74
  investor-owned hospitals and, 322
  management contracts and, 94
  multihospital systems and, 356,
    361-62
  organizational change and, 55-56
  physician contracts and, 295-97, 301

  securing interim, 71
Financial advice, 39-40
Flexner Report (1910), 251, 339
Ford Motor Company, 369
Forecasting trends, 317-19, 395-96,
  437-43
  change in society and, 407-408
  conglomerates and, 396-399
  demand-side economies and, 408-409
  finance and, 405-406
  governmental activities and, 409-410
  inner-city hospitals and, 404-405
  lobbying and, 401-402
  the next decade and, 410-12
  nonprofit systems and, 326-29,
    439-40
  overseas operations and, 400-401
  quality of care and, 399
  rural hospitals and, 402-403
  training and, 401
For-profit systems, 388. *See also*
  Hospital chains; Hospitals;
  Nonprofit systems
  differences and similarities with
    nonprofit systems and, 320-24
  forecasting and, 326-29, 439-40
  holding company, 367
  planning regulation analysis and, 100
  strategic marketing and, 42
  tax burden of, 391
Freestanding medical services, 38, 49,
  345
Functions of an Executive (Barnard),
  110
Fund-raising drive, construction and,
  74

G

Garfield, R. Sidney, 369
Gebhardt, Richard, 314
General Motors, 369
Gephardt-Stockman Bill, 99, 106
Governing boards. *See* Board of
  trustees

Government. *See also* Medicaid;
  Medicare; Regulation
  CEO and state, 193
  change in health care industry and,
    22, 27, 30
  forecasting trends and, 409-410
  health finance and, 386
  HMO development and, 28
  hospital construction and, 45
  industry regulation and, 23
  management contracts and, 94
  medical practice and, 249
  multihospital systems and, 355
  national approach to payment and, 58
  state rate review programs and, 106
Group Health Association (GHA), 27

H

Health administration education. *See*
  Education
Health care system
  capitation plans and, 5-6, 6-7, 29,
    30-31, 324-26
    shared ownership and, 8-9
  competition and, 4-5, 6-7, 24, 25,
    26
  expenditures on, 33
  golden era of, 3-4
  lobbying and, 401-402
  new training concepts and, 401
  restructuring of
    capitation plans and, 29, 30-31
    change process analysis
      government, labor, and
        management and, 22-23
      identifiable options and, 23-25
      the past and, 21-22
  trends in, 317-19, 395-96
    changes in society and, 407-408
    conglomerates and, 396-99
    demand-side economies and, 408-409
    finance and, 405-406
    governmental activities and,
      409-410

    inner-city hospitals and, 404-405
    lobbying and, 401-402
    the next decade and, 410-12
    overseas operations and, 400-401
    quality of care and, 399
    rural hospitals and, 402-403
    training and, 401
Health Frontiers (Kansas), 392
Health insurance, 438. *See also*
  Reimbursement; *names of specific*
  systems
  economic issues and, 387-89
  health plans and, 369
  two-tier care analysis and, 35
Health Insurance Plan (HIP), 27
Health Maintenance Organization Act
  (PL 93-222), 367-68
Health maintenance organizations
  (HMOs), 5, 253, 264, 438, 439
  CEOs and, 68
  cost control and, 116
  forecasting and, 408, 409, 410
  hospital planning and, 104
  hospital revenues and, 365,
    369-74
  Medicare analysis and, 138-42
  prepayment plans and, 441
  productivity analysis and, 219
  restructuring of health care industry
    and, 27-30
  risk-taking example and, 44
Health planning agency, 71, 73. *See*
  also Planning
  construction project approval and,
    76-78
  regulation analysis and, 99, 105
Health system agencies (HSAs), 21, 28,
  30, 406
  cost control and, 112
  hospital planning and, 99, 105
Hill-Burton Law, 386
Holding company structure, 350-51,
  353, 367. *See also* Organizational
  structure
Home care, 150
Hospice care, 150

Hospital chains. *See also* Hospitals
Brown on, 431
capitation plans and, 324-26
CEO education and, 380
CEOs and, 18
consulting services and, 425-26
differences in, 345-47
effective organization and, 357-61
focus of, 351-53
forecasting trends in, 396-99, 439-40
for-profit and nonprofit hospital
values and, 320
differences between, 322-24
similarities of, 320-22
forecasting and, 326-29
growth analysis of, 331-32, 340-43,
392-93
independent development option and,
332-36
integration forms and, 337
internal and external forces and,
337-40
investor-owned, 343, 346, 347, 361
management structure of, 349
matrix-type structure of, 352, 353-55,
362
multiple corporate structure and,
341
organizational flexibility and, 340
organizational structure of, 350-51
overseas operations and, 400-401
parent subsidiary corporate model
and, 340, 345, 367
philosophy and, 343-45
recent trends and, 317-19, 388-89
religious, 342-346
retaining managerial talent and, 326
revenues of, 396-98
second-level functions and, 355-56
services by ownership type and, 327
structural selection and, 361-63
types of ownership and, 318
voluntary hospitals and, 341
weakness of nonprofit, 439-40
Hospital Corporation of America
(HCA), 101, 341

Hospital decertification (Medicare),
122-24
Hospital Insurance Trust Fund. *See*
Medicare, Hospital Insurance Trust
Fund
Hospital Organization and Management
(MacEachern), 420
Hospital planning. *See* Planning
Hospitals. *See also* Chief executive
officers (CEOs); For-profit systems;
Hospital chains; Medical staff;
Nonprofit systems; Physicians
capitation and, 5-6
Catholic, 349-50
CEOs and investor-owned, 182
CEOs and teaching, 19-20, 182-183
choice of (by patient), 40-41
community, 43, 439
medical staff and, 269
community forces and, 38
competition and, 4-5, 34
construction of
assumptions governing, 46-47
forecasting trends in, 45-46
phases in, 47-51
construction project case example
and, 72-79
corporate restructuring and CEOs in,
17-18
cost containment and, 22-23
efficiency in
comparing, 225-26
defining, 223
limitations of concept of, 226-27
measuring, 224-25, 227-34
productivity and, 214-15, 220
professional judgment and, 229
excess capacity and, 441
forecasting middle spectrum activity
and, 402-404
freestanding, 38, 49, 345
health care industry golden era and,
3-4
health-related businesses and, 43
inner-city, 404-405
joint ventures and, 272-74

Medicare and, 128-34
  additional facilities and, 163-64
  demographic and program changes
    and, 153-74
  Hospital Insurance Trust Fund
    and, 135-52
  payment and, 155-59
multihospital management contracts
  and, 91-96
oligopsony analysis and, 6-7
overseas operations and, 400-401
physician conflict with, 250-52
physician-hospital relationship and,
  308
physicians based in, 275-81, 285-87,
  289-92
productivity analysis and, 213-22
religious (chain), 342, 346
reorganization and religious, 60
revenues of
  alternative sources of, 366-68
  capitation plans and, 268-69
  conclusions concerning, 374
  health care conglomerates and,
    396-98
  HMOs and, 365, 369-74
  regulations and, 365-66
rural, 402
shared ownership and, 8-10
Veterans Administration, 349-50
voluntary, 341

I

Iacocca, Lee, 216
INA Corporation, 372
Income of physicians, 286, 307, 440
Independent practitioners associations
  (IPAs), 29
Indigent care, 124
Inglehart, John K., 153
Insurance. *See also* Health Insurance
  cost control and, 112-13
  management contracts and, 95
Investments, 372

J

Johnson, Lyndon, 434
Joint Commission on the Accreditation
  of Hospitals, 228, 265, 403
Joint ventures, 272-74
Judgment in Administration (Brown),
  434

K

Kaiser, Edgar F., 369
Kaiser-Permanente Plan, 27
Kennedy, Edward, 314

L

Labor, change in health care industry
  and, 22, 30. *See also* Unions
Lakeland General Hospital (Florida),
  100-101
Leadership, 218
  CEOs and, 13, 18-19, 190
  internal hospital, 67
Lobbying, 401-402

M

MacEachern, Malcolm, 420
Malpractice, 113, 275, 277-78, 442
  contract and insurance for, 306
Management
  CEOs and shifts in, 194-96
  change and, 11-12, 20
  cost control and, 111
  efficiency and, 225
  evaluation of, 12-13
  hospital-based physician and, 292
  retaining of talented, 326
Management contracts, 326
  elements of sound, 92-95
  general conclusions concerning,
    96

trustees and, 91-92, 96
  control and, 93
Management structure
  multihospital system, 349-50, 353,
    354
  nonprofit hospitals and, 88-90
Marketing plans
  clinical services and, 40-41
  consulting services and, 422
  multihospital systems and, 332,
    333, 344, 355-56
  organizational structure development
    and, 42-44
  skills and techniques used in, 39-40
  use of, 37-39
Market research, 423
Means test (Medicare), 131-32
Medicaid, 4, 34, 101, 105, 338, 366,
    385, 392, 408, 439
  cost control and, 120-22
  entitling the elderly and, 119-20
  reemergence of two-tier health care
    system and, 124-25
  withdrawing from, 122-24
Medical Executive Committee, 260,
    270-71
Medical knowledge, 35, 40
Medical office building, 81, 83, 86
Medical practice
  characteristics changes in, 253-55
  economic factors and, 248-50
  environmental changes in, 247-48
  physician
    and CEO and, 252
    and hospital and, 250-52
Medical staff. *See also* Physicians;
    Specialists
  CEOs and, 17-18, 179-81, 195, 238,
    240
  changing organizational structure
    and, 14
  clinical service selection and, 41
  clinical skills and, 269
  community hospital, 269
  confrontation with management
    costs and, 58-59

  finances and, 57-58
construction programs and, 47, 48,
    50-51
containment of, 351, 389
cost control and, 110
efficiency and, 226, 229
hospital-based physician and, 292
hospital partnership and, 286-87
as independent organization, 259
industry change and, 24
joint ventures and, 272-74
management contracts and, 94
medical practice and, 249, 252-53
multihospital, 360
perceptions of organization of, 269-74
physician contract and, 300, 302, 305
private practice and, 270-72
productivity and, 218
self governance of
  CEO and, 261-63, 267
  characteristics of, 265-66
  differing views on, 258-60
  failure of, 266-67
  patient safety and, 257-58
  physician fears and, 263-65
  trustees and, 198, 258-59, 260-62,
    264
Medicare, 4, 5, 34, 56, 57, 73, 338,
    366, 385, 392, 393, 408, 409, 410,
    442
  basis of crisis in, 127-28, 153-54
  basis of program of
    cost control and, 134
    cost shifting and, 132-33
    free choice of hospital and, 130-31
    means test unacceptability and,
      131-32
    price basis vs. cost basis of, 132
    quality of care and, 131
    right to care and, 128-30
    source of payment and, 133-34
    termination of hospital contract
      and, 133
  Brown and, 429
  case studies and, 161-63
  CEO and, 194

change and, 439
cost control and, 120-22
demographic changes and, 159-61
elderly and, 119-20, 153-54
elective capitation and, 324
entitling the elderly and, 119-20
facilities increases and, 163-64
hospital-based physician and, 311-14
hospital finances and, 339
Hospital Insurance Trust Fund of, 214
  alternate modalities of care and,
    150-51
  development of new programs and,
    142-45
  HMOs and utilization and, 137-42
  options and, 145-50
  rates and, 129
  report to Congress and, 135-37
  utilization pressures and, 151-52
hospital payment and, 155-59
hospital planning regulation and,
  101, 105, 107
physician contract and, 301, 306
physician payments and, 164-65
procompetition bill and, 346
productivity and, 214, 219, 221
reemergence of two-tier health care
  system and, 124-25
responses to changes in, 166-74
withdrawing from, 122-24
Mission statement
management contracts and change in,
  91
multihospital, 352
Modern Healthcare, 341
Multicorporate structures, 65-66, 68.
  See also Organizational structure
Multihospital systems. *See* Hospital
  chains

N

National Council of Community
  Hospitals, 220
New England Journal of Medicine,
  153, 322

Non-profit systems, 18, 388. *See also*
  For-profit systems; Hospital chains;
  Hospitals
  Brown and, 432
  capital costs and, 81, 83-87
  CEOs and, 179, 187-91, 194, 239
  corporate and management structure
    and, 88-90
  creating new business entities and,
    82-83
  debt versus equity and, 81-82
  differences and similarities with
    for-profit systems and, 320-24
  forecasting and, 326-29, 439-40
  hospital design and, 87-88
  reimbursement and, 58-59
  risk taking by CEO and, 15-16
  trustees in, 343
Nurses
  CRNAs, 280
  health administration and, 381
  medical staff organization and, 263
  productivity and, 220-21
Nursing, multihospital system, 355
Nursing homes, 33, 396
  Medicare decertification and, 122

O

Office building (medical), 81, 83, 86
Oligopsony, health care industry
  competition and capitation and, 6-7
Operating costs, 4. *See also* Costs
  CEOs and hospital, 12-13
  hospital chains and, 346
Operations (multihospital system), 356
Organizational effectiveness (Brown),
  427-28, 429
Organizational relationships, changes
  in, 14
Organizational resources, efficiency
  and, 226-27
Organizational structure
  board of trustees and, 59-61
    centralization and, 63-64

giving more authority to CEO and,
62-63
physician board members and,
61-62
CEOs and, 190-91
corporate restructuring and, 17-18
transitional aspects of position of,
235-44
changes in relationships and, 14
confrontation between management
and medical staff
costs and, 58-59
finance and, 57-58
differences in corporate, 323
forecasting change in, 398
governance and, 65-66, 68
health field risk and, 56
holding company, 350-51, 353, 367
horizontal, 337, 342, 350
hospital-based physician and, 292
management changes and, 12-13
medical staff
analysis of, 257-67
corporate, 271
perception of, 269-74
multicorporate, 42, 65-66, 68, 341,
350-51
multihospital theory
corporate, 350-51
effective, 357-61
focus of, 351-53
holding company, 350-51, 353,
367
matrix-type, 353, 353-55
purpose of structure and, 349-50
second-level functions and, 355-56
nonprofit hospitals and corporate,
88-90
parent subsidiary corporate model,
340, 345, 367
physician contracts and, 294
planning and marketing
and changes in, 37-41
and development of, 42-44
restructuring analysis and, 21-31
revenues and multiple corporate, 365

shift from historical roots of hospital,
55-56
two-tier system, 35-36
vertical, 337, 351, 354
Organizational studies, 423-24
Organizational theory, 110
Outpatient care, 87, 217, 374. *See
also* Patients
Ownership. *See also* For-profit systems;
Hospital chains; Hospitals;
Nonprofit systems
hospitals and shared, 8-10
joint venture, 272-74

P

Paige, Satchel, 329
Patients
care program difficulties and, 321,
354
clinical services and, 40-41
competition and pricing of services
and, 34
cost control and, 114-15
forecasting trends and, 398-99, 411,
440
hospital-based physicians and, 291
private practice, 275-76
productivity analysis and, 217, 218,
221
relationship with physician and,
111-12
safety of, 251-52, 257-58, 263,
264, 267, 272
trustees and costs and, 344
Payment systems. *See* Reimbursement
Personnel recruitment, management
contract and, 95
Physical therapy department, 227
Physician-patient relationship, 111-12
Physician recruiting program, 26, 285
management contracts and, 91
Physicians, 13, 56, 92. *See also* Medical
staff; Specialists
advertising and, 254

on board of trustees, 61-62
Brown on, 432-33
capitation plan and shared ownership
    and, 9-10
CEO and, 68, 69, 177, 179-80, 188,
    332
change and, 439
clinical services and, 41
clinical skills and, 269
competition and, 16-17, 33-34
confrontation with management and,
    57-59
consulting services and group
    practices of, 425
contract negotiations and, 293-97,
    299-303, 305-310
cost control and, 109-114, 116
deregulated planning and, 102-103
economic pressures on, 390-92
efficiency and, 229, 230
finance and change and, 56
health administration and, 381
hospital-based, 275-81, 285-87,
    289-92
as hospital-based specialists, 17
income of, 286, 307, 440
increasing supply of, 389, 395-96,
    397, 409-410
industry change and behavioral
    alterations and, 24, 25-26
as investor in hospital system, 82
joint ventures and, 272-74
medical practice
    and CEO and, 252
    and hospital and, 250-52
    and role change of, 247-48
medical staff self governance and
    fears of, 263-65
Medicare and, 129-30
    office visits and, 140-41
    payment and, 164-65
planning practices and, 37
pricing and, 441
private practice and, 250, 270-72,
    275-76
    Medicare and, 312, 313

profit motive and, 86
residency training and specialization
    and, 22, 269
specialist, 22, 38
Planning
    CEOs and, 12
    consulting services and, 424-25, 426
    cooperative, 25
    hospital, 37
        deregulation interim phase and,
            105-107
        deregulation questions and,
            100-102
        frustration with failures in, 99
    hospital construction, 71-72
        case example, 72-79
    multihospital, 354, 355
Planning Act (PL 93-641), 24-25
Planning strategies
    clinical services selection and, 40-41
    organizational structure development
        and, 42-44
    skills and techniques used in, 39-40
    use of (in new organizational era),
        37-39
PL 93-222 (HMO Act), 367-68
PL 93-641 (Planning Act), 24-25
Political skills of CEO, 12
Preferred provider organizations
    (PPOs), 68, 104, 150, 219, 264, 409,
    431, 439
Prepayment plans, 115
Prevention training programs, 115
Price competition, 34, 38, 332.
    See also Competition
Pricing system, 322
Private practice, 250, 270-72, 275-76.
    See also Physicians
    Medicare and, 312, 313
Productivity (hospital)
    CEO and analysis of, 215-18
    conclusions concerning, 221-22
    consulting services and, 424
    efficiency and, 214-15, 220, 224
    financial pressure and, 216, 219-21
    social ethic and, 213-14

Professional Standards Review
  Organizations (PSROs), 111, 409
  hospital planning deregulation and,
    103-104
Profit
  physician and, 86
  productivity and, 217
Prospective payment system, 127
  Medicare and, 312
Public Laws. *See* PL 93-222 (HMO
  Act); PL 93-641 (Planning Act)

Q

Quality of care, 26
  efficiency and, 228
  improvements in, 399
  Medicare and, 131
  multihospital systems and, 352-53
  physician contract and, 307

R

Radiology, Medicare and, 313
Rate review commissions, 21, 24, 29
Rate review programs, 106
Real-estate partnership, 86
Referrals, 300
Regulations, 23, 71
  CEOs and, 178-79, 338
  cost control, 109-117
  hospital planning, 99-107
  hospital revenues and, 365-66
  Medicare
    analysis of, 119-25
    crisis of, 127-34, 153-74
    Hospital Insurance Trust Fund and,
      135-52
    physician (hospital-based) and,
      311-14
Reimbursement, 23, 26, 352, 361, 392.
  See also Capitation plans; Health
  insurance; Medicaid; Medicare
  CEO and, 187, 194

change and, 439
competition and control of, 33
construction programs and, 47
consulting services and, 424
cost control and, 114
economic competition and cost,
  13-14
efficiency and, 228
government and national approach to,
  58
health care financial developments
  (1930-1983) and, 3-4
hospital expansionist period
  (1910-1970s) and, 56, 58-59
hospital payment control and, 145-46
medical staff cooperation and, 16
non-acute medical services and, 39
planning and marketing and, 43
recent restrictions in, 387-88
Religious institutions, 60
  Catholic, 349-50
  chain, 342-346
Remodeling program, 39, 40. *See also*
  Construction projects
  case example of, 72-79
Request for a proposal (RFP)
  capitation plan, 6
  economic competition and, 16
Residency training, 22, 269
Revenues
  alternative sources of, 366-68
  capitation plans and, 368-69
  conclusions concerning, 374
  conglomerates and, 396-98
  HMOs and, 365, 369-74
  regulations and, 365-66
Reynolds Company, 29, 369, 371
Risk, health field and, 56
Risk management, 399
Risk taking, 393
  CEOs and, 15-16, 177, 179, 181, 195
  health care industry and, 320-21,
    325
  hospital, 374
  inadequate, 44
  reimbursement and, 26

S

Salary (CEO), 189. *See also* Income of
physicians
Scheduling, CEO and, 237-40
Securities Exchange Commission, 85
Seminars, consulting services and, 423
Services
ambulatory, 47
clinical
efficiency and, 223, 229, 230-34
hospital revenue and, 366
selection of, 40-41
cost analysis and freezing of, 35
freestanding, 38, 49
hospital-based medicine and, 277
hospital design and, 87
by hospital ownership type, 327
physician contract and, 307
physician-director and, 291
multihospital, 358
price competition and, 34, 38
survival and non-acute, 39
Social Security, 151, 311, 429
Specialists, 22, 253. *See also* Physicians
conclusions concerning, 280-81
consulting services and, 424
ethics and, 278-79
hospital-based implications and, 279-80
increase in, 38
malpractice and, 275, 277-78
medical characteristics of, 276-77
pressure on physicians and, 390
private practice and, 275-76
Stress
CEO and, 236-37
coping with organizational, 241-44
scheduling and, 237-40
Surgical pathology, Medicare and,
312, 313

T

Tax Equity and Fiscal Responsibility Act
(TEFRA), 127, 135, 153, 155, 156,
157, 159, 311, 386, 387, 392
Taxes, 391
Technology, 40, 59, 167, 252, 289,
354, 366
CEOs and, 177, 179
clinical, 16
construction programs and, 48-49
costs and, 35
demand for new, 318
multihospital systems and, 331
new, 344
Termination
CEO case example of, 197-206
physician contract and, 301-302,
306
Training forecasts, 401
Trustees. *See* Board of trustees

U

Unions, 35
cost control analysis and, 112
hospital revenues and, 368-69
Utilization, 41
Brown and, 430
debt and decline in, 81
Medicare analysis and, 135-52
change in, 159-161

V

Value system (nonprofit and
for profit), 320
Veterans Administration hospitals,
349-50